Fundamentals of Manufacturing

Second Edition

Fundamentals of Manufacturing

Second Edition

Philip D. Rufe, CMfgE

Editor

Society of Manufacturing Engineers
Dearborn, Michigan

Table of Contents

Acknowledgments

AUTHORS

Part One—Mathematics and Part Two—Physics and Engineering Science: Philip Rufe, CMfgE

Part Three—Materials: Erik Lokensgard, Ph.D.

Part Four—Product Design: Bob South, Ph.D., CMfgE and Philip Rufe, CMfgE

Part Five— Manufacturing Processes: Philip Rufe, CMfgE; Bob Lahidji, Ph.D., CMfgE; Bob Heller, CMfgE; and Erik Lokensgard, Ph.D.

Part Six—Production Systems: Philip Rufe, CMfgE and Walter Tucker, Ph.D.

Part Seven—Automated Systems and Control: Max Kanagy, Ph.D., CMfgE

Part Eight—Quality: Philip Rufe, CMfgE and Walter Tucker, Ph.D.

Part Nine—Manufacturing Management: Tracy Tillman, Ph.D., CMfgE, CEI

TECHNICAL REVIEWERS

Special thanks to William D. Karr, CMfgT, for reviewing the entire manuscript of this book.

Part One—Mathematics: Bette Warren, Ph.D.

Part Two—Physics and Engineering Science: Alexandria Oakes, Ph.D.; Jamal Bari, Ph.D.; and Frank Gerlitz, Ph.D., PE, CMfgE

Part Three—Materials: Frank Gerlitz, Ph.D., PE, CMfgE

Part Four—Product Design: Kirk Barnes, Ph.D.; Kenny Siler, PE, CMfgE; and Russell Rhoton, CMfgE

Part Five—Manufacturing Processes: Gary Vrsek and Bob Heller, CMfgE

Part Six—Production Systems: Tracy Tillman, Ph.D., CMfgE, CEI

Part Seven—Automated Systems and Control: Russell Rhoton, CMfgE

Part Eight—Quality: Tom Soyster, Ed.D.

Part Nine—Manufacturing Management: Mark Ferris, CMfgE

The efforts of the people responsible for the previous edition are greatly appreciated. Their efforts created the foundation from which this edition has been built. Much of the material from the previous edition has been incorporated into this edition.

Preface

This book was designed to provide a structured review of the fundamentals of manufacturing for individuals planning to take the Fundamentals of Manufacturing Certification Examination. The topics covered are the result of a 1999 survey of manufacturing managers, manufacturing technologists and engineers, and manufacturing educators. Its purpose: to identify fundamental competency areas required by manufacturing technologists and engineers in the field.

While the objective of this book is to help prepare manufacturing managers, technologists, and engineers for the certification process, it is also a primary source of information for individuals interested in learning fundamental manufacturing concepts and practices. This book is a valuable resource for many individuals with limited manufacturing experience or training.

Introduction

MANUFACTURING CERTIFICATION

Manufacturing is concerned with energy, materials, tools, equipment, and products. Excluding services and raw materials in their natural state, most of the remaining gross national product is a direct result of manufacturing.

Modern manufacturing activities have become exceedingly complex because of rapidly increasing technology and expanded environmental involvement. This, coupled with increasing social, political, and economic pressures, has caused successful firms to strive for high-quality manufacturing engineers and managers.

To aid in improving manufacturing, the Society of Manufacturing Engineers' Board of Directors initiated the Manufacturing Engineering Certification Institute (MECI) in 1971. The principal advantage of certification is that it shows the ability to meet a certain set of standards related to the many aspects of manufacturing. These standards pertain to the minimum academic requirements needed, but more importantly, they pertain to the practical experience required of a manufacturing engineer or manager.

Many persons currently employed in industry can successfully measure themselves against these standards, but they cannot provide documentation concerning their ability. The certification program is designed to provide successful candidates with documentary evidence of their abilities. The designations Certified Manufacturing Engineer (CMfgE), Certified Manufacturing Technologist (CMfgT), and/or Certified Enterprise Integrator (CEI) are bestowed upon successful candidates.

Philosophically, the purpose of Manufacturing Certification is to gain increased acceptance of Manufacturing Engineering and Management as a profession and to ultimately improve overall manufacturing effectiveness and productivity.

PURPOSE AND OVERVIEW

The purpose of this text is to provide a structured review for the manufacturing engineer or manager wishing to prepare for certification. The text will serve as a useful review for the experienced manufacturing professional or as an information source and study guideline for the person just entering the field.

The major areas of manufacturing science reviewed include mathematics, physics and engineering science, materials, product design, manufacturing processes, production systems, automated systems and control, quality, and manufacturing management. In each area the topics emphasized are those fundamental to manufacturing.

Sample problems and questions are included at the conclusion of each section for practice. Answers are included for all questions but it is recommended that all problems be attempted before reading the answer.

EXAMINATION SPECIFICS

The Fundamentals of Manufacturing Certification Examination is a three-hour open-book exam consisting of 130 multiple-choice questions. Each major area and its relative emphasis in the exam are listed as follows:

- Mathematics   2.1%
- Physics and Engineering Science   9.1%
- Materials   5.1%
- Product Design   13.4%
- Manufacturing Processes   14.1%
- Production Systems   20.9%
- Automated Systems and Control   5.3%
- Quality   13.0%
- Manufacturing Management   10.8%
- Personal/Professional   6.2%
  Effectiveness

Personal/Professional Effectiveness is a new area in the Fundamentals of Manufacturing Certification Exam. The text does not discuss personal/professional effectiveness because this area is more judgement based rather than knowledge based. Personal/Professional Effectiveness includes:

- Interpersonal skills.
- Negotiating and conflict management.
- Presentation skills and oral communication.
- Written communication skills.
- Innovation and creativity.
- Learning and knowledge transfer.

ADDITIONAL INFORMATION

The bibliography at the end of the book contains appropriate sources for more detailed information on the topics covered. Additional study resources for the Fundamentals of Manufacturing Certification Exam include, but are not limited to, a pencil and paper practice exam and a Windows®-based self-assessment program. The interactive self-assessment program contains 165 questions and answers (based on the same topics as the exam), which will determine your strengths and weaknesses. Built-in bibliographic references suggest study materials for topics where additional help is needed.

For more information regarding the exam or additional resources, please contact the Manufacturing Engineering Certification Institute by calling 313-271-1500, ext. 1811 or e-mail: cert@sme.org. Information can also be obtained on SME's certification website www.sme.org/certification.

Any questions or comments regarding this book are welcome and appreciated. Please direct questions and/or comments to cert@sme.org.

Part 1
Mathematical Fundamentals

Chapter 1
Mathematics

All aspects of engineering require the use of mathematics to analyze and design physical systems. This section provides a brief review of the basic concepts in algebra, geometry, trigonometry, statistics, and calculus. The material presented here is not complete and is not intended to be a resource for learning these topics for the first time.

1.1 ALGEBRA

The study of algebra involves examining the basic properties of numbers. Algebra is founded on several basic laws. These laws or axioms can be used to derive all other concepts in algebra. Three commonly used laws are defined as follows.

Commutative law:

$$a+b = b+a \qquad (1-1)$$

$$ab = ba \qquad (1-2)$$

Associative law:

$$a+(b+c) = (a+b)+c \qquad (1-3)$$

$$a(bc) = (ab)c \qquad (1-4)$$

Distributive law:

$$a(b+c) = ab+ac \qquad (1-5)$$

Certain rules apply when handling exponents in algebra problems. For positive values of x and y, the following rules apply.

$$x^{\frac{m}{n}} = \sqrt[n]{x^m} = \left(\sqrt[n]{x}\right)^m \qquad (1-6)$$

$$x^{-a} = \frac{1}{x^a} \qquad (1-7)$$

$$x^a x^b = x^{a+b} \qquad (1-8)$$

$$(xy)^a = x^a y^a \qquad (1-9)$$

$$x^{ab} = (x^a)^b \qquad (1-10)$$

Logarithms are closely related to exponents. A *logarithm* is the exponent to which a base number is raised to give a particular value. If

$$x = \log_b y \qquad (1-11)$$

then x is the base b logarithm of y or, equivalently, y is b to the xth power

$$y = b^x \qquad (1-12)$$

where base b of the logarithm must be a positive number other than one. It is often helpful to rewrite logarithmic expressions in exponential form.

Engineering applications frequently use two types of logarithms: *common* or *base 10 logarithms* and so-called *natural logarithms* having base e (where $e = 2.7183...$). If x is the natural logarithm of y, then it can be written as:

$$x = \log_e y = \ln y \qquad (1-13)$$

There are several general rules useful in solving problems involving logarithms. These rules apply to logarithms of any base.

$$\log(xy) = \log x + \log y \qquad (1-14)$$

$$\log x^a = a \log x \qquad (1-15)$$

$$\log\left(\frac{x}{y}\right) = \log x - \log y \qquad (1\text{-}16)$$

$$\log_b b = 1 \qquad (1\text{-}17)$$

$$\log 1 = 0 \qquad (1\text{-}18)$$

$$\log x < 0 \qquad \text{if } 0 < x < 1 \qquad (1\text{-}19)$$

$$\log x > 1 \qquad \text{if } x > 1 \qquad (1\text{-}20)$$

$$\log x \text{ is undefined if } x \le 0 \qquad (1\text{-}21)$$

Example 1.1.1. If $\log_a 10 = 0.25$ then what is $\log_{10} a$?

Solution. The expression $0.25 = \log_a 10$ can be rewritten as $10 = a^{0.25}$ (from Equations 1-11 and 1-12),

where:

$$x = 0.25$$
$$\text{base } b = a$$
$$y = 10$$

The base 10 logarithm can be taken of both sides of the expression to give:

$$\log_{10} 10 = \log_{10} a^{0.25}$$

$$\log_{10} 10 = 0.25 \log_{10} a \quad \text{(by Eq. 1-15)}$$

$$1 \quad = 0.25 \log_{10} a \quad \text{(by Eq. 1-17) or}$$

$$\log_{10} a = \frac{1}{0.25} = 4$$

Example 1.1.2. The logarithm of 2 in base 10 is known to be approximately 0.30103. Find the logarithm to the base 10 of 0.5.

Solution. By Eq. 1-16, the expression $\log_{10} \frac{1}{2}$ can be rewritten as:

$$\log_{10} \tfrac{1}{2} = \log_{10} 1 - \log_{10} 2$$

$$= 0 - 0.30103$$

$$= -0.30103$$

One of the most important applications of algebra is solving equations with one vari-able or unknown. The most commonly used forms are: linear equations and quadratic equations. Linear equations with one unknown have the basic form:

$$ax + b = 0 \qquad (1\text{-}22)$$

The unknown quantity x can be solved for by successive application of the following rules, which produce an equivalent equation:

- adding the same number to, or sub-tracting the same number from, both sides of the equation;
- multiplying or dividing both sides of the equation by the same nonzero number.

Another form of an equation of a single variable is the quadratic equation. The basic form of a quadratic equation is given by:

$$ax^2 + bx + c = 0 \, , \, a \ne 0 \qquad (1\text{-}23)$$

There is a standard solution to a quadratic equation given by the quadratic formula:

$$x = \frac{-b \pm \sqrt{b^2 - 4ac}}{2a} \qquad (1\text{-}24)$$

Note that there may be two possible solu-tions. The number of solutions and their type depends on the value of the discrimi-nant (the quantity under the radical). If $b^2 - 4ac > 0$, the quadratic equation has two distinct (different), real solutions. If $b^2 - 4ac = 0$, then the equation has one real solution. If $b^2 - 4ac < 0$, then the equation has two distinct, imaginary (involving i or $\sqrt{-1}$) solutions. Always check your an-swer in the original equation.

Example 1.1.3. Find the value of x.

$$\frac{4x+2}{x+1} + \frac{4}{5} = -\frac{6}{5}$$

Solution. The lowest common denomina-tor is $5(x + 1)$. Both sides of the equation are multiplied by it to obtain:

$$5(x+1)\left(\frac{4x+2}{x+1}+\frac{4}{5}\right)=5(x+1)\left(-\frac{6}{5}\right)$$

$$5(4x+2)+(x+1)4 = (x+1)(-6)$$

$$20x+10+4x+4 = -6x-6$$

$$20x+4x+6x = -6-4-10$$

$$30x = -20$$

$$x=-\frac{2}{3}$$

Example 1.1.4. Find the solution(s) to the following equation.

$$17x^2+41x-74 = 19$$

Solution. The equation is first put in standard form (see Eq. 1-23):

$$17x^2+41x-93 = 0$$

where $a = 17$, $b = 41$, and $c = -93$

Since the discriminant is greater than zero:

$$b^2-4ac = (41)^2-(4)(17)(-93) = 8,005 >0$$

there are two, real solutions.

$$x_{1,2} = \frac{-41\pm\sqrt{41^2-4(17)(-93)}}{2(17)} \approx -3.84,\ 1.42$$

Expanding on the concept of a linear equation with one variable or unknown, a linear equation with two unknowns has the general form given by:

$$ax+by = c \qquad (1-25)$$

This is an equation of a line with slope $-\frac{a}{b}$ and y intercept $\frac{c}{b}$ if $b \neq 0$ as shown in Figure 1-1. If $b = 0$ and $a \neq 0$, it is the equation of the vertical line $x =\frac{c}{a}$.

Two independent linear equations are needed to find a unique solution. A unique solution represents the point where the two lines intersect. There will be no solution if the lines are parallel or both vertical. Parallel lines have identical slopes. If the lines

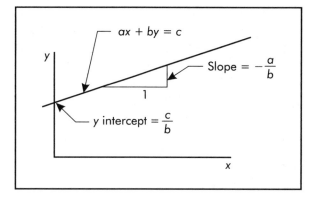

Figure 1-1. Equation of a line.

coincide then infinitely many solutions exist. Consider the following case.

$$a_1x+b_1y = c_1 \qquad (1-26)$$

$$a_2x+b_2y = c_2 \qquad (1-27)$$

If $a_1b_1 \neq a_2b_2$ then a unique solution exists. If $a_1b_1 = a_2b_2$ then there are either no solutions or infinitely many solutions. In this case, the lines are either parallel or the equations are proportional and represent the same line. There are three major approaches to solving these linear, simultaneous systems of equations:

- *Substitution* involves solving for one variable in terms of the other and substituting the result in the other equation.
- *Elimination* can typically be used to solve systems of linear simultaneous equations with two equations and two unknowns by multiplying both equations by an appropriate constant such that one of the unknown terms cancels out when the two equations are added together.
- Systems of linear equations larger than two equations and two unknowns require a different technique called *Gaussian elimination*. Another technique called *Cramer's Rule* uses determinants to solve the system of linear equations. However, it is generally difficult to remember and

is impractical for larger systems of equations. Gaussian elimination uses elementary row operations to reduce an augmented matrix into echelon form to solve the system of linear equations.

Example 1.1.5. Solve the following system of two linear simultaneous equations using substitution.

$$2x + 3y = 1$$

$$3x - 5y = -27$$

Solution. Solve the first equation for y in terms of x.

$$3y = -2x + 1$$

$$y = -\frac{2}{3}x + \frac{1}{3}$$

Substituting, the second equation becomes:

$$3x - 5\left(-\frac{2}{3}x + \frac{1}{3}\right) = -27$$

$$3x + \frac{10}{3}x - \frac{5}{3} = -27$$

Multiplying through by 3 to clear the fractions and then rearranging terms results in the solution for x:

$$9x + 10x - 5 = -81$$

$$19x = -76$$

$$x = -4$$

The resulting value of x is substituted in either equation to obtain the solution for y:

$$2x + 3y = 1$$

$$2(-4) + 3y = 1$$

$$-8 + 3y = 1$$

$$3y = 9$$

$$y = 3$$

Example 1.1.6. Solve the system of equations in example 1.1.5 by elimination.

Solution. Multiply the first equation by 5 and multiply the second equation by 3 to obtain y terms that will cancel each other out:

$$5(2x + 3y = 1) \quad \rightarrow 10x + 15y = 5$$
$$3(3x - 5y = -27) \rightarrow \underline{9x - 15y = -81}$$
$$19x = -76$$
$$x = -4$$

The result is substituted into either equation to obtain a solution for y as in example 1.1.5.

In Gaussian elimination, the equations must be set up in standard form. *Standard form* requires that all the variables and their respective coefficients appear on the left side of the equation. The equations in standard form are used to create an augmented matrix that must then be transformed into echelon form to solve the system of linear equations as demonstrated in Example 1.1.7. In *echelon form*, the leading entry in a row does not have to be one. The leading entry is the leftmost nonzero element in each row. In each column that contains a leading entry, all elements below the leading entry are zero. In any two rows with leading entries, the leading entry of the higher row is farther to the left. Any row that contains all zeros is below any row with some nonzero entries. For example, the following matrix is in echelon form.

$$\begin{matrix} 2 & 1 & -1 \\ 0 & -1 & 2 \\ 0 & 0 & 3 \end{matrix}$$

Elementary row operations include multiplying or dividing individual rows by a nonzero constant and adding or subtracting rows together. The order of the rows also may be changed.

Example 1.1.7. Solve the following equations using Gaussian elimination.

$$10x - 6y - 3z = 11$$

$$5x + 9y + 2z = 3$$

$$15x - 12y - z = 4$$

Solution. Since the equations are in standard form, the augmented matrix can be written as:

$$\begin{bmatrix} 10 & -6 & -3 \\ 5 & 9 & 2 \\ 15 & -12 & -1 \end{bmatrix}\begin{bmatrix} 11 \\ 3 \\ 4 \end{bmatrix}$$

First, arrange the rows so that the leading entries are in decreasing order.

$$\begin{bmatrix} 15 & -12 & -1 \\ 10 & -6 & -3 \\ 5 & 9 & 2 \end{bmatrix}\begin{bmatrix} 4 \\ 11 \\ 3 \end{bmatrix}$$

Replace the third row by the sum of -2 times itself and the second row.

$$\begin{bmatrix} 15 & -12 & -1 \\ 10 & -6 & -3 \\ -2(5)+10 & -2(9)-6 & -2(2)-3 \end{bmatrix}\begin{bmatrix} 4 \\ 11 \\ -2(3)+11 \end{bmatrix}$$

$$\begin{bmatrix} 15 & -12 & -1 \\ 10 & -6 & -3 \\ 0 & -24 & -7 \end{bmatrix}\begin{bmatrix} 4 \\ 11 \\ 5 \end{bmatrix}$$

Multiply the first row by 2.

$$\begin{bmatrix} 30 & -24 & -2 \\ 10 & -6 & -3 \\ 0 & -24 & -7 \end{bmatrix}\begin{bmatrix} 8 \\ 11 \\ 5 \end{bmatrix}$$

Replace the second row by the sum of -3 times itself and the first row.

$$\begin{bmatrix} 30 & -24 & -2 \\ -3(10)+30 & -3(-6)-24 & -3(-3)-2 \\ 0 & -24 & -7 \end{bmatrix}\begin{bmatrix} 8 \\ -3(11)+8 \\ 5 \end{bmatrix}$$

$$\begin{bmatrix} 30 & -24 & -2 \\ 0 & -6 & 7 \\ 0 & -24 & -7 \end{bmatrix}\begin{bmatrix} 8 \\ -25 \\ 5 \end{bmatrix}$$

Replace the third row with the sum of itself and -4 times the second row.

$$\begin{bmatrix} 30 & -24 & -2 \\ 0 & -6 & 7 \\ 0-4(0) & -24-4(-6) & -7-4(7) \end{bmatrix}\begin{bmatrix} 8 \\ -25 \\ 5-4(-25) \end{bmatrix}$$

$$\begin{bmatrix} 30 & -24 & -2 \\ 0 & -6 & 7 \\ 0 & 0 & -35 \end{bmatrix}\begin{bmatrix} 8 \\ -25 \\ 105 \end{bmatrix}$$

Convert the matrix back to equation form:

$$30x - 24y - 2z = 8$$
$$-6y + 7z = -25$$
$$-35z = 105$$

and solve for the variables.

$$-35z = 105$$
$$z = -3$$

$$-6y + 7(-3) = -25$$
$$-6y = -4$$
$$y = \frac{2}{3}$$

$$30x - 24\left(\frac{2}{3}\right) - 2(-3) = 8$$
$$30x = 18$$
$$x = \frac{3}{5}$$

1.2 GEOMETRY

The areas and volumes of common geometric shapes are frequently needed in the solution of engineering problems. The areas of some common two-dimensional shapes are shown in Figure 1-2. The volumes of some common three-dimensional shapes are given in Figure 1-3.

The equation of a straight line can be written in a variety of forms. The general form of an equation of a line is given by:

$$ax + by = c \quad \text{(by Eq. 1-25)}$$

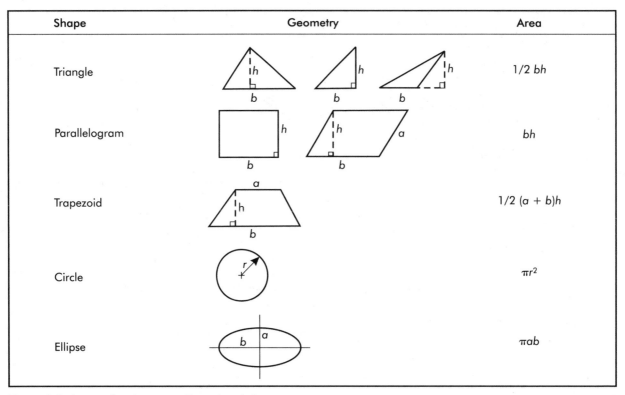

Shape	Geometry	Area
Triangle		1/2 bh
Parallelogram		bh
Trapezoid		1/2 (a + b)h
Circle		πr^2
Ellipse		πab

Figure 1-2. Areas of various two-dimensional shapes.

or

$$ax + by - c = 0 \qquad (1\text{-}28)$$

If $b \neq 0$, the slope of the line with this equation is $-\frac{a}{b}$. In general, the slope, m, can be calculated from any two points with distinct values (x_1, y_1), (x_2, y_2) as:

$$m = \frac{\Delta y}{\Delta x} = \frac{y_2 - y_1}{x_2 - x_1} \qquad (1\text{-}29)$$

If the line is vertical, the slope is not defined, since the denominator $(x_2 - x_1)$ would be zero. Various other forms of the equation of a line are also used. Each has a special relationship with the graph of a line. The point-slope form is given by:

$$y - y_1 = m(x - x_1) \qquad (1\text{-}30)$$

where (x_1, y_1) is any point on the line and m is the slope, as shown in Figure 1-4(a). The slope-intercept form is given by:

$$y = mx + b \qquad (1\text{-}31)$$

where m is the slope and b is the y intercept, as shown in Figure 1-4(b). The two-intercept form is given by:

$$\frac{x}{a} + \frac{y}{b} = 1 \qquad (1\text{-}32)$$

where a is the x intercept and b is the y intercept, as shown in Figure 1-4(c).

Example 1.2.1. Find the equation describing the line shown in Figure 1-5.

Solution. The slope of the line is found as:

$$m = \frac{2.5 - 1}{4 - 1} = \frac{1.5}{3} = \frac{1}{2} \text{ (by Eq. 1-29)}$$

Either given point can be used in the point-slope form to give the equation of the line. Using the point $(x_1, y_1) = (1,1)$

Shape	Geometry	Volume
Rectangular prism		abc
Pyramid		$1/3\ hA$
Cylinder		$\pi r^2 h$
Sphere		$4/3\ \pi r^3$

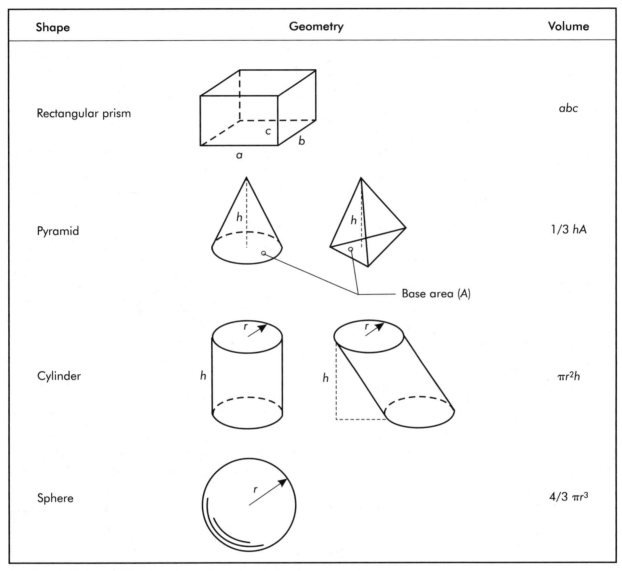

Figure 1-3. Volumes of various three-dimensional shapes.

$y - y_1 = m(x - x_1)$ (Eq. 1-30)

$y - 1 = \dfrac{1}{2}(x - 1)$

$y - 1 = \dfrac{x}{2} - \dfrac{1}{2}$

$y = \dfrac{x}{2} + \dfrac{1}{2}$

For reference, ellipses, parabolas, and hyperbolas are discussed in Appendix A1.

1.3 TRIGONOMETRY

The basic trigonometric functions of acute angles ($0 < \theta < 90°$) can be easily defined as ratios of the sides of a right triangle. Using the right triangle shown in Figure 1-6, the following functions can be defined:

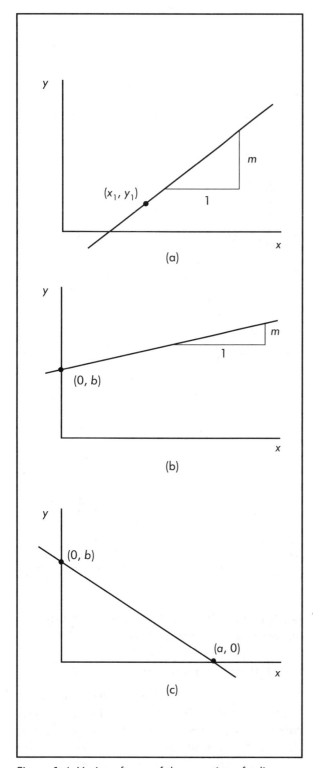

Figure 1-4. *Various forms of the equation of a line.*

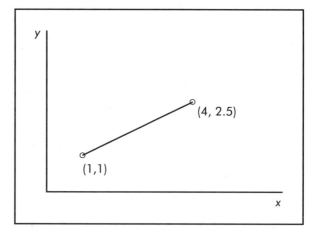

Figure 1-5. *Line described by two known points.*

$$\sin \theta = \frac{a}{c} = \frac{\text{opposite side}}{\text{hypotenuse}} \qquad (1\text{-}33)$$

$$\cos \theta = \frac{b}{c} = \frac{\text{adjacent side}}{\text{hypotenuse}} \qquad (1\text{-}34)$$

$$\tan \theta = \frac{a}{b} = \frac{\text{opposite side}}{\text{adjacent side}} \qquad (1\text{-}35)$$

where c is the hypotenuse of the triangle. By application of the Pythagorean Theorem,

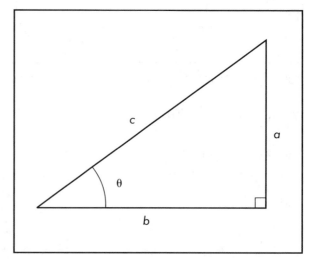

Figure 1-6. *Right triangle.*

$$c^2 = a^2 + b^2 \qquad (1\text{-}36)$$

There are three other trigonometric functions that also can be defined as reciprocals of the three basic functions:

$$\csc\theta = \frac{1}{\sin\theta} \qquad (1\text{-}37)$$

$$\sec\theta = \frac{1}{\cos\theta} \qquad (1\text{-}38)$$

$$\cot\theta = \frac{1}{\tan\theta} \qquad (1\text{-}39)$$

The angle between the adjacent side and hypotenuse can be described in either radians or degrees. Degrees can be converted to radians by multiplying by $\frac{\pi}{180°}$. Radians can be converted to degrees by multiplying by $\frac{180°}{\pi}$. Another important observation is that positive angles are measured counterclockwise with respect to the positive x axis.

The tangent (tan) function asymptotically approaches infinity at odd multiples of $\frac{\pi}{2}$. It has period π. The sine (sin) and cosine (cos) functions are periodic in 2π intervals and are out of phase with each other by $\frac{\pi}{2}$ or 90°.

There are two important formulas that apply to the general triangle shown in Figure 1-7. The *law of sines* describes the relationship of the angles in a triangle to the sides opposite them:

$$\frac{\sin A}{a} = \frac{\sin B}{b} = \frac{\sin C}{c} \qquad (1\text{-}40)$$

where $A + B + C = 180°$. The *law of cosines* describes the relationships between the sides of a triangle and an angle:

$$a^2 = b^2 + c^2 - 2bc\,\cos A \qquad (1\text{-}41)$$

$$b^2 = a^2 + c^2 - 2ac\,\cos B \qquad (1\text{-}42)$$

$$c^2 = a^2 + b^2 - 2ab\,\cos C \qquad (1\text{-}43)$$

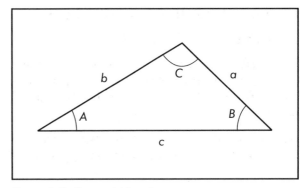

Figure 1-7. General triangle.

Example 1.3.1. If a particular equilateral triangle has a side with a length of 1, what is the perpendicular distance from the side to its center?

Solution. Referring to Figure 1-8, the equilateral triangle can be divided into six smaller right triangles. Applying the definition of the tan function:

$$\tan 30° = \frac{\text{opposite side}}{\text{adjacent side}} = \frac{y}{0.5} \ \text{(by Eq. 1-35)}$$

$$y = 0.5 \tan 30° \approx 0.29$$

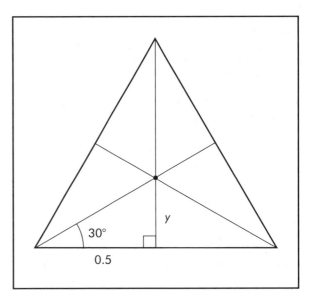

Figure 1-8. Equilateral triangle.

Example 1.3.2. If $\cos \theta = 0.4$, what is θ?

Solution. $\theta = \cos^{-1} 0.4 = 66.4°$

Example 1.3.3. If a triangle has two sides of length 5.3 and 3.8 with a 110° angle between them, what is the length of the third side?

Solution. The triangle is shown in Figure 1-9. The law of cosines can be applied directly as:

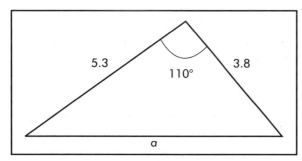

Figure 1-9. Application of the law of cosines.

$$a^2 = b^2 + c^2 - 2bc \cos A \text{ (Eq. 1-41)}$$

where:

b = 3.8
c = 5.3
A = 110°
a^2 = $3.8^2 + 5.3^2 - 2(3.8)(5.3) \cos 110°$
a^2 = 14.4 + 28.1 + 13.8 = 56.3
a = 7.5

Example 1.3.4. Find the unknown side x in the triangle in Figure 1-10.

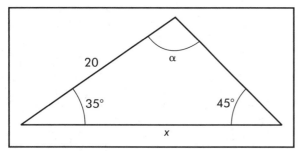

Figure 1-10. Application of the law of sines.

Solution. The angle α can be found since the interior angles in a triangle must sum to 180°.

$$180° = \alpha + 35° + 45°$$

$$\alpha = 100°$$

The law of sines can be applied directly to find the unknown side:

$$\frac{\sin A}{a} = \frac{\sin B}{b} \text{ (Eq. 1-40)}$$

where:

A = 100°
a = x
B = 45°
b = 20

$$\frac{\sin 100°}{x} = \frac{\sin 45°}{20}$$

$$\frac{0.985}{x} = \frac{0.707}{20}$$

$$19.7 = 0.707x$$

$$x = 27.9$$

For reference purposes, common trigonometric identities are listed in Appendix A2.

1.4 PROBABILITY

A *permutation* of any number of items is a group of some or all of them arranged in a definite order. The number of permutations of n things taken r at a time is designated $P(n,r)$ and can be determined by:

$$P(n,r) = \frac{n!}{(n-r)!} \qquad (1-44)$$

where the exclamation point designates a factorial (for example, $4! = 1 \times 2 \times 3 \times 4 = 24$).

A *combination* is a group of n objects taken as any set of r objects without regard to their order. The number of combinations of n things taken r at a time is given by:

$$C(n,r) = \frac{n!}{r!(n-r)!} \qquad (1\text{-}45)$$

A probability $P(A)$ refers to the likelihood of an event A occurring. The probability is always in the range of zero to one.

- The probability of A or B occurring is:

$$P(A \text{ or } B) = P(A) + P(B) - P(A \text{ and } B)$$
$$(1\text{-}46)$$

- If two events cannot occur simultaneously then they are *mutually exclusive*. For example, in a coin tossing experiment, if a head occurs then a tail cannot. Those two events are mutually exclusive. If A and B are mutually exclusive then:

$$P(A \text{ and } B) = 0 \qquad (1\text{-}47)$$

$$P(A \text{ or } B) = P(A) + P(B) \qquad (1\text{-}48)$$

- If two events can occur in a single experimental trial and one event does not affect the probability of the occurence of the other, the events are *independent*. For example, when tossing a pair of dice, rolling a four on the first die and a four on the second die are independent events. Rolling a four with the first die does not affect the probability of rolling a four with the second die. The events are not mutually exclusive since both (two fours) can occur simultaneously. If A and B are independent, then the probability of A and B occuring is the product of the two probabilities:

$$P(A \text{ and } B) = P(A)\,P(B) \qquad (1\text{-}49)$$

- The probability of A not occurring is given by:

$$P(\text{not } A) = 1 - P(A) \qquad (1\text{-}50)$$

Example 1.4.1. There are seven ball bearings packed in a tube. How many different ways can the seven bearings be arranged?

Solution. Since a different order of ball bearings constitutes a different arrangement, order must be taken into account and permutations should be used. This is determined by the number of permutations of seven things taken seven at a time:

$$P(n,r) = \frac{n!}{(n-r)!} \quad \text{(Eq. 1-44)}$$

where:

n = 7 balls total
r = 7 balls per arrangement

$$P(7,7) = \frac{7!}{(7-7)!} = 5,040$$

Example 1.4.2. A three-member committee is to be selected from a group of 10 people. How many different committees are possible?

Solution. The answer does not depend on ordering. It is a combination problem.

$$C(n,r) = \frac{n!}{r!(n-r)!} \quad \text{(Eq. 1-45)}$$

where:

n = 10 people total
r = 3 people per committee arrangement

$$C(10,3) = \frac{10!}{3!(10-3)!} = 120$$

Example 1.4.3. An ordinary die is tossed 100 times. What is the expected number of times a four can be rolled?

Solution. The probability of a four on any toss is $\frac{1}{6}$. It is expected a 4 will be rolled about $\frac{1}{6}$ of the time. Therefore,

$$100 \times \frac{1}{6} \approx 17$$

Approximately 17 fours would appear in 100 tosses.

Example 1.4.4. What is the probability of drawing a king or a one-eyed jack (half of the jacks in the deck are one-eyed) from an ordinary deck of 52 playing cards?

Solution. The events of drawing a king or one-eyed jack are mutually exclusive. The probability of selecting a king or a one-eyed jack is:

$$P(A \text{ or } B) = P(A) + P(B) \quad \text{(Eq. 1-48)}$$

where:

$$P(A \text{ or } B) = P(\text{king or one-eyed jack})$$

$$P(A) = P(\text{king}) = \frac{4 \text{ possible kings}}{52 \text{ cards}} = \frac{4}{52}$$

$$P(B) = P(\text{one-eyed jack})$$

$$= \frac{2 \text{ possible one-eyed jacks}}{52 \text{ card}} = \frac{2}{s5}$$

$$P(\text{king or one-eyed jack})$$

$$= P(\text{king}) + P(\text{one-eyed jack})$$

$$= \frac{4}{52} + \frac{2}{52} = \frac{6}{52} \approx 0.115$$

1.5 STATISTICS

Statistics is the area of mathematics that describes the characteristics of a population by use of parameters that characterize the population. A *statistic* is a single number calculated from a set of sample observations. *Descriptive statistics* are used to describe large bodies of data. *Inferential statistics* are used to draw inferences about a population from a sample or subset of the population.

Measuring *central tendency* means determining a number or value that represents the center of a group of data. Three measures will be discussed here: the mean, median, and mode.

MEAN

The arithmetic *mean* μ is the expected value or average of a group of N observations.

$$\mu = \frac{1}{N} \sum_{i=1}^{N} x_i \quad (1\text{-}51)$$

MEDIAN

The *median* is the middle observation in a group of data ordered by magnitude. The data are ordered in ascending or descending order and counted. The median is halfway through this ordered list. If there are an even number of observations, the median is the average of the two observations in the middle of the ordered list.

MODE

The *mode* is the value that occurs most frequently.

VARIATION

There are several ways to measure the variation within a set of data such as the range, variance, and standard deviation methods described here.

Range

The *range* of any data set is the largest value minus the smallest value.

$$\text{Range } (R) = \text{Maximum } x_i - \text{Minimum } x_i \quad (1\text{-}52)$$

Variance

The measure of *variance* is used where variability of different samples must be combined to calculate overall variances. Variances can be combined where standard deviations cannot. The population variance (σ^2) is defined as:

$$\sigma^2 = \frac{\sum_{i=1}^{N}(x_i - \mu)^2}{N} = \frac{\sum_{i=1}^{N} x_i^2 - N\mu^2}{N} \quad (1\text{-}53)$$

where:

μ = the population mean
x_i = each individual data point
N = population measurements

The population variance assumes that all of the population data is used. If a sample of population data is used, then the sample variance (s^2) is used as defined:

$$s^2 = \frac{\sum_{i=1}^{n}(x_i - \overline{x})^2}{n-1} = \frac{\sum_{i=1}^{n}x_i^2 - n(\overline{x})^2}{n-1} \qquad (1\text{-}54)$$

where:

$\overline{x}$ = the sample mean
x_i = each individual data point
n = sample size

Standard Deviation

The standard deviation is the square root of the variance. Standard deviation is the measure of spread around a data set's mean. It is defined as:

$$\sigma = \sqrt{\sigma^2} = \sqrt{\frac{\sum_{i=1}^{N}(x_i - \mu)^2}{N}} = \sqrt{\frac{\sum_{i=1}^{N}x_i^2 - N\mu^2}{N}}$$
$$(1\text{-}55)$$

Equation 1-55 is the population standard deviation (all of the population data is assumed to be used). If a sample of population data is used, then the sample standard deviation is defined as:

$$s = \sqrt{s^2} = \sqrt{\frac{\sum_{i=1}^{n}(x_i - \overline{x})^2}{n-1}} = \sqrt{\frac{\sum_{i=1}^{n}x_i^2 - n(\overline{x})^2}{n-1}}$$
$$(1\text{-}56)$$

Example 1.5.1. Calculate the mean and standard deviation of 85, 70, 60, 90 and 81. Treat these numbers as a sample drawn from a large population.

Solution. The mean is the average value. Since there are 5 data points, by Eq. 1-51:

$$\overline{x} = \frac{1}{5}\sum_{i=1}^{5}x_i = \frac{1}{5}(85 + 70 + 60 + 90 + 81)$$

$$= \frac{386}{5} = 77.2$$

The sample standard deviation is found as:

$$s = \sqrt{s^2} = \sqrt{\frac{\sum_{i=1}^{n}x_i^2 - n(\overline{x})^2}{n-1}} \quad (\text{Eq. 1-56})$$

$$\sqrt{\frac{(x_1^2 + x_2^2 + x_3^2 + x_4^2 + x_5^2) - n(\overline{x})^2}{n-1}}$$

where:

x_1 = 85
x_2 = 70
x_3 = 60
x_4 = 90
x_5 = 81
n = 5
$\overline{x}$ = 77.2

$$s = \sqrt{\frac{85^2 + 70^2 + 60^2 + 90^2 + 81^2 - 5(77.2)^2}{5-1}}$$

$$s \approx 12.1$$

The Central Limit Theorem states that the distributions of sample means from an infinite population will approach a normal distribution as the sample size increases.

Normally distributed data forms the well-known bell-shaped curve as illustrated in Figure 1-11. However, many distributions are not normal. These data may take many irregular shapes. Analysis of non-normal distributions requires different approaches (with the exception of the median used especially for

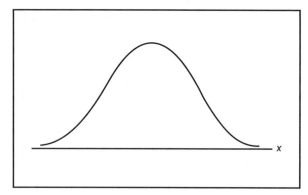

Figure 1-11. Normal distribution.

skewed distributions) from the measures mentioned in this section, which all assume normal distributions.

Some examples of non-normal distributions include skewed and bimodal as illustrated in Figure 1-12(a) and (b).

Because the mean and standard deviation of the normal distribution can take on many

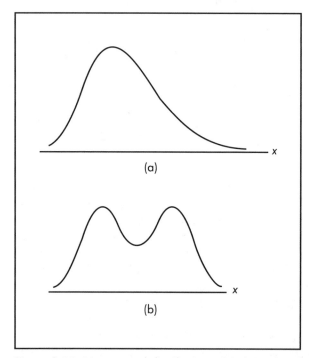

Figure 1-12. Non-normal distributions: (a) skewed and (b) bimodal.

different values from situation to situation, it is convenient to define and work with a standardized normal distribution.

The standard normal random variable is generally denoted by the letter z and the standard normal probability density function by $f(z)$. Because the standard normal distribution has standard deviation equal to one and mean equal to zero, the value for z can be interpreted as the number of standard deviations from the mean.

Figure 1-13 illustrates the standard normal curve. For any normal distribution, 68.27 percent of the values of z lie within one standard deviation of the mean; 95.45 percent of the values lie within two standard deviations of the mean; and 99.73 percent of the values lie within three standard deviations of the mean. The cumulative probabilities of the standardized normal random variable z are provided in Table 1-1. Table 1-1 is left-reading, therefore the areas associated with each value of z are for that portion of the curve from $-\infty$ to a particular value of z. (The cumulative probability value is found by identifying the appropriate ones and tenths place of z in the left-hand column and the hundredths place of z in the top row and finding the number where these two intersect).

The formula for z values or scores is defined as:

$$z_i = \frac{x_i - \mu}{\sigma} \qquad (1\text{-}57)$$

where:

x_i = i^{th} normal random variable
μ = population mean
σ = population standard deviation

Example 1.5.2. The mean lifetime of a 75-watt light bulb is 400 hours. The standard deviation is known to be 30 hours. Assuming the lifetime of the bulbs is normally distributed, what is the probability that a

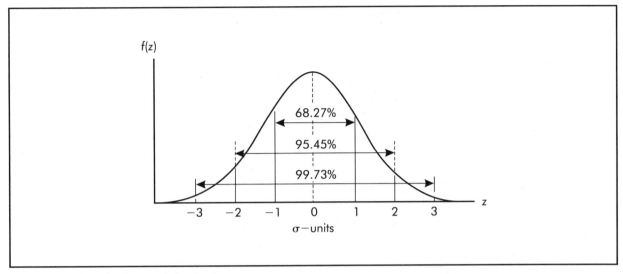

Figure 1-13. Standard normal distribution.

75-watt bulb, randomly selected, will burn out between 350 and 425 hours?

Solution. This is asking for the cumulative probability (under the curve) that the light bulb will burn out between two given points on the normal curve of light bulb lifetimes. These two points must first be translated into standard deviation units, or values of Z:

$$z_i = \frac{x_i - \mu}{\sigma} \text{ (Eq. 1-57)}$$

where:

x_1 = 350 hours
z_1 = number of standard deviations between 350 hours and mean lifetime
x_2 = 425 hours
z_2 = number of standard deviations between 425 hours and mean lifetime
μ = mean lifetime = 400 hours
σ = standard deviation = 30 hours

$$z_1 = \frac{x_1 - \mu}{\sigma} = \frac{350 \text{ hours} - 400 \text{ hours}}{30 \text{ hours}}$$

$$= -1.67 \text{ standard deviations from the mean}$$

$$z_2 = \frac{x_2 - \mu}{\sigma} = \frac{425 - 400}{30}$$

$$= 0.83 \text{ standard deviations from the mean}$$

The area between $z_1 = -1.67$ and $z_2 = 0.83$ on the standard normal distribution curve corresponds to the area between 350 and 425 hours on a normal curve for lightbulb lifetimes with a mean of 400 hours and a standard deviation of 30 hours.

Area one ($-\infty$ to -1.67) = 0.0475
Area two ($-\infty$ to 0.83) = 0.7967

The probability of a randomly selected bulb burning out between 350 and 425 hours is equal to:

Area two $-$ Area one = 0.7967 $-$ 0.0475
$$= 0.7492 \text{ or } 74.92\%$$

Often it is impractical to find the mean or standard deviation of a population and, therefore, inferring information about the population from a sample is necessary. Describing a population through sampling requires that the sample be representative of

Table 1-1. Areas under the standard normal curve

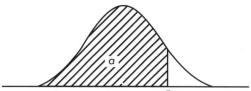

z	0.09	0.08	0.07	0.06	0.05	0.04	0.03	0.02	0.01	0.00
−3.5	0.00017	0.00017	0.00018	0.00019	0.00019	0.00020	0.00021	0.00022	0.00022	0.00023
−3.4	0.00024	0.00025	0.00026	0.00027	0.00028	0.00029	0.00030	0.00031	0.00033	0.00034
−3.3	0.00035	0.00036	0.00038	0.00039	0.00040	0.00042	0.00043	0.00045	0.00047	0.00048
−3.2	0.00050	0.00052	0.00054	0.00056	0.00058	0.00060	0.00062	0.00064	0.00066	0.00069
−3.1	0.00071	0.00074	0.00076	0.00079	0.00082	0.00085	0.00087	0.00090	0.00094	0.00097
−3.0	0.00100	0.00104	0.00107	0.00111	0.00114	0.00118	0.00122	0.00126	0.00131	0.00135
−2.9	0.0014	0.0014	0.0015	0.0015	0.0016	0.0016	0.0017	0.0017	0.0018	0.0019
−2.8	0.0019	0.0020	0.0021	0.0021	0.0022	0.0023	0.0023	0.0024	0.0025	0.0026
−2.7	0.0026	0.0027	0.0028	0.0029	0.0030	0.0031	0.0032	0.0033	0.0034	0.0035
−2.6	0.0036	0.0037	0.0038	0.0039	0.0040	0.0041	0.0043	0.0044	0.0045	0.0047
−2.5	0.0048	0.0049	0.0051	0.0052	0.0054	0.0055	0.0057	0.0059	0.0060	0.0062
−2.4	0.0064	0.0066	0.0068	0.0069	0.0071	0.0073	0.0075	0.0078	0.0080	0.0082
−2.3	0.0084	0.0087	0.0089	0.0091	0.0094	0.0096	0.0099	0.0102	0.0104	0.0107
−2.2	0.0110	0.0113	0.0116	0.0119	0.0122	0.0125	0.0129	0.0132	0.0136	0.0139
−2.1	0.0143	0.0146	0.0150	0.0154	0.0158	0.0162	0.0166	0.0170	0.0174	0.0179
−2.0	0.0183	0.0188	0.0192	0.0197	0.0202	0.0207	0.0212	0.0217	0.0222	0.0228
−1.9	0.0233	0.0239	0.0244	0.0250	0.0256	0.0262	0.0268	0.0274	0.0281	0.0287
−1.8	0.0294	0.0301	0.0307	0.0314	0.0322	0.0329	0.0336	0.0344	0.0351	0.0359
−1.7	0.0367	0.0375	0.0384	0.0392	0.0401	0.0409	0.0418	0.0427	0.0436	0.0446
−1.6	0.0455	0.0465	0.0475	0.0485	0.0495	0.0505	0.0516	0.0526	0.0537	0.0548
−1.5	0.0559	0.0571	0.0582	0.0594	0.0606	0.0618	0.0630	0.0643	0.0655	0.0668
−1.4	0.0681	0.0694	0.0708	0.0721	0.0735	0.0749	0.0764	0.0778	0.0793	0.0808
−1.3	0.0823	0.0838	0.0853	0.0869	0.0885	0.0901	0.0918	0.0934	0.0951	0.0968
−1.2	0.0895	0.1003	0.1020	0.1038	0.1057	0.1075	0.1093	0.1112	0.1131	0.1151
−1.1	0.1170	0.1190	0.1210	0.1230	0.1251	0.1271	0.1292	0.1314	0.1335	0.1357
−1.0	0.1379	0.1401	0.1423	0.1446	0.1469	0.1492	0.1515	0.1539	0.1562	0.1587
−0.9	0.1611	0.1635	0.1660	0.1685	0.1711	0.1736	0.1762	0.1788	0.1814	0.1841
−0.8	0.1867	0.1894	0.1922	0.1949	0.1977	0.2005	0.2033	0.2061	0.2090	0.2119
−0.7	0.2148	0.2177	0.2207	0.2236	0.2266	0.2297	0.2327	0.2358	0.2389	0.2420
−0.6	0.2451	0.2483	0.2514	0.2546	0.2578	0.2611	0.2643	0.2676	0.2709	0.2743
−0.5	0.2776	0.2810	0.2843	0.2877	0.2912	0.2946	0.2981	0.3015	0.3050	0.3085
−0.4	0.3121	0.3156	0.3192	0.3228	0.3264	0.3300	0.3336	0.3372	0.3409	0.3446
−0.3	0.3483	0.3520	0.3557	0.3594	0.3632	0.3669	0.3707	0.3745	0.3783	0.3821
−0.2	0.3859	0.3897	0.3936	0.3974	0.4013	0.4052	0.4090	0.4129	0.4168	0.4207
−0.1	0.4247	0.4286	0.4325	0.4364	0.4404	0.4443	0.4483	0.4522	0.4562	0.4602
−0.0	0.4641	0.4681	0.4721	0.4761	0.4801	0.4840	0.4880	0.4920	0.4960	0.5000

z	0.00	0.01	0.02	0.03	0.04	0.05	0.06	0.07	0.08	0.09
+0.0	0.5000	0.5040	0.5080	0.5120	0.5160	0.5199	0.5239	0.5279	0.5319	0.5359
+0.1	0.5398	0.5438	0.5478	0.5517	0.5557	0.5596	0.5636	0.5675	0.5714	0.5753
+0.2	0.5793	0.5832	0.5871	0.5910	0.5948	0.5987	0.6026	0.6064	0.6103	0.6141
+0.3	0.6179	0.6217	0.6255	0.6293	0.6331	0.6368	0.6406	0.6443	0.6480	0.6517
+0.4	0.6554	0.6591	0.6628	0.6664	0.6700	0.6736	0.6772	0.6808	0.6844	0.6879
+0.5	0.6915	0.6950	0.6985	0.7019	0.7054	0.7088	0.7123	0.7157	0.7190	0.7224
+0.6	0.7257	0.7291	0.7324	0.7357	0.7389	0.7422	0.7454	0.7486	0.7517	0.7549
+0.7	0.7580	0.7611	0.7642	0.7673	0.7704	0.7734	0.7764	0.7794	0.7823	0.7852
+0.8	0.7881	0.7910	0.7939	0.7967	0.7995	0.8023	0.8051	0.8079	0.8106	0.8133
+0.9	0.8159	0.8186	0.8212	0.8238	0.8264	0.8289	0.8315	0.8340	0.8365	0.8389
+1.0	0.8413	0.8438	0.8461	0.8485	0.8508	0.8531	0.8554	0.8577	0.8599	0.8621
+1.1	0.8643	0.8665	0.8686	0.8708	0.8729	0.8749	0.8770	0.8790	0.8810	0.8830
+1.2	0.8849	0.8869	0.8888	0.8907	0.8925	0.8944	0.8962	0.8980	0.8997	0.9015
+1.3	0.9032	0.9049	0.9066	0.9082	0.9099	0.9115	0.9131	0.9147	0.9162	0.9177
+1.4	0.9192	0.9207	0.9222	0.9236	0.9251	0.9265	0.9279	0.9292	0.9306	0.9319
+1.5	0.9332	0.9345	0.9357	0.9370	0.9382	0.9394	0.9406	0.9418	0.9429	0.9441
+1.6	0.9452	0.9463	0.9474	0.9484	0.9495	0.9505	0.9515	0.9525	0.9535	0.9545
+1.7	0.9554	0.9564	0.9573	0.9582	0.9591	0.9599	0.9608	0.9616	0.9625	0.9633
+1.8	0.9641	0.9649	0.9656	0.9664	0.9671	0.9678	0.9686	0.9693	0.9699	0.9706
+1.9	0.9713	0.9719	0.9726	0.9732	0.9738	0.9744	0.9750	0.9756	0.9761	0.9767
+2.0	0.9773	0.9778	0.9783	0.9788	0.9793	0.9798	0.9803	0.9808	0.9812	0.9817
+2.1	0.9821	0.9826	0.9830	0.9834	0.9838	0.9842	0.9846	0.9850	0.9854	0.9857
+2.2	0.9861	0.9864	0.9868	0.9871	0.9875	0.9878	0.9881	0.9884	0.9887	0.9890
+2.3	0.9893	0.9896	0.9898	0.9901	0.9904	0.9906	0.9909	0.9911	0.9913	0.9916
+2.4	0.9918	0.9920	0.9922	0.9925	0.9927	0.9929	0.9931	0.9932	0.9934	0.9936
+2.5	0.9938	0.9940	0.9941	0.9943	0.9945	0.9946	0.9948	0.9949	0.9951	0.9952
+2.6	0.9953	0.9955	0.9956	0.9957	0.9959	0.9960	0.9961	0.9962	0.9963	0.9964
+2.7	0.9965	0.9966	0.9967	0.9968	0.9969	0.9970	0.9971	0.9972	0.9973	0.9974
+2.8	0.9974	0.9975	0.9976	0.9977	0.9977	0.9978	0.9979	0.9979	0.9980	0.9981
+2.9	0.9981	0.9982	0.9983	0.9983	0.9984	0.9984	0.9985	0.9985	0.9986	0.9986
+3.0	0.99865	0.99869	0.99874	0.99878	0.99882	0.99886	0.99889	0.99893	0.99896	0.99900
+3.1	0.99903	0.99906	0.99910	0.99913	0.99915	0.99918	0.99921	0.99924	0.99926	0.99929
+3.2	0.99931	0.99934	0.99936	0.99938	0.99940	0.99942	0.99944	0.99946	0.99948	0.99950
+3.3	0.99952	0.99953	0.99955	0.99957	0.99958	0.99960	0.99961	0.99962	0.99964	0.99965
+3.4	0.99966	0.99967	0.99969	0.99970	0.99971	0.99972	0.99973	0.99974	0.99975	0.99976
+3.5	0.99977	0.99978	0.99978	0.99979	0.99980	0.99981	0.99981	0.99982	0.99983	0.99983

* Proportion of total area under the curve that is under the portion of the curve from $-\infty$ to $(X_i - \mu)/\sigma$ (X_i represents any desired value of the variable X).

the statistical universe it purports to describe. A simple random sample must be arbitrarily taken from the lot it will represent. This means that every element in the population has an equal chance of being chosen for the sample. In addition to a simple random sample, examples of other sampling methods include stratified sampling, cluster sampling, and systematic sampling.

Stratified sampling involves forming strata within a population and then randomly picking a sample from each stratum. Strata could be people who own cars valued from $10,000 to $20,000 and people who own cars valued from $20,001 to $30,000, for example. *Cluster sampling* involves grouping individuals into clusters and randomly selecting clusters. Clusters could be groups of people who eat lunch at different restaurants. *Systematic sampling* implies selecting one value at random and then selecting additional values at evenly spaced intervals.

Sampling error is the error attributed to the difference between the sample and the population. Typically, large samples have smaller sampling errors than small samples. The accuracy of the sample does not vary in a linear fashion with the sample size. If the sample is selected randomly and its size is less than 10% of the population size, then precision depends primarily on the absolute size of the sample rather than the sample size expressed as a percentage of the population size. Nonsampling errors occur when acquiring, recording, or calculating statistical data.

1.6 CALCULUS

Knowledge of calculus is the cornerstone of a sound engineering education. Calculus is briefly reviewed here in its most basic elements.

Differential calculus involves the examination of how something changes relative to something else. For example, if the position of an object is known as a function of time, then differentiation of that function (or the derivative of the function) will give the velocity. The slope of a function $y = f(x)$ at a point (the slope of the tangent line at the point) is the first derivative of the function written as:

$$\frac{dy}{dx} = Dy = y' \qquad (1\text{-}58)$$

The slope of a function can be found at a point if the derivative of the function can be evaluated at that point.

The second derivative of a function is written as:

$$\frac{d^2y}{dx^2} = D^2y = y'' \qquad (1\text{-}59)$$

The second derivative at a point measures the degree to which the function's graph is bending around the point.

Some derivative formulas are given next. The notation assumes that f and g are functions of x, and k is a constant. Additional derivative formulas, if needed, are in Appendix A3.

$$\frac{dk}{dx} = 0 \qquad (1\text{-}60)$$

$$\frac{d(kx^n)}{dx} = nkx^{n-1} \qquad (1\text{-}61)$$

$$\frac{d}{dx}(f + g) = f' + g' \qquad (1\text{-}62)$$

Example 1.6.1. Find the derivative of the function $x^3 - 4x$.

Solution. The function can be broken down into two individual components of x and Equation 1-62 can be applied.

$$\frac{d}{dx}(f + g) = f' + g' \quad (\text{Eq. 1-62})$$

where:

$f = x^3$
$g = -4x$

Now each component can be solved separately.

$$f' = \frac{df}{dx} = \frac{d\left(kx^n\right)}{dx} = nkx^{n-1} \text{ (Eq. 1-61)}$$

where:

$$k = 1, n = 3$$

$$\frac{df}{dx} = \frac{d\left(x^3\right)}{dx} = (3)(1)x^{3-1}$$

$$\frac{df}{dx} = 3x^2$$

$$g' = \frac{dg}{dx} = \frac{d\left(kx^n\right)}{dx} = nkx^{n-1} \text{ (Eq. 1-61)}$$

where:

$$k = -4, n = 1$$

$$\frac{dg}{dx} = \frac{d(-4x)}{dx} = (1)(-4)x^{1-1}$$

$$\frac{dg}{dx} = -4$$

These results are substituted back into Eq. 1-62 for the final result:

$$\frac{d}{dx}\left(x^3 - 4x\right) = 3x^2 - 4$$

One of the most important applications for derivatives is finding the maximum and minimum points in a function $f(x)$. The following tests can be applied to determine the location of a maximum or minimum point:

- $f'(x) = 0$ or undefined at a maximum or minimum point;
- If $f''(x_0) > 0$ then f has a relative minimum at x_0;
- If $f''(x_0) < 0$ then f has a relative maximum at x_0.

Example 1.6.2. Find the maximum and minimum points in the function:

$$f(x) = x^3 - 3x^2 + 3$$

Solution. First, the derivative of the function is found, as in Example 1.6.1.

$$f'(x) = \frac{df}{dx} = \frac{d}{dx}\left(x^3 - 3x^2 + 3\right)$$

By Eq. 1-62,

$$f'(x) = \frac{d}{dx}(x^3) + \frac{d}{dx}\left(-3x^2\right) + \frac{d}{dx}(3)$$

By Eq. 1-61,

$$f'(x) = 3(1)x^{3-1} + 2(-3)x^{2-1} + 0$$

$$f'(x) = 3x^2 - 6x$$

The derivative of the function is set to zero to reveal the extreme (maximum/minimum) points in the function.

$$f'(x) = 3x^2 - 6x = 0$$

Solving for the values of x:

$$3x(x-2) = 0$$

$$3x = 0 \text{ or } x - 2 = 0$$

$$x = 0 \text{ or } x = 2$$

The second derivative is used to test whether these extreme points are local maximum or local minimum. The second derivative is found by taking one more derivative of the first derivative.

$$f''(x) = \frac{df'}{dx} = \frac{d}{dx}\left(3x^2 - 6x\right)$$

By Eq. 1-62,

$$f''(x) = \frac{d}{dx}\left(3x^2\right) + \frac{d(-6x)}{dx}$$

By Eq. 1-61,

$$f''(x) = 2(3)x^{2-1} + 1(-6)x^{1-1}$$

$$f''(x) = 6x - 6$$

Substituting in the extreme points:

$$f''(x = 0) = 6(0) - 6 = -6$$

$f''(0) < 0$, so f has a relative maximum at $x = 0$

$$f''(x = 2) = 6(2) - 6 = 6$$

$f''(2) > 0$, so f has a relative minimum at $x = 2$

This is confirmed by the graph of the function in Figure 1-14.

Integral calculus is the inverse of differentiation. Differentiation finds the slope of a curve, whereas integration finds the area under the curve. In an earlier example, differentiating a position function produced the velocity function. Integrating the velocity function will result in the original position function. If the derivative of a function is integrated, the original function plus a constant of integration is the result:

$$\int f'(x)dx = f(x) + C \qquad (1\text{-}63)$$

This is referred to as an indefinite integral. A definite integral is one that is evaluated between two limits of integration. With definite integrals, the constant of integration cancels out and the integral is evaluated by:

$$\int_a^b f'(x)dx = f(x)\Big|_a^b = f(b) - f(a) \qquad (1\text{-}64)$$

If a function describing a curve is given by $y = f(x)$ and $f(x) \geq 0$ for all x in the integral (a, b), then the area under the curve from a to b is given by:

$$A = \int_a^b f(x)dx \qquad (1\text{-}65)$$

as shown in Figure 1-15.

Some common integration formulas are given next. The notation assumes that c is a constant of the function and C is a constant added in after integration. More integration formulas, if needed, are listed in Appendix A1.3.

$$\int dx = x + C \qquad (1\text{-}66)$$

$$\int cf(x)dx = c\int f(x)dx \qquad (1\text{-}67)$$

$$\int x^n dx = \frac{x^{n+1}}{n+1} + C \quad n \neq -1 \qquad (1\text{-}68)$$

Example 1.6.3. Find the area between the x axis and the function $y = x^2$ from 1 to 7.

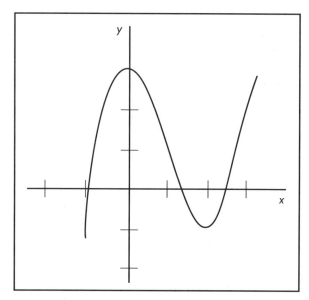

Figure 1-14. Plot of the function in Example 1.6.2.

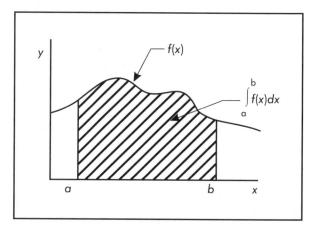

Figure 1-15. Definite integral.

Solution. The area can be found by application of a definite integral.

$$A = \int_a^b f(x)dx \text{ (Eq. 1-65)}$$

where:

$a = 1$
$b = 7$
$f(x) = x^2$

$$A = \int_1^7 x^2 dx$$

$$= \frac{x^{2+1}}{2+1}\Big|_1^7 = \frac{x^3}{3}\Big|_1^7 \text{ (by Eq. 1-68)}$$

$$= \frac{(7)^3}{3} - \frac{(1)^3}{3} \text{ (by Eq. 1-64)}$$

$$= \frac{343}{3} - \frac{1}{3} = \frac{342}{3}$$

REVIEW QUESTIONS

Solve the equations in Problems 1.1 to 1.4 for x:

1.1) $3x + 2 = 4x - 6 + x$

1.2) $\dfrac{1}{6}x - \dfrac{2}{3} = \dfrac{3}{4}x + \dfrac{1}{2}$

1.3) $\dfrac{x}{y} = 2x + 3$

1.4) $\dfrac{3}{x} - \dfrac{2}{x-1} = \dfrac{1}{2x}$

1.5) The length of a rectangle is 4 ft less than two times its width. The perimeter is 46 ft. What is the width?

1.6) A student must have an average grade from 80–90% on four tests to receive a grade of B. Grades on the first three tests were 83%, 76%, and 79%. What grade on the fourth test will guarantee a grade of B?

Solve the equations in Problems 1.7 to 1.9 by the quadratic formula.

1.7) $y^2 + 5y = -5$

1.8) $(g+2)(g-3) = 1$

1.9) $6r^2 = 7 - 19r$

1.10) A pool is 30 ft × 40 ft. Wood chips are to be spread in a uniform width around the perimeter of the pool. If there are enough wood chips to cover 296 ft^2, how wide can the strip be?

1.11) A rectangular piece of sheet metal has a width that is 4 in. less than its length. A piece 2 in. × 2 in. square is cut from each corner. The sides are turned up to form an uncovered box of 256 in.^{3} volume. Find the dimensions of the original piece of metal.

Solve the systems of equations in Problems 1.12 to 1.14.

1.12) $2x + 3y = 5$
$\ 2x + 2y = 5$

1.13) $3x - 2y = 5$
$\ -4x + 5y = 5$

1.14) $x - 2y + z = 5$
$\ -2x + 3y + z = 1$
$x + 3y + 2z = 2$

Solve the equations in Problems 1.15 to 1.17 for x:

1.15) $25^x = 125$

1.16) $\log_2 x = 3$

1.17) $\log_{10} x + \log_{10} \dfrac{3x}{2} = 5$

1.18) The outside of a 10-m diameter cylindrical tank that sits on the ground is to be painted. The tank is 10 m high. If 1 L of paint covers 5 m^2, how many liters are required? Include the top.

1.19) A line with a slope of -2 intersects the x axis at 2. Find the equation of the line.

1.20) A line intercepts the x axis at 4 and the y axis at -6. Find the equation of the line.

1.21) If $\cos \theta = 0.8$ and θ is an acute angle, what is θ?

1.22) Two legs of a right triangle are three and four units long. How long is the hypotenuse?

1.23) Find the interior angles of a triangle with sides two, three, and four.

1.24) A triangle has two sides of length six and eight units. The angle between these two sides is 60°. Find the length of the side opposite the 60° angle.

1.25) A card is drawn from a well-shuffled deck of 52 cards. Find the probability that the card is:

   a) a seven
   b) a red seven
   c) a spade
   d) the seven of spades
   e) a face card

1.26) Two dice are rolled. Find the probability that:

   a) the sum is seven
   b) a sum greater than two is rolled
   c) an odd sum is rolled

1.27) How many ways can six people be seated in a row of six seats?

1.28) A club has 30 members. If a committee of three is selected in a random manner, how many committees are possible?

1.29) Two fair coins are tossed. Find the probability of tossing both heads or both tails.

1.30) A teacher gives the following scores on an examination:

Frequency	Score
1	35
3	45
6	55
8	65
10	75
4	85
2	95

   a) What is the mode of the scores?
   b) What is the mean?
   c) What is the standard deviation?

1.31) A turning center produces shafts with diameters that are normally distributed with a mean and standard deviation of 0.497 and 0.004 respectively. If the specifications require that the shaft diameters be 0.500 ± 0.004, what percentage of the production will be acceptable?

1.32) Differentiate $3x^5 + 7x^2$

1.33) Find the slope of the function $y = 2x^3 - 3x$ at $x = 1$.

1.34) Where does the local maximum and minimum value of $y = x^3 - 12x^2$ occur?

1.35) Find the area under the curve $y = 4x^3$ from $x = 1$ to $x = 2$.

Part 2
Physics and Engineering Sciences

The two most common measurement systems used in the United States are the U.S. Customary System and the International System of Units (SI system, or the metric system). While the United States uses both systems, many other countries have adopted the SI system exclusively.

The International System of Units (SI) was first released by the Conference Generale des Poids et Mesures (CGPM) in 1960 under the French title, Le Systeme International d'Unites. It has since been referred to in all languages as SI. The United States and approximately 36 other countries participated in the international conference.

In 1975, Congress passed the Metric Conversion Act to coordinate and plan for increased use of the metric system in the United States. The Act defined the basis for the United States' compliance with international SI standards. The U.S. Metric Board was formed to carry out the intent of the Act. However, due to the ineffectiveness of the Board, it was disbanded in 1982.

Still realizing the need for conformance with international standards for trade, Congress passed the Omnibus Trade and Competitiveness Act of 1988. This Act designated the metric system as the preferred system of weights and measures for the United States.

As with any system available throughout the world, the metric system deals in base and derived units. The following discussion defines the units of measurement and multiples or divisions of the base units in the metric SI system.

The SI system is based on decimal arithmetic. Each physical quantity consists of units of different sizes, which are formed or created by multiplying or dividing a single base value by powers of 10. Thus, changes can be made very simply by adding zeros or moving decimal points.

2.1 SI BASE UNITS

There are seven base units. They represent the quantities of length, mass, time, electric current, thermodynamic temperature, amount of substance, and luminous intensity. Table 2-1 represents these units and their respective base of definition. From these seven units all other quantities can be derived.

LENGTH

The base unit of length in the SI system is the meter. The millimeter (mm) ($\frac{1}{1,000}$ of a meter), is used as a standard unit of length for most drafting operations. One *meter* (m) is the length of the path traveled by light in a vacuum during a time interval of $\frac{1}{299,792,458}$ of a second.

TIME

The base unit of time in the SI system is the second (s). The *second* is defined as the duration of 9,192,631,770 cycles of the vibration of the isotope cesium 133. Minutes,

Table 2-1. SI base units and their symbols

Quantity	Unit	Symbol
Length	meter	m
Mass	kilogram	kg
Time	second	s
Electric current	ampere	A
Thermodynamic temperature	Kelvin	K
Amount of substance	mole	mol
Luminous intensity	candela	cd

hours, and days are also acceptable forms in non-SI units. Table 2-2 shows the relationship of these units.

MASS

The SI unit for mass is the kilogram (kg). The term *mass* reflects the amount of matter an object contains. The standard unit is a cylinder of platinum-iridium alloy. The kilogram only represents mass; weight and force are represented by other SI units that are derived.

In addition to objects having mass, liquids also have a mass equivalency. In the metric system there is a direct relationship between volume and mass of water. It has been established that one decimeter cubed (1 dm^3) of water has a mass of one kilogram (1 kg), and one centimeter cubed (1 cm^3) of water has a mass of one gram (1 g). The liter (L), an acceptable non-SI term, is equal to one decimeter cubed (1 dm^3).

TEMPERATURE

The SI unit for temperature is the *Kelvin* (K). It is defined as $\frac{1}{273.16}$ of the thermodynamic temperature of the triple point of water. The Kelvin scale is developed from the Celsius scale (° C); Kelvin temperatures are exactly 273.16° above Celsius temperatures. In the Celsius scale, 0° C (or 273.16 K) equals the freezing point of pure water and 100° C (or 373.16 K) equals the boiling point of pure water at controlled atmospheric pressure.

Zero on the Kelvin scale (0 K) represents absolute zero, the temperature at which there is absence of heat. Absolute zero on the Celsius scale, therefore, is −273.16° C. (Note, when writing temperatures in Kelvin, the degree symbol [°] is not used.) Since there is a correlation between Kelvin and Celsius, the use of Celsius is preferred and it is a non-SI acceptable unit.

ELECTRIC CURRENT

The base unit for electric current in the SI is the ampere (A). The *ampere* is defined as the amount of current between two straight parallel wires placed one meter apart. The result is 2×10^{-7} Newton/meter (N/m) of wire force between those two wires.

LUMINOUS INTENSITY

The SI unit for luminous intensity is the candela (cd). The *candela* is defined as the luminous intensity, in a given direction, of a light source producing single-frequency light at 540×10^{12} hertz with a power of $\frac{1}{683}$ watt per steradian.

AMOUNT OF SUBSTANCE

The mole (mol) is the base SI unit for the amount of substance. The *mole* is defined as the amount of substance of a system containing the same amount of elementary entities as there are atoms in carbon 12 having

Table 2-2. The relationship of the various units of time

Units	Symbol	Equals
1 minute	min	60 seconds
1 hour	hr	60 minute or 3,600 seconds
1 day	d	24 hours or 1,440 minutes or 86,400 seconds

a mass of 0.012 kilogram, or 6.023×10^{23} entities. Hence, one mole of water molecules would be 6.023×10^{23} molecules, etc.

2.2 SI PREFIXES

One of the most beneficial aspects of the SI system is the ability to multiply the base unit by powers of 10 to express multiples or sub-multiples of the base unit. These units are expressed by adding a prefix to the name of the base unit. For example, one thousandth of a meter is expressed as a millimeter, and one thousand meters is expressed as a kilometer. Table 2-3 represents the expression of metric values as noted by the multiplication factors, the prefix names, and the SI symbols.

Example 2.2.1. Express 207×10^3 MPa as Pa.

Solution.

$$207 \times 10^3 \text{ MPa} = 207 \times 10^3 (10^6) \text{ Pa}$$
$$= 207 \times 10^{3+6} \text{ Pa (Eq. 1-8)}$$
$$= 207 \times 10^9 \text{ Pa}$$

2.3 SI DERIVED AND SUPPLEMENTARY UNITS

When measuring quantities such as density, pressure, speed, acceleration, and area, it becomes necessary to use combinations of the seven base-SI units. These combinations are called *derived units*.

Supplementary units are units that have not been specifically classified as base or derived units. At present, there are only two supplementary units and they both refer to angular measurement. These units are the radian and steradian. Plane angles are measured in radians. Solid angles are measured in steradians. The form of angular measurement using degrees did not become an SI supplementary unit. However, the degree (°), the minute ('), and the second (") are acceptable non-SI units. There are 60 seconds per minute, 60 minutes per degree, and 360 degrees in a complete revolution. Hence a 360° turn is equivalent to 21,600' or 1,296,000". These units and equivalencies are shown in Table 2-4.

Table 2-5 lists derived SI units and their respective definitions. Table D-1 in Appendix D lists derived SI units and their respective formulas. Converting from one system to another can be accomplished using a conversion table such as Table D-2 found in Appendix D.

Example 2.3.1. Convert 1.250 inches to millimeters.

Solution. First use Table D-2 in Appendix D to convert inches into the standard SI unit for length, meters.

$$1.250 \text{ in.} \times \frac{0.0254 \text{ m}}{1 \text{ in.}} = 0.03175 \text{ m}$$

Now use Table D-2 to convert into mm.

$$0.03175 \text{ m} \times \frac{1 \text{ mm}}{0.001 \text{ m}} = 31.75 \text{ mm}$$

$$1 \text{ mm} = (10^{-3}) \text{ m} = 0.001 \text{ m}$$

2.4 U.S. CUSTOMARY SYSTEM

In the U.S. Customary System, the base units are length (feet), force (pounds), and time(seconds). The *foot* is defined as exactly 0.3048 m. The *pound* is defined as the weight

Table 2-3. The expression of metric values

SI Symbol	Prefix	Multiplication Factors
T	tera	$10^{12} = 1\ 000\ 000\ 000\ 000$
G	giga	$10^{9} = 1\ 000\ 000\ 000$
M	mega	$10^{6} = 1\ 000\ 000$
k	kilo	$10^{3} = 1\ 000$
h	hecto*	$10^{2} = 100$
da	deka*	$10^{1} = 10$
d	deci*	$10^{-1} = 0.1$
c	centi*	$10^{-2} = 0.01$
m	milli	$10^{-3} = 0.001$
μ	micro	$10^{-6} = 0.000\ 001$
n	nano	$10^{-9} = 0.000\ 000\ 001$
p	pico	$10^{-12} = 0.000\ 000\ 000\ 001$
f	femto	$10^{-15} = 0.000\ 000\ 000\ 000\ 001$
a	atto	$10^{-18} = 0.000\ 000\ 000\ 000\ 000\ 001$

* To be avoided when possible

Table 2-4. Supplementary units and their equivalency

Units	Symbol	Equals
1 degree	°	$= \dfrac{\pi}{180}\ \text{rad}$
1 minute	′	$= \dfrac{1}{60}^{\circ} = \dfrac{\pi}{10,800}\text{rad}$
1 second	″	$= \dfrac{1}{60}^{\prime} = \dfrac{1}{3,600}^{\circ} = \dfrac{\pi}{648,000}\text{rad}$

of a platinum standard, with a mass of 0.45359243 kg, at sea level and 45 degrees latitude. The *second* is defined as the duration of 9,192,631,770 cycles of the vibration of the isotope cesium 133. Table 2-6 provides a list of the U.S. Customary base units including their symbols.

In the U.S. Customary System the unit of mass is derived and called a *slug*. A slug is the mass of material accelerated at one foot per second squared by a force of one pound. From Newton's second law, the following expression is obtained.

$$1\ \text{slug} = \frac{1\ \text{lb-s}^{2}}{\text{ft}} \qquad (2\text{-}1)$$

It should be noted that the unit of force is the pound (lb) and the unit of mass, which is derived, is the slug (slug). In some engineering applications, an alternative unit of mass called the pound mass (lbm) is used. When pound mass is used, the corresponding unit of force is the pound force (lbf). In this text, the unit of force will be either pounds (lb) or newtons (N). The unit of mass will be either slugs (slug) or kilogram (kg).

Table 2-5. Derived SI units and their descriptions

SI Unit	Description
Coulomb	The quantity of electricity transported in one second by a current of one ampere.
Farad	The electric capacitance of a capacitor that has a difference of potential of one volt between its plates when it is charged by a quantity of electricity equal to one coulomb.
Henry	The electric inductance of a closed circuit in which an electromotive force of one volt is produced when the electric current in the circuit varies uniformly at a rate of one ampere per second.
Hertz	A frequency of one cycle per second.
Joule	The work done (that is, energy expended) when the point of application of a force of one newton is displaced a distance of one meter in the direction of the force.
Lumen	The luminous flux emitted in a solid angle of one steradian by a point source having a uniform intensity of one candela.
Lux	The illuminance produced by a luminous flux of one lumen uniformly distributed over a surface of one square meter.
Newton	That force which, when applied to a body having a mass of one kilogram, gives it an acceleration of one meter per second squared.
Ohm	The electric resistance between two points of a conductor when a constant difference of potential of one volt, applied between these two points, produces a current of one ampere.
Pascal	The pressure or stress of one newton per square meter.
Siemens	The electrical conductance of a conductor in which a current of one ampere is produced by an electric potential difference of one volt.
Tesla	The magnetic flux density given by a magnetic flux of one weber per square meter.
Volt	The unit of electric potential difference and electromotive force, which is the difference of electric potential between two points of a conductor carrying a constant current of one ampere when the power dissipated between these points is equal to one watt.
Watt	The power that gives rise to the production of energy at the rate of one joule per second.
Weber	The magnetic flux which, linking a circuit of one turn, produces in it an electromotive force of one volt as it is reduced to zero at a uniform rate in one second.

Table 2-6. U.S. Customary System base units and their symbols

Quantity	Unit	Symbol
Length	foot	ft
Mass	slug	slug
Time	second	s
Electric current	ampere	A
Thermodynamic temperature	rankine	R
Amount of substance	mole	mol
Luminous intensity	foot candle	ft-C

Pound mass (lbm) and pound force (lbf) will not be used except in Chapter 9, where units of specific heat are defined as btu/lbm-°R or J/kg-K.

Table 2-7 specifies some common conversions within the U.S. Customary System.

Table 2-7. Common weight and measurement conversions within the U.S. Customary System

Length
1 mile = 1,760 yards (yd) = 5,280 feet (ft)
1 yd = 3 ft = 36 inches (in.)
1 ft = 12 in.
1 mil = 0.001 in.

Square measure
1 square yard (yd^2) = 9 square feet (ft^2)
1 ft^2 = 144 square inches (in.^{2})

Cubic measure
1 cubic yard (yd^3) = 27 cubic feet (ft^3)
1 ft^3 = 1,728 cubic inches (in.^{3})

Liquid measure
1 U.S. gallon (gal) = 0.1337 ft^3 = 231 in.^{3}

Commercial weight
1 net ton = 2,000 pounds (lb)
1 lb = 16 ounces (oz)

Pressure
1 pound per square inch (lb/in.^{2} or psi) = 144 pounds per square foot (lb/ft^2)
1 atmosphere = 14.7 lb/in.^{2} or psi

REVIEW QUESTIONS

2.1) How many millimeters are in 5 meters?

2.2) What SI unit of length is most commonly used for machining practices?

2.3) One inch is equal to how many millimeters?

2.4) Fifty cycles per second equals how many hertz?

2.5) One meter equals how many feet?

2.6) What SI symbol is used to represent pressure?

2.7) What SI symbol is used to represent energy?

2.8) Convert a feed rate of 0.022 inches per revolution to millimeters per revolution.

Chapter 3

Light

3.1 ELECTROMAGNETIC RADIATION

Light is electromagnetic radiation. Light is the portion of the electromagnetic spectrum that is visible to the human eye. The different components of the electromagnetic spectrum are illustrated in Figure 3-1. The eye has varying sensitivity to different wavelengths of light as shown in Figure 3-2. The eye is most sensitive to yellow-green colors. This is the rationale behind the yellow color of some fire trucks and self-adhesive note papers.

The speed of light in a given material is constant. In a vacuum or air, the speed of light is approximately 984×10^6 ft/s (300×10^6 m/s). The wave nature of light allows it to be characterized in terms of wavelength and frequency. The product of the wavelength and frequency of light is equal to its speed:

$$c = \lambda f \qquad (3\text{-}1)$$

where:

c = speed of light in a vacuum (ft/s [m/s])
λ = wavelength (ft [m])
f = frequency (cycles per second or Hz)

3.2 RAY THEORY

Many aspects of the physical behavior of light can be explained in terms of ray theory. A ray of light is a straight path that the light travels in from one point to another. Reflection and refraction are two phenomena readily explained by ray theory.

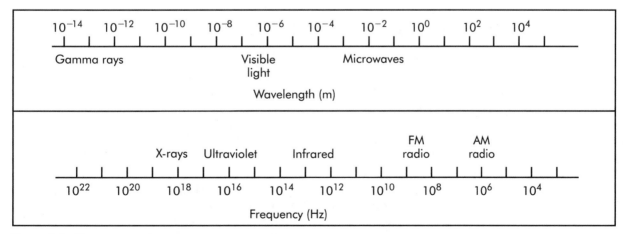

Figure 3-1. Electromagnetic spectrum.

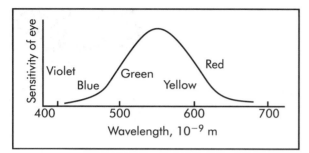

Figure 3-2. Sensitivity of the eye to light.

REFLECTION

Consider a light ray impinging on an object. A portion of the light wave is redirected away from the object, while the other portions are absorbed by the object and transmitted through it. Reflected light is the portion of the light wave redirected away from the object. If a line is drawn normal to the surface, the angle of incidence θ_1 (measured between the normal line and the incoming ray) is equal to the angle of reflection θ_2 as shown in Figure 3-3:

$$\theta_1 = \theta_2 \qquad (3-2)$$

REFRACTION

Light travels at different speeds in different media. When a ray of light is transmitted through two materials, the line of travel of the light wave is changed at the interface

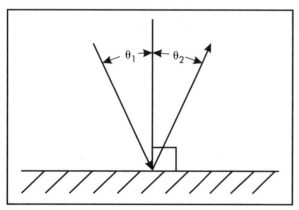

Figure 3-3. Reflected light.

of the two materials. Figure 3-4 shows a ray of light traveling through one media with angle of incidence θ_1. The line of travel is changed at the interface of the two materials having an angle of refraction θ_2. Refraction is the basis for the action of lenses. For the situation depicted in Figure 3-4, the speed of light would be greater in material 1 than in material 2. The angles of incidence and refraction are related by Snell's Law:

$$\eta_1 \sin \theta_1 = \eta_2 \sin \theta_2 \qquad (3-3)$$

where:

η_1 and η_2 = the indices of refraction for the two media

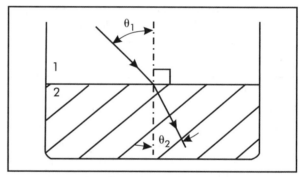

Figure 3-4. Light refracted.

Various refraction indices are given in Table 3-1.

Table 3-1. Various indices of refraction

Material	η
Air	1.00
Water	1.33
Fused quartz	1.46
Flint glass	1.66
Diamond	2.42

Example 3.2.1. Light enters a pool of water from the air as in Figure 3-5. Find the angle of refraction for water using Snell's Law if the angle of incidence, $\theta_1 = 45°$.

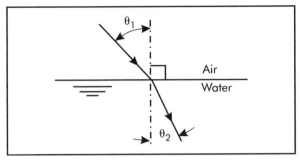

Figure 3-5. Example 3.2.1

Solution. Using the data for indices of refraction, Snell's Law may be applied directly:

$$\eta_1 \sin \theta_1 = \eta_2 \sin \theta_2 \text{ (Eq. 3-3)}$$

where:

η_1 = indice of air = 1.00
θ_1 = angle of incidence = 45°
η_2 = indice of water = 1.33
θ_2 = angle of refraction (°)

$$1.00 \sin 45° = 1.33 \sin \theta_2$$
$$0.53 = \sin \theta_2$$
$$\theta_2 = \sin^{-1} 0.53 = 32°$$

REVIEW QUESTIONS

3.1) Is the frequency of visible light higher or lower than FM radio?

3.2) What is the longest wavelength of light that can be seen with the human eye?

3.3) A manufacturer's specifications indicate that a light-emitting diode is 880 nanometers (880×10^{-9} m). Is the emission of the LED visible? What is the frequency of the emission?

3.4) A machine shop is repainting its tools. Would blue or green be a better choice for safety? Assume a safer color is one that is more visible to the human eye.

3.5) A remote control uses an infrared light beam to turn on and off a TV set. The user wants to turn off a TV set by bouncing the beam off a mirror as shown in Figure Q3-1. The remote control is positioned somewhere along the centerline of the wall. How far from the edge of the wall (what distance x) can the remote control be located and still turn off the set?

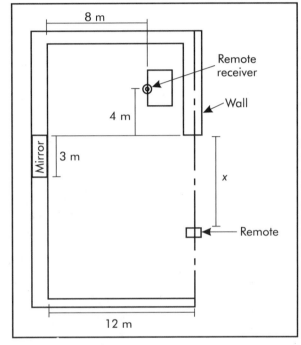

Figure Q3-1. Question 3.5.

3.6) A spotlight is located at the bottom of a decorative fountain as shown in Figure Q3-2. How far from the surface of the water will the spot be projected on the wall?

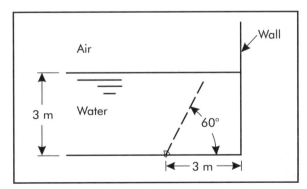

Figure Q3-2. Question 3.6.

Chapter 4

Sound

Sound is the transmission of mechanical waves in matter. It can only be transmitted through matter and cannot be transmitted in a vacuum. The human ear is sensitive to certain frequencies of sound waves, typically in the range of 20–20,000 cycles/second or hertz (Hz). The ear detects mechanical vibrations in the air and the nervous system transmits them to the brain.

4.1 WAVE NATURE OF SOUND

Sound is comprised of longitudinal mechanical waves travelling through matter. Sound waves are generated by the successive compression and rarefaction of the media that is transmitting it. The generation of sound in air can be visualized by the action of a piston in a cylinder as illustrated in Figure 4-1.

When a crank is rotating at ω radians/second, a series of compressed bursts of air resulting from the forward (left-to-right) motion of the piston will be emitted from the cylinder. These compressed bursts will alternate with rarified bursts of air resulting from the retraction of the piston. The

bursts will be separated by a wavelength given by:

$$\lambda = a \sin \omega t \qquad (4\text{-}1)$$

where:

a = radius of the crank (in.[m])
ω = frequency of the sound waves (Hz)
t = time

Sound waves propagate through a gas at a speed given by:

$$v = \sqrt{\frac{kP}{\rho}} \qquad (4\text{-}2)$$

where:

k = specific heat ratio for the gas
P = pressure (lb/in.^{2} [Pa])
ρ = density of the gas (slug/in.^{3} [kg/m^3]

The values of specific heat for various gases are given in Table 4-1.

4.2 INTENSITY OF SOUND

Sound waves represent a successive increase and decrease in pressure in the media transmitting them. This process transmits energy (power) through the media over a

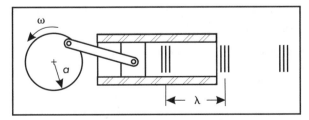

Figure 4-1. Generation of sound waves.

Table 4-1. Specific heat ratio of various gases

Gas	Specific Heat Ratio (k)
Air	1.40
CO_2	1.30
CH_4	1.31
He	1.66

given area. The intensity of sound is a measure of the energy that it transmits. *Intensity* is defined as:

$$I = \frac{P}{A} \qquad (4\text{-}3)$$

where:

I = actual intensity (w/m²)
P = power, which is the amount of energy divided by the amount of time the energy is expended (W)
A = surface area exposed to the energy source (m²)

The intensity of sound waves passing through an open window is the power transmitted through the area of the open window.

In most cases, the intensity of sound is expressed in terms of *relative intensity* or power level:

$$\text{Relative Intensity (dB)} = 10\log\left(\frac{I}{I_0}\right) \quad (4\text{-}4)$$

where:

I = actual intensity (w/m²)
I_0 = intensity of sound at the threshold of human hearing, typically $I_0 = 10^{-12}$ W/m². Relative intensity has units of decibels (dB), whereas actual intensity is described in terms of watts per square meter.

Example 4.2.1. Find the actual intensity in W/m² of a 45-dB sound.

Solution. The relative intensity in decibels is the logarithmic ratio of the actual intensity to the threshold of human hearing:

$$\text{Relative intensity} = 45 \text{ dB} = 10 \log \frac{I}{I_0}$$
(Eq. 4-4)

where:

I = actual intensity
I_0 = intensity at threshold of human hearing = 10^{-12} W/m²

This equation can be solved for I:

$$45 = 10 \log\frac{I}{10^{-12} \text{ W/m}^2}$$

$$\log\frac{I}{10^{-12} \text{ W/m}^2} = 4.5$$

$$\frac{I}{10^{-12} \text{ W/m}^2} = 10^{4.5} = 3.16 \times 10^4$$

$$I = 3.16 \times 10^{-8} \text{ W/m}^2$$

The relative intensities of various types of sound are shown in Table 4-2.

4.3 FREQUENCY OF SOUND

The frequency of sound is normally referred to as its *pitch*. Pitch describes the audible effect that a frequency of sound waves has on the human ear. Pitch is normally measured in hertz (Hz) or cycles/second. The frequency of sound is determined by the rate of oscillation of the physical phenomena that produces the sound waves.

Example 4.3.1. A simple siren can be constructed by blowing air through a small-diameter tube at a rotating disk that has a series of holes spaced evenly around its outer edge. If the disk has 48 holes in it and is rotating at 1,200 rpm, find the pitch of the sound produced by the siren.

Solution. A single cycle of the sound wave produced by the siren occurs when a hole passes the location of the air jet. The pitch can be determined by calculating the num-

Table 4-2. Typical sound intensities

Sound Type	Intensity W/m²	dB
Jet aircraft (close range)	100	140
Jackhammer	10^{-2}	100
Automobile on highway	10^{-4}	80
Normal speech	10^{-6}	60
Whisper	10^{-10}	20

ber of times a hole passes the blowing air in a second.

$$\text{pitch} = \left(\frac{1,200 \text{ rev}}{1 \text{ min}}\right)\left(\frac{1 \text{ min}}{60 \text{ s}}\right)\left(\frac{48 \text{ holes (cycles)}}{\text{rev}}\right)$$

$$\text{pitch} = \frac{960 \text{ cycles}}{\text{s}} = 960 \text{ Hz}$$

4.4 RESPONSE OF THE HUMAN EAR TO SOUND

The sensitivity of the human ear to sound is a function of frequency. The perceived loudness is strongly influenced by pitch. The threshold of hearing is approximately 0 dB for most sounds in the range of frequencies associated with human speech (200–5,000 Hz). Frequencies lower and higher than this range must have a higher intensity before they are detected by the human ear. Figure 4-2 illustrates the range of audibility of the human ear. Sounds with intensities less than the lower limit cannot be detected by the average human ear. If a sound has an intensity greater than 120 dB, it generally produces pain rather than hearing. *Ultrasonic sound* is at a frequency above the range of human hearing. *Infrasonic sound* has a frequency below the range of human hearing.

REVIEW QUESTIONS

4.1) What is the lowest intensity of sound at 10,000 Hz that can be detected by the typical human ear?

4.2) What is the loudest (highest intensity) sound that occurs in typical human speech? At what approximate frequency does this sound occur?

4.3) Find the intensity of 80 dB sound in W/m^2.

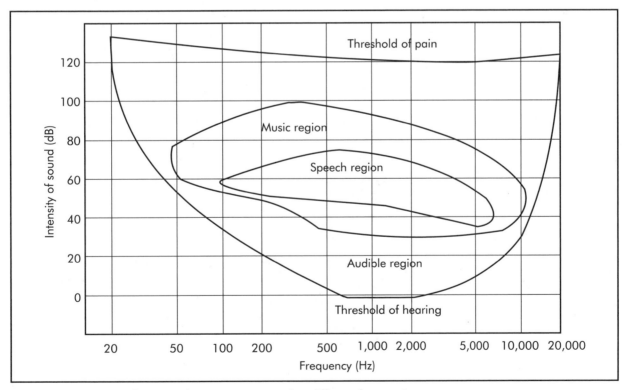

Figure 4-2. Response of average human ear to sound at different frequencies.

4.4) What is the relative intensity of sound with an actual intensity of 4×10^{-6} W/m²?

4.5) A 2×4 m sheet of plastic is in front of a speaker that is emitting sound at 90 dB. Assuming all the power is transferred to the sheet, how much is transferred?

4.6) Wind blows through a wheel with five slots spaced evenly around the edge. The wheel has a diameter of 18 in. with the tire mounted. The wheel is mounted on a vehicle moving at 60 miles/hour. Find the pitch of the sound produced.

Chapter 5

Electricity/Electronics

Electricity and electronics are involved in the generation, transmission, and storage of power in numerous applications. The field of study in these topics is very large. The coverage here will be limited to a brief discussion of circuits and power flow.

5.1 ELECTRICAL CIRCUITS

Electrical circuits are the interconnection of components for generating and distributing electrical power, converting electrical power to another form (such as light, heat, or motion), or processing information. Electrical circuits contain a source of electrical power, passive components, which dissipate or store energy, and active components, which change the amount of electrical power. Circuits can be broadly classified as direct current (DC) where currents and voltages do not vary with time, and as alternating current (AC) where currents and voltages vary (usually sinusoidally) with respect to time.

There are several quantities used in electrical circuits: charge, current, voltage, energy, power, resistance, inductance, and capacitance.

CHARGE (Q)

Electrical charge is an energy carrying quantity measured in units of coulombs. The smallest unit of electrical charge is the electron, which carries a charge of 1.6022×10^{-19} coulombs. Charges can be either positive or negative. Opposite charges attract each other and like charges repel each other. Charges exert a force on each other, which is the basis of electrical power.

CURRENT (I)

Electrical current is the time rate of flow of charge past a point in a circuit. It is measured in amperes. Analogous to a fluid system, electrical current can be compared to the volumetric flow rate of water through a pipe. A higher electric current implies a greater "volume" of energy being delivered in a given period of time.

VOLTAGE (V)

Voltage is the change in energy per unit charge. The unit of measure is the volt. Voltage can increase or decrease as current flows through circuit elements. Some sources, such as batteries, can increase voltage. Resistors and other loads decrease voltage as current flows through them. Voltage is analogous to pressure in a fluid system.

ENERGY (W)

Electrical energy is the capacity to do work. Energy is measured in joules. Electrical energy can be stored in circuit elements such as batteries, capacitors, or coils. It can be transformed into mechanical energy in a motor or dissipated as heat through a resistor.

POWER (P)

Electric power is the time rate of energy flow. It is measured in watts. The energy consumed by a household in a billing cycle is commonly expressed in units of kilowatt-hours, indicating an amount of power for a period of time. This unit is actually the number of joules per second. The power supplied by a circuit component can be found as the product of the voltage rise across the component and the current that flows through it:

$$P = IV \qquad (5\text{-}1)$$

where:

P = power (watts)
I = current (amperes)
V = voltage (volts)

The power consumed by a component can be found by the same formula as the product of the voltage drop across the component and the current that flows through it:

$$P = IV \text{ (Eq. 5-1)}$$

Alternately, the power consumed in a resistive load can be found as the product of the resistance and the square of the current that flows through it:

$$P = I^2R \qquad (5\text{-}2)$$

where:

R = resistive load (ohms)

The power consumed in a resistive load can also be found by:

$$P = \frac{V^2}{R} \qquad (5\text{-}3)$$

There are many types of components that can be used to form an electrical circuit. Some examples of sources that generate electrical energy are: batteries, generators, and power supplies (devices that convert one type of voltage/current combination into another). Some of the passive components used in circuits are: resistors, inductors, and capacitors. These components are illustrated in Figure 5-1 in the context of a DC circuit.

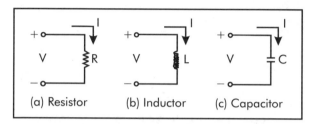

Figure 5-1. Circuit components.

RESISTANCE (R)

Resistors are energy absorbing components. As current flows through a resistor, the voltage drops. A resistor is symbolized in Figure 5-1(a). Resistance is measured in ohms (Ω). The relationship between current and voltage in a resistor is given by:

$$I = \frac{V}{R} \qquad (5\text{-}4)$$

where:

I = current (amperes)
V = voltage (volts)
R = resistance (ohms)

INDUCTANCE (L)

Inductors are energy-storing components where energy is stored in a magnetic field. An inductor is illustrated in Figure 5-1(b). Inductance is measured in henries. The relationship between current and voltage in an inductor is given by:

$$I = \frac{1}{L}\int V dt \qquad (5\text{-}5)$$

$$\text{or amperes} = \frac{\text{volts} \times \text{seconds}}{\text{henries}}$$

where:

I = current (amperes)
L = inductance (henries)

V = voltage (volts)
dt = derivative of time function

CAPACITANCE (C)

Capacitors are energy-storing components where energy is stored in an electric field. A capacitor is shown in Figure 5-1(c). Capacitance is measured in farads. One farad is very large. A typical capacitor used in a circuit for consumer electronics has a value measured in the microfarads. The relationship between current and voltage in a capacitor is given by:

$$I = C\frac{dV}{dt} \qquad (5\text{-}6)$$

$$\text{or amperes} = \frac{\text{farads} \times \text{volts}}{\text{seconds}}$$

where:

I = current (amperes)
C = capacitance (farads)
$\dfrac{dV}{dt}$ = derivative of voltage function with respect to time

5.2 TYPES OF CIRCUIT CONNECTIONS

The two basic types of circuit connections, parallel and series, are illustrated in Figure 5-2. In a parallel connection, the same voltage is present across all components. In a series connection, the same current flows through all components.

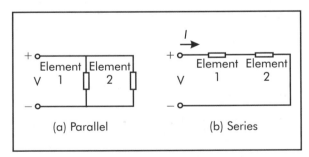

Figure 5-2. Parallel and series connections.

Components in a circuit may be combined and analyzed as a simpler circuit containing fewer elements. The rules for combining circuit components vary depending on the type of component and whether they are connected in parallel or series. An equivalent component can be found that has the same performance as a set of components in the circuit. The rules for combining components are summarized in Figure 5-3. Some comment should be made about combining sources in parallel and series. Sources can be combined in series to obtain an additive equivalent voltage. Sources having equal voltages can be combined in parallel to supply a large current without demanding an excessive current from any single source. The equivalent voltage in a parallel connection of equal voltage sources is equal to that of any individual source. Sources having appreciably different voltages are not connected in parallel since wasteful circulating currents would occur, even if there was not external connection to the sources.

Example 5.2.1. Find the single equivalent resistance to the interconnected resistors shown in Figure 5-4.

Solution. Step 1: the 6Ω and 3Ω resistors are combined in parallel.

$$\frac{1}{R_{eq}} = \frac{1}{R_1} + \frac{1}{R_2} \text{ (from Figure 5-3)}$$

where:

R_{eq} = new equivalent resistor (replacing 6Ω and 3Ω)
R_1 = 6Ω
R_2 = 3Ω

$$\frac{1}{R_{eq}} = \frac{1}{6\Omega} + \frac{1}{3\Omega} = \frac{1}{6} + \frac{2}{6} = \frac{3}{6} = \frac{1}{2}$$

$$R_{eq} = 2\Omega$$

Step 2: The 4Ω and the resulting 2Ω resistors are combined in series.

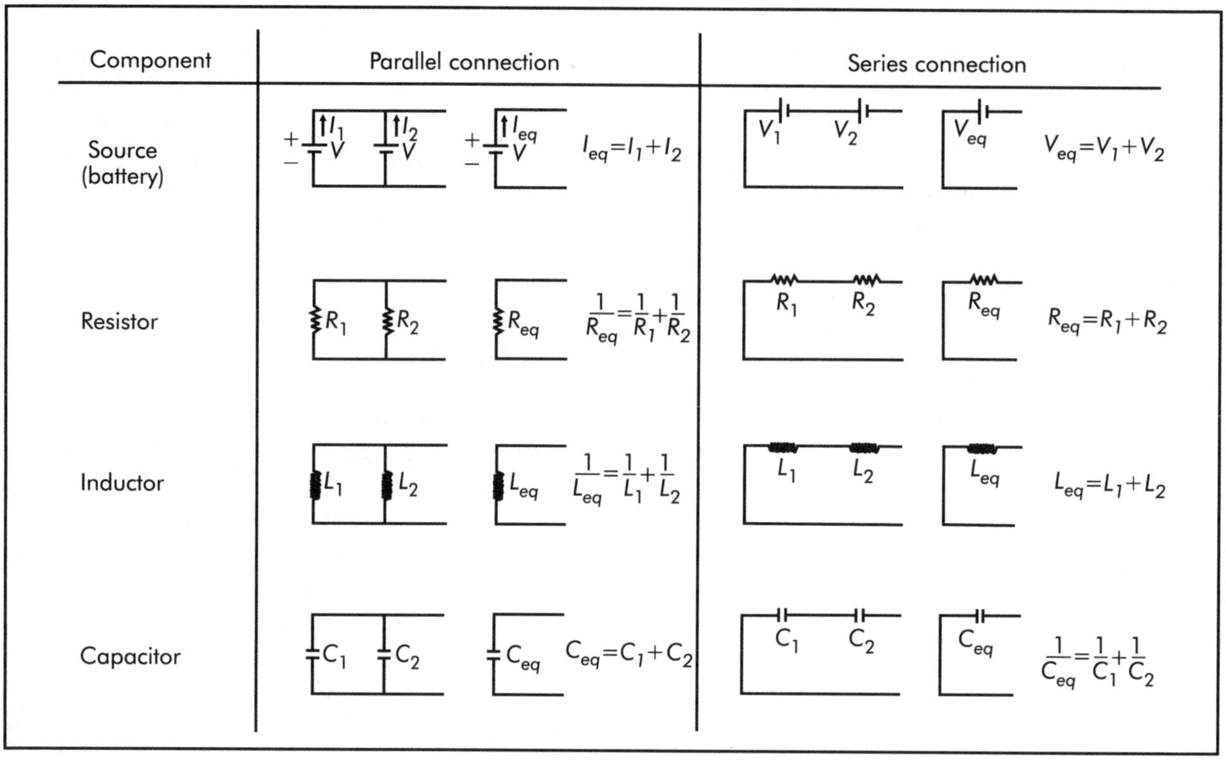

Component
Parallel connection
Series connection
Source (battery)
$I_{eq}=I_1+I_2$
$V_{eq}=V_1+V_2$
Resistor
$\frac{1}{R_{eq}}=\frac{1}{R_1}+\frac{1}{R_2}$
$R_{eq}=R_1+R_2$
Inductor
$\frac{1}{L_{eq}}=\frac{1}{L_1}+\frac{1}{L_2}$
$L_{eq}=L_1+L_2$
Capacitor
$C_{eq}=C_1+C_2$
$\frac{1}{C_{eq}}=\frac{1}{C_1}+\frac{1}{C_2}$

Figure 5-3. Parallel and series connections of various components.

Step 1:
Step 2:
Step 3:
Step 4:

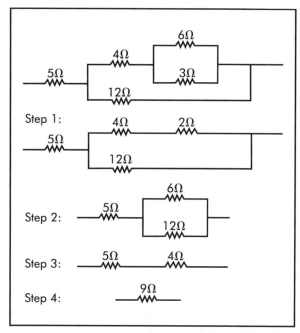

Figure 5-4. Network of resistors.

$R_{eq} = R_1 + R_2$ (from Figure 5-3)

where:

R_{eq} = new equivalent resistor (replacing 4Ω and 2Ω)
R_1 = 4Ω
R_2 = 2Ω
R_{eq} = 4Ω + 2Ω = 6Ω

Step 3: The resulting parallel branch of 6Ω and 12Ω resistors is combined.

$$\frac{1}{R_{eq}} = \frac{1}{R_1} + \frac{1}{R_2} \text{ (from Figure 5-3)}$$

where:

R_{eq} = new equivalent resistor (replacing 6Ω and 12Ω)
R_1 = 6Ω
R_2 = 12Ω

$$\frac{1}{R_{eq}} = \frac{1}{6\Omega} + \frac{1}{12\Omega} = \frac{2}{12} + \frac{1}{12} = \frac{3}{12} = \frac{1}{4}$$

$$R_{eq} = 4\Omega$$

Step 4: The resulting 4Ω and 5Ω resistors are combined in series to obtain the overall equivalence.

$$R_{eq} = R_1 + R_2 \text{ (from Figure 5-3)}$$

where:

R_{eq} = overall equivalent resistor
R_1 = 4Ω
R_2 = 5Ω
R_{eq} = $4\Omega + 5\Omega = 9\Omega$

5.3 CIRCUIT ANALYSIS USING KIRCHOFF'S LAWS

There are two tools used in analyzing simple electrical circuits. These tools are based on two conservative laws that govern the behavior of basic circuits: Kirchoff's Loop Rule and Kirchoff's Point Rule.

KIRCHOFF'S LOOP RULE (KLR)

Kirchoff's Loop Rule is a statement of conservation of energy. It states that the sum of voltage rises or drops in a particular direction around a closed path or loop must be zero.

KIRCHOFF'S POINT RULE (KPR)

Kirchoff's Point Rule is a statement of conservation of charge. It states that the flow of charges (current) into or out of a point (junction of electrical connections) must add to zero.

Example 5.3.1. For the circuit shown in Figure 5-5, find (a) the current I; (b) the power sourced by the batteries, and (c) the power dissipated by each resistor.

Solution. (a) Since it is a closed loop, the current I is the same throughout the circuit.

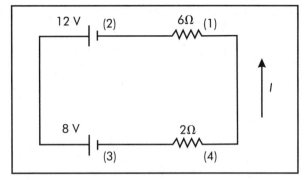

Figure 5-5. Circuit for example 5.3.1.

The voltage changes with every element, but the net changes must sum to zero according to Kirchoff's Loop Rule. The elements are numbered for clarity and the voltage changes are taken in the direction of the current.

$$\Sigma V_{changes} = V_1 + V_2 + V_3 + V_4 = 0 \quad (5\text{-}7)$$

Resistors cause a voltage drop, so the sign for elements (1) and (4) will be negative. The voltage change across the resistors can be found by:

V = IR (see Eq. 5-4)
V_1 = $-I(6\Omega)$
V_4 = $-I(2\Omega)$

The voltages of the batteries are given but their polarity must be determined. Current flows through battery (2) from negative to positive, so it provides a voltage increase.

$$V_2 = +12V$$

Battery (3) is aligned in the opposite way so it provides a voltage decrease.

$$V_3 = -8V$$

$$\Sigma V_{changes} = -I(6\Omega) + 12V - 8V - I(2\Omega) = 0$$

$$4V = I(8\Omega)$$

$$I = \frac{4V}{8\Omega} = 0.5 \text{ A}$$

(b) The power sourced by the batteries is a sum of the power supplied by each battery. Remember that battery (3) is in the circuit backwards and is supplying power in a direction opposite to the current flow, so its power contribution is negative.

$$P_{sourced} = \Sigma P_{batteries} = P_2 + P_3$$
$$= IV_2 + IV_3 \text{ (Eq. 5-1)}$$

where:

I = current through circuit = 0.5 A
V_2 = change in voltage across battery (2) = +12 V
V_3 = change in voltage across battery (3) = −8 V
$P_{sourced} = (0.5 \text{ A})(+12 \text{ V}) + (0.5 \text{ A})(−8 \text{ V})$
$= 6 \text{ W} − 4 \text{ W}$
$= 2 \text{ W}$

(c) The power dissipated by each resistor can be found by either Equation 5-2 or 5-3. However, since the current flowing through the circuit is known, but not the voltage across each resistor, Equation 5-2 is used.

$$P_{dissipated} = \Sigma P_{resistors} = P_1 + P_4$$
$$= I^2R_1 + I^2R_4 \text{ (Eq. 5-2)}$$

where:

I = current through circuit = 0.5 A
R_1 = resistance of resistor (1) = 6Ω
R_4 = resistance pf resistor (4) = 2Ω

$$P_{dissipated} = (0.5 \text{ A})^2(6Ω) + (0.5 \text{ A})^2(2Ω)$$
$$= 2\text{W}$$

The power dissipated by the resistors is equal to the power sourced by the batteries.

Example 5.3.2. For the circuit shown in Figure 5-6, find the voltage that must be supplied by source X if the ammeter indicates that a 0.5-ampere current is flowing in the circuit.

Solution. Kirchoff's Point Rule is applied at point P. The 0.5-ampere current and I_1 flow into the junction and I_2 flows out of the junction. If the direction of I_1 and I_2 is not given, their direction must be assumed.

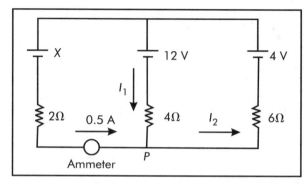

Figure 5-6. Circuit for example 5.3.2.

$$0.5 \text{ A} + I_1 − I_2 = 0 \text{ (Kirchoff's Point Rule)}$$

Kirchoff's Loop Rule is applied to the left loop first. Since the Loop Rule must be applied in one particular direction around the loop, and the left loop has currents flowing in both directions, some of the voltage changes in the left loop must be found against the current flow. In this example, the loop rule will be applied counter-clockwise starting from point P.

$$\Sigma \Delta V = V_{4Ω} + V_{12V} + V_x + V_{2Ω} = 0$$
(Kirchoff's Loop Rule)

where:

$$V_{4Ω} = IR = I_1(4Ω) \text{ (by Eq. 5-4)}$$

Resistors decrease voltage in the direction of current flow. But, since this loop is evaluated against the current, the sign is positive.

$$V_{12V} = +12V$$

The loop is evaluated across the 12 volt battery in the negative-to-positive direction so the voltage is positive—remember the direction in which a battery increases voltage does not depend on the direction of the current.

$$V_x = −X$$
$$V_{2Ω} = IR = −(0.5 \text{ A})(2Ω) = −1V$$
$$\text{(by Eq. 5-4)}$$

This resistor is evaluated in the direction of the current flow, so it causes a decrease in voltage.

$$\Sigma \Delta V = I_1(4\Omega) + 12V - X - 1V = 0$$
$$11V - X + I_1(4\Omega) = 0$$

Similarly, the Loop Rule is applied in the right loop starting form point P. Since all currents in the right loop flow counter-clockwise, it is easiest to evaluate this loop with the flow of current.

$$\Sigma \Delta V = V_{6\Omega} + V_{4V} + V_{12V} + V_{4\Omega} = 0$$

where:

$$V_{6\Omega} = IR = -I_2(6\Omega)$$
$$V_{4V} = +4 \text{ V}$$
$$V_{12V} = -12 \text{ V}$$
$$V_{4\Omega} = IR = -I_1(4\Omega)$$

$$\Sigma \Delta V = -I_2(6\Omega) + 4 \text{ V} - 12 \text{ V} - I_1(4\Omega) = 0$$
$$8 \text{ V} + I_1(4\Omega) + I_2(6\Omega) = 0$$

Now there are three variables and three equations that can be solved simultaneously:

$$0.5 \text{ A} + I_1 - I_2 = 0$$
$$11 \text{ V} - X + I_1(4\Omega) = 0$$
$$8 \text{ V} + I_1(4\Omega) + I_2 (6\Omega) = 0$$

Solving for I_1 in the first equation and replacing it into the third equation produces a value for I_2:

$$0.5 \text{ A} + I_1 - I_2 = 0$$
$$I_1 = I_2 - 0.5 \text{ A}$$

$$8 \text{ V} + I_1(4\Omega) + I_2(6\Omega) = 0$$
$$8 \text{ V} + (I_2 - 0.5 \text{ A})(4\Omega) + I_2(6\Omega) = 0$$
$$8 \text{ V} + I_2(4\Omega) - 2 \text{ V} + I_2(6\Omega) = 0$$
$$I_2(10\Omega) = -6 \text{ V}$$
$$I_2 = -0.6 \text{ A}$$

Now I_1 can be found from I_2:

$$I_1 = I_2 - 0.5 \text{ A}$$
$$I_1 = -0.6 \text{ A} - 0.5 \text{ A}$$
$$I_1 = -1.1 \text{ A}$$

And finally, replacing I_1 into the second equation solves for X:

$$11 \text{ V} - X + I_1(4\Omega) = 0$$
$$11 \text{ V} - X + (-1.1 \text{ A})(4\Omega) = 0$$
$$11 \text{ V} - 4.4 \text{ V} = X$$
$$X = 6.6 \text{ V}$$

Note that the negative signs on the currents indicate that the directions shown in Figure 5-6 are opposite to the actual flow of current in each case.

REVIEW QUESTIONS

5.1) An automotive electrical system operating at 12 volts contains a light bulb that draws 2 amperes. What is the power consumed by the light bulb?

5.2) A resistor rated at 100 ohms is placed across the terminals of a 12-volt battery. How much current does the resistor draw from the battery?

5.3) A household electric heater operates at 110 volts. The unit is rated at 1,000 watts. What is the resistance of the heater and the current that flows through it?

5.4) What physical quantity is measured in kilowatt-hours?

5.5) Two 1.5-volt batteries are to be connected to supply a total of 3.0 volts to an electrical load. Should the batteries be connected in series or parallel?

5.6) Find the total equivalent resistance between points A and B in the circuit shown in Figure Q5-1.

5.7) Find the current I in the circuit shown in Figure Q5-2.

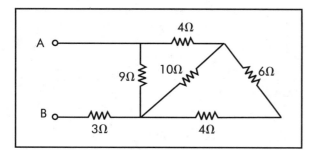

Figure Q5-1. Question 5.6.

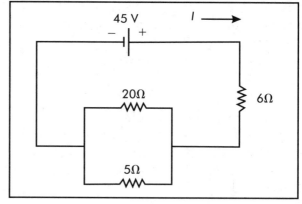

Figure Q5-2. Question 5.7.

Statics refers to the analysis of the mechanical equilibrium of rigid bodies subjected to force systems. The term *statics* is used because the analysis is restricted to bodies at rest. Traditionally, engineering statics requires an understanding of forces, the transmissibility of forces, Newton's laws, and the construction of free-body diagrams. For reference purposes, centroids are discussed in Appendix D.

6.1 FORCE

Force is a vector quantity. It is specified by both a magnitude and a direction. The study of statics depends on several basic principles: transmissibility, parallelogram law, and Newton's laws.

TRANSMISSIBILITY

Transmissibility is the principle that the equilibrium of a rigid body will remain unchanged if a force F on a rigid body is replaced by a force F' with the same magnitude, direction, and line of action acting at a different point. A force may be transmitted along its line of action without changing the effect it has on a body as seen in Figure 6-1.

PARALLELOGRAM LAW

Two forces acting on a particle can be replaced by a single force known as the *resultant*. The resultant is obtained by vector addition of the two forces. This can be visualized as drawing the diagonal of the paral-

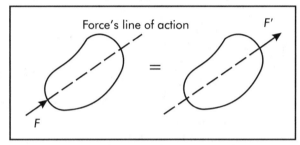

Figure 6-1. Transmissibility of forces.

lelogram having sides given by the force vectors shown in Figure 6-2.

NEWTON'S LAWS

First Law

A particle will remain at rest or will move in a straight line at a constant speed when the resultant force acting on the particle is zero. This can be summarized as:

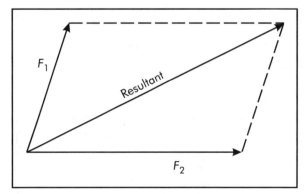

Figure 6-2. Resultant of two forces.

$$\Sigma F = 0 \qquad (6\text{-}1)$$

This equation can be read as "the summation of all forces acting on a particle is equal to zero."

Second Law

If the resultant force acting on a particle is not equal to zero, the particle will have an acceleration with a magnitude proportional to the resultant force and a direction along the resultant force. The constant of proportionality is the mass of the particle, m. This law is summarized as:

$$F = ma \qquad (6\text{-}2)$$

where:

F = force (lb [N])
m = mass of particle (slug [kg])
a = acceleration (ft/s^2 [m/s^2])

This concept is described in greater detail in Chapter 7, Dynamics.

Third Law

The forces of action and reaction between bodies in contact have the same magnitude, same line of action, and opposite sense. Figure 6-3 shows a block being pushed against a wall with force F applied on the left side. The wall reacts against the right side of the block with an equal force, with opposite sense along the same line of action.

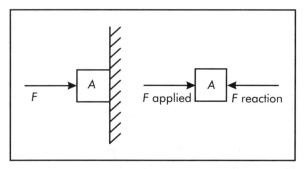

Figure 6-3. Reaction to an applied force.

6.2 RECTANGULAR COMPONENTS OF A FORCE

It is often useful to resolve a force into components that are along perpendicular coordinate axes. In Figure 6-4, the force F has been resolved into two rectangular components. The magnitudes of these components are given by:

$$F_x = F \cos \theta \qquad (6\text{-}3)$$
$$F_y = F \sin \theta \qquad (6\text{-}4)$$

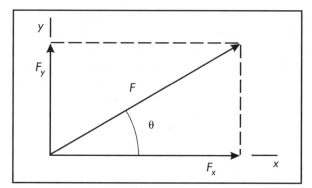

Figure 6-4. Rectangular components of a force.

This result is often useful in adding together the forces acting on a particle. It is the analytical equivalent to the parallelogram law. The rectangular components of the resultant force (R) acting on a particle are given by:

$$R_x = \Sigma F_x \qquad (6\text{-}5)$$
$$R_y = \Sigma F_y \qquad (6\text{-}6)$$

Example 6.2.1. Three forces act on the eyebolt as shown in Figure 6-5. Find the resultant force.

Solution. Refer to Table 6-1. Each of the individual forces is broken down into its x- and y-components and these components are summed to find the resultant force.

$$R_x = 73 \text{ N} \qquad R_y = 150 \text{ N}$$

The magnitude of the resultant force can be found by Pythagorean Theorem:

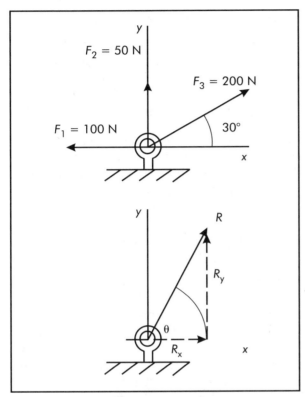

Figure 6-5. Forces applied to an eyebolt.

$$R = \sqrt{R_x^2 + R_y^2}$$

$$R = \sqrt{(73 \text{ N})^2 + (150 \text{ N})^2}$$

$$R = 167 \text{ N}$$

And the angle can be found by trigonometry:

$$\tan \theta = \frac{R_y}{R_x} = \frac{150}{73}$$

$$\theta = \tan^{-1} \frac{150}{73}$$

$$\theta = 64°$$

6.3 MOMENT OF FORCE

A *moment* is the tendency to rotate that a force imparts to a rigid body. The *magnitude of the moment* is the product of the magnitude of the force and the perpendicular distance between the line of action of the force and the point or axis of rotation. The *axis of rotation* would be an imaginary axis passing through the point of rotation and perpendicular to the plane the force is acting in. The *perpendicular distance* is also known as the *moment arm*. For example, in Figure 6-6 the moment about point O is given by:

$$|M_o| = |F| d \tag{6-7}$$

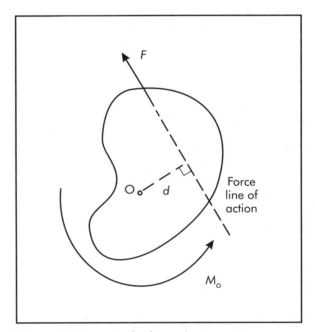

Figure 6-6. Moment of a force about a point.

Table 6-1. Forces applied to the eyebolt in Figure 6-5

Force F	Magnitude (N) $|F|$	x-Component (N) $F_x = F \cos \theta$	y-Component (N) $F_y = F \sin \theta$
F_1	100	$F_{1x} = 100 \cos 180° = -100$	$F_{1y} = 100 \sin 180° = 0$
F_2	50	$F_{2x} = 50 \cos 90° = 0$	$F_{2y} = 50 \sin 90° = 50$
F_3	200	$F_{3x} = 200 \cos 30° = 173$	$F_{3y} = 200 \sin 30° = 100$
	Resultant:	$R_x = 73$	$R_y = 150$

where:

$|M_o|$ = magnitude of the moment about point O (ft-lb [N-m])
$|F|$ = magnitude of the force (lb [N])
d = perpendicular distance between the line of action of the force and the point of rotation (ft [m])

Note: The magnitude of the moment can also be expressed in other units such as in.-lb, lb-ft, and lb-in. It is immaterial which unit is stated first.

A moment that generates a tendency to rotate clockwise is negative and a moment that generates a tendency to rotate counter-clockwise is positive. The force in Figure 6-6 creates a tendency for the rigid body to rotate counterclockwise with respect to point O. Therefore, the moment created by force F with respect to point O is positive.

6.4 FORCE COUPLES

Two forces of equal magnitude and opposite sense with parallel lines of action form a *couple*. Figure 6-7 shows a couple of forces acting on an object. These two forces can be resolved into a moment of magnitude given as:

$$|M_o| = |F|d \text{ (Eq. 6-7)}$$

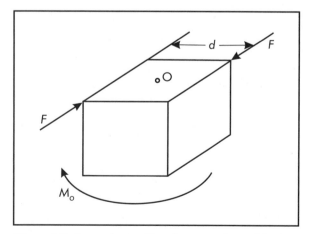

Figure 6-7. A couple resulting from a system of forces.

where:

$|M_o|$ = magnitude of moment (ft-lb [N-m])
d = perpendicular distance between the lines of action of the two forces (ft [m])
$|F|$ = magnitude of one of the forces (lb [N])

This equation is the same as Equation 6-7 except the definitions of d and F are different. A couple such as this one results when there is a moment generated by two balanced forces.

6.5 NEWTON'S FIRST LAW AND MOMENTS

Newton's First Law may be extended to a rigid body with one additional observation about static equilibrium. As in the case of a particle, the summation of all forces acting on the body in the x-, y-, and z-directions must sum to zero. In addition, the summation of all moments acting about any point in the rigid body must sum to zero. These statements may be expressed as:

$$\Sigma F_x = 0 \qquad (6\text{-}8)$$

$$\Sigma F_y = 0 \qquad (6\text{-}9)$$

$$\Sigma F_z = 0 \qquad (6\text{-}10)$$

$$\Sigma M_o = 0 \qquad (6\text{-}11)$$

6.6 FREE-BODY DIAGRAMS

A free-body diagram (FBD) is the technique used to identify the relevant forces and moments that affect a body. When drawing one, the body is isolated from all contacting bodies. Next, all forces acting on the body and external reactions are depicted. The general procedure for creating a free-body diagram is:

- Isolate the body from the ground or any bodies in contact with it.
- Indicate all external forces acting on a body.

- Identify the magnitude and direction of reactions from the ground or other bodies in contact by the application of Newton's First Law. In all cases, a set of appropriate coordinate axes, which are fixed to the body, should be selected.

Example 6.6.1. Draw the corresponding free-body diagram for the simply supported beam in Figure 6-8.

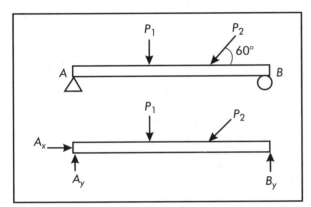

Figure 6-8. Simply supported beam and corresponding free-body diagram.

Solution. The pin provides reactions (support) in the x- and y-directions. The roller only provides a reaction (support) in the y-direction.

Example 6.6.2. A simple structure that is fixed to the ground is shown in Figure 6-9 (on the left). Find the reactions at the ground.

Solution: A free-body diagram is drawn showing all forces on the structure (see Figure 6-9). At point B where the structure is in contact with the ground, the forces are not known yet. There is a possible reaction force and a possible moment at point B, so these are drawn in the FBD (the reaction force is broken into x- and y-components). By Newton's First Law, all forces in the FBD can be summed in the x- and y-directions and set equal to zero. Sign conventions are defined in Figure 6-10.

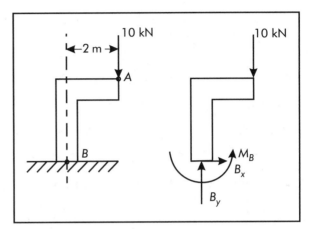

Figure 6-9. Loaded structure and corresponding free-body diagram.

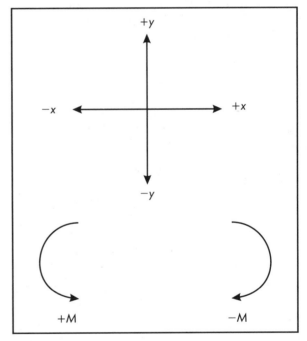

Figure 6-10. Sign conventions.

$$\Sigma F_x = B_x = 0 \quad \text{(Eq. 6-8)}$$
$$B_x = 0$$

$$\Sigma F_y = B_y - 10 \text{ kN} = 0 \quad \text{(Eq. 6-9)}$$
$$B_y = 10 \text{ kN}$$

All moments can also be summed and set equal to zero.

$\Sigma M_o = M_B - (10 \text{ kN})(2 \text{ m}) = 0$ (Eq. 6-11)

$M_B = 20 \text{ kN-m}$

Since M_B and B_y are both positive, they are drawn in the correct directions.

6.7 FRICTION

The force required to overcome friction resulting from bodies in contact is important in many statics problems. In almost all cases, the concept of dry or Coulomb friction is assumed to apply. The force of *friction* acts opposite to the direction of any impending motion that would result from an applied force. Hence, an object moving or resting against a frictionless surface experiences no forces against its motion, only forces normal to it. The maximum possible force of friction is defined as:

$$F_F = \mu N \qquad (6\text{-}12)$$

where:

   μ = coefficient of friction
   N = force that acts normal to the surfaces in contact (lb [N])

It should be noted that this discussion applies to static friction. A similar relationship exists for dynamic friction between bodies in relative motion. The coefficient of friction is a function of the two surfaces in contact. To overcome friction and cause a body to move, a force F must be applied that is greater than or equal to the force of friction as illustrated in Figure 6-11.

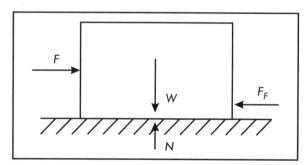

Figure 6-11. Conditions for frictional forces.

Example 6.7.1. The block shown in Figure 6-11 has a mass of 200 kg and the coefficient of friction between the block and the floor is 0.3. How large must the force F be to start the block in motion?

Solution. In this case, the normal force acting on the frictional contact surfaces is equal to the weight of the block. Weight is a force that can be found by Newton's Second Law:

$$F = ma \quad (\text{Eq. 6-2})$$
$$W = mg \qquad (6\text{-}13)$$

where:

   F = force (N)
   m = mass of block = 200 kg
   g = acceleration of gravity = 9.81 m/s^2
   $W = (200 \text{ kg})(9.81 \text{ m/s}^2)$
   $W = 1{,}962 \text{ N}$

Since the block is not moving in the y-direction (vertical):

$$\Sigma F_y = 0 \quad (\text{Eq. 6-9})$$
$$N - 1{,}962 \text{ N} = 0$$
$$N = 1{,}962 \text{ N}$$

The frictional force can then be found by Equation 6-12.

$$F_F = \mu N$$

where:

   μ = coefficient of friction = 0.3
   N = normal force = 1,962 N
   $F_F = (0.3)(1{,}962 \text{ N})$
   $F_F = 589 \text{ N}$

The horizontal force, F, must be equal to or greater than the force of friction.

$$F \geq 589 \text{ N}$$

REVIEW QUESTIONS

6.1) Find the reaction at the right side (roller) of the beam shown in Figure Q6-1. The left side is pin connected.

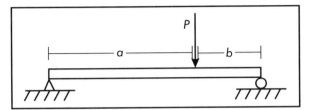

Figure Q6-1. Question 6.1.

6.2) A pulley is mounted at the end of a beam as shown in Figure Q6-2. The pulley weighs 20 lb. The load suspended on the cable weighs 40 lb. Find the force the beam exerts on the pulley.

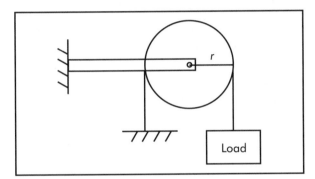

Figure Q6-2. Question 6.2.

6.3) Find the tension in the cable supporting the beam shown in Figure Q6-3.

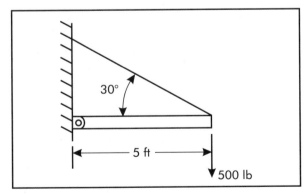

Figure Q6-3. Question 6.3.

6.4) What moment must be applied to the member shown in Figure Q6-4 to keep it in equilibrium?

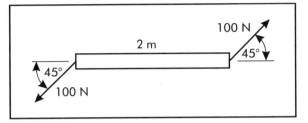

Figure Q6-4. Question 6.4.

6.5) The coefficient of friction between the box and the ramp shown in Figure Q6-5 is 0.25. Will the box slide down the ramp?

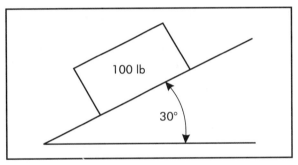

Figure Q6-5. Question 6.5.

6.6) A box shown in Figure Q6-6 is resting on a ramp with a coefficient of friction equal to 0.3. What is the magnitude of the force P that will prevent the box from sliding down the ramp?

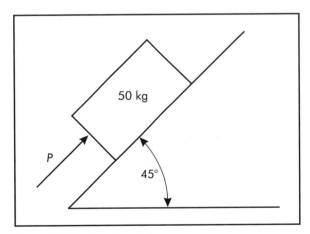

Figure Q6-6. Question 6.6.

Dynamics is the study of bodies in motion. There are two major topics in the study of dynamics:

- *kinematics* is the study of the motion of particles and bodies, and
- *kinetics* is the study of the forces and moments required to induce motion.

The motion of particles can be categorized as rectilinear and curvilinear. These types of motion also apply to rigid bodies. The motion of rigid bodies also can be described by angular motion. For reference purposes, curvilinear motion and momentum are discussed in Appendix D.

7.1 RECTILINEAR MOTION

Rectilinear motion describes the action of a particle in a straight line. The acceleration (a), velocity (v), and displacement (s) of a particle are described by the following relationships.

The average velocity (v_{AVG}) in a time interval (Δt) is expressed as:

$$v_{AVG} = \frac{\Delta s}{\Delta t} \tag{7-1}$$

The average acceleration (a_{AVG}) in a time interval (Δt) is expressed as:

$$a_{AVG} = \frac{\Delta v}{\Delta t} \tag{7-2}$$

The following equations are for systems with constant acceleration (such as the action of gravity), with initial conditions $t_0 = 0$, $v = v_0$, and $s_0 = 0$.

$$v = v_0 + at \tag{7-3}$$

$$s = v_0 t + \frac{at^2}{2} \tag{7-4}$$

$$v^2 = v_0^2 + 2as \tag{7-5}$$

Example 7.1.1. An automobile skids to a stop in 200 ft after its brakes are applied when it was moving at 60 miles/hour. Find the deceleration in units of ft/s^2, assuming the deceleration rate is constant.

Solution. The initial velocity must be put in appropriate units:

$$v_0 = \frac{60 \text{ miles}}{1 \text{ hour}} = \frac{1 \text{ hour}}{3,600 \text{ s}} \times \frac{5,280 \text{ ft}}{1 \text{ mile}} = 88 \frac{\text{ft}}{\text{s}}$$

The following equation of rectilinear motion will be applied:

$$v^2 = v_0^2 + 2as \text{ (Eq. 7-5)}$$

where:

v = final velocity = 0 ft/s
v_0 = initial velocity = 88 ft/s
a = acceleration (ft/s^2)
s = distance traveled = 200 ft

$$(0 \text{ ft/s})^2 = (88 \text{ ft/s})^2 + 2a(200 \text{ ft})$$
$$-7,744 \text{ ft}^2/\text{s}^2 = a \times 400 \text{ ft}$$
$$a = -19.4 \text{ ft/s}^2$$

The negative sign indicates that the vehicle is decelerating.

7.2 ANGULAR MOTION

A rigid body can be characterized by angular motion where the angular displacement of the body about a point is measured relative to a datum (usually the positive x axis). Figure 7-1 shows a body rotating about point O with angular displacement θ, angular velocity ω, angular acceleration α, and the radius of rotation r. These terms are related by:

$$\omega = \frac{\Delta\theta}{\Delta t} \qquad (7\text{-}6)$$

$$\alpha = \frac{\Delta\omega}{\Delta t} \qquad (7\text{-}7)$$

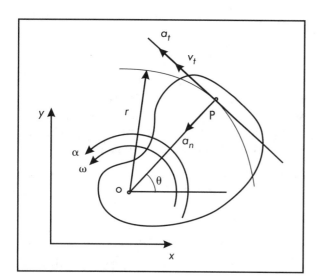

Figure 7-1. Angular motion.

The tangential velocity and acceleration at point P are given by:

$$v_t = r\omega \qquad (7\text{-}8)$$

$$a_t = r\alpha \qquad (7\text{-}9)$$

where:

v_t = tangential velocity (ft/s [m/s])
r = radius of rotation (ft [m])
ω = angular velocity (rad/s)
a_t = tangential acceleration (ft/s^2 [m/s^2])
α = angular acceleration (rad/s^2)

Tangential means the vectors have a direction tangent to the arc of rotation at point P. The normal acceleration of point P has a direction that points inward toward the center point, O, and is given by:

$$a_n = \frac{v_t^2}{r} = r\omega^2 \qquad (7\text{-}10)$$

where:

a_n = normal acceleration (ft/s^2 [m/s^2])

If the angular acceleration α is constant, and the initial conditions are $t_0 = 0$, $\omega = \omega_0$, and $\theta_0 = 0$, then the following equations of motion will apply:

$$\omega = \omega_0 + \alpha t \qquad (7\text{-}11)$$

$$\theta = \omega_0 t + \frac{\alpha t^2}{2} \qquad (7\text{-}12)$$

$$\omega^2 = \omega_0^2 + 2\alpha\theta \qquad (7\text{-}13)$$

7.3 NEWTON'S SECOND LAW

Newton's Second Law describes the relationship between the forces acting on a particle or body and how it will accelerate:

$$\Sigma F = ma \qquad (7\text{-}14)$$

where:

F = force (lb [N])
m = mass of particle (slug [kg])
a = acceleration (ft/s^2 [m/s^2])

The mass of the body is assumed to be constant and a is the acceleration of the centroid (or center of mass) of the object. Note: When the mass of an object is required for an object, it must be expressed in the proper units. In the metric system, mass is measured in kilograms. In the United States Customary System (USCS), mass (m) is measured in lb $\times$ s^2/ft or slugs and can be found by:

$$m = \frac{W}{g} \qquad (7\text{-}15)$$

where:

W = weight (lb)
g = gravitational acceleration (32.2 ft/s^2)

Example 7.3.1. Find the acceleration of the block shown in Figure 7-2. The coefficient of friction, $\mu = 0.3$.

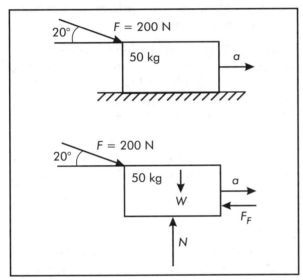

Figure 7-2. Sliding block.

Solution. The 200 N applied force can be separated into horizontal and vertical components and then forces can be summed in each direction.

$$F_x = 200N \times \cos 20° = 187.9N$$
$$F_y = 200N \times \sin 20° = 68.4N$$

The sum of the vertical forces is zero because the block experiences no net force in a vertical direction.

$$\Sigma F_y = N - W - F_y = 0$$

where:

N = normal force (N)
W = weight of block = (50 kg)(9.81 m/s^2)
$\quad$ = 491N
F_y = 68.4N
ΣF_y = N − 491N − 68.4N = 0
N = 558.9N

Now that the normal force has been found, the frictional force can be determined from it:

$$F_F = \mu N \text{ (Eq. 6-14)}$$

where:

μ = coefficient of friction = 0.3
N = normal force = 558.9N
F_F = frictional force = (0.3)(558.9N)
F_F = 167.7N

Summing the horizontal forces produces the net horizontal force causing the block to accelerate.

$$\Sigma F_x = F_x - F_F$$

where:

F_x = horizontal component of applied force = 187.9N
F_F = frictional force = 167.7N
ΣF_x = 187.9N − 167.7N
ΣF_x = 20.2N

Since the net force and the weight of the block are known, the acceleration can be determined by Newton's Second Law.

$$F = ma$$

where:

F = net force = 20.2N
m = mass of block = 50 kg
a = acceleration of block (m/s^2)

$$20.2N = (50 \text{ kg})a$$
$$a = 0.40 \text{ m/s}^2$$

7.4 ENERGY METHODS

Energy methods are important tools for solving kinetics problems that would be cumbersome to solve by the application of Newton's Laws. These techniques use the concepts of *conservation of energy* (energy can neither be created nor destroyed) and the definition of work (energy is the capability to do work).

Work is defined as the product of an applied force (F) and the distance over which the force is applied (s). For a constant force, this relation is given by:

$$W = Fs \qquad (7\text{-}16)$$

For a rotating body, work is the product of an applied moment (M) and the angle (θ) (in radians) through which the moment is applied. The net work done on an object is equal to the change in energy in the object. The energy change can occur by kinetic energy or potential energy.

For a body in linear motion, kinetic energy is given by:

$$K_E = \tfrac{1}{2}mv^2 \qquad (7\text{-}17)$$

where:

K_E = kinetic energy (ft-lb [J])
m = mass (slug [kg])
v = velocity (ft/s [m/s])

For a body in angular motion, kinetic energy is given by:

$$K_E = \tfrac{1}{2}I\omega^2 \qquad (7\text{-}18)$$

where:

I = mass moment of inertia (slug $-$ ft^2 [kg $-$ m^2])
ω = angular velocity (rad/s)

Potential energy is the stored energy associated with the body or the potential to do work. One form of potential energy is the position of an object relative to a datum in a gravitational field. The potential energy is given by the product of the weight of the object ($W = mg$) and its distance from the selected datum (h).

$$P_E = mgh \qquad (7\text{-}19)$$

where:

P_E = potential energy (ft-lb [J])
m = mass (slug [kg])
g = (ft/s^2 [m/s^2])
h = distance from datum (ft [m])

In the case of the energy stored in a linear spring, the potential energy is given by:

$$P_E = \tfrac{1}{2}kx^2 \qquad (7\text{-}20)$$

where:

k = spring constant (lb/ft [N/m])
x = distance that the spring is compressed or extended (ft [m])

Example 7.4.1. A 50 kg block is attached to a relaxed spring with a spring constant of 40 N/m and is then abruptly dropped. Find the velocity of the 50 kg block shown in Figure 7-3 after it falls 2 m from rest.

Solution. Since energy in a system is conserved, the initial energy of the system is equal to the final energy of the system.

$$KE_i + PE_i = KE_f + PE_f$$

where:

KE_i = initial kinetic energy of system
PE_i = initial potential energy of system
KE_f = final kinetic energy of system
PE_f = final potential energy of system

$KE_i = \tfrac{1}{2}mv_0^2$ (Eq. 7-17)

$\quad = \tfrac{1}{2}(m)(0^2)$ ($v_o = 0$ since block is at rest)

$\quad = 0$

$PE_i = mgh + \tfrac{1}{2}kx^2$ (Eqs. 7-19 and 7-20)

$\quad = mgh + \tfrac{1}{2}k(0^2)$ ($x = 0$ since spring is relaxed)

$\quad = mgh$

$KE_f = \tfrac{1}{2}mv^2$

$PE_f = mgh + \tfrac{1}{2}kx^2$

$\quad = mg(0) + \tfrac{1}{2}kx^2$ ($h = 0$ since block is at the bottom of the selected datum)

$\quad = \tfrac{1}{2}kx^2$

The equation becomes:

$$0 + mgh = \tfrac{1}{2}mv^2 + \tfrac{1}{2}kx^2$$

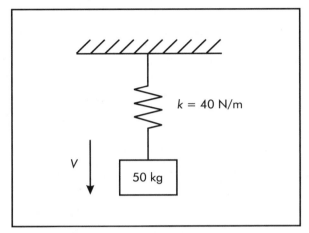

Figure 7-3. Mass/spring system.

where:

m = mass of block (kg)
g = acceleration of gravity = 9.81 m/s^2
h = height of block above datum = 2 m
v = velocity of block at final position
k = spring constant = 40 N/m
x = distance spring is stretched = 2 m

$$0 + (50 \text{ kg})(9.81 \text{ m/s}^2)(2 \text{ m})$$

$$= \tfrac{1}{2}(50 \text{ kg})v^2 + \tfrac{1}{2}(40 \text{ N/m})(2 \text{ m})^2$$

$$981 \text{ N-m} = 25 \text{ kg} \times v^2 + 40 \text{ N-m}$$
$$v^2 = 37.6 \text{ m}^2/\text{s}^2$$
$$v = 6.1 \text{ m/s}$$

The final velocity of the block after falling 2 m is 6.1 m/s.

REVIEW QUESTIONS

7.1) An object is moving with an initial velocity of 30 m/s. If it is decelerating at 5 m/s^2, how far will it travel before it stops?

7.2) A particle is shot straight up with an initial velocity of 50 m/s. After how many seconds will it return if the drag is neglected?

7.3) A gear at rest is accelerated at 6 radian/s^2. How many times will the gear revolve in ten seconds?

7.4) A 1.5-ft-long lever is hinged at one end and is rotating at 0.5 radian/s. It is accelerating at 1 radian/s^2. How many seconds will it take for the free end to reach 10 ft/s?

7.5) What is the kinetic energy of a 7-lb bowling ball traveling at 300 ft/min?

7.6) A weight (W) will cause a spring to deflect 1 in. if it rests on top of it. If the weight is dropped from a height of 10 in. above the free position of the spring, how much will the spring deflect?

Chapter 8

Strength of Materials

Strength of materials comprises the study of deformable bodies subject to applied forces and moments. Some of the important questions addressed in the study of the strength of materials are:

- How much load can be safely applied to a structure or component?
- What material should be chosen to fabricate a component to safely withstand a particular load?
- How much will a component deflect under load?

For reference purposes, Poisson's ratio and beam loading are discussed in Appendix D.

8.1 STRESS AND STRAIN

Stress and *strain* are quantities used to characterize the strength and deformation of a component. When the properties of an engineering material are tested and recorded in a handbook, the definition of stress and strain allow the test data to be applied to virtually any structure.

In a mechanical strength test of a material such as steel, a test specimen is loaded with a controlled amount of force, applied perpendicular to the cross sectional area, and the amount of resulting deformation is recorded until it fractures. Figure 8-1 shows a prismatic (constant cross section) bar of length L. Cross-sectional area A is subjected to axial force P. The applied force causes the bar to stretch by ΔL.

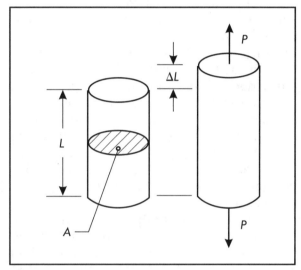

Figure 8-1. Loaded prismatic bar.

The normal or longitudinal strain ε is defined as:

$$\varepsilon = \frac{\Delta L}{L} \tag{8-1}$$

Strains are positive if the specimen is elongated and negative if it is shortened. The normal or axial stress, σ is defined as:

$$\sigma = \frac{P}{A} \tag{8-2}$$

where:

P = external load (lb [N])
A = cross-sectional area perpendicular to the load (in.^{2} [m^2])

Stress has units of force per unit area. Common stress units are psi (abbreviation for pounds per square inch) and the Pascal or Pa (defined as one Newton per square meter). Since psi and the Pascal are relatively small, stress is usually expressed in thousands of psi (ksi) and megapascals (MPa).

8.2 AXIAL LOADING

If the specimen shown in Figure 8-1 is subjected to a tensile test, an increasing axial force will be applied and the resulting deformation will be recorded. This data is transformed into stress and strain and plotted to depict important material properties characterizing the strength of the material. A typical stress/strain curve resulting from a tensile test of a ductile material (capable of withstanding significant strain prior to fracture) is shown in Figure 8-2. Steel, aluminum, and brass are some examples of ductile materials.

As the force is initially applied, the stress increases proportionally with strain. If the material is a linear elastic material, stress and strain in the elastic range will be related by Hooke's Law:

$$\sigma = E\varepsilon \qquad (8\text{-}3)$$

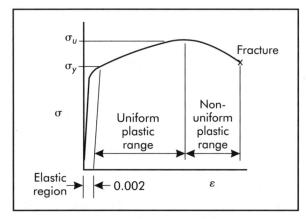

Figure 8-2. Stress-strain diagram.

where:

σ = normal or axial stress (lb/in.^{2} [Pa])
E = material constant called Young's modulus or modulus of elasticity (lb/in.^{2} [Pa])
ε = normal or longitudinal strain (in./in. [m/m])

The component will return to its original undeformed shape if the load is removed in the elastic range. Clearly, most mechanical design is done within the elastic range of materials. As the material continues to deform under increasing applied load, the elastic behavior will cease and the material will take on a permanent set if the load is released. This phenomenon is known as plastic deformation. The stress corresponding to the transition from the elastic region to the plastic region is called the yield strength (σ_y). For consistent test results, the yield point is defined as where a line drawn parallel to the elastic region with a 0.2% strain offset intersects the stress/strain curve. The transition point between the elastic and plastic regions is also called the proportional limit.

Table 8-1 shows the significant material properties that can be collected from a tensile test for various materials.

The definitions of stress and strain can be combined to derive a useful formula for the amount of elongation that occurs in a tensile member when axially loaded in the elastic region:

$$\Delta L = \frac{PL}{AE} \qquad (8\text{-}4)$$

where:

ΔL = amount of elongation (in. [m])
P = external load (lb [N])
L = original length (in. [m])
A = original cross-sectional area (in.^{2} [m^2])
E = Young's modulus or modulus of elasticity (psi [Pa])

Table 8-1. Typical material properties

Material	Modulus of Elasticity E 10^6 psi	Modulus of Rigidity G 10^6 psi	Ultimate Tensile Strength (σ_u) 10^3 psi	Yield Strength σ_y 10^3 psi	Poisson's Ratio v
Mild steel	30	12	58	36	0.30
Aluminum	10	3.9	16	14	0.33
Magnesium	6.5	2.4	55	40	0.35
Titanium	15	6	130	120	0.34
Brass	15	6	48	15	0.33

Notes: 1. Units of psi can be approximately converted to kPa by multiplying by 7,000.
2. This data is for example purposes only. It should not be used for design.

One form of factor of safety in the design of a component is the ratio of the yield stress to the allowable stress:

$$F_S = \frac{\sigma_y}{\sigma_a} \qquad (8\text{-}5)$$

where:

F_S = factor of safety
σ_y = yield strength
σ_a = allowable stress

Example 8.2.1. A hinged beam weighs 2,000 lb and is supported by a single steel wire as shown in Figure 8-3. Using the material property data from Table 8-1 and a factor of safety of two, find the required diameter of the wire and the amount of elongation in the wire.

Solution. The structure is reduced to a free-body diagram and the tension in the wire is found by summing moments about the wall connection, R:

$$\Sigma M_R = 0$$
$$-[2{,}000 \text{ lb } (5 \text{ ft})] + [T \sin 30° \, (10 \text{ ft})] = 0$$
$$T = 2{,}000 \text{ lb}$$

where:

ΣM_R = sum of the moments about pin R
T = tensile force in wire

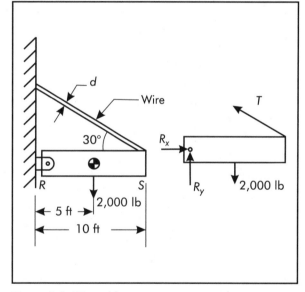

Figure 8-3. Hinged beam.

R_x = horizontal force of wall pushing on beam
R_y = vertical force of wall pushing on beam

The allowable stress is found by applying the factor of safety to the yield strength of steel from Table 8-1:

$$F_S = \frac{\sigma_y}{\sigma_a} \quad (\text{Eq. 8-5})$$

where:

F_S = factor of safety = 2
σ_y = yield strength of steel = 36×10^3 psi
σ_a = maximum allowable stress in wire

$$2 = \frac{36{,}000 \text{ psi}}{\sigma_a}$$

$\sigma_a = 18{,}000$ psi

The allowable stress is used to size the wire based on the normal stress formula:

$$\sigma_a = \frac{P}{A} \quad \text{(Eq. 8-2)}$$

where:

σ_a = maximum allowable stress
   = 18,000 psi
P = external load (lb)
   = tensile force in wire = T = 2,000 lb
A = cross-sectional area of wire
   $= \dfrac{\pi d^2}{4}$ (d = diameter)

$$18{,}000 \text{ psi} = \frac{2{,}000 \text{ lb}}{\dfrac{\pi d^2}{4}} = \frac{8{,}000 \text{ lb}}{\pi d^2}$$

$$d^2 = \frac{8{,}000 \text{ lb}}{\pi \left(18{,}000 \dfrac{\text{lb}}{\text{in.}^2}\right)} = 0.141 \text{ in.}^2$$

$$d = 0.376 \text{ in.}$$

The elongation can be readily found since the factor of safety assures loading in the elastic range:

$$\Delta L = \frac{PL}{AE} \quad \text{(Eq. 8-4)}$$

where:

ΔL = elongation of wire
P = external load = tension in wire
   = T = 2,000 lb
L = original length of wire

$$= \frac{10 \text{ ft}}{\cos 30°} = \frac{120 \text{ in.}}{\cos 30°} = 130.6 \text{ in.}$$

A = cross-sectional length of wire

$$= \frac{\pi d^2}{4} = \frac{\pi (0.376 \text{ in.})^2}{4} = 0.111 \text{ in.}^2$$

E = modulus of elasticity for steel
   = 30×10^6 psi (Table 8-1)

$$\Delta L = \frac{(2{,}000 \text{ lb})(130.6 \text{ in.})}{(0.111 \text{ in.}^2)(30 \times 10^6 \text{ psi})} = 0.078 \text{ in.}$$

The wire stretches approximately 0.078 in. under the applied load.

8.3 TORSIONAL LOADING

Shafts and other machine elements subjected to equilibrating couples at each end (torque) are in torsion. A circular shaft in torsion is shown in Figure 8-4.

Applied torque creates a shear stress that causes the shaft to twist. In the elastic range of the material, the shear stress τ is related to the shear strain γ by a modified version of Hooke's Law:

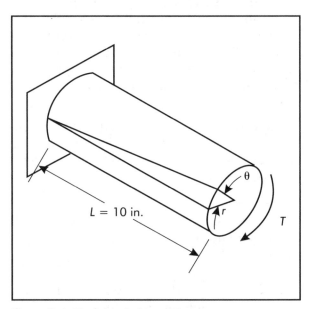

Figure 8-4. Shaft loaded in torsion.

$$\tau = G\gamma \qquad (8\text{-}6)$$

where:

G = modulus of rigidity (psi [Pa])

The maximum shear stress in the shaft occurs at the surface and is given by:

$$\tau_m = \frac{Tr}{J} \qquad (8\text{-}7)$$

where:

τ_m = maximum shear stress (lb/in.^{2} [N/m^2])
T = applied torque (in-lb [N-m])
r = radius of the shaft (in. [m])
J = polar moment of inertia (in.^{4} [m^4])

The polar moment of inertia for a solid circular cross section is given by:

$$J = \frac{\pi d^4}{32} \qquad (8\text{-}8)$$

For a hollow shaft, the polar moment of inertia can be found by:

$$J = \pi\left(\frac{d_o{}^4 - d_i^4}{32}\right) \qquad (8\text{-}9)$$

where:

d_o = outer diameter (in. [m])
d_i = inner diameter (in. [m])

The angle of twist θ (units in radians) for an elastically loaded shaft can be found by:

$$\theta = \frac{TL}{JG} \qquad (8\text{-}10)$$

where:

T = applied torque (in-lb [N-m])
L = length of shaft (in. [m])
J = polar moment of inertia (in.^{4} [m^4])
G = modulus of rigidity (psi [Pa])

Example 8.3.1. A circular steel rod supports a handle with a 1,000-lb force on the end, as shown in Figure 8-5. The length of the rod shaft L is 10 in. Find the maximum shear

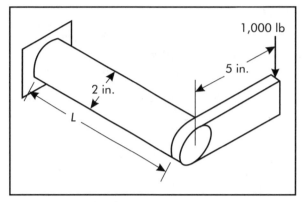

Figure 8-5. Steel rod in torsion.

stress in the rod and the angle of twist of the rod.

Solution. The torque (T) applied to the rod and the polar moment of inertia (J) of the rod must both be found before either formula (maximum shear stress or angle of twist in the rod) can be applied. The torque applied to the rod is given by:

$$T = Fd \quad \text{(Eq. 6-8)}$$

where:

F = applied force = 1,000 lb
d = perpendicular distance from rod to force = 5 in.
T = (1,000 lb)(5 in.)
T = 5,000 in.-lb

The polar moment of inertia of the rod is given by:

$$J = \frac{\pi d^4}{32} \quad \text{(Eq. 8-8)}$$

where:

d = diameter of rod = 2 in.

$$J = \frac{\pi(2 \text{ in.})^4}{32} = 1.57 \text{ in.}^4$$

The maximum shear stress occurs at the surface of the rod and is given by:

$$\tau_m = \frac{Tr}{J} \quad \text{(Eq. 8-7)}$$

where:

T = applied torque = 5,000 in.-lb
r = radius of rod = 1 in.
J = polar moment of inertia = 1.57 in.^{4}

$$\tau_m = \frac{(5{,}000 \text{ in.-lb})(1 \text{ in.})}{1.57 \text{ in.}^4}$$

$$\tau_m = 3{,}183 \text{ lb/in.}^2 = 3{,}183 \text{ psi}$$

The angle of twist is found by:

$$\theta = \frac{TL}{JG} \text{ (Eq. 8-10)}$$

where:

T = applied torque = 5,000 in.-lb
L = length of rod = 10 in.
J = polar moment of inertia = 1.57 in.^{4}
G = modulus of rigidity for steel
    = 12×10^6 psi (from Table 8-1)

$$\theta = \frac{(5{,}000 \text{ in.-lb})(10 \text{ in.})}{(1.57 \text{ in.}^4)(12 \times 10^6 \text{ psi})}$$

$$\theta = 0.0026 \text{ rad} \times \frac{360°}{2\pi \text{ rad}}$$

$$\theta = 0.15°$$

REVIEW QUESTIONS

8.1) A 2,000-lb load is supported by a 3/4-in.-diameter eyebolt. Find the stress in the straight section of the bolt.

8.2) The eyebolt in Question 8.1 is made of mild steel. If using a safety factor of 2, find the maximum stress permitted.

8.3) An outdoor sculpture is supported by a 50-ft-long mild steel wire. The wind can cause the sculpture to place a 200 lb load on the wire. The deflection of the sculpture is limited to 0.5 in. What is the required diameter of the wire?

8.4) Determine the rod diameter required to support a tensile load of 35,000 lb if the tensile stress cannot exceed 22,000 psi.

8.5) A hollow circular steel shaft has an 80-mm outside diameter and a 50 mm inside diameter. Calculate the allowable torque that can be transmitted if the allowable shear stress is 60 MPa.

8.6) An extension on a socket wrench may be represented as a 0.5 in.-diameter solid steel cylinder 8 in. long. A 75 in.-lb torque is applied to the end of the wrench extension. How much does the extension twist?

Chapter 9

Thermodynamics and Heat Transfer

The thermal properties of matter are controlled by temperature. Temperature is a measure of the tendency of an object to absorb or dissipate energy in the form of heat.

9.1 TEMPERATURE CONVERSIONS

There are several scales commonly used for measuring temperature. Temperature measurements can be relative or absolute. Relative measurements of temperature are referenced to a physical phenomenon, typically the freezing point of water. Temperature in the Fahrenheit scale T_F (part of the United States Customary System [USCS] units) is related to the Celsius scale T_C (part of the metric or Systeme International [SI] units) by the equation:

$$T_C = \frac{5}{9}(T_F - 32) \qquad (9\text{-}1)$$

Absolute temperatures are referenced to the minimum achievable temperature, absolute zero. The value of absolute zero can be found by a simple experiment where a closed volume of gas is reduced in temperature. The pressure in the closed volume will drop with decreasing temperature. Absolute zero is the temperature found if the pressure-temperature curve is extrapolated to a pressure of zero. This temperature is a single value, independent of the gas used, as shown in Figure 9-1. At this temperature (approximately $-273°$ C or $-460°$ F) all atomic motion ceases, removing the kinetic energy

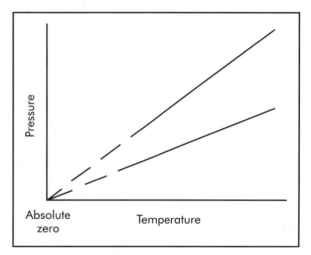

Figure 9-1. Determining the value of absolute zero.

necessary for a gas to create a pressure against a surface.

The United States Customary System scale for absolute temperature is Rankine (T_R), defined as:

$$T_R = T_F + 460 \qquad (9\text{-}2)$$

The metric scale for absolute temperature is Kelvin (T_K), defined as:

$$T_K = T_C + 273 \qquad (9\text{-}3)$$

9.2 THERMAL EXPANSION

The dimensions of most solid materials will expand and contract with increasing and decreasing temperatures. Increasing the temperature of an object increases the motion of

---

the atoms in the object, causing increased atomic separation and the object to grow as depicted in Figure 9-2.

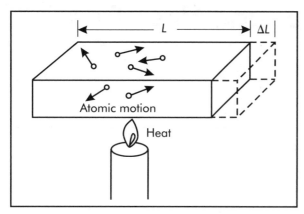

Figure 9-2. Expansion of an object by increase of temperature.

The change in a linear dimension, such as length or diameter, is proportional to the change in temperature of the object ΔT, its original length L, and the coefficient of expansion α. The change in length ΔL can be found as:

$$\Delta L = \alpha L \Delta T \qquad (9\text{-}4)$$

Also, the change in diameter, ΔD, can be found by:

$$\Delta D = \alpha D \Delta T \qquad (9\text{-}5)$$

where:

    α = coefficient of expansion (m/m/° F [m/m/° C])
    D = original diameter (in. [mm])
    ΔT = change in temperature (° F [° C])

The coefficients for some common materials are shown in Table 9-1. They are based on a particular temperature scale. Conversion of temperatures into the appropriate scale is necessary to apply them.

The expansion and contraction of materials with temperature is useful for making

Table 9-1. Coefficients of expansion

Material	α(m/m/° C = 1/° C)
Glass	9×10^{-6}
Concrete	10×10^{-6}
Iron	12×10^{-6}
Brass	19×10^{-6}
Aluminum	25×10^{-6}

shrink fits between parts. In addition, two strips of metal with dissimilar coefficients are bonded together to create the bimetal strips widely used in thermostats. A bimetal strip will bend with a large deflection under a relatively small temperature change.

Example 9.2.1. A brass sheet has a 2.000-in.-diameter hole at 70° F. The sheet is heated to 300° F. Find the new diameter of the hole.

Solution. The change in diameter can be found as:

$$\Delta D = \alpha D \Delta T \qquad (\text{Eq. 9-5})$$

where:

    ΔD = change in diameter (in. [m])
    α = coefficient of expansion
        = 19×10^{-6} 1/° C
    D = original diameter
        = 2.000 in.
    ΔT = change in temperature

To use the values in Table 9-1, the temperatures must be converted to Celsius.

$$T_F = \frac{5}{9}(300 - 32) \quad (\text{by Eq. 9-1})$$
$$= 148.9° \text{ C}$$
$$T_i = \frac{5}{9}(70 - 32)$$
$$= 21.1° \text{ C} \quad (\text{by Eq. 9-1})$$
$$\Delta T = T_F - T_i = 148.9° \text{C} - 21.1° \text{C} = 127.8° \text{C}$$
$$\Delta D = (19 \times 10^{-6}/° \text{ C})(2.000 \text{ in.})(127.8° \text{ C})$$
$$\Delta D = 0.005 \text{ in.}$$

Thus, the new diameter is 2.005 in.

9.3 HEAT CAPACITY

The *heat capacity* of a material defines the amount of energy that is needed to change its temperature. Conversely, heat capacity describes the temperature change that will occur with a given amount of energy. The typical engineering units for heat, a form of energy, are the British thermal unit (Btu) and the joule (J). In chemistry, however, the calorie (cal) is also used.

Unit heat capacity is typically quantified as *specific heat* (c_p), which is the quantity of heat required to change the temperature of a unit mass of substance by one degree. Units for specific heat typically used in thermodynamics and heat transfer are Btu/lbm-° R and J/ kg-K. In some situations, the units for specific heat can be defined as Btu/lbm-° F and J/kg-° C. The specific heats of various substances are shown in metric units in Table 9-2. Using the definition of specific heat, the heat contained in a quantity of substance is given by:

$$Q = mc_p\Delta T \qquad (9\text{-}6)$$

where:

m = mass of the substance (lbm [kg])
c_p = specific heat (Btu/(lbm-° R) [J/(kg-K)])
ΔT = change in temperature (° R [K])

Specific heats are used in the study of *calorimetry*, the analysis of heat content or chemical energy in fuels, foods, and other media. Known quantities of two substances, one of which is typically water, are placed in an insulated chamber known as a calorimeter. The heat gained by one substance is lost (or generated) by the other substance.

Example 9.3.1. How much water at 15° C must be used to cool a 200 g part made of copper from an initial temperature of 80° C to a final temperature of 25° C? Assume the contact takes place in an insulated calorimeter.

Solution. The heat lost by the copper must be equal to the heat gained by the water, which will also have a final temperature of 25° C. The equation relating the two quantities of heat is:

$$Q_l = Q_g$$

$$(mc_p\,\Delta T)_c = (mc_p\,\Delta T)_w \quad (\text{Eq. } 9\text{-}6)$$

where:

Q_l = heat lost by copper
Q_g = heat gained by water
m_c = mass of copper = 200 g = 0.2 kg
C_{pc} = specific heat of copper = 386 J/kg-K
ΔT_c = temperature change of copper (Kelvin)
  = (273 + 80 °C) K – (273 + 25 °C) K
  = 55 K
m_w = mass of water
C_{pw} = specific heat of water = 4,190 J/ kg-K
ΔT_w = temperature change of water (Kelvin)
  = (273 + 25 °C) K – (273 + 15 °C) K
  = 10 K

$$(0.2 \text{ kg})(386 \text{ J/kg-K})(55 \text{ K})$$
$$= m_w(4{,}190 \text{ J/kg-K})(10 \text{ K})$$
$$4{,}246 \text{ J} = m_w\,(41{,}900 \text{ J/kg})$$
$$m_w = 0.101 \text{ kg} = 101 \text{ g}$$

Table 9-2. Specific heats of various materials

Material	Specific Heat $\left(\dfrac{\text{J}}{\text{kg - K}}\right)$
Aluminum	900
Glass	840
Iron	447
Copper	386
Water	4,190

9.4 THERMODYNAMICS

Thermodynamics is the study of energy in transition. A knowledge of thermodynamics is critical in analyzing the operation of steam power plants, refrigerators, and other devices associated with energy. An extensive study of thermodynamics is beyond the scope of this book. However, some basic principles of thermodynamics will be described to provide a more complete discussion of thermal sciences.

There are two basic physical laws of thermodynamics that can be applied to all processes involving heat, work, and energy. The first law of thermodynamics is commonly known as *conservation of energy*. Energy cannot be created nor destroyed; it can only be changed in form. In the context of thermodynamics, this law is stated as:

$$Q = \Delta U + W \qquad (9\text{-}7)$$

where:

Q = quantity of heat
ΔU = change in internal energy
W = work performed

Heat (Q) added into a system (IN) is positive. Heat leaving a system (OUT) is negative. Work (W) performed on a system (IN) is negative. Work performed by a system (OUT) is positive.

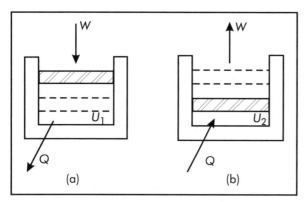

Figure 9-3. The first law of thermodynamics.

The consequences of the first law can be illustrated by a quantity of gas contained in a cylinder with a perfectly sealing piston as shown in Figure 9-3. In Figure 9-3(a), work is done on the system as the piston is being forced down. This work input can result in an increase in the internal energy of the gas (ΔU) (as evidenced by an increase in temperature) and or heat (Q) being transferred out of the cylinder. If the cylinder is insulated and no heat transfer occurs, all of the work input will result in raising the internal energy of the gas, causing a rise in its temperature and pressure. A smaller change in internal energy will occur if heat exchange to the surroundings occurs. In Figure 9-3(b), heat is added to the system from the surroundings. The heat will cause the gas to expand, doing work by raising the piston. If the piston is prevented from being raised, all of the heat input will result in a change in internal energy of the gas, causing a rise in temperature and pressure.

The second law of thermodynamics describes the *relationship of work and heat*. One consequence of the second law is that heat flows spontaneously from a hot object to a cold object and not vice versa. Work must be done to transfer heat from a cold object to a hot object. A quantity of heat Q_H may be extracted from a hot object at temperature T_H and a lesser quantity of heat Q_L will be dissipated into a corresponding cold object at T_L. The difference between the two quantities of heat can be captured as useful work (W_{OUT}) as illustrated in Figure 9-4(a).

$$W_{OUT} = Q_H - Q_L \qquad (9\text{-}8)$$

A quantity of heat Q_L can be extracted from a cold object and through the action of the input of work, a larger quantity of heat Q_H is dissipated to the surroundings. The quantity of work (W_{IN}) required to move the heat is given by:

$$W_{IN} = Q_H - Q_L \qquad (9\text{-}9)$$

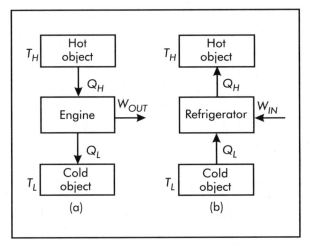

Figure 9-4. Thermodynamic cycles.

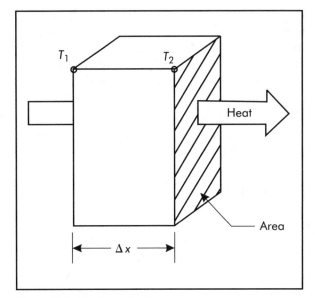

Figure 9-5. Heat conduction.

A refrigerator operates under these conditions, requiring work input to move heat from the interior of the refrigerator to the surroundings as shown in Figure 9-4(b).

9.5 HEAT TRANSFER

Heat can be transferred between two objects in three modes: conduction, convection, and radiation. Heat will spontaneously flow from a hot object to a cold object through one or more of these three modes.

Heat *conduction* describes the transfer of energy from a high-temperature region to a low-temperature region through a solid object, as shown in Figure 9-5. The rate of the energy transfer is dependent on the area of conduction (A), the temperature difference between the hot and cold regions ($\Delta T = T_1 - T_2$), the thickness of the material (Δx), and the thermal conductivity, k, of the material. Large values of k indicate good heat conductors and conversely small values indicate poor heat conductors.

Heat *convection* describes the transfer of energy from a surface by the flow of a fluid over the surface. Figure 9-6 shows heat loss from a wall by the flow of a fluid. The fluid velocity has a gradient such that it has zero velocity at the wall and reaches

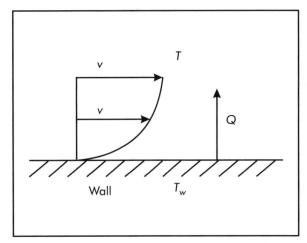

Figure 9-6. Heat transfer by convection.

maximum velocity v_∞ in the free stream where the flow of fluid is unaffected by the presence of the wall. The temperature of the wall is T_w and the temperature of the free stream is T_∞.

The third mode of heat transfer is *radiation*. Electromagnetic radiation carries energy from one body to another. The rate of energy transfer is based on the performance of ideal radiators and absorbers called black bodies. An ideal black body would be an infinitely large black plate. Other objects with different geometries and emissivities (the ability to emit radiation) determine the amount of heat transfer that will occur.

REVIEW QUESTIONS

9.1) Convert a temperature of 295° F into the following temperature scales:

    a) Celsius
    b) Rankine
    c) Kelvin

9.2) A shrink fit is needed for two mating aluminum parts (a shaft and a hole). The diameter of the hole is 2.000 in. and the shaft is 2.002 in. at 70° F. Only the female part will be heated. What temperature should the female part be heated to for 0.001 in. of clearance at assembly?

9.3) An iron part is being heat-treated. The part will be heated to 1,200° F and plunged into water at 55° F. Two kilograms of water will be used. The part has a mass of 250 g. What is the final temperature of the water and the part?

9.4) A quantity of gas is contained in a cylinder with a perfectly sealing piston. The piston performs five units of work by compressing the gas. A total of four units of heat were transferred to the surroundings of the cylinder. Did the internal energy of the gas increase or decrease?

9.5) What mode of heat transfer is used by most heat exchangers?

10.1 FLUID PROPERTIES

There are several common fluid properties used to describe fluid behavior.

- *Density* (ρ) is the ratio of mass (*m*) to volume (*V*) of a substance.

$$\rho = \frac{m}{V} \qquad (10\text{-}1)$$

- *Specific volume* (*v*) is the volume occupied by a unit mass of substance.

$$v = \frac{1}{\rho} \qquad (10\text{-}2)$$

- *Specific weight* (γ) is the force of gravity on a mass per unit volume.

$$\gamma = \rho g \qquad (10\text{-}3)$$

- *Specific gravity* (*Sg*) is the ratio of the density of a substance to the density of water.

$$Sg = \frac{\rho}{\rho_W} \qquad (10\text{-}4)$$

Specific gravity can also be defined as the ratio of the specific weight of a substance to the specific weight of water.

$$Sg = \frac{\gamma}{\gamma_w} \qquad (10\text{-}5)$$

10.2 FLUID STATICS

The study of fluid statics often involves the change of fluid pressure due to the change in depth of the fluid.

The pressure associated with a fluid is the force it exerts on a body per unit of area. There are several definitions of pressure depicted in Figure 10-1.

Gages typically measure pressures relative to atmospheric pressure either as a gage pressure or as a vacuum pressure. Typically, the relationship between absolute pressure and gage pressure is given by:

$$P_{abs} = P_{atm} + P_{gage} \qquad (10\text{-}6)$$

where:

P_{abs} = absolute pressure
P_{atm} = atmospheric pressure
P_{gage} = gage pressure

Absolute pressure is measured relative to an absolute zero datum pressure.

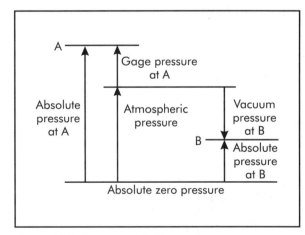

Figure 10-1. Pressure definitions.

If a fluid has a constant specific weight, pressure (p) at any depth (h) in the fluid is given by:

$$p = \gamma h \qquad (10\text{-}7)$$

where:

$$p = 0 \text{ at } h = 0$$

This relationship is useful for measuring pressures by measuring the height of a column of fluid in a manometer.

Example 10.2.1. A 300-gallon tank is mounted above a pump to produce a positive head at the inlet. If the static pressure at the inlet needs to be 10 psi, and the fluid has a specific gravity of 0.89, how high must the average fluid level be above the pump inlet? The specific weight of water is $62.4 \dfrac{\text{lb}}{\text{ft}^3}$.

Solution.

$$p_i = \gamma_f h_f \text{ (Eq. 10-7)}$$

where:

p_i = inlet pressure
γ_f = specific weight of the fluid
h_f = average height of the fluid

Solving Eq. 10-7 for the fluid height yields

$$h_f = \frac{p_i}{\gamma_f}$$

From Eq. 10-5,

$$Sg = \frac{\gamma_f}{\gamma_w}$$

where:

γ_f = specific weight of fluid
γ_w = specific weight of water = 62.4 lb/ft³

$$Sg_{fluid} = 0.89 = \frac{\gamma_f}{62.4 \text{ lb/ft}^3}$$

$$\begin{aligned} \gamma_f &= 0.89 \,(62.4 \text{ lb/ft}^3) \\ &= 55.5 \text{ lb/ft}^3 \end{aligned}$$

Substituting the specific weight into the original equation yields:

$$h_f = \frac{p_i}{\gamma_f} = \frac{10\dfrac{\text{lb}}{\text{in.}^2}\left(\dfrac{144 \text{ in.}^2}{1 \text{ ft}^2}\right)}{55.5\dfrac{\text{lb}}{\text{ft}^3}} = 26.0 \text{ ft}$$

10.3 FLUID POWER

Fluid power uses a pressurized fluid in a sealed system to do work. Most hydraulic systems use a synthetic oil that acts as a solid to transmit power. The power can be used to move actuators some distance from the power source. The fluid power system can also easily move actuators with some degree of accuracy and precision.

Figure 10-2 illustrates *Pascal's Law*, which states that pressure exerted by a confined fluid acts the same in all directions at right angles to the inside of the container wall. Pressure against a wall or piston is a function of force and area:

$$P = \frac{F}{A} \qquad (10\text{-}8)$$

where:

P = pressure (lb/in.² [Pa])
F = force on the wall or piston (lb [N])
A = surface area of the wall or piston the force acts on (in.² [m²])

One of the major attributes of hydraulic systems is force multiplication. The work performed by either the input cylinder or output cylinder is defined as:

$$W = F \times L \qquad (10\text{-}9)$$

where:

W = work performed (in.-lb [N-m])
F = force (lb [N])
L = distance traveled (in. [m])

The relationship between the input (pump) and output (ram) cylinders in Figure 10-3 is defined as:

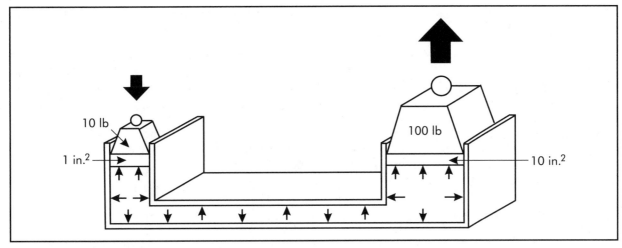

Figure 10-2. Pascal's Law.

$$F_1 \times L_1 = F_2 \times L_2 \qquad (10\text{-}10)$$

where:

F_1 and L_1 = input cylinder
F_2 and L_2 = output cylinder

Example 10.3.1 An operator exerts 50 lb on the pump piston in Figure 10-3. If the ram must lift 1,000 lb of weight 1 in., how far must the operator's pump piston travel?

Solution. To solve for L_1, rearrange Eq. 10-10.

$$F_1 \times L_1 = F_2 \times L_2 \text{ (Eq. 10-10)}$$

$$L_1 = \frac{F_2 \times L_2}{F_1}$$

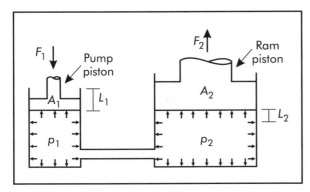

Figure 10-3. Force multiplication.

where:

L_1 = distance operator's pump piston travels (in.)
F_1 = force applied by operator = 50 lb
L_2 = distance weight travels = 1 in.
F_2 = weight (force) on ram
  = 1,000 lb

$$L_1 = \frac{1,000 \text{ lb} \times 1 \text{ in.}}{50 \text{ lb}}$$

L_1 = 20 in.

Example 10.3.2. Using the system in Figure 10-3, how much weight can be lifted by the ram if the force on the pump piston is 300 lb? The ram diameter is 2 in. and the pump piston diameter is 0.5 in.

Solution. Relate the pressure on the pump piston and the ram using Pascal's Law and Eq. 10-8. Pascal's Law states that pressure within a confined fluid acts the same on all surfaces.

$$P_1 = \frac{F_1}{A_1} = P_2 = \frac{F_2}{A_2} \text{ (from Eq. 10-8)}$$

$$\frac{F_1}{A_1} = \frac{F_2}{A_2}$$

where:

F_1 = input force = 300 lb

A_1 = pump piston area = $\dfrac{\pi d^2}{4}$

  = $\dfrac{\pi(0.5 \text{ in.})^2}{4}$ = 0.20 in.^{2}

F_2 = weight lifted by ram

A_2 = ram area = $\dfrac{\pi d^2}{4}$ = $\dfrac{\pi(2 \text{ in.})^2}{4}$

  = 3.14 in.^{2}

$\dfrac{300 \text{ lb}}{0.20 \text{ in.}^2} = \dfrac{F_2}{3.14 \text{ in.}^2}$

F_2 = 4,710 lb

10.4 FLUID DYNAMICS

The study of fluid dynamics considers the flow of fluids. The main issues in fluid flow center on the velocity, pressure, and force necessary to cause the fluid to move. Most fluid flow problems are analyzed in the form of an imaginary system, called a control volume, into which and from which the fluid flows. There are three main principles that govern fluid dynamics: conservation of mass, conservation of energy, and conservation of momentum (Newton's Second Law). It must be emphasized that the following development only applies to fluids that can be regarded as incompressible. Water and oil are examples of fluids typically regarded as incompressible.

Conservation of mass is described by the continuity equation:

$$A_1 v_1 = A_2 v_2 \qquad (10\text{-}11)$$

where:

A = area that the fluid flows through (in.^{2} [m^2])

v = velocity of the fluid (in./s [m/s])

The subscripts refer to the point where the fluid enters and exits the system.

Example 10.4.1. Water flows through a 100-mm diameter pipe at 8 m/s. Downstream, the pipe is reduced in diameter to 40 mm. Find the velocity of the water in the smaller diameter pipe.

Solution. The continuity equation is applied directly:

$$A_1 v_1 = A_2 v_2 \quad (\text{Eq. 10-11})$$

where:

area $A = \dfrac{\pi d^2}{4}$ (d = pipe diameter)

$$\dfrac{\pi d_1^2}{4} v_1 = \dfrac{\pi d_2^2}{4} v_2$$

Canceling π and 4 from the equation, there is a direct relationship between diameter and velocity:

$$d_1{}^2 v_1 = d_2{}^2 v_2$$

$$v_2 = v_1 \dfrac{d_1{}^2}{d_2{}^2}$$

where:

d_1 = inflow diameter = 100 mm
v_1 = velocity at inflow = 8 m/s
d_2 = outflow diameter = 40 mm
v_2 = velocity at outflow

$$v_2 = 8 \text{ m/s} \dfrac{(0.100 \text{ m})^2}{(0.040 \text{ m})^2}$$

$$v_2 = 50 \text{ m/s}$$

Conservation of energy is described by the energy equation, also known as the Bernoulli equation:

$$\dfrac{v_2{}^2}{2g} + \dfrac{p_2}{\gamma} + z_2 = \dfrac{v_1{}^2}{2g} + \dfrac{p_1}{\gamma} + z_1 \qquad (10\text{-}12)$$

where:

p = pressure of the fluid (lb/in.^{2} [Pa])
z = elevation of the system relative to a datum (in. [m])
g = acceleration of gravity
γ = specific weight

It will be assumed that flow is in a steady state and incompressible with a uniform velocity profile.

Example 10.4.2. Water is flowing at a rate of 10 m/s into a pipe with an inside diameter of 50 mm that narrows to a diameter of 25 mm as illustrated in Figure 10-4. The pressure at point 1 is 6 MPa. Assuming that no work is done nor energy lost, compute the pressure at point 2.

Solution. Since point 1 and point 2 are at the same elevation, z_1 and z_2 in Bernoulli's equation cancel.

$$\frac{v_2^2}{2g} + \frac{p_2}{\gamma} = \frac{v_1^2}{2g} + \frac{p_1}{\gamma} \text{ (Eq. 10-12)}$$

where:

v_1 = velocity at point 1 = 10 m/s
p_1 = pressure at point 1 = 6 MPa
v_2 = velocity at point 2
p_2 = pressure at point 2
g = acceleration of gravity = 9.81 m/s^2
γ = specific weight of water

γ = ρg (by Eq. 10-3)
   = $(1,000 \text{ kg/m}^3)(9.8 \text{ m/s}^2)$
   = 9,810 N/m^3

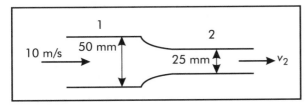

Figure 10-4. Fluid flow through pipe.

To solve for the pressure at point 2, both velocities must be found. This can be found by the continuity equation:

$$A_1v_1 = A_2v_2 \text{ (Eq. 10-11)}$$

or as reduced:

$$d_1^2v_1 = d_2^2v_2$$

$$v_2 = v_1\frac{d_1^2}{d_2^2}$$

$$= 10 \text{ m/s}\frac{(0.050 \text{ m})^2}{(0.025 \text{ m})^2}$$

$$= 40 \text{ m/s}$$

Substituting into Bernoulli's equation yields,

$$=\frac{(40 \text{ m/s})^2}{2(9.81 \text{ m/s}^2)} + \frac{P_2}{9,810 \text{ N/m}^3} = \frac{(10 \text{ m/s})^2}{2(9.81 \text{ m/s}^2)} + \frac{6\times10^6 \text{ Pa}}{9,810 \text{ N/m}^3}$$

$$81.56 \text{ m} + \frac{P_2}{9,810 \text{ N/m}^3} = 5.10 \text{ m} + 611.62 \text{ m}$$

$$P_2 = 5.25 \times 10^6 \text{ Pa}$$

REVIEW QUESTIONS

10.1) Atmospheric pressure at sea level is approximately 14.7 psi. A vacuum pump is rated at drawing a 10 psi vacuum. What is the absolute pressure created by the vacuum pump?

10.2) A tank 2 ft wide and 4 ft long is being built to hold 250 gallons of water. What should the minimum height of the tank be (refer to Table 2-7)?

10.3) A cylinder with an area of 4 in.^{2} raises a load of 1,000 lb using fluid supplied by a single-acting hand pump with a cylinder area of 0.250 in.^{2}. Find the force exerted on the pump by the operator.

10.4) Water is flowing at a rate of 5 m/s through a 500 mm-diameter pipe. The pipe reduces in diameter to 400 mm. Find the velocity of the water in the reduced section of the pipe.

10.5) What water pressure is needed to pump water up to the top of a 100 m tall building? Assume the water pressure at the top of the building is zero.

Part 3
Materials

Chapter 11

Material Properties

11.1 STRUCTURE OF MATTER

Matter can be defined as anything that has mass and occupies space. Matter may consist of one element alone, or elements in combinations called *compounds*. Whether elemental or as compounds, matter can exist as a solid, or in gaseous or liquid forms. These are the three states of matter.

GASES

Gases are substances that have no definite shape and no definite volume. They are fluid and take on the volume of the container that holds them. Gases, sometimes also called *vapors*, expand and can be compressed. When gases mix, the mixtures are homogeneous or uniform throughout. Mixtures of gases are *solutions* because gases are soluble in each other. The term *miscible*, soluble in each other, is thus appropriate for gases.

LIQUIDS

Liquids are substances that have no definite shape, but do have a definite volume. In contrast to a gas, the volume of a liquid does not change much with changes in temperature and pressure. In fact, many liquids are considered incompressible, because even large changes in pressure cause negligible changes in volume. When liquids mix, they may form a solution if they are miscible. If the liquids are immiscible, such as oil and water, they will form a heterogeneous mixture.

SOLIDS

Solids are substances that have a definite shape and a definite volume. If the atoms in the solid are arranged in orderly geometric patterns, the substance is called *crystalline*. Metals are crystalline solids. If the atoms are arranged in disordered, sometimes random patterns, the substance is called *amorphous*. Glass is an example of an amorphous solid.

Many substances are common in all three states. The magnitude of the forces between the atoms, also called the *energy level*, determines which state the substance is in. At high energy levels, a material may exist in a gaseous state. As atoms become less mobile with a decreasing energy level, the material may change to a liquid or solid phase. In a pure substance, there is a special condition of temperature and pressure where solid, liquid, and gas phases may exist simultaneously called the *triple point*. This is shown in Figure 11-1.

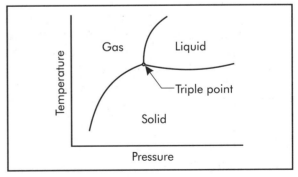

Figure 11-1. Phase diagram.

11.2 MATERIAL TESTING AGENCIES

Any discussion of material properties relies on methods to determine these properties. Although numerous agencies create and publish standards for testing, two of the most important agencies are the International Organization for Standardization (ISO) and the American Society for Testing and Materials (ASTM). The ISO, which includes standards organizations from over 90 countries, has as its goal "to promote the development of standards in the world with a view to facilitating international exchange of goods and services, and to developing cooperation in the sphere of intellectual, scientific, technological, and economic activity." The ASTM, an international technical society, is focused on ". . . the promotion of knowledge of the materials of engineering, and the standardization of specifications and methods of testing."

Although there are differences between the ISO and ASTM methods, many manufacturing companies need to utilize both methods. For example, many companies producing plastics parts for automobiles conduct tests on the tensile strength of materials according to ASTM D638 and ISO R527. Both methods specify the sample size, testing environment, testing procedure, and report format.

11.3 PHYSICAL PROPERTIES

A distinction between physical and chemical properties of substances provides a starting point for a discussion of material properties. Chemical properties involve the ways substances act when the amounts or nature of the substances change. In contrast, physical properties are related to any change in which the amounts or nature of the substances do not change. This definition of physical properties is so broad that it is frequently divided into narrower categories. In the following discussion, the overall physical properties will be subdivided into two groups, physical properties, and mechanical properties. A list of physical properties is shown in Table 11-1.

Table 11-1. Physical properties of materials

Color
Density
Electrical conduction
Magnetism
Melting temperature
Thermal conduction
Thermal expansion
Specific gravity
    (The ratio of the density of a given material to the density of pure water)
Specific heat
    (The amount of heat required to change the temperature of a unit mass of substance one degree)

11.4 MECHANICAL PROPERTIES

In contrast to physical properties, the mechanical properties indicate the way a substance reacts when acted upon by a mechanical force. Many tests reveal these properties, but only a few will be selected for thorough discussion in the next section. Table 11-2 defines a variety of mechanical properties.

11.5 MECHANICAL TESTING METHODS

There are many tests used to reveal the mechanical properties defined in Table 11-2. However only a few will be selected for thorough discussion. They are tensile properties, hardness properties, and fatigue properties.

TENSILE TESTING

The tensile test as specified by the American Society for Testing and Materials (ASTM) determines mechanical properties of materials in relation to stress and strain. A tensile test will reveal several mechanical

Table 11-2. Mechanical properties of materials

Brittleness	The tendency of a material to fail suddenly by breaking, without any permanent deformation of the material before failure. Deformation is a generic term used whenever a material changes shape by twisting, bending, stretching, etc. It is important to note that brittleness is not an indicator of the strength of a material.
Compressive strength	The resistance of a material to a force that is tending to deform or fail it by crushing.
Creep	The slow deformation of a metal under prolonged stress (for example, elongation). Not to be confused with deformation that results immediately upon application of a stress. Creep is very evident in plastics and metals at elevated temperatures.
Ductility	The ability of a material to become permanently deformed without failure. The term *failure* can mean cracking or even surface blemishes depending on the application.
Elastic limit	The maximum stress to which a material can be subjected without permanent deformation or failure by breaking.
Elasticity	The ability of a material to return to original shape and dimensions after a deforming load has been removed. All materials are elastic to some extent, some more than others.
Elongation	The stretching of a material, by which any straight-line dimension increases.
Endurance limit	The maximum stress that a material will support indefinitely under variable and repetitive load conditions.
Fatigue failure	The cracking, breaking, or other failure of a material as the result of repeated or alternating stressing below the material's ultimate tensile strength.
Fatigue strength	The resistance of a material to repetitive or alternating stressing, without failure.
Hardness	The ability of a material to resist indentation, penetration, abrasion, and scratching.
Impact strength	The ability of a metal to withstand a sharp, high-velocity blow without failure.
Load	The amount of force applied to a material or structure.
Malleability	The property of being permanently deformed by compression without rupturing; that is, the ability to be rolled or hammered into thin sheets.
Mechanical property	A material's ability to resist or withstand a particular kind of physical force applied against the material.
Modulus of elasticity	The ratio of tensile stress to the strain it causes, within that range of elasticity where there is a straight-line relationship between stress and strain.

Table 11-2. Mechanical properties of materials (*continued*)

Notch toughness	The resistance of a metal to adverse effects from the presence of notches or similar irregularities.
Physical property	An inherent physical characteristic of a material that is not directly an ability to withstand a physical force of any kind.
Plasticity	The property of a material being deformed under the action of a force and not returning to its original shape after removal of the force.
Proportional limit	The stress point beyond which an increase in stress is no longer proportionate to an increase in strain.
Strain	The physical effect of stress, usually evidenced by stretching or other deformation of the material.
Strength	The ability to resist physical forces imposed upon material.
Stress	The load, or amount of force, applied per unit area.
Tensile strength	The resistance of a material to a force that is acting to pull it apart.
Toughness	The ability of a metal to withstand the shock of a rapidly applied load.
Ultimate tensile strength	The maximum pulling force to which the material can be subjected without failure.
Yield point	The point at which the material will continue to elongate without increase in the force applied.
Yield strength	The stress level at which permanent deformation results.

properties that play a major role in engineering design: proportional limit, elastic limit, yield point, yield strength, ultimate strength, breaking (rupture) strength, ductility, and modulus of elasticity.

Proportional Limit

The early part of the stress-strain graph may be approximated by a straight line *OP* in both Figures 11-2 and 11-3. In this range, the stress and strain are proportional, so any increase in stress results in a proportionate increase in strain. The stress at the limit of proportionality (point *P*) is known as the *proportional limit*.

Elastic Limit

If a small load is applied to a material and then removed, that material will indicate a

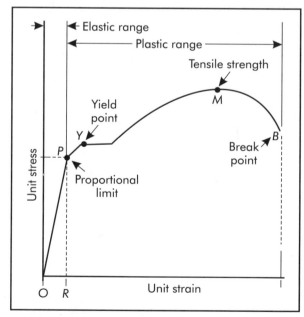

Figure 11-2. Stress-strain diagram for ductile steel.

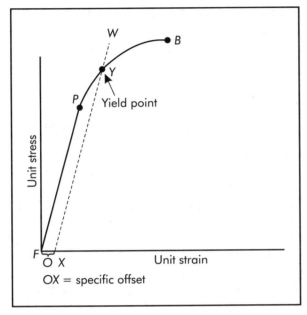

Figure 11-3. Stress-strain diagram for brittle material.

zero deformation. This means the strain is elastic. If the load is increased enough, a point will be reached where the material experiences a permanent deformation. This is called the elastic limit. Therefore, the definition of *elastic limit* is the minimum stress at which permanent deformation occurs. For most materials, the numerical value of the elastic limit and proportional limit are nearly the same.

Yield Point

Point Y in Figure 11-2 represents the yield point of a ductile material. The *yield point* can be defined as the point at which permanent deformation continues without an increase in stress. In some ductile materials, the stress (load) may actually decrease momentarily, resulting in an upper and lower yield point.

Yield Strength

Most nonferrous materials and high-strength steels do not possess a well-defined yield point. Therefore, the yield strength must be determined by the offset method. The *yield strength* is the stress at which a material exhibits a specified limiting deviation from the proportionality of stress to strain. Figure 11-3 illustrates the offset method. *OX* is laid off along the strain axis, then a line *XW* is drawn parallel to *OP*, thus locating *Y* (yield point). The offset is generally 0.2% strain or 0.002 strain.

Ultimate Strength (Tensile Strength)

As the load on the test piece increases still further, the stress and strain increase, as indicated by the portion of the curve *YM* in Figure 11-2. The maximum stress is reached at point *M*. The *ultimate strength* or tensile strength is the maximum stress developed by the material based on the original cross-sectional area. A brittle material breaks when stressed to the ultimate strength (point *B* in Figure 11-3), whereas a ductile material will continue to stretch. Tensile strength is measured in psi (pounds per square inch) or Pa (pascals).

Breaking Strength

The *breaking* or *rupture strength* is that point of the curve where the specimen actually fails. At maximum stress, ductile materials experience a localized deformation. As the cross-sectional area decreases at a rapid rate, the stress decreases. The deformation and elongation occur rapidly until failure. With a brittle material, the ultimate strength and breaking strength coincide.

Modulus of Elasticity

The *modulus of elasticity (E)* is an indication of the stiffness of a material. The formula for computing *E* is:

$$E = \frac{\text{Stress}}{\text{Strain}} = \frac{\sigma}{\varepsilon} \qquad (11\text{-}1)$$

It is important to remember that E represents the slope of the curve only in the elastic region of the stress-strain diagram.

Two important material properties are based on tensile testing. They are ductility and toughness. *Ductility*, defined as the amount of deformation a material can withstand until failure, is determined by the tensile test. It is measured by determining the percent of elongation or reduction in cross-sectional area at fracture.

$$\% \text{ elongation} = \frac{L_f - L_o}{L_o} \times 100 \qquad (11\text{-}2)$$

where:

L_f = final length (in. [mm])
L_o = original gage length (in. [mm])

$$\% \text{ reduction in area} = \frac{A_o - A_f}{A_o} \times 100 \quad (11\text{-}3)$$

where:

A_o = original cross-sectional area (in.^{2} [mm^2])
A_f = final cross-sectional area (in.^{2} [mm^2])

Toughness is the ability of a material to absorb energy prior to failure. Toughness can be derived from stress/strain graphs such as those depicted in Figure 11-2 and Figure 11-3. The material in Figure 11-2 is considered to be tougher than the material in Figure 11-3 since the total area under the stress/strain curve is larger. Toughness is mainly a property of the plastic range since only a small part of the total energy absorbed is elastic energy that can be recovered when the stress is released.

Toughness can also be determined by an impact test. This method uses a machine with a swinging pendulum of fixed weight raised to a standard height. The principle is that the pendulum swings with a definite kinetic energy; upon striking and breaking the specimen, the amount of energy used is recorded in foot-pounds. The more energy used to break the specimen, the tougher it is.

HARDNESS TESTING

The two hardness tests most commonly used in industry are the Brinell and the Rockwell.

Brinell Hardness Test

The Brinell hardness number (BHN) is the ratio of the load in pounds (kilograms) to the impressed area in square inches (square millimeters). The Brinell test consists of pressing a 0.4 in. (10 mm) diameter ball into a material under a specified load for a specific amount of time. (For nonferrous materials, the load is 1,100 lb [500 kg] for 10 seconds; ferrous materials require 6,600 lb [3,000 kg] for 10 seconds.) The diameter of the impression is measured by means of a microscope containing a scaled ocular, permitting estimates to the nearest 0.0004 in. (0.01 mm). The following formula is used to calculate BHN:

$$\text{BHN} = \frac{L}{(\pi D/2) \ (D - \sqrt{D^2 - d^2})} \qquad (11\text{-}4)$$

where:

L = test load (lb [kg])
D = diameter of ball (in. [mm])
d = diameter of impression (in. [mm])

Rockwell Hardness Test

The Rockwell test uses a direct reading instrument based on the principle of differential depth measurement. There are two basic types of Rockwell machines: the normal tester for relatively thick sections and the superficial tester for thin sections. The Rockwell machine operates by placing a minor load on a specimen (22 lb [10 kg] for normal and 6.6 lb [3 kg] for superficial) and zeroing the gage. The major load is then applied. After the gage comes to a rest, the major load is reset and the reading taken. The major load is usually 110 lb (50 kg), 220 lb (100 kg), and 331 lb (150 kg) for normal testing, and 31 lb (14 kg), 66 lb (30 kg), and

99 lb (45 kg) for superficial testing. The penetrators consist of steel balls of various sizes and a 120° conical diamond. The most commonly used Rockwell scales are B (220 lb [100 kg] major load, 0.0625 in. [1.6 mm] ball) and C (331 lb [150 kg] major load, diamond cone or brale).

FATIGUE RESISTANCE

If a material is subjected to fluctuation or to a number of cycles of stress reversal, failure may occur. This failure may occur even though maximum stress at any cycle is less than the value at which failure would occur under constant stress. By subjecting test specimens to stress cycles and, in turn, counting the number of cycles to failure, fatigue properties may be determined.

With a series of these tests and when the maximum stress values are reduced in a progressive manner, S-N diagrams can be plotted. The S (fully reversed cyclic stress) is on the vertical axis and the N (number of cycles to failure) is on the horizontal axis. A sample S-N diagram is shown in Figure 11-4. At stress levels below the endurance limit, the material, ideally, will not fail due to fatigue regardless of the number of cycles. For a material without an endurance limit, standard practice is to specify fatigue strength at a stress value. This stress value corresponds to the number of stress reversals.

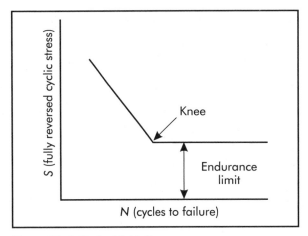

Figure 11-4. Typical S-N diagram.

REVIEW QUESTIONS

11.1) What are the three states of matter?

11.2) Define the term "liquid."

11.3) What are the two most important agencies that create and publish standards for material testing?

11.4) What properties of a material are revealed in a tensile test?

11.5) What is the elastic limit?

11.6) Define the "modulus of elasticity."

11.7) What are the two basic types of hardness tests?

11.8) What type of information does an S-N diagram provide the design engineer?

Most elements in the periodic table are metals. They share some important characteristics. Generally, metals are:

- solid at room temperature;
- good conductors of heat;
- good conductors of electricity;
- shiny and become highly reflective when smooth; and
- malleable and ductile.

12.1 CRYSTALLINE STRUCTURE

When a pure metal is hot enough to be in liquid form, the arrangement of the atoms is constantly changing. As the metal cools, the atoms take on a very orderly, three-dimensional, geometric arrangement. This arrangement is called a *crystalline structure*. There are several possible crystalline structures, but the most common are face-centered cubic (fcc), body-centered cubic (bcc), and hexagonal close-packed (hcp). Figure 12-1 illustrates the common crystalline structures.

During cooling, the crystallization begins at many points, called *nuclei*, and proceeds in the bcc, fcc or hcp structure. The initial orientation of the crystal is random, so when the crystals are large enough to "bump into" neighboring crystals, they retain their original orientation. The result is crystals with differing orientations. These crystals are called *grains*. The edge where one crystal meets another is called the *grain boundary*. It is a weak area in a crystalline solid and, consequently, has large effects on properties. Figure 12-2 depicts the growth of crystals and the development of grains. Two metallic specimens may have the same chemical composition, but they may exhibit radically different hardnesses because of the grain structure.

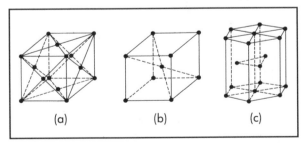

Figure 12-1. Common crystalline structures: (a) face-centered cubic (fcc); (b) body-centered cubic (bcc); and (c) hexagonal close-packed (hcp).

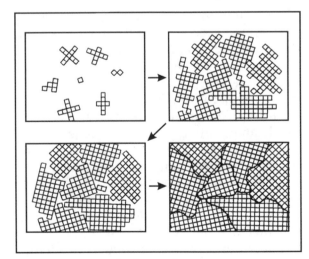

Figure 12-2. Growth of crystalline grains.

In general, a material with a fine grain structure will be harder and less ductile than a material with a coarse grain structure.

12.2 PHASE DIAGRAMS

The phase diagram is a tool for understanding the phase changes for a metal. Pure metals have a clearly defined melting point. Solidification or "freezing" occurs at a constant temperature. As a pure liquid metal is cooled, its temperature drops to the solidification temperature and remains at that temperature until all of the liquid has solidified. Figure 12-3 is a cooling curve typical of a pure metal.

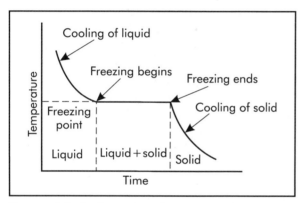

Figure 12-3. Cooling curve of a pure metal.

If two miscible metals with differing melting points are melted and mixed together, the resulting cooling curve, as indicated in Figure 12-4, will show solidification beginning at one temperature and ending at a differing temperature. Since the cooling curves for mixtures of metals, or alloys, often differ dramatically as the percentages of the metals change, alloy diagrams present the results of many cooling curves at once.

Alloys or mixtures of metals solidify over a range of temperatures based on the composition of the alloy. As an alloy is cooled, the mixture will begin to solidify at the liquidus temperature. It completes solidification at the solidus temperature as shown

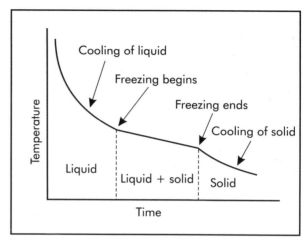

Figure 12-4. Cooling curve of an alloy.

in Figure 12-5. The mixtures will be in a slush state when they are cooling from the liquidus to solidus temperatures. The material illustrated in Figure 12-5 is an example of a binary alloy (two components). This particular example is an alloy made of components that exhibit complete solid solubility. *Solid solubility* refers to a situation in which two metals are each completely soluble in the other while in the solid state.

Other binary alloys can have different phase diagrams where single phases of solid solutions can occur. Solid solutions can be visualized as a uniform distribution of two

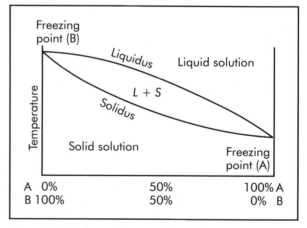

Figure 12-5. Phase diagram of an alloy.

types of crystalline structures. A solid solution has all of the macroscopic properties of a solid. However, it is composed of two different internal arrangements of atoms in the form of crystals. Figure 12-6 shows a phase diagram for an alloy that exhibits a *eutectic point* (meaning "easy to melt"). A particular composition of the two components has a melting temperature that is lower than the melting temperature of either component. Lead-tin alloys, such as solder, make use of this characteristic.

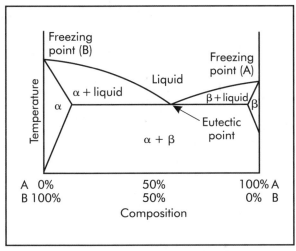

Figure 12-6. Phase diagram of an alloy with a eutectic point.

12.3 IRON-CARBON DIAGRAM

One of the most important phase diagrams in engineering applications is the iron-carbon system. Steels, cast iron, and cast steels are very common engineering materials because of their versatile properties and relatively low cost. Virtually all iron products contain some carbon resulting from the production of the iron. Commercially used pure iron contains up to 0.008% carbon. Steels contain typically less than 1% carbon. Cast irons contain between 2.11% and 6.7% carbon. The iron-carbon diagram is shown in Figure 12-7.

SOLID PHASES

There are three solid phases of the iron-carbon mixture that are important in understanding the metallurgy of iron and steel. They are ferrite, austenite, and cementite.

Ferrite

Ferrite, or α-iron, is a soft and ductile body-centered-cubic phase of iron. The solid solution contains only about 0.008% carbon at room temperature and a maximum of 0.022% carbon at 1,341° F (727° C). It is the softest structure that is formed in the iron-carbon system. The typical hardness is approximately 80 BHN.

Austenite

Austenite or γ-iron is a solid solution containing up to 2.11% carbon at 2,098° F (1,148° C). Austenite is a face-centered-cubic phase. It is ductile at elevated temperatures and exhibits good formability. Steel can be austenitized or transformed into a homogeneous structure of austenite by elevating its temperature according to the iron-carbon phase diagram. This is the usual starting point for virtually all heat treatment processes.

Cementite

Cementite is iron carbide (Fe_3C). It contains up to 6.67% carbon by weight. Cementite is a very hard and brittle structure that can have a significant influence on the properties of steels.

12.4 MICROSTRUCTURES OF STEEL

The region of the iron-carbon diagram for steels is shown in Figure 12-8. Various microstructures can be formed by heating and controlled cooling of a steel specimen. For example, consider a sample of steel with a eutectoid composition (0.77% C) that is heated from room temperature past the

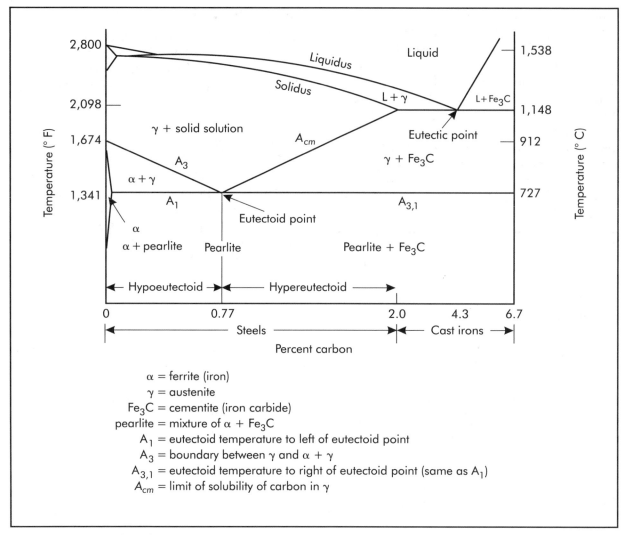

Figure 12-7. Iron-carbon diagram.

austenitizing temperature (from Figure 12-8, 1,341° F [727° C]). The sample will transform into a uniform mass of γ-iron. If the sample is cooled slowly (to maintain equilibrium conditions), a phase transformation will occur when the temperature drops below 1,341° F (727° C). The austenite will be transformed into a mixture of ferrite and cementite. At the eutectoid composition, the mixture of ferrite and cementite is called *pearlite*. The structure of pearlite is characterized by alternating layers (lamellae) of crystals of ferrite and cementite (under approximately 700× magnification, the structure appears like a fingerprint). Most significantly, the resulting structure has mechanical properties between ferrite (soft and ductile) and cementite (hard and brittle).

In the heat treatment of *hypoeutectoid steel* (with carbon content less than 0.77%), the resulting structure consists of a mixture of ferrite and pearlite (giving a correspondingly softer and more ductile composition than pure pearlite). *Hypereutectoid steels* (with carbon content greater than 0.77%) produce a structure of cementite and pearlite, which is correspondingly more brittle and hard than pure pearlite. As can be seen in Figure 12-8, both hypoeutectoid and hypereutectoid steels have austenitizing temperatures greater than 1,341° F (727° C).

If the crystal structure of the pearlite after heat treatment is thin and closely packed, it is called *fine pearlite*. If the crystals are large and loosely packed, it is called *coarse*

pearlite. Most heat treatment involves the formation of pearlite in a controlled way. The mechanical properties of the steel can be controlled by heating the steel into the austenitizing range and cooling it at a rate that gives the desired pearlite structure. Large crystals take time to grow (as anyone who has tried to make rock candy has discovered). Consequently, coarse pearlite results from a relatively slow cooling process and fine pearlite results from a rapid cooling process. As described earlier, fine crystal structures tend to be more difficult to

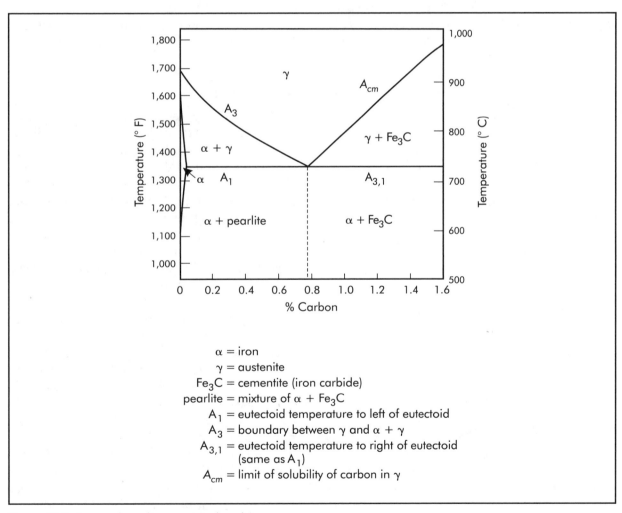

Figure 12-8. Iron-carbon diagram (steels only).

deform, so they are harder and have a high tensile strength.

Three types of pearlite are typically formed by heat treatment processes:

1. Furnace cooling—coarse pearlite (pure form: 14 Rockwell C or 240 BHN).
2. Air cooling—medium pearlite (pure form: 25 Rockwell C or 280 BHN).
3. Oil quench—fine pearlite (pure form: 38 Rockwell C or 380 BHN).

Unless a steel is a eutectic composition, the pearlite is mixed with ferrite (pure form: 80 BHN) or cementite (pure form: 1,000 BHN). The mix between ferrite/cementite and pearlite in a plain carbon steel can provide an estimate of the steel hardness. The following formula can be applied to estimate the hardness of a hypoeutectoid plain carbon steel after heat treatment based on carbon content and type of cooling process:

$$H = H_F \left(\frac{0.77 - \%C}{0.77} \right) + H_P \left(\frac{\%C}{0.77} \right) \quad (12\text{-}1)$$

where:

H = Brinell hardness number (BHN)
H_F = BHN for ferrite
H_P = BHN for the particular type of pearlite that is formed
$\%C$ = percentage of carbon

The tensile strength of a plain carbon steel can be estimated by the formula:

$$U_T = 500 \times \text{BHN} \quad (12\text{-}2)$$

where:

U_T = ultimate tensile strength (psi)
BHN = BHN of steel

12.5 HEAT TREATMENT PROCESSES

Heat treatment may be defined as any process whereby metals are better adapted to desired conditions or properties, in predictably varying degrees, by means of controlled heating and cooling in their solid state without altering their chemical composition. Heat treatment can be applied to a variety of metals: iron, steel, aluminum, copper, and numerous others. However, because of the versatility and broad use of ferrous alloys in industry, the treatments applied to steel are, by far, the most widely used.

Heat treatment may be employed to improve tensile strength, ductility, toughness, wear resistance, machinability, formability, bending quality, corrosion resistance, magnetic properties, and other properties. Heat-treatment temperatures usually range from room temperature to 2,350° F (1,287° C) but can be as low as –324° F (–198° C).

The major heat-treatment processes can be grouped into two categories, hardening and annealing (softening).

HARDENING

If steel is heated to the 100% austenite range, then hardening of steel generally requires two factors, the appropriate composition of the material and the cooling rate of the heated pieces. In the composition, the percentage of carbon can determine the greatest hardness achievable. Although hardening increases the natural attributes of steel, it also creates a structure of *martensite*, a supersaturated solid solution of carbon and iron, which is extremely hard and brittle. Formed by rapid cooling from the upper critical temperature (A_3 or A_{cm}) or austenite range to room temperature, martensite appears as a needle-like structure when viewed under a microscope. The carbon atoms are trapped in a solid solution of iron before they are able to diffuse out of solution. The resultant structure is body-centered tetragonal, which is a highly stressed condition.

A major cause of the stress is that the volume of parts increases as much as 4% during the martensite transformation. These expansions, coupled with thermal gradients, result in internal stresses and can cause quench cracking. Consequently, it is important that the surface of the material be clean and completely free of nicks, pits, seams, or tool marks, because these imperfections can become stress risers during the hardening process.

The rate of cooling also effects the resulting hardness. Generally, the faster the cooling, the higher the hardness. In practical terms, the key to rapid cooling is the medium used for quenching. The relative severity of quenching for different media is defined in Table 12-1. From the table, agitated brine can cool a sample 250 times faster than still air.

Table 12-1. Relative severity of quenching for different media

Relative Severity	Quenching Media
5	agitated brine
1	still water
0.3	still oil
0.02	still air

Hardenability depends on composition and cooling rate. Consequently, it is possible to achieve a specified hardness either by increasing carbon content and decreasing cooling rate, or by decreasing the carbon content and increasing the cooling rate. The time-temperature-transformation curve (TTT curve) modified for continuous cooling shows these relationships graphically in Figure 12-9.

In Figure 12-9, the broken line labeled A_1 at 1,341° F (727° C) indicates the start of the austenitic range. Steels must be heated into this range to become fully austenite. If cooling occurs rapidly enough, the sample will become martensite and remain martensite at room temperature. In other words, the sample will reach its maximum hardness when the amount of martensite is high. In pure form, martensite has hardness values

of 55 Rockwell C or 700 BHN. In Figure 12-9, the region for this is to the left of the line labeled critical cooling rate. If the cooling is less rapid, the sample will end up at room temperature as a combination of martensite and pearlite, as shown by the area between the critical cooling rate line and the line labeled 35° C/s. A sample following this trajectory will be softer than the rapidly cooled sample. If the cooling rate is slower yet, the sample will become pearlite at room temperature, in effect showing no increase in hardness.

It is important to understand that Figure 12-9 represents the transformations that occur in a steel with a carbon content of 0.77%. To know what happens when the carbon content is changed, a metallurgist would refer to another TTT curve.

Example 12.5.1. What temperature is needed to completely austenitize a sample of plain carbon steel with 0.4% carbon? Estimate the hardness after austenitizing and oil quenching.

Solution. From Figure 12-8, the sample is completely austenitized at approximately 1,480° F (804° C). The hardness can be found using Equation 12-1:

$$H = H_F \left(\frac{(0.77 - \%C)}{0.77} \right) + H_P \left(\frac{\%C}{0.77} \right)$$

where:

H = Brinell hardness number (BHN)
H_F = 80 BHN for ferrite
H_P = 380 BHN for oil quench (fine pearlite)
$\%C$ = 0.4

$$H = 80 \left(\frac{(0.77 - 0.4)}{0.77} \right) + 380 \left(\frac{0.4}{0.77} \right)$$

$$H = 236 \text{ BHN}$$

Example 12.5.2. Estimate the tensile strength of plain carbon steel with 0.2% carbon after austenitizing and air cooling.

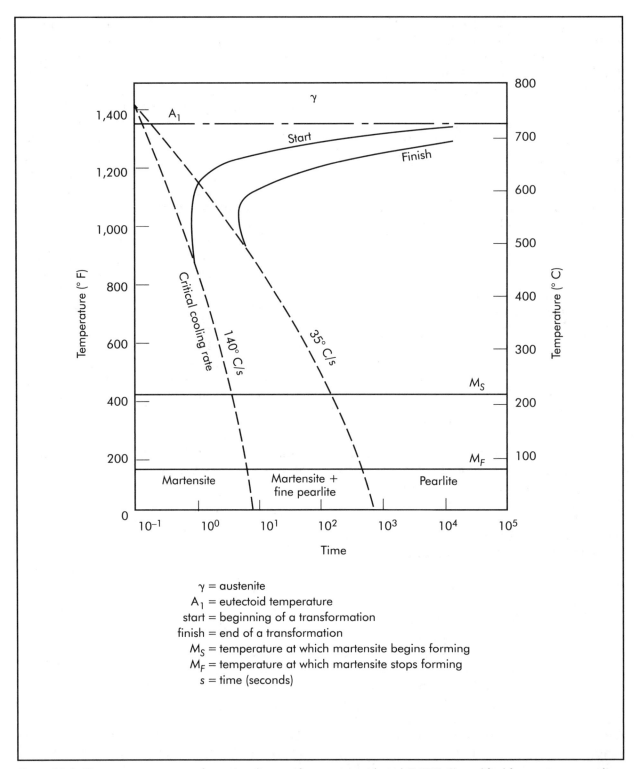

Figure 12-9. Time-temperature-transformation diagram for a euctectoid steel (0.77% C) modified for continuous cooling.

Solution. The tensile strength can be estimated based on the BHN. The BHN can be found from Equation 12-1:

$$H = H_F \left(\frac{(0.77 - \%C)}{0.77} \right) + H_P \left(\frac{\%C}{0.77} \right)$$

where:

H = Brinell hardness number (BHN)
H_F = 80 BHN for ferrite
H_P = 280 BHN for air-cooling (medium pearlite)
$\%C = 0.2$

$$H = 80 \left(\frac{(0.77 - 0.2)}{0.77} \right) + 280 \left(\frac{0.2}{0.77} \right)$$

$$H = 132 \ \text{BHN}$$

The tensile strength is estimated by Equation 12-2:

$$\begin{aligned} U_T &= 500 \times \text{BHN} \\ &= 500 \times 132 \\ &= 66{,}000 \ \text{psi} \end{aligned}$$

Surface Hardening

Surface hardening treatments are used to add carbon, nitrogen, or both to the surface of steel parts to provide a hardened layer or case of a definite depth. Sometimes called *case hardening*, these treatments create a surface with high wear resistance but maintain a ductile inner core for impact strength or toughness. The five principal methods of case hardening are carburizing, cyaniding, nitriding, flame hardening, and induction hardening.

Carburizing. The oldest and one of the least expensive methods of case hardening, *carburizing*, consists of placing a low-carbon steel, usually about 0.2% carbon or lower, in contact with substantial amounts of carbon. The usual carburizing temperature is 1,700° F (927° C). At that temperature, carbon is completely dissolved into the austenite.

Commercial carburizing may be accomplished by pack carburizing, gas carburiz-ing, or liquid carburizing. In pack carburizing, the work is surrounded by a carburizing compound (charcoal, for example) in a closed container. With gas carburizing, the work is placed in contact with gases rich in carbon monoxide and hydrocarbons, such as methane, butane, and propane. Liquid carburizing is performed in a bath of molten salt containing up to 20% sodium cyanide. The cyanide is a source of carbon and nitrogen. The case obtained by this method is composed largely of carbon with only a small amount of nitrogen.

Cyaniding. *Cyaniding* consists of immersing the steel in a molten bath containing about 30% sodium cyanide at temperatures between 1,450° F (788° C) and 1,600° F (871° C). It is usually followed by water quenching. Cyaniding differs from liquid carburizing in the composition and character of the case. The process creates a high-nitrogen and low-carbon case, quite the reverse of liquid carburizing. Used mainly where a light case is required, cyaniding requires only one hour for a 0.010 in. (0.3 mm) deep case.

Nitriding. In *nitriding*, the part is placed in an airtight container through which ammonia is passed continuously at a temperature between 900° F (482° C) and 1,150° F (621° C). Under these conditions, the ammonia partially decomposes into nitrogen and hydrogen. The nitrogen penetrates the steel surface and combines with iron to form nitrides. Nitriding produces the hardest surface of the case-hardening processes. However, it is the most time-consuming process (50 hours = approximately 0.014 in. [0.356 mm] case depth).

Flame hardening. *Flame hardening* involves rapidly heating a selected surface area of medium or high-carbon steel and immediately cooling it in water or by air blast.

Induction hardening. *Induction hardening* is similar to flame hardening. They are both shallow hardening and do not change the chemical composition of the steel.

Induction hardening is used mainly on medium-carbon steels. In this method, the part to be hardened is made the secondary of a high-frequency induction apparatus. The primary or work coil consists of several turns of water-cooled copper tubing. When a high-frequency alternating current is passed through the coil, a magnetic field is set up, inducing a high-frequency eddy current in the metal. The losses due to these currents produce the required heat. Quenching immediately follows.

ANNEALING

Annealing is a general term for restoration of the cold-worked or heat-treated material to its original properties. It may be performed to increase ductility and reduce hardness and strength. It is also done to relieve residual stresses in a manufactured part to improved machinability. Annealing steel is done by heating the part to a temperature higher than the austenitizing temperature. The material is "soaked" at that temperature for a period of time and allowed to slowly cool. The resulting structure is coarse pearlite (soft and ductile with uniform grains). Some variations of annealing are:

- full annealing;
- spheroidize annealing;
- stress relief annealing;
- normalizing; and
- tempering.

Full Annealing

Full annealing consists of heating the steel to the proper temperature and then cooling slowly through the transformation range, preferably in the furnace or in any good heat-insulating chamber. The purpose of annealing may be to refine the grain, induce softness, improve electrical and magnetic properties and, in some cases, improve machinability.

The proper annealing temperature for a hypoeutectoid (low-carbon) steel is 50° F (10° C) above the upper-critical-temperature (A_3) line shown in Figure 12-10. Refinement of the grain size of hypereutectoid (high-carbon) steel will occur about 50° F (10° C) above the lower-critical-temperature ($A_{3,1}$) line. Heating above this temperature will coarsen the austenitic grains, which, on cooling, will transform to large pearlitic areas surrounded by a network of cementite. This creates a plane of weakness, brittleness, and usually poor machinability. Annealing never should be a final heat treatment for hypereutectoid steels.

Spheroidize Annealing

Spheroidize annealing is a process sometimes used to improve the properties of hypereutectoid steels. It involves holding the material for a prolonged period at a temperature just below the lower-critical temperature ($A_{3,1}$) or heating and cooling alternately between temperatures slightly above and slightly below the lower critical line. Spheroidize annealing allows cementite to assume the form of round particles (spheroids) instead of pearlitic plates. This structure not only gives good machinability but also high ductility.

Stress-relief Annealing

Also referred to as subcritical annealing, *stress-relief annealing* is useful in removing residual stresses due to heavy machining, cold-working processes, casting, and welding. It is usually carried out at temperatures between 1,000° F (538° C) and 1,200° F (649° C).

Normalizing

Normalizing is carried out by heating the material approximately 100° F (38° C) above the upper-critical-temperature (A_3 or A_{cm}) line, followed by cooling in still air to room

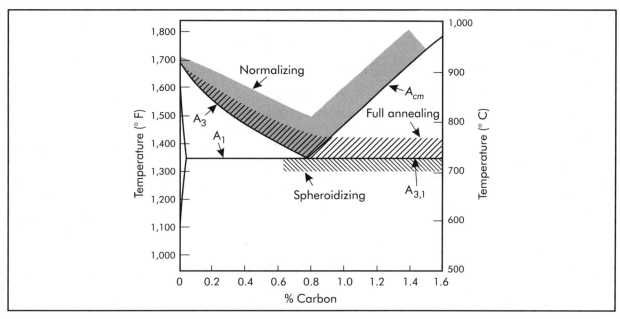

Figure 12-10. Typical heat-treatment temperatures for steel.

temperature. The purpose of normalizing is to produce a steel harder and stronger than full annealing, refine the grain, homogenize the structure, and improve machinability, particularly in low-carbon (hypoeutectoid) steels. Cooling in air causes the austenite to transform into pearlite at a lower temperature, resulting in a pearlite structure finer than that of annealing. Figure 12-10 shows a relationship between annealing and normalizing.

Tempering

Previously hardened steels are heated to prescribed temperatures to reduce brittleness, increase ductility and toughness and reduce residual stresses. Temperatures below 400° F (204° C) are typically used for applications requiring high wear resistance and above 800° F (427° C) are used for applications requiring high toughness.

12.6 ALLOY STEELS

Various elements are added to steel to tailor its properties. Alloying elements can en-

hance the strength, hardness, toughness, wear resistance, and many other properties. The most common alloying elements are presented in Table 12-2 with a summary of their effects.

There are standard designations for steel alloys. The most widely used system is the AISI-SAE system (American Iron and Steel Institute and Society of Automotive Engineers). The first two digits indicate the major alloying elements. The last two digits indicate the percentage of carbon by weight. For example, 1020 steel is a plain carbon steel with 0.2% carbon by weight. The characteristics of the AISI-SAE steel series are given in Table 12-3.

12.7 STAINLESS STEELS

Stainless steels are used for applications where corrosion resistance, high strength, and heat resistance are important. These steels are characterized by high chromium content. They are called stainless because a thin, airtight film of chromium oxide forms on the surface to isolate the metal

Table 12-2. Steel alloying elements

Element	Effect
Carbon	Improves hardenability, strength, and wear resistance. Reduces ductility and weldability.
Chromium	Improves toughness, wear and corrosion resistance, and high-temperature strength.
Cobalt	Improves strength and hardness at elevated temperatures.
Lead	Improves machinability. Causes embrittlement.
Molybdenum	Improves hardenability, wear resistance, toughness, elevated temperature strength, and creep resistance.
Nickel	Improves strength, toughness, and corrosion resistance.
Vanadium	Improves strength, toughness, abrasion resistance, and hardness at elevated temperatures.

Table 12-3. Characteristics of AISI-SAE steel series

AISI Number	Characteristics
10XX	Plain carbon
13XX	Manganese—increases strength in as-rolled state and increases ductility after heat treatment
23XX-25XX	Nickel—increases tensile strength without loss of ductility
3XXX	Nickel/chromium—tough and ductile due to nickel, wear and corrosion due to chromium
4XXX	Molybdenum—significant increase in tensile strength and hardenability
5XXX	Chromium—high wear resistance
6XXX	Chromium/vanadium—high yield strength, good fatigue properties
8XXX-9XXX	Chromium/nickel/molybdenum—exhibits benefits of each

from corrosion. Chromium oxidizes very rapidly. The protective film reappears quickly if the surface is scratched. There are several types of stainless steels, identified by an AISI three-digit numbering system. The significance of the last two digits varies, but the first digit indicates the series. The numbering system is shown in Table 12-4.

The characteristics of the stainless steel metallurgy are austenitic, ferritic, and martensitic.

AUSTENITIC

Austenitic stainless steels are typically nonmagnetic and do not harden by heat treatment. They have superior corrosion resistance and are hardened by cold working. Austenitic stainless is the most ductile type of stainless steel. Typical applications are kitchen utensils, fittings, and welded construction.

FERRITIC

The *ferritic* stainless steels are magnetic and have good corrosion resistance, but they are less ductile than austenitic stainless steels. They cannot be hardened by heat treatment. Typical applications are nonstructural applications in corrosive environments.

Table 12-4. Stainless steels

AISI Number	Characteristics
2XX	Chromium/nickel/manganese composition, nonhardenable by heat treatment, austenitic and nonmagnetic
3XX	Chromium/nickel composition, nonhardenable by heat treatment, austenitic and nonmagnetic
4XX	Chromium composition, hardenable by heat treatment, martensitic and magnetic or nonhardenable by heat treatment, ferritic and magnetic
5XX	Low chromium composition, hardenable by heat treatment and martensitic

MARTENSITIC

The *martensitic* stainless steels do not contain nickel. These steels are hardenable by heat treatment. They are magnetic and exhibit high strength, hardness, fatigue resistance, and ductility. However, they have only moderate corrosion resistance. Typical applications are valves, springs, and cutlery.

12.8 CAST IRON

Cast iron is basically an alloy of iron and carbon. It contains between 2% and 6.67% carbon. The high carbon content tends to make cast iron brittle. Cast iron cannot be rolled, drawn, or otherwise worked unless it is done at an elevated temperature. The desirable characteristics it incorporates are its low-melting temperature and its castability (ease of pouring into complicated shapes).

There are several basic types of cast iron. They are gray, white, malleable, and nodular. The characteristics are determined by carbon content, form, alloy content, and heat treatment.

GRAY IRON

In *gray iron*, the carbon content is in a free state (flakes of graphite). This is the most widely used cast iron due to its machinability and high shear strength. The graphite is formed by the addition of silicon and phosphorus. The free graphite acts as a lubricant in the machining process.

WHITE IRON

White or *chilled iron* is made by casting gray iron against a metal heat sink. The localized rapid cooling results in a hard, abrasion-resistant surface with a softer gray iron core. No free graphite is formed upon rapid cooling. Instead, the carbon forms cementite. Limited depths of chill are possible due to the physical limitations in transferring heat away from the molten metal.

MALLEABLE IRON

Malleable iron is made by heat treating white iron. Free graphite is formed by holding the white iron component at a high temperature. The resulting product has higher strength, ductility, and machinability.

NODULAR IRON

Nodular iron or ductile iron contains carbon in the form of tiny nodules or spheres. The composition is similar to gray iron except the addition of magnesium or cerium causes the formation of spheres of graphite rather than flakes. The nodular structure gives this material excellent impact properties.

12.9 ALUMINUM

Aluminum is an important engineering material because of its high strength-to-weight ratio, resistance to corrosion, high thermal and electrical conductivity, appearance, machinability, and formability.

Aluminum is used for packaging, structures, electrical conductors, and consumer goods.

Various types of aluminum are used in the form of wrought products (made into various shapes by rolling, extrusion, drawing, and forging) and cast alloys. Wrought aluminum alloys are identified by four digits and a temper designation (indicating the processing of the material). The major alloying element determines the first digit. The second digit refers to other alloying elements, and the third and fourth digits indicate a particular alloy within the series. In the 1XXX series, the last two digits indicate the purity of the aluminum. For example, 1070 contains 99.70% aluminum and 1090 contains 99.90% aluminum. The various types of wrought aluminum are shown in Table 12-5.

The designations for cast aluminum alloys also use four digits. A decimal point is added between the third and fourth digit. In the 1XX.X series, the second and third digits indicate the aluminum content. The fourth digit, which is to the right of the decimal, indicates the product form: 1XX.0 indicates castings and 1XX.1 indicates ingot. In the other series, these digits vary in usage. The cast aluminum alloy numbering system is shown in Table 12-6.

The temper designations used for aluminum apply to both wrought and cast alloys. Temper designations indicate the form of secondary processing done to the aluminum at the mill. The following letter designations are used:

- F—as fabricated;
- O—annealed;
- H—strain hardened by cold work; and
- T—heat treated.

Aluminum, like all nonferrous metals, does not harden by heat treating the same way steel does. Heat-treating processes for aluminum include strain hardening (cold working), annealing, solution heat treatment, and precipitation hardening.

STRAIN HARDENING

Strain hardening caused by cold working occurs in all metals to some degree. However, it is more prominent in nonferrous metals such as aluminum, copper, and brass. When a metal is deformed below its recrystallization temperature, it becomes harder. The recrystallization temperature is the temperature at which metal grains reform or recrystallize into an unstrained condition.

ANNEALING

After aluminum has been strain hardened, annealing, or more specifically, recrystallization, will return it to a soft and ductile condition. For example, heating 1100 aluminum at approximately 650° F (343° C) and quenching will restore its softness and ductility. The

Table 12-5. Wrought aluminum alloy designations

Number	Alloy	Properties
1XXX	Commercially pure	Corrosion resistant, high electrical and thermal conductivity, good workability, low strength
2XXX	Copper	High strength-to-weight ratio, low corrosion resistance
3XXX	Manganese	Good workability, moderate strength
4XXX	Silicon	Low melting point
5XXX	Magnesium	Good corrosion resistance, weldable, high strength
6XXX	Magnesium and silicon	Good weldability, machinability, and formability, corrosion resistant, medium strength
7XXX	Zinc	High strength

Table 12-6. Aluminum casting alloys

Number	Alloy	Properties
1XX.X	Commercially pure	Corrosion resistant
2XX.X	Copper	High strength and ductility
3XX.X	Silicon	Good machinability (with copper or magnesium)
4XX.X	Silicon	Good castability, corrosion resistant
5XX.X	Magnesium	High strength
6XX.X	Unused	
7XX.X	Zinc	High strength, excellent machinability

quenching rate is not important for pure aluminum. For wrought aluminum alloys of the precipitation hardening grades, for example 2017, the cooling rate must be 50° F (10° C) per hour or less to achieve the annealed condition. Slow cooling of 2017, alloyed with copper, allows the second phase ($CuAl_2$) to precipitate out of the solution as coarse particles. For aluminum-copper alloys this condition is considered the annealed state.

SOLUTION HEAT TREATMENT

Solution heat treatment involves creating a solid solution of aluminum and an alloying element by heating and quenching. For example, if the aluminum-copper alloy 2017 is heated at 950° F (510° C) for 12 hours, a solid solution of aluminum and copper will form. A supersaturated solution is then formed by rapid quenching. The aluminum in this quenched state has higher corrosion resistance and ductility. However, its hardness may be increased by precipitation hardening or aging.

PRECIPITATION HARDENING

Precipitation hardening or aging takes solution heat treatment one step further. Precipitation hardening increases aluminum's hardness by the precipitation of very fine $CuAl_2$ particles. The fine particles of $CuAl_2$ precipitate at the grain boundaries and increase slip resistance in the aluminum. Particle precipitation, known as *aging*, takes

place after the aluminum-copper alloy is solution heat treated. Natural aging means that the precipitation of $CuAl_2$ occurs at room temperature and artificial aging implies that the precipitation occurs at an elevated temperature. Overaging is possible if the aging time or temperature is too high. Overaging results in lower strength and corrosion resistance.

REVIEW QUESTIONS

12.1) How are grain boundaries formed in a metal?

12.2) How does the addition of salt affect the solidus temperature of water?

12.3) What is the range of carbon content in typical steels?

12.4) What is the lowest possible austenitizing temperature for steel?

12.5) Why is oil sometimes used in preference over water in quenching heat-treated samples?

12.6) Estimate the hardness of a specimen of plain carbon steel with 0.5% carbon (AISI 1050) after austenitizing and subsequent oil quenching.

12.7) Recommend a full annealing temperature for a steel with 0.2% carbon.

12.8) What metal can be alloyed with steel to improve its machinability?

12.9) What category of stainless steels is typically used for making knives?

　a) ferritic
　b) austenitic
　c) nodular
　d) martensitic

12.10) A C-clamp is to be made from cast iron and the manufacturer wants the part to resist being broken when dropped. What type of cast iron should be selected?

12.11) What type of wrought aluminum should be chosen when strength is not a consideration but high electrical conductivity is?

12.12) Which of the following treatments of metal is not used for surface hardening?

　a) carburizing
　b) cyaniding
　c) nitriding
　d) normalizing

Chapter 13

Plastics

Nonmetallic materials cover three broad categories, namely plastics, composites, and ceramics. In many applications, considerable overlap occurs between plastics and composites, because the composite matrix is a plastic material. The overlap between composites and ceramics usually centers on the use of glass fibers. Composites and ceramics will be discussed in the next two chapters respectively.

13.1 PLASTICS

The terms polymer, plastics, polymers, resins, rubber, and elastomer are often confused. Polymers are organic compounds that come from natural sources or are synthetic. The word *polymer* means many (poly) mers. *Mers* are small units, generally simple organic molecules. Mers are also called monomers when only one type of molecule is present. The division between simple organic molecules, such as the automobile fuel octane, and polymers depends on the number of mers linked together. A rule-of-thumb is that a polymer must contain at least 100 mers.

The word *plastics* is rather difficult to define. The Greek word "plastikos" means moldable, but that meaning does not separate plastics from moldable materials such as clay. A tighter definition used by the Society of the Plastics Industry (SPI) describes plastics as basically organic materials that are solid in the finished state, but were formed with heat and pressure. This definition provides a distinction between resins, which are gum-like semisolid substances, and plastics, which have to be solids. However, this definition does not address the problem of elasticity.

In the past, the word "rubber" referred to natural latex and products made of natural latex. Natural rubber and other elastomers are polymeric materials that can stretch to at least twice their original length and then snap back. In contrast, the word "plastics" referred to those polymeric materials that were less elastic, harder, and stiffer. This simple distinction between plastics and rubber is now difficult to maintain. A new family of materials often called *thermoplastic elastomers* (TPEs) now fills the gap between traditional rubber and rigid plastics.

Although the difficulties with definitions persist, plastics fall into two major groups, thermoplastics and thermosets. *Thermoplastics* are those plastics that are solid at room temperature, but when heated they soften and can be reformed. These materials can be reused and recycled easily. *Thermosets* are those plastics that soften during original processing, but once finished, they can not easily be reprocessed.

POLYMERIZATION

Crude oil and natural gas supply the chemicals required for the production of plastics. When crude oil is "cracked" by fractional distillation, some fractions, such as octane, kerosene, and oils, are immediately useful. The companies producing plastics take the very small molecules, such as methane and ethane, and chemically combine them to make the large macromolecules of plastics. Figure 13-1 shows a progression from small to very large hydrocarbon molecules.

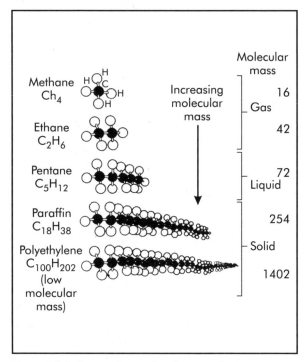

Figure 13-1. Increasing molecular mass from a gas to a solid plastic (Richardson and Lokensgard 1997).

The key to polymerization is to bring the selected small molecules together and then force them to chemically combine with each other. The force can result from various combinations of heat, pressure, and chemical catalysts. Since polymerization is an exothermic reaction, the process must be able to effectively control the heat generated. One way to control the heat is to dissolve the monomer in a large bath of solvent. The temperature of the bath can be controlled to remove unwanted heat.

At the chemical level, the reaction proceeds in two ways, either by addition polymerization, or condensation polymerization.

Addition Polymerization

Addition polymerization is also called *chain growth polymerization*. The monomers join together in a manner that leaves no by-products. The image of a freight train is appropriate. The train is created when many boxcars join together. No additional parts are needed and nothing remains behind. Addition polymerization is the process that creates most thermoplastics.

Condensation Polymerization

Condensation polymerization is also called *stepwise growth*. In condensation polymerization, a by-product is usually produced when the monomers join together. This by-product is called *condensate*. Removing the condensate so that it will not slow or contaminate the reaction is important in this process. In a stepwise reaction, monomers combine to form a unit two mers long. Then, the two mer units combine to form four mer units. This continues until the process is terminated.

13.2 POLYMER STRUCTURES

The possible combinations of monomers to create polymers are virtually endless. However, three possibilities are most common, homopolymers, copolymers, and terpolymers.

HOMOPOLYMERS

Homopolymer plastics come from only one basic kind of building block or monomer. Some of the most common homopolymers are polyethylene, polypropylene, polyvinyl chloride, and polystyrene. Homopolymers can have either amorphous or semicrystalline arrangements of the molecular chains. In amorphous plastics, the molecular chains are coiled, twisted, and kinked. They have no long-range order. When no fillers, colors, or other additives are present, amorphous plastics are transparent. Polystyrene (PS) and polyvinyl chloride (PVC) fall in this group.

Semicrystalline homopolymers include high-density polyethylene (HDPE), low-density polyethylene (LDPE), and polypropylene (PP). In crystalline regions, the molecular chains take on a highly ordered structure. Generally, the way this occurs is that the chains fold back and forth causing increased density in the crystalline regions. These regions have major effects on the properties of the plastic. The crystalline regions cause diffraction in light transmission, causing semicrystalline materials to be translucent or opaque, not transparent. Semicrystalline materials exhibit greater mold shrinkage than amorphous materials. Mold shrinkage is the change in length, measured as in. per in. or mm per mm. When the semicrystalline materials take on the orderly arrangement, the volume required diminishes and the shrinkage increases.

COPOLYMERS

Copolymers contain two chemically differing mers. An example is the plastic known as styrene-acrylonitrile (SAN). It contains both the styrene monomer and the acrylonitrile monomer. Because there are two kinds of building blocks, several possibilities arise. In alternating copolymers, the structure is similar to ABABABABABABAB. In block copolymers, the structure reveals a group of one type, followed by the other type, such as AAAAABBBAAAAABBBAAAA. In graft copolymers, the backbone is usually one type, and the other becomes a short branch off the main chain. In random copolymers, there is no apparent order of the two types. As with homopolymers, copolymers can be either amorphous or semicrystalline.

TERPOLYMERS

In terpolymers, three basic mers combine to create a polymer. One example is ASA, which brings together acrylic, styrene, and acrylonitrile monomers. The possible structures are more complex than with copolymers. The terpolymers also can have amorphous or semicrystalline arrangements.

13.3 THERMOPLASTICS

Table 13-1 lists properties of a number of common plastics. Please note that most of the plastics in the table are thermoplastics, with only epoxy and phenolic representing the thermosets. In addition, the thermoplastics are listed according to amorphous and crystalline structures. An alternative approach is to group the thermoplastics into the categories of commodity thermoplastics and engineering thermoplastics.

COMMODITY THERMOPLASTICS

Commodity thermoplastics are those materials that receive wide-scale use in expendable products. Containers for foods, cosmetics, and beverages are usually made of commodity thermoplastics. The recycling codes provide a convenient listing of the most common commodity plastics. These codes are defined in Table 13-2.

The thermoplastics listed in Table 13-2 account for almost three-fourths of the total annual plastics consumption in the USA. However, only a small percentage of that volume returns through the recycling stream to find reuse. The materials that have the highest percentage of recycling are those used for beverage containers.

The most widely used commodity thermoplastics are polyethylene (PE), polypropylene (PP), polyvinyl chloride (PVC), polystyrene (PS), and polyethylene terephthalate (PETE).

Polyethylene

Polyethylene has been the number-one selling plastics materials since the 1950s. It is manufactured in two major forms, low-density

Table 13-1. Properties of selected industrial plastics

Type of Plastic	Molecular Packing	Specific Gravity	Mechanical Properties (Room Temperature)				
			ASTM D-638 Tensile Strength psi (MPa)	ASTM D-638 Elongation %	ASTM D-695 Compressive Strength, psi (MPa)	ASTM D-256 Impact Strength (Izod), ft-lb/in. (J/cm)	
Polystyrene	Amorphous	1.10	7,500 (51.7)	2	14,000 (96.5)	0.3 (0.2)	
High-impact polystyrene	Amorphous	1.15	5,000 (34.5)	10	7,500 (51.7)	0.6–10.0 (0.3–5.3)	
Acrylics	Amorphous	1.15	10,000 (69.0)	6	15,000 (103.4)	0.4 (0.2)	
Polycarbonate	Amorphous	1.20	9,000 (62.1)	100	10,000 (69.0)	15.0 (8.0)	
ABS	Amorphous	1.05	6,000 (41.4)	30	8,000 (55.2)	6.0 (3.2)	
Acetal (homopolymer)	Crystalline	1.40	10,000 (69.0)	40	18,000 (124.1)	1.8 (1.0)	
Nylon 6/6 at 50% RH*	Crystalline	1.15	11,000 (75.8)	400	10,000 (69.0)	2.1 (1.1)	
Polypropylene	Crystalline	0.91	4,500 (31.0)	500	7,000 (48.3)	1.0 (0.5)	
Polyethylene (high density)	Crystalline	0.95	4,000 (27.6)	600	3,000 (20.7)	10.0 (5.3)	
Polyethylene (medium density)	Crystalline with amorphous regions	0.93	2,400 (16.5)	600	3,000 (20.7)	8.0 (4.3)	
Polyethylene (low density)	Semicrystalline	0.91	1,500 (10.3)	700	3,000 (20.7)	No break	
Epoxy	Cross-linked network	1.25	10,000 (69.0)	3	20,000 (137.9)	0.8 (0.4)	
Phenolic	Cross-linked network	1.35	7,000 (48.3)	2	10,000 (69.0)	0.4 (0.2)	

*RH = relative humidity

Table 13-2. Recycling codes

Number	Abbreviation	Name
1	PETE	Polyethylene terephthalate
2	HDPE	High-density polyethylene
3	V	Vinyl (polyvinyl chloride)
4	LDPE	Low-density polyethylene
5	PP	Polypropylene
6	PS	Polystyrene
7	Other	

polyethylene (LDPE) and high-density polyethylene (HDPE). Both forms have high solvent resistance, high flexibility, and good electrical insulation properties. However, they are also both susceptible to environmentally induced damage and have low softening points.

About three-fourths of the annual production of low-density polyethylene becomes film. It is flexible and tear resistant and, if thin, it is rather clear. Dry-cleaner bags are usually LDPE. In contrast to HDPE, LDPE is more flexible and has lower crystallinity.

HDPE finds use in both injection molding and blow molding. Most milk containers and detergent bottles are HDPE. The quart containers of motor oil are generally recycled HDPE bottles. In contrast to LDPE, HDPE has greater crystallinity, higher strength, and greater rigidity.

Polypropylene

Polypropylene (PP) is very important in injection molding and blow molding. Many interior automobile parts are PP. In addition, PP is significant in the fiber market. Post-industrial scrap PP carpet material is frequently reprocessed for automotive applications. In comparison to HDPE, PP has a higher melting point and also a higher softening point. PP is tougher and more rigid than HDPE, but it is very susceptible to oxidative degradation and damage from ultraviolet (UV) light. Additives can prevent these problems from occurring for extensive lengths of time.

Polyvinyl Chloride

Polyvinyl chloride (PVC) can be flexible for use as vinyl upholstery material or very rigid as found in PVC pipes and plumbing fittings. The difference is that the flexible PVC has been plasticized. *Plasticized* means that various special oils have been mixed into the PVC. These oils cause the material to be almost rubbery. Wire insulation material is frequently flexible PVC. The advantages of PVC are its excellent solvent resistance and its resistance to burning. Flame-retardant PVC is used for computer housings.

Polystyrene

Polystyrene (PS) is a glassy material. When no fillers or additives are present, polystyrene (called crystal PS) is very transparent, stiff, and brittle. To reduce the brittleness of crystal polystyrene, general-purpose PS contains rubber additives. If more rubber is added, the material becomes high-impact polystyrene (HIPS). Polystyrene is the base for a family of materials called *styrenics*. One of the most popular styrenics is ABS, a material that contains rubber, acrylic, and polystyrene. The advantages of polystyrene include translucency when thicker than film and its ability to be readily foamed, as in the production of Styrofoam®. Its major disadvantages are poor solvent resistance and brittleness.

Polyethylene Terephthalate

Polyethylene terephthalate (PETE) is also called thermoplastic polyester. PETE is widely used for carbonated beverage containers. A filled two-liter PETE container is at least one-quarter lighter than a comparable glass bottle. This property, in addition to its amenability to high-speed manufacturing, makes PETE dominant in beverage applications. PETE has excellent transparency, toughness, and flexibility. It addition, it is stiff enough so that pressure-tight closures can prevent the loss of carbonation. PETE is recycled into other containers and into various fibers. Many sleeping bags contain insulating bats made from recycled beverage bottles. PETE has good resistance to many solvents. A major disadvantage is its tendency to absorb moisture from the air. Consequently it must be thoroughly dried (to less than 0.005% moisture) before processing.

ENGINEERING THERMOPLASTICS

Many materials have special characteristics that make them appropriate to applications with high demands. Thermoplastic engineering resins are characterized as those resins with the following combination of properties:

- thermal, mechanical, chemical, and corrosion resistance, and usability;
- ability to sustain high mechanical loads, in harsh environments, for long periods of time; and
- predictable, reliable performance.

The most common engineering thermoplastics are nylon, acetal, and polycarbonate.

Nylon

Nylon is a trade name for polyamide plastics. Polyamide plastics were first developed by Wallace Carothers at DuPont and commercialized in 1938. Polyamides require combining an amine group and an adipic acid group. They are categorized by the number of carbon atoms in the amine and acid groups. For example, nylon 6,6 has six carbon atoms in the amine group and six carbons in the acid. Nylon is available in various combinations, including nylon-6, nylon-6,10, nylon-11, and nylon-12.

Nylons are semicrystalline materials with high strength, stiffness, and heat resistance. Nylon-6 is used for sewing thread, fishing line, household/industrial brushes, and level-filament paint brushes. Nylon-6,6 is stiffer than nylon-6.

Nylon strapping began replacing steel strapping in the early 1960s, even at higher cost, because of the general advantages of nonmetallic strapping. In recent years, nylon has met increasing competition in this market from polypropylene and PET.

Nylon is also extruded into rods, tubes, and shapes for machining. Nylon-11 is used for powder coatings and flexible tubing. Nylon-12 is used for the same purposes, but to a greater extent in Europe than in the U.S. These resins have exceptional moisture resistance, but they are considerably less stiff than nylon-6 or 6,6.

Acetal

The chemical name for acetal is polyoxymethylene (POM). Acetals are highly crystalline polymers. They are commercially available as both homopolymers and copolymers. Acetal has high mechanical strength and rigidity, natural lubricity, the highest deflection temperature of any common unreinforced engineering plastic, excellent toughness, and resistance to creep and repeated impacts. It also has excellent resistance to moisture, gasoline, solvents, and many other neutral chemicals. Acetal is frequently used for gears, cams, valves, switches, springs, and pumps.

The major manufacturing process that uses acetal is injection molding. Although an acetal terpolymer is available for injection blow molding, it has found little use except for some carburetor floats. Although difficult, acetal can be extruded into shapes for subsequent machining.

The most common manufacturer of the homopolymer, E. I. du Pont de Nemours and Company, sells it under the trade name Delrin®. A popular version of the copolymer is made by Ticona and sold under the trade name Celcon®. The homopolymer has better physical properties, but the copolymer has a wider processing window and is less subject to thermal degradation during service life.

Polycarbonate

Polycarbonate is an amorphous engineering thermoplastic. The transparency of polycarbonate, combined with its extrudability and impact resistance, makes it a strong competitor for acrylic sheet in replacing flat glass. Extruded sheet for glazing, lighting, and signs accounts for approximately 25% of polycarbonate's volume. Its use in extruded profiles is minor, but polycarbonate is widely used in blow molding water bottles, milk bottles, baby nursing bottles, and miscellaneous packaging.

Automotive manufacturers are investing considerable time and money into efforts to substitute polycarbonate for glass windows. The major technical hurdle is to provide the polycarbonate with a tough, scratch resistant coating. Uncoated polycarbonate windows are very strong, but scratch easily.

13.4 THERMOSET PLASTICS

THERMOSETS

Thermosets are plastics containing molecules that are chemically linked to each other. The chemical bonds between molecules are called *cross-links*. These bonds cause thermosets to be unmeltable and, consequently, they are not readily recycled. To make products, many thermoset materials are manufactured in a two-stage process. First, the raw materials are partially polymerized, but not cross-linked. When heated and pressed into a finished form, cross-linking occurs. Classic rubber products are thermosetting polymers, which are above the glass transition point. Hard, brittle thermosets, such as phenolics, are usually below the glass transition point. The *glass transition point* or *transition temperature* is a point or temperature where a material's mechanical properties change from flexible and ductile to hard and brittle.

Rubber

Natural rubber comes from the Hevea brasiliensis tree, which grows readily in Southeast Asia. It can be cross-linked by mixing powdered sulfur into the rubber and then applying heat. This process is called *vulcanizing*. Synthetic rubber products are copolymers of a diene monomer and another monomer, such as styrene or acrylonitrile. Styrene-butadiene rubbers (SBR) usually contain about 25% styrene. SBR rubbers, which contain fillers, are often superior to natural rubbers in abrasion resistance.

Natural rubber, which is often more expensive than SBR, is still in demand because it has higher resilience and generates less heat when flexed. Automobile tires use both natural and synthetic rubber to achieve the desired characteristics.

Hard Thermosets

The four dominant hard thermosets are phenolics, urea-formaldehydes, epoxides and polyesters. Phenolics are very hard, heat-resistant, and dark in color. They can be injection and compression molded. Often used in knobs and handles for cookware, phenolics are not highly resistant to strong acids or bases. Urea-formaldehydes are cheaper and lighter in color than phenolics. However, they are less heat-resistant than phenolics, and find numerous applications in electrical fittings. Epoxides are tough and have high adhesion properties. Polyesters form the matrix that bonds many composite materials together. Large-size automotive and truck parts are often made with sheet-molding compounds, which are polyesters with reinforcing fibers in sheet form. To cross-link the sheet-molding compounds, large compression-molding machines apply heat and pressure.

REVIEW QUESTIONS

13.1) Which of the following is not a property of plastics?

a) Organic
b) Solid in its finished state
c) Can be shaped by flow
d) Has a small molecular chain

13.2) What are the two major types of polymerization reactions?

13.3) What are the possible arrangements of mers in a copolymer?

13.4) What kind of plastic material bears the recycling code number 2?

13.5) When do organic molecules warrant the name polymers?

13.6) Which shrink more, amorphous or semicrystalline plastics?

13.7) What is the chemical name for nylon?

13.8) Do polyesters fall above or below the glass transition point?

REFERENCE

Richardson, Terry L., and Erik Lokensgard. 1997. *Industrial Plastics: Theory and Application*, Third Edition. Albany, NY: Delmar, a division of Thomson Learning.

Chapter 14

Composites

A *composite material* is created by the combination of two or more materials: a reinforcing element and a compatible resin binder (matrix) to obtain specific characteristics and properties. The components do not dissolve completely into each other or otherwise chemically merge, although they do act synergistically. Normally, the separate components can be physically identified, as well as the interface between components.

14.1 COMPOSITE MATERIALS

A common type of a composite material is fiberglass. Glass fibers, though very strong, fracture readily if notched. And if put in compression, they buckle easily. But, by encapsulating the glass fibers in a resin matrix, they are protected from damage. At the same time, the resin matrix transfers applied loads to the unified fibers so that their stiffness and strength can be fully used in tension and compression. The arrangement of the glass fibers influences the strength of the composite. Figure 14-1 shows three possible arrangements of glass fiber.

The more advanced structural composites use fibers of glass, carbon/graphite, boron, Kevlar® (aramid), and other organic materials. These fibers are very stiff and strong, yet lightweight. The strengthening effects of the fiber reinforcements in composites are derived from (a) the percentage of fibers (fiber-resin ratio); (b) the type of fibers; and (c) the fiber orientation with respect to the direction of the loads.

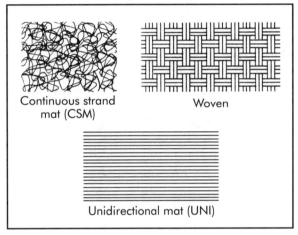

Figure 14-1. Common forms of fiberglass (Bakerjian and Mitchell 1992).

While advanced fiber and resin-matrix composites are classified as reinforced thermosets, a special technology sets them somewhat apart from other reinforced thermosets. Called "advanced composites," resin-matrix composites can include hybrids, which are mixtures of fibers in various forms in the resin (usually epoxy) matrix.

To engineers in the field, an *advanced composite* denotes a resin-matrix material reinforced with high-strength, high-modulus fibers of carbon/graphite, aramid, or boron. It is usually fabricated in layers to form an engineered component. More specifically, the term is applied largely to epoxy-resin matrix materials reinforced with oriented, continuous fibers of carbon and fabricated in a multilayer form to make extremely rigid, strong structures. Another characteristic distinguishing composites from reinforced plastics is the fiber-to-resin ratio. This ratio is generally greater than 50% fiber by weight. However, the ratio is sometimes indicated by volume since the weight and volume in composites are similar.

14.2 COMPOSITE CONSTRUCTION

Composites use a matrix design with different types of fibers and are either of a laminate or sandwich construction.

THE MATRIX

The *matrix* serves two important functions in a composite: (1) it holds the fibers in place and (2) under an applied force, it deforms and distributes the stress to the high-modulus fibrous constituent. The matrix material for a structural fiber composite must have a greater elongation at break than the fibers for maximum efficiency. Also, the matrix must transmit the force to the fibers and change shape as required to accomplish this, placing the majority of the load on the fibers. Furthermore, during processing, the matrix should encapsulate the fibrous phase with minimum shrinkage, placing an internal strain on the fibers. Other properties of the composite, such as chemical, thermal, electrical, and corrosion resistance, also are influenced by the type of matrix used.

The two main classes of polymer resin matrices are thermoset and thermoplastic. The principal thermosets are epoxy, phenolic, bismaleimide, and polyimide. Thermoplastic matrices are many and varied, including nylon (polyamide), polysulfone, polyphenylene sulfide, and polyetheretherketone. The matrix material must be carefully matched for compatibility with the fiber material and for application requirements. The selection process should cover factors such as thermal stability, impact strength, environmental resistance, processability, and surface treatment of the reinforcing fibers (sizing).

FIBER TYPES

The unique fiber geometry provides many advantages in an advanced composite. In their fiber form, materials such as carbon/graphite and boron (also known as polycrystalline ceramic fibers) show near-perfect crystalline structure. Parallel alignment of these crystals along the filament axis provides the superior strengths and stiffness characteristics of advanced composites. Various production methods are used for the different fiber types.

COMPOSITE CATEGORIES

Composites can be divided into laminates and sandwiches. *Laminates* are composite materials consisting of layers bonded together. *Sandwiches* are multiple-layer structural materials containing a low-density core between thin faces (skins) of composite materials. Figure 14-2 shows a sandwich with a cellular core and surface layers created by liquid composite molding (LCM). In some applications, particularly in the field of advanced structural composites, the constituents (individual layers) may themselves be composites (usually of the fiber-matrix type).

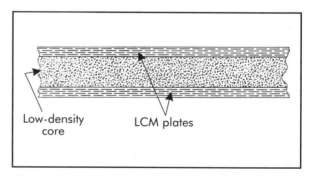

Figure 14-2. Sandwich construction (Bakerjian and Mitchell 1992).

14.3 COMPOSITE APPLICATIONS

By tailoring the materials and fabrication methods, and by modifying structural designs to accommodate their unique properties, advanced composites can be used for applications requiring high strength, high stiffness, or low thermal conductivity. The beneficial feature in many aerospace uses is that the new materials weigh less than the metallic materials they replace.

Advanced composites containing materials such as carbon/graphite, boron, or aramid fibers in an organic resin matrix are currently used mainly by the aerospace industries. However, these stiff, strong, lightweight materials are also used in various other commercial and industrial applications, ranging from aircraft structures to automobiles and trucks, from spacecraft to printed circuit boards, and from prosthetic devices to sports equipment. Products run the gamut from boat hulls and hockey shin guards to an advanced composite hinge for the retractable arm of the space shuttle.

Carbon/graphite-reinforced composites are used in a variety of applications that require thermal stability, high temperature strength, good ablation characteristics, and good insulating capability. Carbon fibers are physically stable at elevated temperatures and are used in rocket nozzle throats and ablation chambers. Graphite fibers are typically used when greater strength is required. Graphite fibers have six times the tensile strength of carbon fibers. However, they have higher thermal conductivity.

REVIEW QUESTIONS

14.1) A composite material is a combination of a reinforcing element and _____.

14.2) Advanced composites are distinguished from reinforced plastics in that:

   a) They use fibers in a resin binder for strength.
   b) Their polymer resin matrices are thermoset only.
   c) Their fiber-to-resin ratio by weight is greater than 50%.
   d) They can be machined dry.

14.3) The fibers in advanced composites are usually made of what materials?

14.4) What two functions does the matrix of a composite serve?

14.5) Under what conditions should graphite fibers versus carbon fibers be used?

15.1 CERAMIC APPLICATIONS

The word "ceramics" derives from a Greek word *keramos,* which means clay or items made of fired clay. By scientific definition, a *ceramic* is an inorganic compound containing metals, semimetals, and nonmetals. Ceramics include a wide range of materials. The clay-based applications include bricks, tiles, clay pipe, porcelain, stoneware, and earthenware. A special category of clay is fire clay, designed to resist high temperatures. These materials are also knows as *refractory materials.* Glass is a ceramic used for windowpanes, lenses, bottles, light bulbs, and fibers. Cement used in concrete for construction and roadways is also a ceramic. Most abrasives and grinding wheels are made of ceramics. Many metal cutting tools are ceramic, such as tungsten carbide.

One major advantage of many ceramics is their ability to resist corrosion. Many materials that corrode metals have no effect on ceramics. Table 15-1 shows the corrosion resistance of several ceramics. The corrosive agents listed are extremely active and will attack most non-ceramic materials.

Ceramic properties also include high hardness and brittleness, low impact strength, no plastic deformation before reaching tensile strength, and a high modulus of elasticity (high stiffness).

15.2 CERAMIC STRUCTURES

Frequently, ceramics exhibit ionic bonding at the atomic level. The ionic bonds are extremely strong and stable. This type of bonding partially explains the high melting temperature of many ceramics.

Ceramics are often crystalline in structure, but in contrast to metals, the crystalline structure is very complex. Cubic and hexagonal structures describe a number of metals. However, with ceramics, the number of structures is much higher because the atoms in ceramics tend to be of greatly differing sizes.

Some ceramics are amorphous in structure. For example, when a glass windowpane breaks, the lines of fracture follow the path of least resistance. Since the structure is amorphous, the fracture pattern is not straight, but often wanders along gently curving lines.

15.3 GLASS

Glass refers to an inorganic, generally nonmetallic compound, which has been cooled without crystallizing. The main raw material for glass is silica. A rather pure form of silica is silica sand, commonly used in foundry sand. When silica is melted and then cooled, it forms a glass. The temperature required to melt pure silica is very high, so to reduce the temperature, other materials are added to the silica. For example, window glass, a type of soda-lime glass, contains about 75% silica, 14% soda, and 10% lime. The purpose of the soda and lime are to reduce melting temperatures, to make the molten glass more fluid for easier processing,

Table 15-1. Corrosion resistance of ceramics

	Hydrochloric Acid	Hydrofluoric Acid	Hot Sodium Hydroxide	Fused Sodium Hydroxide
Glass	A	D	D	D
Quartz	A	D	C	D
Aluminum oxide (99.5%)	A	B	C	D
Mullite	A	C	D	D
Zirconium oxide	B	C	A	A
Silicon carbide (sintered)	A	A	A	C
Silicon nitride	A	C	A	C
Titanium diboride	C	C	C	C

Key: A: No reaction
B: Slight reaction
C: Appreciable attack
D: Dissolves

(Bakerjian and Mitchell 1992)

and to retard crystallization. If the glass crystallizes, it will not be transparent.

Glass fibers require a differing formula for the glass. To make a glass appropriate for fibers, less soda, more lime, and additional aluminum oxide are added to the formula. Various types of fibers are manufactured using altered formulas. Glass fibers for reinforcing plastics are mostly E-glass. It is called E-glass because it has high electrical resistance. To make fibers with greater tensile strength, aluminum oxide and magnesium oxide are added to the silica.

15.4 ADVANCED CERAMICS

Advanced ceramics generally refer to ceramic materials that have been synthetically created. Three categories of advanced ceramics are oxides, carbides, and nitrides. Table 15-2 shows the physical properties of several advanced ceramics.

OXIDES

Aluminum oxide, or alumina, has been used for thousands of years. It is called an advanced ceramic because it is currently produced synthetically. The synthetic production allows control of impurities, particle sizes, and exact blending. As a consequence, the new alumina has improved physical properties.

CARBIDES

Carbides include silicon carbide, tungsten carbide, titanium carbide, and tantalum carbide. These materials have extreme hardness and wear resistance. Consequently, the major use of these materials is for cutting tools and abrasives. Tungsten carbide, the oldest of these materials, was developed in Germany and the United States in the 1920s. Cutting tools made of tungsten carbide provided a huge improvement over the high-speed steel tools available at the time. Carbide cutters allowed machining at higher speeds and greater depths of cut because the carbide remained harder and sharper at higher temperatures than steel cutters.

NITRIDES

The most important nitrides are boron nitride, silicon nitrite, and titanium nitride. A popular use for titanium nitride is as a surface coating for cutting tools. It has a very

Table 15-2. Properties of advanced ceramic materials

Property	Alumina	Partially Stabilized Zirconia	Mullite	Silicon Carbide	Silicon Nitride	Titanium Diboride
Density, lb/in.^{3} (g/cc)	0.141 (3.90)	0.208 (5.75)	0.101 (2.80)	0.11 (3.1)	0.11 (3.1)	0.162 (4.48)
Color	White	Ivory	Tan	Black	Gray	Black
Flexural strength, ksi (MPa)	55 (379)	90 (620)	25 (172)	80 (552)	80 (552)	50 (345)
Elastic modulus, Mpsi (GPa)	54 (372)	35 (241)	22 (152)	58 (400)	40 (276)	78 (538)
Poisson's ratio	0.22	0.22	0.22	0.20	0.22	0.19
Hardness, kg/mm^2	1,440	1,200	750	2,800	1,500	2,700
Fracture toughness, MPa $\times$ m$^{0.5}$	3.5	12	2	4	6	5
Coefficient of thermal expansion, $10^{-6}\,°F$ ($10^{-6}\,°C$)	4.6 (8.3)	5.7 (10.3)	2.9 (5.2)	2.4 (4.3)	1.7 (3.0)	4.6 (8.3)

(Bakerjian and Mitchell 1992)

low coefficient of friction with steel, but like other nitrides, it is rather brittle. To utilize its properties, yet avoid problems with brittleness, titanium nitride is applied as a very thin coating on the cutter. Boron nitride in cubic form, often called cubic boron nitride (CBN), is also used for cutting tools.

REVIEW QUESTIONS

15.1) What is the oldest carbide?

15.2) What does "refractory" mean?

15.3) What type of chemical bonding is typical of many ceramics?

15.4) What is the purpose of adding soda and lime during the manufacture of glass?

15.5) What does the abbreviation CBN represent?

Part 4
Product Design

Chapter 16

Engineering Drawing

Engineering drawings are the graphical representations of ideas. Graphical representations are recognized as an efficient and nearly universal means of communicating designs, instructions, and plans. These documents graphically describe shapes, sizes, and materials used in a product. Drawings are the primary method used to control production.

In this chapter, all dimensions are in millimeters unless otherwise stated. The following are general rules for specifying dimensions in metric units.

- The decimal point and zero are omitted when the metric dimension is a whole number. For example, a hole size of 30 mm is dimensioned as 30 not 30.0.
- When a metric dimension is less than 1 mm, a zero proceeds the decimal point. For example, four-tenths of a millimeter is dimensioned as 0.4. As a note on a drawing in the inch system, when a dimension is less than 1 in. the proceeding zero before the decimal point is omitted. For example, one-tenth of an inch is dimensioned as .100.

It is also important to note that on drawings, a note indicates if dimensions are millimeters or inches. When dimensions are contained in text, such as the text contained in this book, a zero always proceeds the decimal point regardless of which system of measurement is being used.

16.1 DRAWING STANDARDS

Standard practices are used in engineering drawings to avoid confusion and improve the effectiveness of communication. This chapter provides an overview of some of the recommended practices and standards used in the graphical language of engineering drawings. These practices and standards are developed by organizations such as the American Society of Mechanical Engineers (ASME), the American National Standards Institute (ANSI), and the American Welding Society (AWS). The six common standards most used are:

- metric drawing sheet size and format—ANSI/ASME Y14.1M-1992;
- line conventions and lettering—ANSI/ASME Y14.2M-1992;
- multiview and sectional view drawings—ANSI/ASME Y14.3M-1994;
- pictorial drawing—ANSI/ASME Y14.4M-1989(R1994);
- dimensioning and tolerancing—ANSI/ASME Y14.5M-1994, and
- welding—ANSI/AWS A2.4 (1986).

Engineering drawings make use of standard lines to aid in showing the details associated with a part. The standard lines are shown in Figure 16-1 and their application is described in Table 16-1.

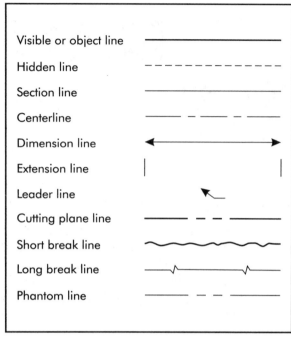

Figure 16-1. Types of lines used in engineering drawings.

16.2 PROJECTION SYSTEMS

There are two systems of projection recognized internationally for multiview drawings. The American system places the front view under the top view. The European sys-

tem places the top view under the front view. The American system is known as *third-angle projection* and the European system is known as *first-angle projection*. The terms are derived from the trigonometric quadrants relative to the front and top viewing planes of a part as illustrated in Figure 16-2. Figure 16-3 shows the standard symbols used on drawings to indicate the projection convention in use.

There are six principal views for a drawing in third angle projection. The standard arrangement for these views is shown in Figure 16-4. A minimum number of views should be used to represent any part in an engineering drawing. All views are assumed to be rotated by 90° from one another unless otherwise indicated on the drawing. The view that shows the most detail is typically selected as the front view. The front view is shown with an accompanying top or right-side view to show detail that cannot be seen in the front view. If three views of a part are needed, the most common arrangement is to show the top, front, and right-side views in the standard arrangement shown in Figure 16-4. No superfluous views should be included in a drawing.

Table 16-1. Application of various line types

Line Type	Application
Visible or object	Visible edges of parts
Hidden	Hidden edges of parts that are not directly visible in a view
Section	Cut surfaces of a cross section
Center	Center positions of holes, shafts, radii, and arcs
Dimension	Size and location of part features
Extension	Locate the extent of the dimension
Leader	Special details, notes, or specifications
Cutting plane	Position and path of an imaginary cut made to form a sectional view
Short break	End of the partially illustrated portion of a small detail
Long break	End of the partially illustrated portion of a large detail
Phantom	Position and relationship of adjacent parts and alternate positions of moving parts

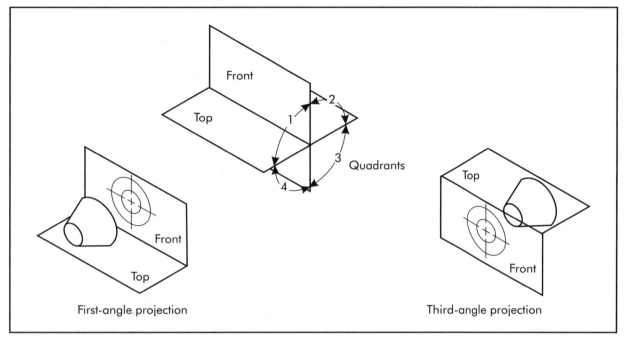

Figure 16-2. Standards for multiview projection.

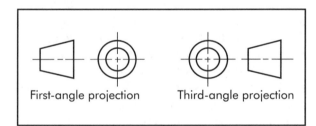

Figure 16-3. Drawing symbols for type of projection.

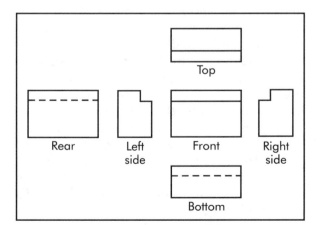

Figure 16-4. Six principal views in third-angle projection.

16.3 AUXILIARY AND SECTION VIEWS

Auxiliary views are used to show the true size and shape of features not parallel to any principal views. Primary auxiliary views are projected from a principal view. Secondary auxiliary views also can be used by making a projection from a primary auxiliary view. Figure 16-5 shows an example of a slot seen in its true size and shape (TSS) in a primary auxiliary view.

Sectional views are drawn to show interior details. They are often clearer than exterior views, which contain numerous hidden lines. The location and position of a *sectional view* is indicated by a cutting plane line and arrows indicating the line of sight in the section. Section lines are used to show the solid material in a sectional view. General sectioning is indicated by thin lines at a 45° angle. Special sectioning symbols may be used for specific materials. An example of a full section is shown in Figure 16-6.

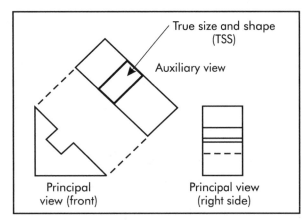

Figure 16-5. Auxiliary view.

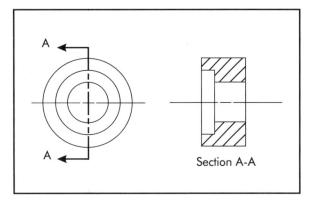

Figure 16-6. Sectional view.

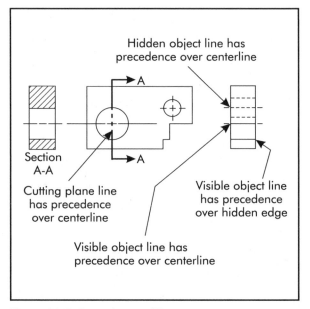

Figure 16-7. Precedence of lines.

More than one line may occupy the same position in a view as illustrated in Figure 16-7. The following precedence of lines should be applied in these cases:

- Object lines take precedence over hidden lines and centerlines.
- Hidden lines take precedence over centerlines.
- Cutting plane lines take precedence over centerlines when showing the path of a sectional view.
- Notice in the right-side view that whenever a hidden line has precedence over a centerline, the centerline is still drawn in the view by leaving a space and then extending it beyond the edge.

16.4 DIMENSIONING

Dimensions describe the details of a part so it can be constructed to the proper size. They show the sizes and locations necessary to manufacture and inspect the part. Dimensions are placed between points that have a specific relationship to each other to ensure the function of the part. More than one view may illustrate a feature. The dimension of the feature should be placed in the view that best describes the feature. Dimensions are not repeated in different views.

The international system of units (SI) is now commonly used in the United States on engineering drawings to conform to global trade and multinational company affiliations. The SI linear unit on engineering drawings is the millimeter, abbreviated as mm. However, the U.S. linear unit of decimal inches is still being used as we make the transition to all metric. All drawings should clearly state by a note that, unless otherwise specified, all dimensions are in millimeters or inches. ANSI/ASME Y14.5M-1994 is the current standard for dimensioning.

All dimensions are subjected to a *tolerance* (amount of permissible variability unless noted as basic dimensions or reference dimensions). Basic dimensions are identified by an enclosing frame symbol as illustrated in Figure 16-8. The basic dimension is the theoretically exact size or location of a feature. It is the basis from which permissible variations are established by tolerances. Reference dimensions are supplied for information only. They represent intended sizes, but they do not govern the manufacture or inspection of the part. Figure 16-9 shows an example of a part with three holes dimensioned in a series. The dimension that is not to be used in manufacturing the part is enclosed in parentheses. Tolerances are applied to the 20 and 60 mm dimensions. These two dimensions are used to control the manufacturing process applied to produce the part.

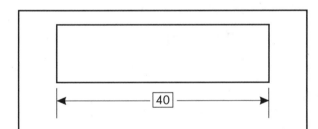

Figure 16-8. Basic dimension symbol.

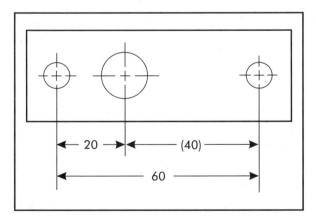

Figure 16-9. Application of a reference dimension.

Dimensions are related by three primary methods. *Chain dimensions* are used when the tolerance between adjacent features is more important than the overall tolerance accumulation. *Baseline dimensions* are used when the location of features must be controlled from a common reference plane. *Direct dimensioning* is applied to control specific feature locations. These three types of dimensioning methods are shown in Figure 16-10. A general tolerance is applied to all dimensions.

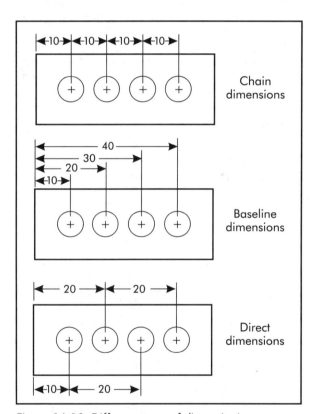

Figure 16-10. Different types of dimensioning.

16.5 TOLERANCING

Modern mass production calls for parts made at remote locations to be brought together for assembly and to fit properly without modification. Manufacturers depend on the capability of a part to be assembled with its intended mating part. Assembly would be no problem if all parts could be made exactly to size. Some parts, such as gage blocks, can be made very close to a target dimension, but such accuracy is very expensive.

Exact sizes of parts are impossible to produce. For practical reasons, parts are made to varying degrees of accuracy depending on their functional requirements. A tolerance refers to the degree of accuracy that is required in a dimension. In general, the cost of manufacturing a component increases with smaller tolerances on its dimensions.

The major terms used in tolerancing are defined as follows:

- *Nominal size* is the stated designation used for the purpose of general identification. A 9/32 drill is an example of a nominal size.
- *Basic size* is that size from which limits of size are derived by the application of allowances and tolerances. The basic size for a 9/32 drill is 0.28125 in.
- *Limits* are the extreme allowable sizes for a feature. In Figure 16-11, the limits for the shaft are 1.247 and 1.248 in.
- *Tolerance* is the permissible variation in a dimension. It is the difference between the largest and smallest acceptable sizes for a feature. The difference in diameters, 0.001 in., is the tolerance on the shaft diameter in Figure 16-11.
- *Allowance* is the minimum clearance between mating parts. In the case of a shaft and mating hole, it is the difference in the diameters of the largest shaft and smallest hole as shown in Figure 16-12.
- *Maximum material condition* (MMC) is the condition of a part when it contains the most amount of material. The MMC of an external feature of size, such as a shaft, is the upper limit. The MMC of an internal feature of size, such as a hole, is the lower limit.

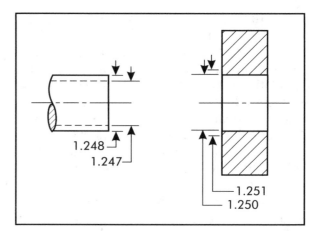

Figure 16-11. Tolerancing of mating parts (units are inches).

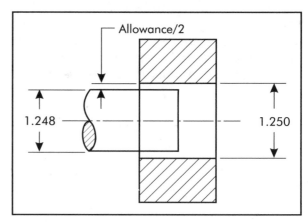

Figure 16-12. Tightest fit in mating parts (units are inches).

- *Least material condition* (LMC) is the condition of a part when it contains the least amount of material possible. The LMC of an external feature of size is the lower limit. The LMC of an internal feature of size is the upper limit.

Figure 16-13 shows three methods that can be used to express tolerances for dimensions: limit dimensioning, unilateral tolerances, and bilateral tolerances.

- *Limit dimensioning*—the maximum and minimum sizes of a feature are specified as shown in Figure 16-13(a).

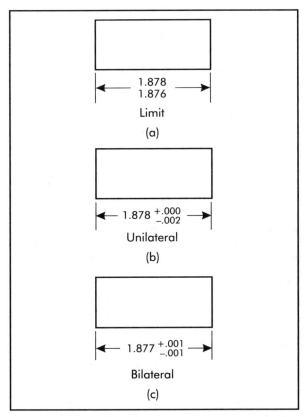

Figure 16-13. Different methods for expressing tolerances (units are inches).

The maximum value is placed over the minimum value.

- *Unilateral tolerances*—a basic size is followed by a plus and minus expression of tolerance where variations are allowed in only one direction from the nominal size. Figure 16-13(b) shows an example of unilateral tolerances where all the tolerance is toward the smaller size.
- *Bilateral tolerances*—a basic size is followed by a plus and minus expression where variations are permitted in both directions from the nominal size. Figure 16-13(c) illustrates a dimension with bilateral tolerances.

Two criteria must be used for determining tolerance for a dimension: (1) the tolerance should be chosen to permit the assembly of randomly selected mating parts and (2) the tolerance should be as large as possible. The cost of producing any manufactured component increases with smaller tolerances.

16.6 FITS

A fit signifies the type of clearance that exists between mating parts. The three most common types of fits are clearance, interference, and transition. *Clearance fits* provide some gap between mating parts. *Interference fits* have no clearance and force is required for the assembly to occur. *Transition fits* are toleranced to result in either a clearance or an interference fit. Standard systems of fits are applied to holes and shafts that govern the tolerances according to the basic size of the components. Fits can either be based on a standard hole system or a standard shaft system. In a standard hole system, the smallest allowable hole is taken as the basic size from which the limits of tolerance are applied. In a standard shaft system, the largest allowable shaft is taken as the basic size.

There are standardized American National Standard and metric sizes for holes and shafts to achieve different types of fits. The American National Standard system is a set of classes of fits based on the basic hole system. The basic hole system is widely used because drills and reamers are used to produce standard-sized holes. The types of fit covered by this standard are:

- RC—running and sliding fits;
- LC—clearance locational fits;
- LT—transition locational fits;
- LN—interference locational fits, and
- FN—force and shrink fits.

Tables of standard sizes and tolerances are needed to use this system. Since the system is organized on a hole basis, the basic shaft size and the type of fit are needed to determine the dimension and tolerance for the mating parts. For example, an RC 4 fit refers to a close running fit, whereas RC 9 refers to a loose running fit. Tables will supply the tolerances (in number of thousandths) to add to the basic size to determine the upper limit on the hole and to subtract from the basic size to determine the upper and lower limits on the shaft. The standard tables are too extensive to be reprinted here, but should be available in any text on engineering drawing or the *Machinery's Handbook*.

Example 16.6.1. Find the dimensions and tolerances for a 2.500 in. diameter hole and shaft with an RC 9 fit.

Solution. Table 16-2 (based on American National Standard fits—ANSI B 4.1-1967, 1979) provides the following information (Oberg et al. 2000).

Table 16-2. ANSI RC9 fit

Limits of Clearance	Hole	Shaft
9.0	7.0	−9.0
20.5	0	−13.5

(Units are thousandths of an inch)
(Oberg et al. 2000)

The lower limit of the hole has no tolerance since it represents the basic size. The limit dimensions on the hole are found as:

Upper limit: 2.5000 + 0.0070 = 2.5070 in.
Lower limit: 2.5000 + 0.0000 = 2.5000 in.

The limit dimensions on the shaft are found as:

Upper limit: 2.5000 − 0.0090 = 2.4910 in.
Lower limit: 2.5000 − 0.0135 = 2.4865 in.

The limits of clearance represent the largest and smallest clearances that can result in assembly. They can be readily verified by calculating the extreme shaft and hole combinations:

LMC hole − LMC shaft = largest clearance (loosest fit)

2.5070 − 2.4865 = 0.0205 in.

MMC hole − MMC shaft = smallest clearance (tightest fit or allowance)

2.5000 − 2.4910 = 0.0090 in.

The metric system of fits is organized in a fashion similar to the American National Standard system. The metric system can operate on a hole basis or shaft basis. An International Tolerance (IT) Grade is associated with a particular size and level of accuracy. For example, the designation 40H8 refers to a 40 mm basic-size hole with an IT grade of 8. The designation 40f7 refers to a 40 mm basic-size shaft with an IT grade of 7. The combination of 40H8/f7 refers to a particular fit, in this case, a close running fit. Tables of standard metric values are needed to determine the appropriate tolerances.

16.7 TOLERANCES FOR 100% INTERCHANGEABILITY

The most common requirement of a tolerance on a dimension calls for parts to be 100% interchangeable. Any random combination of mating parts will be guaranteed to assemble. The extreme or most difficult conditions for assembly are used to find the unknown tolerance. In the extreme condition, internal dimensions are taken at the minimum value and external dimensions are taken at the maximum value. A path equation is used to add signed dimensions to find the value of an unknown tolerance.

Example 16.7.1. Figure 16-14 shows a car radio tuner knob (k) being assembled with a bearing (b) and a spacer (s) in a cavity (c). For the knob to turn freely, a 0.003 in. clearance (g) must exist between the knob flange (a) and the top of cavity. Find the tolerance x of the depth of the cavity.

Solution. A sign convention is used. Dimensions are positive going from the bottom to the top. Starting at the bottom of the cavity in Figure 16-14, the signed dimensions for

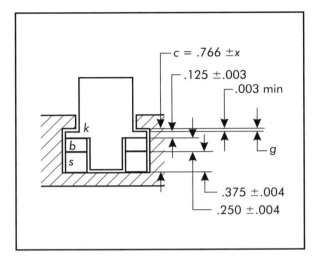

Figure 16-14. Car tuner knob assembly (units are in inches).

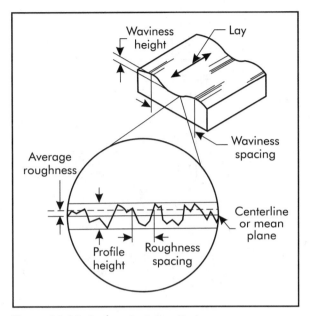

Figure 16-15. Surface texture criteria.

the extreme conditions are added to form a closed path. The extreme conditions are found when the maximum-size knob, bearing, and spacer are combined with a minimum clearance (g) and minimum cavity (c):

$$s_{max} + b_{max} + k_{max} + g_{min} - c_{min} = 0$$

or:

$$0.379 + 0.254 + 0.128 + 0.003 - (0.766 - x) = 0$$

$$x = 0.002$$

16.8 SURFACE FINISH SYMBOLS

Surface texture is the variation of height, width, and orientation of the irregularities on a surface. Surface texture can strongly affect the performance of a part in service. Surface texture specifications are critical to assuring the proper function of parts such as bearings or dies. Figure 16-15 illustrates standard surface texture criteria. The important terms used in surface texture specification are defined as follows:

- *Roughness* refers to the finest irregularities in a surface. Roughness is strongly dependent on the type of manufacturing process used to generate a surface.

- *Average roughness* is the arithmetic average of the absolute values of height deviations from the mean plane or centerline of a surface. It is typically measured in microinches or micrometers.
- *Roughness spacing* is the average spacing between successive peaks within the roughness sampling length.
- *Cutoff* is the sampling length used for calculation of the average roughness. When it is not specified, a value of 0.030 in. (0.8 mm) is assumed.
- *Waviness* is the widely spaced, repeated variation on a surface.
- *Waviness height* is the peak-to-valley distance between waves.
- *Waviness spacing* is the average spacing between successive peaks within the waviness sampling length.
- *Lay* is the direction of the surface pattern. This is dependent on the method used to generate the surface.

Figure 16-16 illustrates standard lay designations. Figure 16-17 illustrates applications of surface texture symbols.

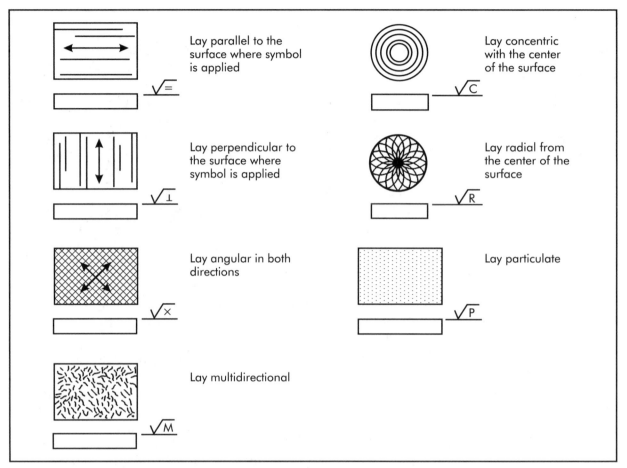

Figure 16-16. Standard lay designations.

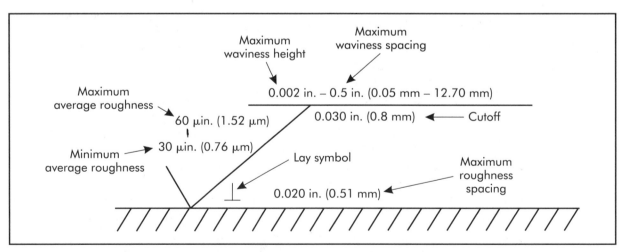

Figure 16-17. Application of surface texture symbols: average roughness is given in microinches. All other values are given in inches.

REVIEW QUESTIONS

16.1) What type of view is used to show the true size and shape of features not parallel to any principle views?

16.2) Draw the sectional view passing through points A-A in Figure Q16-1.

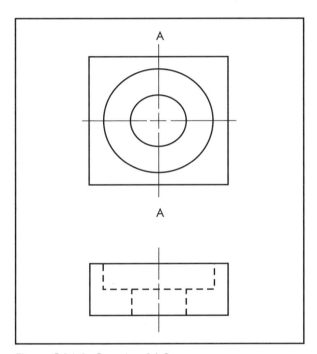

Figure Q16-1. Question 16.2.

16.3) The part in Figure Q16-2 must be manufactured so that the location of the top surface of each step is accurately located with respect to the edge 1-2. What type of dimensioning should be used?

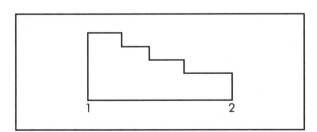

Figure Q16-2. Question 16.3.

16.4) A 1 in.-diameter pin is placed in a 1.3 in.-diameter hole. The dimensions of both the pin and the hole may vary ±0.1 in. What is the allowance?

16.5) Is the American National Standard system based on shafts, holes, or both?

16.6) Interpret the symbols in the following IT designation: 50f6.

16.7) A dimension may vary between 0.505 and 0.509 mm. Express this information in the form of a unilateral tolerance and bilateral tolerance.

16.8) Provide proper dimensions and tolerances for a piston and a cylinder according to the following specifications. The nominal dimension of the piston is 1.000 in. The allowance in the assembly is 0.001 in. The piston and cylinder each have bilateral tolerances of 0.001 in.

16.9) Find tolerance X in Figure Q16-3 for 100% interchangeability.

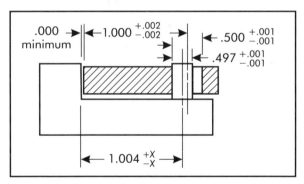

Figure Q16-3. Question 16.9 (units are inches).

16.10) Identify the indicated parts of the surface texture specification shown in Figure Q16-4.

REFERENCE

Oberg, Erik, Franklin Jones, Holbrook Horton, and Henry Ryffell. 2000. *Machinery's Handbook*, 26th Edition. New York: Industrial Press.

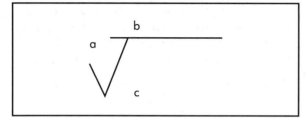

Figure Q16-4. Question 16.10.

Chapter 17

Geometric Dimensioning and Tolerancing

Geometric dimensioning and tolerancing (GD&T) developed over the past 40 years as a tool to define parts and features more efficiently. GD&T considers the function of the part, as well as its fit with related parts. This allows the designer to define the part's features more accurately, without increasing the tolerances.

For many years, GD&T saw limited use on engineering drawings and, even when used, there was, and still is, disagreement on the actual meaning of the symbols and terms. However, in recent years this international language and dimensional philosophy has seen a great increase in use. The current wide use of statistical process control (SPC) and compliance with ISO 9000 standards are just two reasons for growth in the use of GD&T. The two greatest advantages are: product tolerances can be increased and there is the ability to maximize producibility to implement total cost reductions.

In this chapter, all dimensions are in millimeters unless otherwise stated.

17.1 GD&T STANDARDS

Geometric dimensioning and tolerancing is a method of defining parts based on how they function. It is almost always used to refine other tolerances rather than to control features by themselves. The current standard for GD&T is ASME Y14.5M-1994, which is a revision of ANSI Y14.5M-1982. Two major symbol changes in the 1994 standard are: the universal (ISO) datum feature symbol is adopted and replaces the previous one, and the symmetry tolerance symbol is now back in the standard. Another significant change is the elimination of the material symbol for regardless of feature size (RFS). The RFS condition applies when the symbols for MMC and LMC are not stated on features of size.

There are two general rules in ASME Y14.5M-1994. The first rule establishes default conditions for features of size. The second rule establishes a default material condition for feature control frames.

RULE 1—SET DEFAULT CONDITIONS FOR FEATURES OF SIZE

Where only a tolerance of size is specified, the limits of size for an individual feature prescribe the extent to which variations in its form, as well as its size, are allowed. Rule 1 is a dimensioning rule used to ensure that features of size (FOS) will assemble with one another. A feature of size can be a cylinder or spherical surface or a set of opposed elements or surfaces associated with a size dimension. Features are simply part surfaces. When Rule 1 applies, the maximum boundary for an external FOS is its maximum material condition (MMC). The minimum envelope for an internal FOS is its MMC. To determine if two features of size will assemble, the designer compares the MMCs of the features of size.

RULE 2—SET DEFAULT MATERIAL CONDITION FOR FEATURE CONTROL FRAMES

With respect to the individual tolerance, datum reference, or both, RFS applies where no modifying symbol is specified. MMC or least material condition (LMC) must be specified on the drawing where required. Where a geometric tolerance is applied on an RFS basis, the tolerance is limited to the specified value regardless of the actual size of the feature.

Figure 17-1 depicts many of the common symbols found in ASME Y14.5-1994. The symbols are a universal method of specifying requirements without the use of notes or words. The symbols are designed to be intuitive and look like the requirement they are identifying.

Repetitive features such as holes, slots, and tabs often can be specified by stating the required number of features or places and an "X" and then following with the requirement. A space is used between the "X" and the requirement. Where used with a basic dimension, the number of places and the X may be placed either inside or outside the basic dimension frame.

The symbol for diameter is a circle with a slash. The symbol for radius is the letter "R." The symbol for square features is a square box. The symbol for counterbore, illustrated

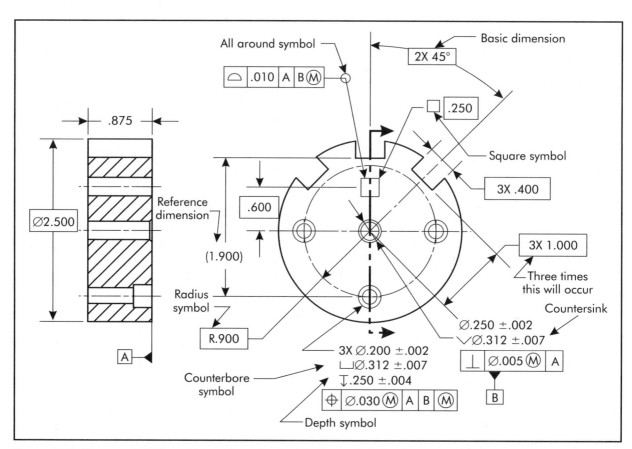

Figure 17-1. Common GD&T symbols and applications (units are in inches).

in Figure 17-1, and spot face are the same. A spot face will have no depth indicated while the counterbore symbol will always have a depth specified. The countersink symbol is shown as a 90° "V." The deep or depth symbol will identify the depth of the indicated feature.

Figure 17-2 illustrates the 14 symbols used in GD&T and also groups together the five types of tolerances relative to their use.

17.2 FEATURE CONTROL FRAME

The feature control frame, illustrated in Figure 17-3, is probably the most important symbol in the geometric tolerancing system. It states the requirements or instructions for the features to which it is attached.

The first compartment of a feature control frame will always contain one of the 14 geometric characteristics symbols.

The second compartment of a feature control frame will contain the total tolerance for the feature. If the tolerance is preceded by a diameter symbol ∅, the tolerance will be a diameter or cylindrically shaped tolerance zone as in the location of a hole. If there is no symbol preceding the tolerance, the tolerance zone may be two parallel lines or planes, depending on the feature. Following the feature tolerance, a feature modifier such as MMC or LMC may be specified. The symbol for MMC is an M inside a circle and the symbol for LMC is an L inside a circle.

The third and following compartments of a feature control frame contain the specified datums, if datums are applicable. The datums are specified in their order of importance, such as primary, secondary, and tertiary.

The placement of a feature control frame is very important. If the feature control frame is attached or directed to a surface, it controls that surface as in a flatness or profile control.

17.3 FIVE CLASSIFICATIONS OF TOLERANCES

Tolerances can be categorized in terms of form, orientation, runout, profile, and location.

TOLERANCES OF FORM

Tolerances of form include controls for flatness, straightness, circularity (roundness), and cylindricity. In all of these, the part geometry is compared to the true geometric counterpart specified and held to within limits of acceptable variance specified by a statement of tolerance zone width. Form tolerances describe how an actual feature may vary from a geometric ideal feature.

Flatness

A surface is ideally flat if all its elements are coplanar. The *flatness* specification describes the tolerance zone formed by two parallel planes that contain all the elements on a surface. A 0.1 mm tolerance zone is described by the feature control symbol in Figure 17-4. The distance between the highest point on the surface to the lowest point on the surface may not be greater than 0.1 mm.

Straightness

A straightness control can be applied to a surface or to a feature of size (FOS). The surface straightness tolerance is represented by connecting the feature control frame to the surface with a leader or by connecting the feature control frame to an extension line in the view where the controlled surface is shown as an edge.

A surface is perfectly straight if all its elements are collinear. *Straightness* is specified by two parallel lines that contain all the elements of a surface. A straightness tolerance is typically applied to cylindrical features. A 0.03 mm tolerance zone is described by the feature control symbol in Fig-

	Type of Tolerance	Characteristic	Symbol
For individual features	Form	Flatness	▱
		Straightness	—
		Circularity (roundness)	◯
		Cylindricity	⌭
For individual or related features	Profile	Profile of a surface	⌓
		Profile of a line	⌒
For related features	Orientation	Angularity	∠
		Perpendicularity	⊥
		Parallelism	∥
	Location	Position	⌖
		Concentricity	◎
		Symmetry	⌯
	Runout	Circular runout	↗
		Total runout	⤴↗

Figure 17-2. Five types of tolerances and the 14 symbols used in GD&T.

ure 17-5. All elements on the surface must lie between two parallel lines spaced 0.03 mm apart.

When a straightness control is applied to an FOS, it controls axis or center plane straightness. Axis straightness, for example, is shown in Figure 17-6 by placing the feature control frame below the diameter dimension. A diameter symbol is placed before the geometric tolerance to specify a cylindrical tolerance zone. The size of the cylindrical tolerance zone is 0.4 mm.

Axis straightness may be specified with an MMC modifier in the feature control frame after the tolerance size in Figure 17-7. This allows the cylindrical tolerance zone to increase in size as the produced size departs from MMC to LMC.

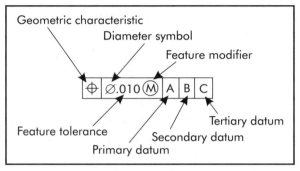

Figure 17-3. Feature control frame (units are in inches).

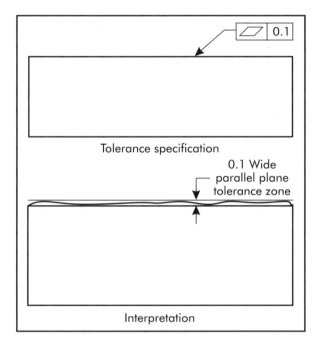

Figure 17-4. Flatness.

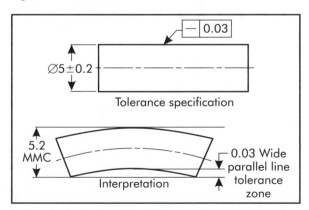

Figure 17-5. Surface straightness.

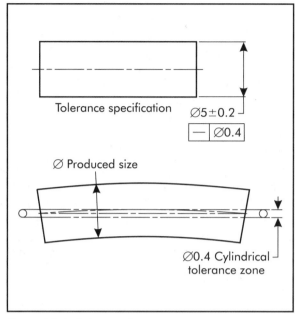

Figure 17-6. Axis straightness.

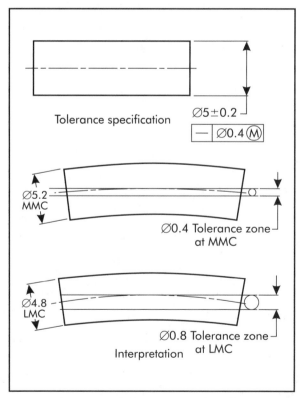

Figure 17-7. Axis straightness at MMC and LMC.

Circularity

Circularity or roundness compares a circular element to a perfect circle. The tolerance zone is two perfect circles, concentric, and the tolerance value apart. The tolerance is applied to only one sectional element at a time (see Figure 17-8).

Cylindricity

Cylindricity compares a cylinder to a perfect cylinder. The tolerance zone is two perfect cylinders, concentric, and the tolerance value apart. In Figure 17-9, the cylinder has a 0.15 mm cylindrical tolerance zone. Cylindricity can be considered a blanket tolerance covering the entire feature.

TOLERANCES OF ORIENTATION

Tolerances of orientation enable the clear specification of relationships between part features and acceptable limits of variation. There are three orientation tolerances that control the relationship of features to one another: parallelism, perpendicularity, and angularity. Orientation tolerances require the placement of a datum reference in the feature control frame.

Parallelism

A *parallelism* tolerance specifies a tolerance zone defined by two parallel planes that are mutually parallel to a datum. All elements of the toleranced surface must lie

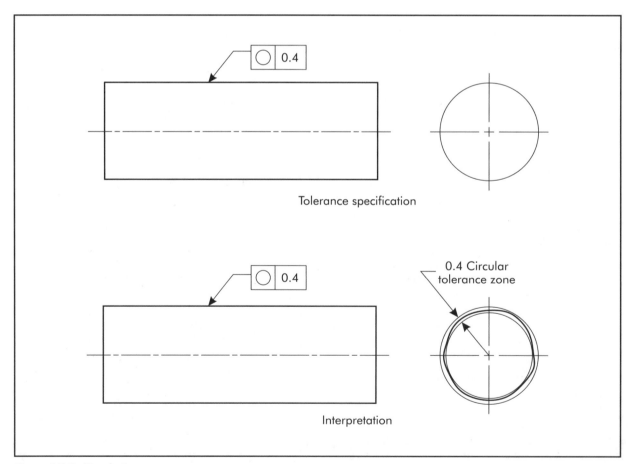

Tolerance specification

0.4 Circular tolerance zone

Interpretation

Figure 17-8. Circularity.

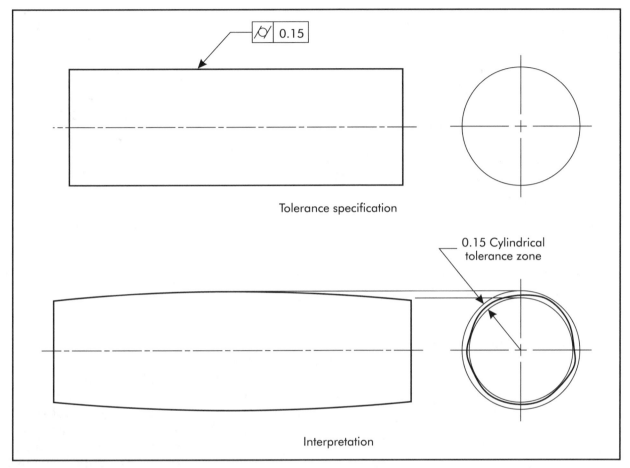

Figure 17-9. Cylindricity.

within the specified tolerance zone. In Figure 17-10, the parallel zone is two planes 0.1 mm apart that can float between the MMC limit of 6.2 mm and LMC limit of 5.8 mm.

Perpendicularity

A *perpendicularity* tolerance specifies a tolerance zone, which is typically defined by two parallel planes mutually perpendicular to a datum or a cylinder perpendicular to a datum. All elements of the toleranced surface must lie within the specified tolerance zone. An example of a perpendicularity specification is shown in Figure 17-11 with the surface oriented between two parallel planes, 0.15 mm apart, and perfectly perpendicular to datum A.

Angularity

An *angularity* geometric tolerance zone is established by two parallel planes at a specified basic angle other than 90° and referenced to a datum plane. In Figure 17-12, the inclined surface is oriented between two parallel planes, 0.15 mm apart, and 60° from datum A.

TOLERANCES OF RUNOUT

Runout is a tolerance used to express relationships between surfaces of features in the many applications in which acceptable part deviation is best observed in terms of rotation about an axis. Thus, the runout

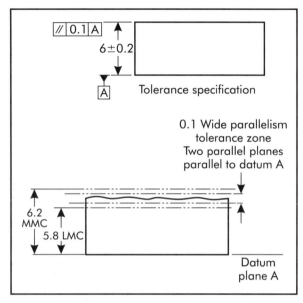

Figure 17-10. Parallelism.

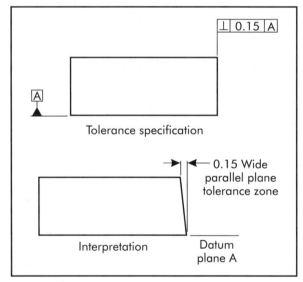

Figure 17-11. Perpendicularity.

tolerances, both circular runout and total runout, are expressed in terms of limits of full indicator movement (FIM). Runout is a combination of geometric tolerances used to control the relationship of one or more features to a datum axis. There are two types of runout: circular and total.

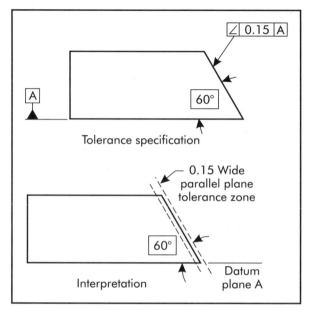

Figure 17-12. Angularity.

Circular Runout

Circular runout provides control of a single circular element of a surface. Circular runout is shown as a single arrow in the first compartment of the feature control frame. It is similar to circularity in that it only controls one circular element. When applied to surfaces around a datum axis, circular runout controls circularity and coaxiality. *Coaxiality* is two or more features sharing a common axis. In Figure 17-13, the control would be measured plus or minus 0.05 mm FIM of a dial indicator.

Total Runout

Total runout is a tolerance that blankets the surface to be controlled. Total runout is used to control the combined variations of circularity, straightness, and coaxiality when applied to surfaces around a datum. Total runout is indicated by two arrows in the feature control frame. It is comparable to cylindricity in that it controls an entire surface rather than a single element. Figure 17-14 depicts a total runout control.

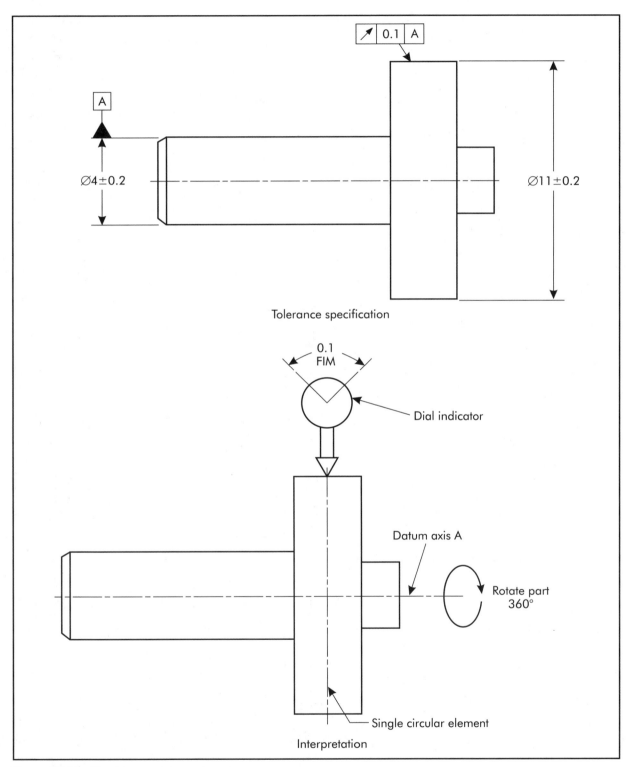

Figure 17-13. Circular runout.

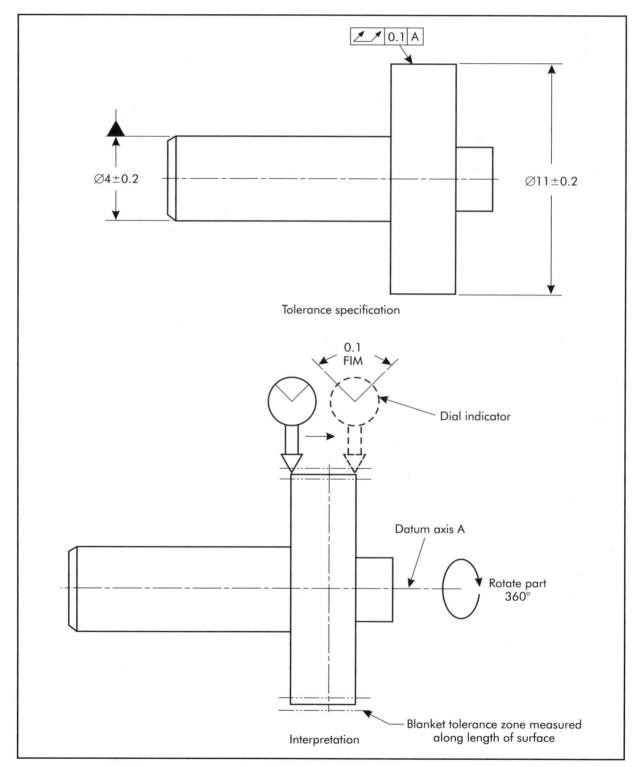

Figure 17-14. Total runout.

TOLERANCES OF PROFILE

Profile tolerancing provides an effective means of controlling irregular lines, surfaces, or unusual part profiles. Tolerances of profile include profile of a line and profile of a surface.

The profile tolerance specifies a uniform tolerance along the true profile that the elements of a surface must lie within. In most applications, the true profile is dimensioned using basic dimensions and is assumed to be bilateral unless otherwise indicated on the drawing.

Profile of a Line

The profile of a line tolerance is a two-dimensional tolerance that extends the length of the feature. In Figure 17-15, note that the tolerance is 0.05 mm on each side of the true profile line from point A to point B.

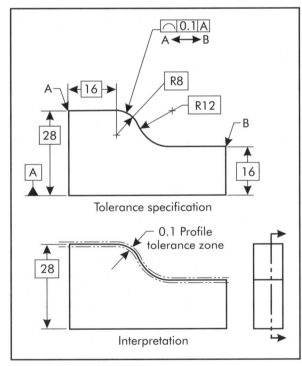

Figure 17-15. Profile of a line.

Profile of a Surface

The profile of a surface tolerance is a three-dimensional surface boundary considered to be a blanket tolerance to control the entire surface of a single entity. In Figure 17-16, note that the tolerance is bilateral in nature from point A to B.

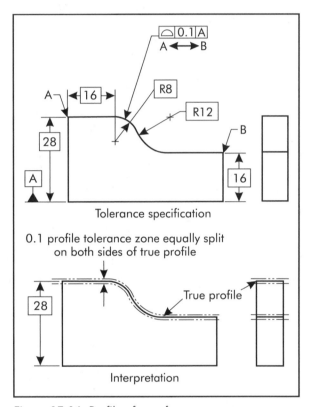

Figure 17-16. Profile of a surface.

LOCATION CONTROLS

The location tolerances are concentricity, symmetry, and position. These provide a means of clearly expressing the limits of variation of the location of an axis or center plane of a part feature from a theoretically perfect location.

Concentricity

Concentricity is a condition that specifies the relationship between one cylinder and another. The specification of concentricity is typically the permitted variation between the centerlines of two cylinders. One cylinder is flagged as the datum (indicating that its centerline will be used as a reference) and the permissible variation of the centerline of the other cylinder is specified. Figure 17-17 shows the larger-diameter cylinder as a datum. The axis of this tolerance zone coincides with the datum axis A. The centerline of the smaller-diameter cylinder is permit-

ted to vary within a cylindrical tolerance zone with a diameter of 0.1 mm.

Symmetry

Symmetry geometric tolerances ensure that the controlled feature is centered on the datum. In Figure 17-18, the parallel planes are ±0.2 mm from the true centerline of datum B.

Tolerance of Position

Tolerance of *position* is the single most valuable and versatile geometric control and, therefore, it is the most used. Position tolerancing takes maximum advantage of using MMC bonus tolerancing. The MMC application is most common. However, LMC or RFS is also used.

In Figure 17-19, a positional tolerance symbol is placed in the first compartment of the feature control frame. In the second compartment is the size of the tolerance, its shape, and appropriate modifier. In the remaining compartments are the primary, secondary, and tertiary datum references. Perpendicularity of the true position center-line is controlled relative to the primary datum with the secondary and tertiary datums used as location datums for true position. These location dimensions are basic dimensions as opposed to the old-style plus and minus dimensions.

The lower half of Figure 17-19 depicts the two extreme hole sizes and their effect on the positional tolerance zone. A positional tolerance at MMC implies that the diameter of this cylindrical tolerance zone is equal to the specified positional tolerance at MMC. However, as the hole is allowed to increase in size to LMC, bonus tolerance allows the size of the tolerance zone to increase to its maximum size. At MMC the size of the tolerance zone is $\varnothing0.1$ mm and at LMC the size of the tolerance zone is $\varnothing0.5$ mm.

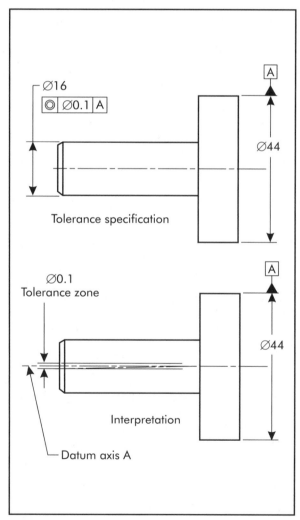

Figure 17-17. Concentricity.

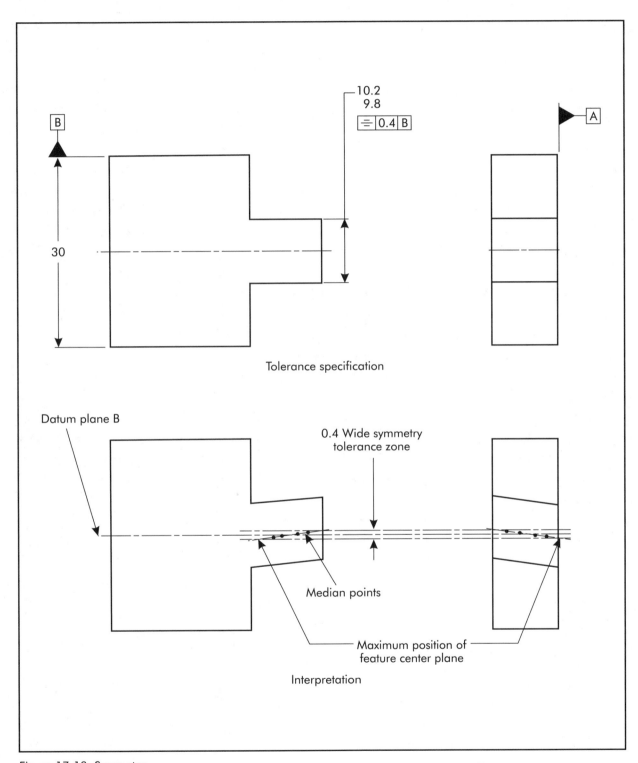

Figure 17-18. Symmetry.

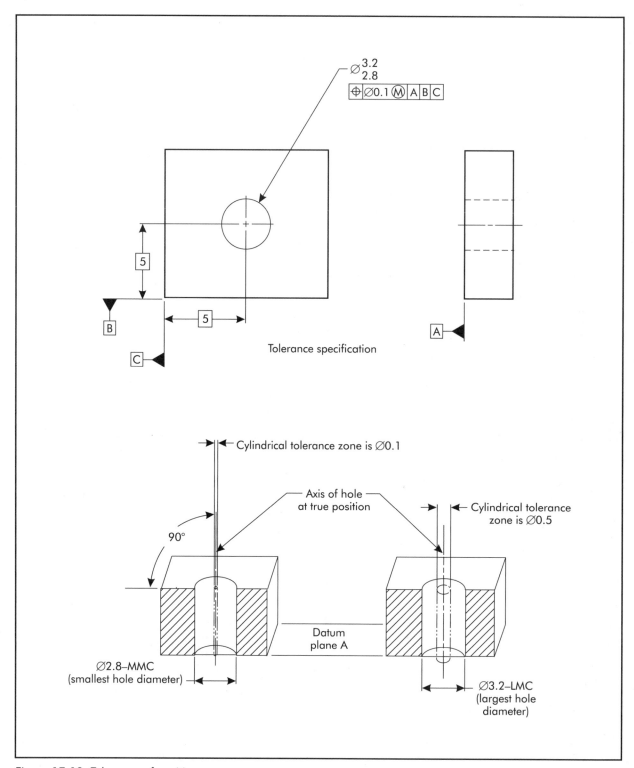

Figure 17-19. Tolerance of position.

REVIEW QUESTIONS

17.1) Which of the following is the MMC of a hole with a dimension of ∅0.625 ±0.005 in.?

a) 0.625 in.
b) 0.630 in.
c) 0.620 in.
d) 0.615 in.

17.2) The symbols used in GD&T to provide specific controls related to the form, orientation, or outline of features; the relationship of features to an axis; or the location of features are called _____ symbols.

a) geometric characteristic
b) feature control frame
c) datum feature
d) material condition

17.3) The symbols used in the feature control frame to modify the geometric tolerance other than the implied condition are _____.

a) MMC and RFS
b) LMC and RFS
c) MMC and GDT
d) MMC and LMC

17.4) A(n) _____ dimension is a theoretically perfect dimension.

a) untoleranced
b) specified
c) basic
d) exact

17.5) With respect to surface straightness, _____ is required at MMC.

a) Perfect form
b) Extreme form variation
c) Perfect variation
d) Perfect size

17.6) What is the size of the geometric tolerance zone for a shaft with a size dimension of ∅0.625 ±0.005 in. and surface straightness of 0.001 in. produced at ∅0.630 in.?

a) 0.000 in.
b) 0.001 in.
c) 0.005 in.
d) 0.010 in.

17.7) _____ is the condition of a surface where all of the elements are in one plane.

a) Flatness
b) Profile
c) Straightness
d) Perfect form

17.8) _____ is controlled by a single cross-sectional tolerance zone defined by two concentric circles.

a) Circularity
b) Cylindricity
c) Profile all around
d) Profile of a line

17.9) The _____ tolerance zone is two parallel planes that are perfectly 90° to a datum.

a) angularity
b) perpendicularity
c) parallelism
d) runout

17.10) _____ provides combined control of circularity, straightness, coaxiality, angularity, taper, and profile when applied to surfaces around a datum axis.

a) Circular runout
b) Total runout
c) Profile of a line
d) Profile of a surface

Chapter 18

Computer-aided Design

18.1 WIREFRAME, SURFACE, AND SOLID MODELING

Computer-aided design/computer-aided manufacturing (CAD/CAM) has become a significant factor in the design and manufacturing process. Once perceived only as a tool for Fortune 500 companies, CAD/CAM now has become affordable by all. Most CAD systems are designed and intended to automate manual functions, whether they are engineering analysis, conceptual design, drafting, or documentation. The need for shorter product development cycles has driven companies to focus on computer systems to automate design processes. As a result, many software packages were developed independently to suit specific needs and objectives. However, because of the proprietary nature of the formats of such software, system-to-system compatibility became a big problem when electronic transfer of information was needed. Therefore, a joint government/industry force was created in 1979 to develop a method for data exchange. Through their efforts, the Initial Graphics Exchange Specification (IGES) was published in 1980 to facilitate data exchange independent of CAD/CAM systems. The IGES methodology enables manufacturers to exchange CAD data between different CAD systems. CADD, CAD/CAM, CAE, CIM, and a host of other computer-driven technologies have provided industry with tremendous time savings and flexibility. Development of these systems is one of the most significant engineering breakthroughs in decades.

Three-dimensional (3-D) modeling gives a full and complete CAD/CAM representation. *Three-dimensional CAD* systems consist of wireframe, surface, and solid modeling systems. Their 3-D capability is necessary to thoroughly describe all but the simplest of mechanical parts and provide multi-axis computer numerical control of machine tools.

Wireframe drawings store the geometry of the 3-D model as edges and points. A wireframe is transparent in nature, requiring some skill and expertise in interpreting the model. The points on the surface are implied. Precise surface representations or information must be passed through line and offset-type information. One advantage of a wireframe is the infinite number of views and drawings that can be generated from a single model. However, it is moderately difficult to clean up the drawing to make a finished engineering drawing. Wireframe drawings are giving way to solid and hybrid modellers.

Surface modeling adds varying degrees of accuracy in a CAD/CAM model when compared to wireframe models. Planar or ruled surfaces or surfaces of revolution have increased accuracy, while sculptured surfaces have lesser degrees of accuracy than wireframes. The additional surface information gives improved graphical imaging when it is linked to 2-½, 3, and 5-axis manufacturing applications and numerical control processes.

Solid modeling consists of constructive solid geometry (CSG) or boundary representation solids (BREP). CSG uses primitives (cubes, cylinders, cones, tori, etc.) to create solid images. In the CSG system, the solids are created by storing construction parameters and size to specified primitives. These primitives are combined to form a composite solid object. CSG is most appropriate for regular prismatic components. The number of primitives available is increasing on many systems.

BREP solids can be stored as true surfaced or faceted. The true surface form is stored as true surface representation and topology. The faceted form stores the faceted surface representation and true surface data is generated when needed by other applications. Generally, the construction sequence of the BREP solid is stored with the associated BREP solid.

Solid modeling provides CAD/CAM systems with a wealth of knowledge. Topological models give CAD/CAM systems the capability of understanding the inside and the outside of a model, including maximum and minimum material conditions. Solid modeling requires more computer power than surfaces or wireframe, but drafting, engineering analysis, and CAM functions can be executed faster from solid models than the other systems.

18.2 CIRCUIT BOARD LAYOUT

CAD software designed for printed circuit boards (PCB) has features unique to that application. Current surface mount technology (SMT) and the continued miniaturizing of integrated-circuit products makes the design of most PCBs a complex task. Contributing to the complexity of designing PCBs are:

- the number of layers in a final board assembly (single-sided, double-sided, and multilayered);

- the miniaturization of components and the effect on pin spacing and number of pins in a conductor;
- conductor routing and board layers;
- the frequency of the current in the different circuits and the resulting inductance;
- heat dissipation, and
- the placement of similar types of components.

PCB-oriented CAD software can assist in board layout and routing and in accommodating the preceding points. It is preferred over attempting PCB design manually or with non-PCB CAD software. Manual layout gives greater flexibility in component placement and in determining if conductor placement is an inductive or capacitive issue, but it requires electrical expertise. For an automatic system to be useful, the rules constraining the layouts (for example, board size, components, component placement, etc.) must be established. This may be time consuming. However, the advantage is that once they are developed, they are done for that type of board.

18.3 RAPID PROTOTYPING

Rapid prototyping uses modern technology to produce a physical prototype from a CAD file in a matter of hours instead of days or weeks. The evolution of rapid prototyping technology has made it possible to create different methods/techniques such as:

- stereolithography apparatus (SLA);
- solid ground curing (SGC);
- laminated object manufacturing (LOM);
- fused deposition modeling (FDM);
- selective laser sintering (SLS), and
- ballistic particle manufacturing (BPM).

Advantages of rapid prototyping are to:

- produce three-dimensional parts within hours;

- create masters and patterns;
- accelerate prototype production;
- achieve major savings in production of soft and hard tooling;
- increase manufacturing capabilities with low-volume production runs;
- add impact to marketing concept presentations with hands-on models, and
- improve the accuracy of vendor bid response.

Disadvantages of rapid prototyping are:

- Parts typically cannot be used for physical testing.
- Parts have surface finish quality and tolerance limitations.
- Special techniques and materials are required of some systems.
- Equipment is expensive.

STEREOLITHOGRAPHY APPARATUS

A *stereolithography apparatus* (SLA) creates three-dimensional plastic parts directly from CAD/CAM data. It builds the physical models one layer at a time. An ultraviolet (UV) laser traces a thin cross section of the object onto a liquid resin surface, selectively hardening the polymer. The layer is lowered into a polymer vat, and its surface is recoated in preparation for building the next cross section. Successive layers are built until the object is complete.

SOLID GROUND CURING

The *solid-ground curing* (SGC) process builds three-dimensional objects, layer by layer, in a solid environment. To build each layer, a photocurable resin is spread across the work area of the workpiece. The resin is exposed to ultraviolet light through a mask. Any unsolidified liquid resin is carefully drawn away from the work area by an aerodynamic wiper. A water-soluble wax, serving as a support material, is then spread over all the polymer-free areas. After cooling, each layer is milled to an exact thickness. Following completion, the models are removed from the wax support material by using heat to melt the wax or by dissolving the wax in an acidic solution.

LAMINATED OBJECT MODELING

Laminated object modeling (LOM) produces 3-D parts of various complexities directly form CAD data by successive deposition, bonding, and laser cutting of sheet or film materials. A laser is guided over an *x-y* axis table by the data from CAD files and cuts a 2D cross section in the sheet material. A platform under the table drops an increment equal to the thickness of a single layer of the material. The material is then advanced from a supply roller to a pickup roller over the top of the previously cut cross-section and a heated roller presses and bonds the material against the previous layer. The next layer is cut by the laser beam and the cycle is repeated until the 3D object is completed.

FUSED-DEPOSITION MODELING

Fused-deposition modeling (FDM) involves depositing thin layers of thermoplastic material from a lightweight extruder head/nozzle onto a fixtureless base. The thermoplastic material is supplied in the form of wirelike filaments from a spool. The plastic is fed into the extruder head/nozzle and heated so that each layer fuses to the previously deposited one. The head/nozzle moves in an *x-y* plane to build each layer.

SELECTIVE LASER SINTERING

Selective laser sintering (SLS) is similar to SLA except the part is not created in a liquid vat but from heat-fusible wax or metal powder. As the process begins, a very thin layer of heat-fusible powder is deposited into a work space container and heated to just below its melting point. An initial cross-section of the object under fabrication is traced on the layer of powder by a laser. The temperature of the powder impacted by the laser beam is raised to the point of "sintering," forming a solid mass. As the process is repeated, each layer fuses to the underlying layer, and successive layers of powder are deposited and sintered until the object is complete.

BALLISTIC PARTICLE MANUFACTURING

The *ballistic particle manufacturing* (BPM) system deposits material in an organized pattern to build a part. The material delivery system is attached to a robotics system and driven by data generated from a CAD model. Droplets of wax are delivered by an ink-jet mechanism and polyethylene glycol is used for the support material. After all the layers are deposited, the object is placed in a warm-water bath that dissolves the support material, leaving the finished part intact (Bakerjian and Mitchell 1992).

REVIEW QUESTIONS

18.1) What exchange standard is used to exchange CAD data between different CAD systems?

18.2) Which type of 3-D CAD modeling is transparent in nature?

18.3) Which type of solid modeling uses primitives to create solid images?

18.4) Which type of CAD modeling requires the most computer power?

18.5) Which type of rapid prototyping uses a laser and an ultraviolet light-sensitive polymer?

18.6) Can rapid prototyping create a part that can be physically tested?

REFERENCE

Bakerjian, Ramon and Philip Mitchell, eds. 1992. *Tool and Manufacturing Engineers Handbook*, Fourth Edition, *Volume 6: Design for Manufacturability*. Dearborn, MI: Society of Manufacturing Engineers.

19.1 PRODUCT DEVELOPMENT STRATEGIES

To be successful in product development, different organizations have adopted various strategies to accommodate fast-changing markets. Many firms believe that initiation and innovation strategies are most likely to succeed over imitation. Some of these strategies include, but are not limited to:

- customer responsiveness;
- entrepreneurial manufacturing;
- time-based, and
- managing for product speed to market.

Common to all is the objective of producing a quality product at a competitive price. Firms with a traditional mass-production strategy acknowledge that to remain competitive, they must develop a flexible specialization approach that enables them to accommodate and create rapid market changes.

These strategies are not packaged, off-the-shelf items offering turnkey implementation. With each, a feasibility study to ensure applicability is needed. Implementation without planning could drive up costs and leave a negative impact that may be detrimental to the existence and survival of a company.

CUSTOMER-RESPONSIVE STRATEGY

A *customer-responsive strategy* targets quality improvement and customer service. It integrates an effective organizational structure with good human resource management and efficient production processes. The manufacturing function plays a big role in this approach and cultivates employee involvement and departmental partnering, where internal cooperation, not competition, is what is necessary to succeed. This scheme sets the stage for short-run manufacturing to be attained through the utilization of the work cell concept. By gaining this flexibility, and by implementing total quality control, companies have combined the necessary elements to produce products in just-in-time (JIT) mode, thus capturing a competitive edge.

ENTREPRENEURIAL MANUFACTURING STRATEGY

The *entrepreneurial manufacturing strategy* is based on a concept similar to that of customer responsiveness. It requires flexible manufacturing capable of shifting from one product to another on short notice. It provides a continuous stream of new products to specialized markets and creates an integrative organizational structure to allow smooth operation across functional activities. It instills in workers an entrepreneurial spirit built on pride, commitment, collaboration, and teamwork. The success of this strategy is based on a company's capacity to create new markets for specialized high-value-added products rather than continuing with standardized products at lower prices.

TIME-BASED STRATEGY

A *time-based strategy* is designed to achieve high productivity and low cost. Fundamental to its success is its focus on offering variety rather than volume. This approach is founded on three basic elements:

1. Organization of process components and standardization.
2. Length of production run.
3. Complexity of scheduling procedures.

This strategy favors smaller increments of improvement in new products but introduces them more often. The product development work uses factory cells staffed by cross-functional teams and stresses local responsibility in scheduling.

MANAGING A PRODUCT'S SPEED TO MARKET

The strategy that manages a product's speed to market revolves around:

- organizing product development for speed;
- organizing product manufacturing for speed;
- using miscellaneous techniques for speed, and
- using computer-aided technology for speed.

This strategy requires that all departments be in proximity to one another and depends on individual discipline as well as team effort to ensure simultaneous consideration of all interfunctional requirements. All possible modern manufacturing techniques and computer aids are taken into account to enhance process speed. For workers, broader task orientation and up-to-date skills are required to accommodate the flexibility of the system.

19.2 CONCURRENT ENGINEERING

Concurrent engineering is based on the integrated design of products and manufac-turing and support processes. The design of the product and the process must be integrated to assure a more optimum approach to the manufacture of the product. Additional considerations for integration include test and inspection processes, product service and support processes (reliability and maintainability), spare parts requirements and logistics, human factors requirements, environmental and safety requirements, operation and maintenance documentation, and disposal requirements.

A starting point for concurrent engineering is developing a better understanding of the customer. This does not necessarily mean gathering additional data on customers and performing more market research. It means that the personnel involved in product development need to understand the customer's requirements to effectively develop products to meet these requirements. Marketing and program management functions need to be involved in product development to provide this type of customer/market input, assure proper dissemination of specification/contract requirements, and provide coordination with customers to review and obtain feedback on product concepts and designs. In addition to this, concurrent engineering involves many other basic principles and concepts. These essential principles are presented in Table 19-1.

Table 19-1. Essential principles of concurrent engineering

1. Understand your customer.
2. Use product development teams.
3. Integrate process design.
4. Involve suppliers and subcontractors early.
5. Use digital product models.
6. Integrate CAE, CAD, and CAM tools.
7. Use quality engineering and reliability techniques.
8. Create an efficient development approach.
9. Improve the design process continuously.

Courtesy DRM Associates

19.3 DESIGN FOR MANUFACTURE

Design for manufacture (DFM) is a methodology that simultaneously considers all of the design goals and constraints for products that will be manufactured. DFM is sometimes equated with design for assembly (DFA), but that is only one aspect of DFM. Other aspects include all the other "design fors" or "abilities," for example, design for testability, quality, reliability, serviceability, style, appearance, shipping, etc. These are sometimes referred to as "design for X" (DFX).

DFM can increase profits by improving sales and decreasing costs. Production costs can be cut by designing less expensive parts that can be assembled at lower total cost. Products designed in group technology families with common parts can be built with lower inventory, in less factory space, and on fewer machines. Products designed for flexible manufacturing can quickly respond to changing market conditions while eliminating finished goods inventory. Quality and reliability can be assured by design and process controls rather than expensive testing, diagnostics, and rework.

Development costs will be lower with maximum use of reusable engineering, modular design, catalog parts, and vendor assistance. Products will reach the market sooner because they are designed right the first time. The result is a timely, quality product that will satisfy customer needs at a competitive price. DFM alone may make the difference between being competitive or not succeeding in the marketplace. Most markets are highly competitive, and slight competitive advantages or disadvantages can have a significant effect. DFM can have enormous positive impact on product cost, quality, and time-to-market with very little capital investment (Bakerjian and Mitchell 1992).

19.4 DESIGN FOR ASSEMBLY

Design for assembly (DFA) is a component of DFM. DFA objectively evaluates the design efficiency of a product or subassembly. Equation 19-1 quantifies design efficiency (Boothroyd and Dewhurst 1983).

$$D_e = \frac{N_{min}\left(t_{avg}\right)}{t_{act}} \qquad (19\text{-}1)$$

where:

D_e = design efficiency
N_{min} = theoretical minimum number of parts
t_{avg} = average time to assemble one part
t_{act} = actual time to assemble all parts

The DFA methodology for decreasing the number of parts in an assembly by combining several parts into one and increasing design efficiency can be based on the answers to three questions (Bakerjian and Mitchell 1992):

1. During product operation, does the part move relative to all other parts already assembled?
2. Does the part need to be made from a different material or isolated from all other parts already assembled?
3. Must the part be separate from all other parts already assembled because of necessary assembly or disassembly of other parts?

19.5 FAILURE MODE AND EFFECTS ANALYSIS

There are two types of failure mode and effects analysis (FMEA): *design failure mode and effects analysis* (DFMEA) and process failure mode and effects analysis (PFMEA). DFMEA is a systematic method to identify and correct known or potential failure modes before the first production run. A first production run is viewed as the run that produces a product and/or service for a specific customer. Customers could include the company that does the final assembly or the public who purchases and uses the product. The DFMEA reduces the risks of failure by:

- objectively evaluating design alternatives;
- considering potential failure modes and their effects;
- establishing a prioritized list of potential failure modes to be addressed by part revisions, and
- providing a reference if and/or when field failures occur.

The *process failure mode and effects analysis* (PFMEA) evaluates the manufacturing process for potential failure modes and their causes. Its purpose is to identify and eliminate potential process failure modes or to minimize the risk of those that cannot be avoided. Actions that may be taken include process redesign, process control improvements, and design revisions to facilitate manufacturing.

DFMEAs and PFMEAs can be performed by asking the following five basic questions whose answers are tabulated on a form illustrated in Figure 19-1. The form can be used for either a design or process FMEA.

1. What are the potential modes of failure for the product as designed or how does the process fail to meet specifications (cracking, sticking, leaking, etc.)?
2. What are the potential effects of the failure (poor appearance, does not fit, noise, partial operation, unstable, etc.)?
3. What is the likelihood that a specific cause will result in a failure mode (range from 1 to 10 with 1 being very unlikely and 10 being almost inevitable)?
4. What is the seriousness of the effect of the potential failure mode (range from 1 to 10 with 1 being minor and 10 being very severe)?
5. What is the likelihood of detection by the current control program (range from 1 to 10 with 1 being almost inevitable and 10 being very unlikely)?

After the questions are answered, a risk priority number (RPN) is calculated using the following equation:

$$\text{Risk Priority Number} = R \times P \times N \quad (19\text{-}2)$$

where:

R = likelihood of occurrence
P = severity of effect
N = likelihood of detection

Companies will typically have a minimum RPN required for corrective action to be implemented. For example, if the minimum RPN were 30, then any potential failure mode with an RPN greater than or equal to 30 would require corrective action. Any failure mode with an RPN less than 30 would not require any corrective action.

19.6 QUALITY FUNCTION DEPLOYMENT

Quality function deployment (QFD) is a technique of listening to the "voice of the customer." It allows the customers' requirements, desires, and preferences to be taken into account throughout all processes, beginning with the design development activities and continuing through the production operations on the factory floor.

Benefits of using the QFD approach usually include:

- earlier determination of key product characteristics;
- documentation of actual customers' needs rather than decisions based on opinions;
- reduction in product development costs;
- reduction in time required to bring a new product to market;
- greater customer satisfaction due to lower costs and improved responsiveness, and
- reduction in number of engineering changes across the product's life cycle.

Part/ process name Part number	Part/ process function	Potential failure mode	Potential effect(s) of failure	▷	Potential cause(s)/ mechanism(s) of failure	Current controls	Occurrence	Severity	Detection	RPN	Recommended action(s) status	Actions taken	Area responsible for actions taken	Occurrence	Severity	Detection	RPN

Figure 19-1. A typical form used for a design or process failure mode and effects analysis.

QFD provides a structured, proactive method for successful transition from customer requirements to production requirements. This transition is accomplished in four stages: product planning to transform customer requirements to design requirements, product deployment to transform design requirements to actual product characteristics, process planning to link product characteristics to process requirements, and production planning to create detailed operating instructions. The relationship between these stages, and the information passed from stage to stage, is shown in Figure 19-2.

The first stage, product planning, is typically accomplished using the "house of quality" matrix as illustrated in Figure 19-3. This matrix identifies customer requirements or "wants" and translates them into specific "hows" (design characteristics) with specific target values. The house of quality matrix also ranks customer requirements by relative importance, identifies the relationship between customer requirements and design characteristics, and identifies the relationship between the design characteristics (Wick and Veilleux 1987).

Figure 19-4 shows a set of typical QFD matrices.

19.7 GROUP TECHNOLOGY

Group technology (GT) is an approach to reduce manufacturing system information content by identifying and exploiting the sameness or similarity of parts based on their geometrical shape and/or similarities in their production process. GT is implemented by using classification and coding systems to identify and understand part similarities and to establish parameters for action. Manufacturing engineers can decide on more efficient ways to increase system

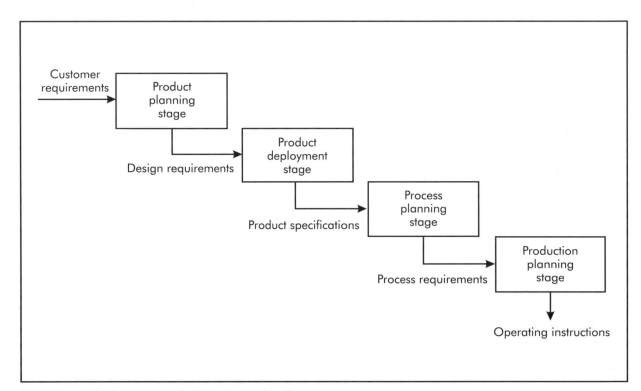

Figure 19-2. The four stages of QFD (Wick and Veilleux 1987).

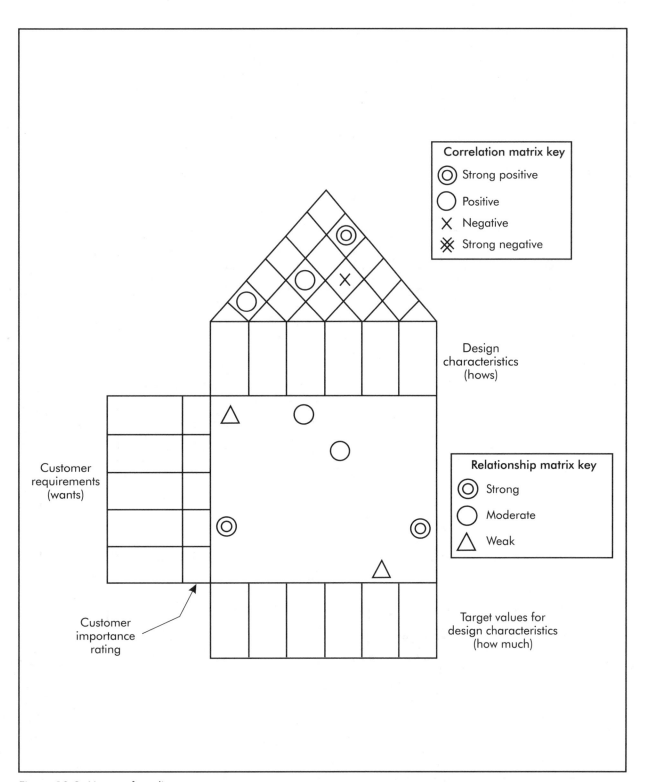

Figure 19-3. House of quality.

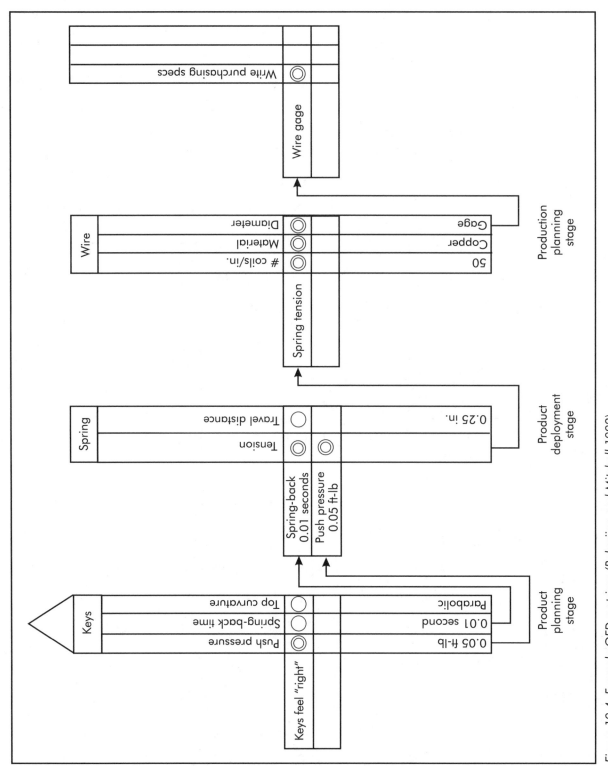

Figure 19-4. Example QFD matrices (Bakerjian and Mitchell 1992).

flexibility by streamlining information flow and reducing setup time and floor space requirements. Design engineers can focus on producibility and help eliminate tooling duplication and redundancy.

GT can be applied in many ways to produce significant design efficiency and product performance and quality improvements. One use is for facilitating significant reductions in design time and effort. In design, it is often erroneously deemed easier to design new parts, tooling, and jigs rather than try to locate similarly designed parts. The ease with which parts can be designed using CAD systems exacerbates the problem. A GT database helps reverse this tendency by enabling the quick and easy retrieval and review of existing parts similar to the new part being designed. With GT, the design engineer only needs to identify the code describing the desired part. A search of the GT database reveals whether a similar part exists. If a similar part is found—and this is most often the case—the designer can simply modify the existing design to design the new part. In essence, GT enables the designer to start the design process with a nearly complete design. For example, a designer may find a gear identical to the one being designed but of a different thickness. Simply copying the existing design and making minor changes saves substantial design time and effort by helping to prevent "redesigning the wheel."

Group technology also facilitates standardization and rationalization (S&R), which helps control part proliferation and eliminates redundant part designs. It is common for a company to have many similar versions of the same part, such as a gear. When the company implements GT, similarities among gears can be identified, and it is possible to create standardized gears that are interchanged in a variety of applications and products. S&R such as this pays big dividends in that it simultaneously creates economies of scale by increasing part volume and economies of scope because the same gear can be used in a variety of applications.

The grouping of related parts into part families is the key to group technology implementation. The family of parts concept not only provides the information necessary to design individual parts in an incremental or modular manner, but also provides information for rationalizing process planning and forming machine groups or cells that process the designated part family. A *part family* may be defined as a group of related parts possessing some specific sameness and similarity. *Design-oriented part families* have similar design features, such as geometric shape. *Manufacturing-oriented part families* can be based on any number of different considerations. Such considerations may include parts manufactured by the same plant, parts that serve similar functions, such as shafts or gears, or parts fabricated from the same material. All these parts could conceivably be grouped into part families.

Three methods of grouping parts are commonly used: visual inspection, production flow analysis (PFA), and classification and coding. Visual inspection of parts and their drawings is quite simple but limited in effectiveness when a large number of parts is involved. Production flow analysis assesses the operation sequence and the routing of the part through the machines in the plant. Using the data from operation sheets or route cards instead of part drawings, part families are formed. Part classification and coding is perhaps the most effective and widely used method. In this approach, parts are examined abstractly to identify generic features that are captured using an agreed-on classification and coding system. Though they are the most costly to implement, classification and coding systems are the most accurate.

CODING SYSTEMS

The two main coding systems in use today are attribute-based (polycodes) and hierarchical-based (monocodes).

In *attribute coding*, the simpler of the two, code symbols are independent of each other. Codes of fixed length span parts families and each position in the code corresponds to the same variable. Because of this, each attribute to be coded must be represented by one digit, which can make the code quite long in some

cases. Figure 19-5 illustrates an attribute coding scheme.

A *hierarchical code structure* is designed so that each digit in the sequence is dependent on the information carried in the digit just preceding it. Generally, the first digit holds the most basic information, and each succeeding digit contains more specific information. This makes it possible to capture a great deal of information in a relatively short code. Figure 19-6 illustrates a hierarchical-based coding scheme (Bakerjian and Mitchell 1992).

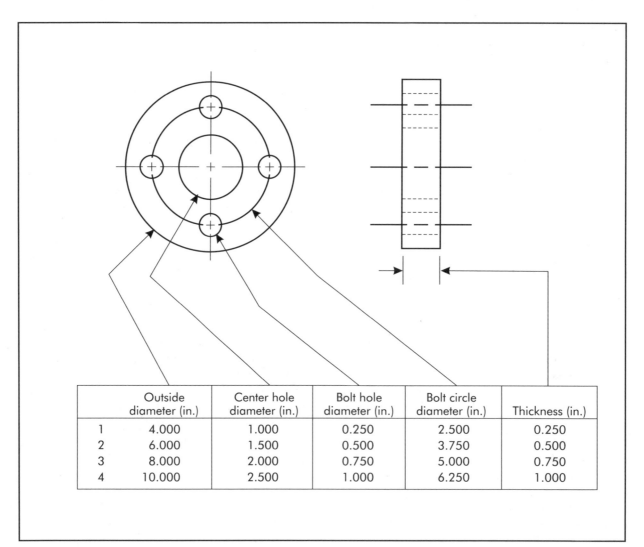

	Outside diameter (in.)	Center hole diameter (in.)	Bolt hole diameter (in.)	Bolt circle diameter (in.)	Thickness (in.)
1	4.000	1.000	0.250	2.500	0.250
2	6.000	1.500	0.500	3.750	0.500
3	8.000	2.000	0.750	5.000	0.750
4	10.000	2.500	1.000	6.250	1.000

Figure 19-5. Attribute-based coding.

	1st digit		2nd digit		3rd digit		4th digit
1	Shaft	1	Diameter < 1 in.	1	Length < 6 in.	1	Carbon steel
						2	Stainless steel
				2	Length > 6 in.	1	Carbon steel
						2	Stainless steel
		2	Diameter > 1 in.	1	Length < 6 in.	1	Carbon steel
						2	Stainless steel
				2	Length > 6 in.	1	Carbon steel
						2	Stainless steel
2	Bushing	1	Inside diameter < 1 in.	1	Outside diameter < 1 in.	1	Metal
						2	Plastic
				2	Outside diameter > 1 in.	1	Metal
						2	Plastic
		2	Inside diameter > 1 in.	1	Outside diameter < 2 in.	1	Metal
						2	Plastic
				2	Outside diameter > 2 in.	1	Metal
						2	Plastic
3	Sheet	1	Thickness < 0.030 in.	1	Length < 20 in.	1	Metal
						2	Plastic
				2	Length > 20 in.	1	Metal
						2	Plastic
		2	Thickness > 0.030 in.	1	Length < 20 in.	1	Metal
						2	Plastic
				2	Length > 20 in.	1	Metal
						2	Plastic

Group number = ___ ___ ___ ___ + part number

Figure 19-6. Hierarchical-based coding.

REVIEW QUESTIONS

19.1) What are the three basic elements of the time-based strategy?

19.2) At what stage in product development is it least costly to make product changes?

 a) design
 b) manufacturing
 c) sales
 d) customer service

19.3) What does the "X" in DFX stand for?

19.4) Will increasing the number of discrete fasteners in an assembly increase or decrease the design efficiency?

19.5) What three factors affect the RPN value?

19.6) Using the "house of quality" refers to which stage of the QFD process?

19.7) What group technology methods can be employed for grouping parts into families?

REFERENCES

Bakerjian, Ramon and Philip Mitchell, eds. 1992. *Tool and Manufacturing Engineers Handbook*, Fourth Edition, *Volume 6: Design for Manufacturability*. Dearborn, MI: Society of Manufacturing Engineers.

Boothroyd, Geoffrey and Peter Dewhurst. 1983. *Product Design for Assembly*. Amherst, MA: Department of Mechanical Engineering, University of Massachusetts.

Wick, Charles and Raymond Veilleux, eds. 1987. *Tool and Manufacturing Engineers Handbook*, Fourth Edition, *Volume 4: Quality Control and Assembly*. Dearborn, MI: Society of Manufacturing Engineers.

Part 5
Manufacturing Processes

Chapter 20

Cutting Tool Technology

20.1 TOOL NOMENCLATURE

Solid single-point cutting tools can be made of a variety of materials, such as high-speed steel, carbide, and diamond. A carbide-tipped, single-point cutting tool, as opposed to a solid high-speed steel tool, has the cutting material brazed onto a less expensive material for the tool body. The nomenclature is the same for both solid- and carbide-tipped tools, as shown in Table 20-1. A single-point tool embodies several geometrical elements as illustrated in Figure 20-1.

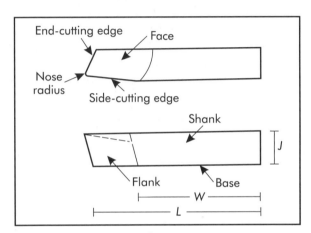

Figure 20-1. Tool nomenclature.

Table 20-1. Tool nomenclature

Size	The size of a tool with a square or rectangular section is expressed by giving, in the order named, width of shank, W; the height of shank, J; and total tool length, L, in inches (mm), such as $3/4 \times 1\frac{1}{2} \times 8$ in. ($19 \times 38 \times 203$ mm).
Shank	The shank is the holding portion of the tool.
Base	The base is a flat surface on the tool shank, parallel or perpendicular to the tool reference plane and useful for locating or orienting the tool in its manufacture, sharpening, and measurement.
Face	The face is the surface that the chip contacts as it is separated from the workpiece.
Tool point	The tool point (cutting part) is the part of the tool shaped to produce the cutting edges, face, and flank.
Cutting edge	The cutting edge is the portion of the face edge that separates the chip from the workpiece. It usually consists of the side-cutting-edge, nose, and end cutting edge.
Nose	The nose is the corner, arc, or chamfer joining the side-cutting and the end-cutting-edges.
Flank	The flank is the surface or surface below and adjacent to the cutting edge.

20.2 TOOL ANGLES

The Tool angles shown in Figure 20-2 are "normal." That is, taken with reference to the cutting edges, because these are the ones specified in grinding a single-point tool.

The face of the tool consists of a back-rake angle and a side-rake angle. The rake angles determine how the chip will flow from the workpiece and across the face or rake face. The *back-rake angle*, as illustrated in Figure 20-2, is positive if the face slopes downward from the point toward the shank, tending to reduce the included angle of the tool point. It is negative if the face slopes upward toward the shank. It is important to point out that,

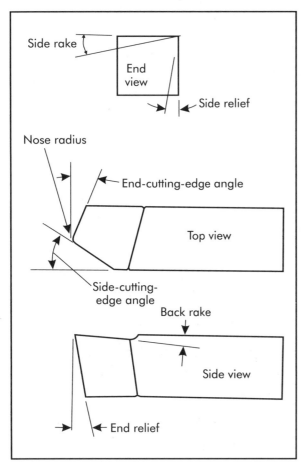

Figure 20-2. Single-point cutting-tool angles.

in general, the negative rake angle is more suited for brittle cutting-tool materials such as ceramic. However, a negative rake angle requires more cutting force and more power in a cutting process. The *side-rake angle* is the inclination of the face with respect to the side-cutting edge angle. If the face slopes down and away from the side-cutting edge angle, as illustrated in Figure 20-2, the angle is positive. If it slopes upward, the side-rake angle is negative.

The relief angles consist of the side-relief angle and the end-relief angle. Relief angles provide clearance between the cut surface of the workpiece and the tool. *The side-relief angle* indicates the relief below the side-cutting edge and the *end-relief angle* indicates the relief below the end-cutting edge as illustrated in Figure 20-2.

The cutting-edge angles consist of the side-cutting-edge angle and the end-cutting-edge angle. The *side-cutting-edge angle* is the angle between the side-cutting edge and the side of the tool shank or holder. It influences the tool entry into the workpiece. The *end-cutting-edge angle* is the angle between the end-cutting edge of the tool and a line at right angles to the side of the tool shank. It prevents the end-cutting edge from rubbing the workpiece.

20.3 TOOL FAILURE AND TOOL LIFE

In metal cutting, *tool failure* can be categorized as gradual tool wear or catastrophic failure. There are two basic areas on the tool where gradual tool wear can occur: on the relief face of the tool, referred to as *flank wear*, and on the rake face of the tool, called *crater wear* as illustrated in Figure 20-3. Flank wear is caused by abrasion, plastic deformation of the tool's cutting edge, and adhesion. Diffusion, chemical reaction, and adhesion cause crater wear. *Diffusion* is the transfer of atoms across the interface between the workpiece and the cutting tool.

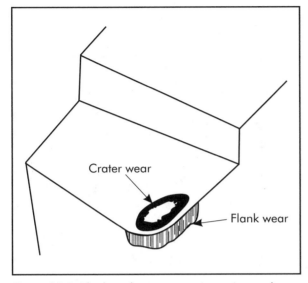

Figure 20-3. Flank and crater wear in cutting tool.

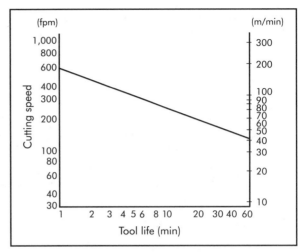

Figure 20-4. Log-log plot of tool life vs. cutting speed (Drozda and Wick 1983).

Adhesion occurs when two surfaces are brought together under high pressure and high temperature. At sufficiently higher temperatures and pressures, welding occurs between the chip and the tool face; when these welds fracture, minute pieces of tool material are carried away with the chip.

Chipping is considered to be a catastrophic failure that occurs when a small piece breaks away from the cutting edge of the tool. Mechanical shock and thermal fatigue are two major causes of tool chipping.

A *built-up edge* (BUE), consisting of material from the workpiece, may collect on the cutting edges of the tool. The BUE can form and break free continuously during cutting. The built-up edge has a large influence on the surface finish of the workpiece.

Tool life is defined as the period of the cutting time that the tool can be used. Among all the variables that affect tool life, such as depth of cut, feed rate, workpiece material, and tool material, cutting speed is the most significant. Figure 20-4 illustrates an example log-log plot of tool life in relation to cutting speed for a given workpiece material and cutting tool material.

An estimation of tool life based on specific conditions can be calculated using Taylor's tool life equation.

$$VT^n = C \qquad (20\text{-}1)$$

where:

V = cutting speed, ft/min (m/min)
T = tool life, min

n and C are parameters that depend on feed rate, depth of cut, work material, tooling material, and tool life criteria. The range of n values, observed in practice, is presented in Table 20-2.

Table 20-2. Average numerical values
for tool life exponent n

Material to be Machined	Carbide Tools	HSS Tools
Steel	0.3	0.15
Cast iron	0.25	0.25
Light metals	0.41	0.41
Brass and cast brass		0.25
Copper		0.13

(Drozda and Wick 1983)

Example 20.3.1 Using the Taylor equation for tool wear, let $n = 0.125$, $V = 100$ ft/min and $C = 200$ ft/min (C is the cutting speed at $T = 1$ min). Find the tool life.

Solution:

$$VT^n = C$$

$$100T^{0.125} = 200$$

$$T^{0.125} = 2$$

$$\ln T^{0.125} = \ln 2$$

$$0.125 \ln T = 0.693$$

$$\ln T = 5.544$$

$$T = e^{5.544}$$

$$T = 256 \text{ min}$$

20.4 CUTTING TOOL MATERIALS

Of the many variables affecting any machining operation, the cutting tool is one of the most critical. Important requirements for any cutting tool material are good wear resistance, toughness, and hot hardness. Resistance to the various wear mechanisms is essential for the tool to retain its sharpness and cutting efficiency, as well as to provide long life.

Cutting-tool materials have a wide range of properties. Figure 20-5 illustrates how cutting-tool hardness changes with temperature. Table 20-3 defines other performance attributes for cutting-tool materials.

Cutting-tool materials are usually divided into the following general categories:

- high-speed steels,
- cast cobalt alloys,
- carbides,
- coated carbides,
- ceramics,
- cubic boron nitride, and
- diamond.

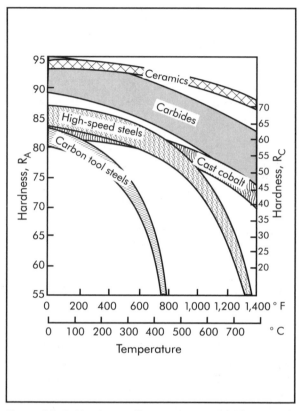

Figure 20-5. Hardness of various cutting-tool materials as a function of temperature (Drozda and Wick 1983).

HIGH-SPEED STEELS

High-speed steels (HSS) are the most highly alloyed of the tool steels, and they were developed to cut at higher speed. HSS are capable of maintaining hardness at a higher temperature better than carbon and medium alloy steel. However, they are not as good as other available tool materials.

CAST-COBALT ALLOYS

Also referred to as *stellite tools*, *cast cobalt alloys* have good wear resistance and maintain their hardness at high temperature, but thy are not as tough as high-speed steels. Their composition ranges from 38–53% cobalt, 30–33% chromium, and 10–20% tungsten.

Table 20-3. Relative cutting-tool material properties

	High-speed Steel	Cast Cobalt Alloys	Carbide	Coated Carbide	Ceramic	Cubic Boron Nitride	Diamond
Impact strength	Good	Fair	Fair	Fair	Poor	Poor	Poor
Wear resistance	Poor	Poor	Fair	Fair	Good	Good	Very good
Cutting speed	Low	Low	Moderate	Moderate	High	High	Very high
Depth of cut	Light to moderate	Light to heavy	Light to heavy	Light to heavy	Light to heavy	Light to heavy	Very light
Workpiece finish	Rough	Rough	Good	Good	Very good	Very good	Excellent
Cost	Low	Low	Moderate	Moderate	High	High	Very high

CARBIDES

Carbides, also referred to as *cemented* or *sintered carbides*, were introduced in the 1930s to meet the need for higher speeds and higher production rates. Carbide tools have high hardness over a wide range of temperatures, with a high elastic modulus and thermal conductivity, and low thermal expansion. Carbides are used for many applications in industry because they can be versatile and cost-effective. Two basic groups of carbides used for machining operations include: tungsten carbide and titanium carbide.

COATED CARBIDES

An important step was taken for cutting material when, in the early 1960s, coated carbides were introduced to industry. The introduction of cemented carbide, with a very thin coating of other carbides, changed the performance of carbide tools drastically. It improved tool life of the cutting tool, increased the cutting speed and feed and, more importantly, a higher temperature was tolerated in the cutting operation. The main coating materials used are titanium carbide (TiC), titanium nitride (TiN), aluminum oxide-ceramic (Al_2O_2) and titanium carbonitride (TiCN). Coated cemented carbides are manufactured by applying layers of 80–400 μin. (2–10 μm) coating onto inserts by chemical vapor deposition (CVD).

CERAMICS

A major advantage of using ceramic cutting tools is increased productivity. *Ceramic cutting tools* are operated at higher cutting speeds than tungsten-carbide tools. In many applications, this results in increased metal-removal rates. Favorable properties of ceramic tools that promote these benefits include good hot hardness, low coefficient of friction, high wear resistance, chemical inertness, and low coefficient of thermal conductivity. Another important advantage is that improved-quality parts can often be produced because of better size control resulting from less tool wear. Also, ceramic tools are capable of machining many hard metals, often eliminating the need for subsequent grinding.

Despite the many improvements in the physical properties and uniformity of ceramic tools, careful application is required because ceramic tools are more brittle than carbides.

CUBIC BORON NITRIDE

Cubic boron nitride (CBN) was developed in the 1960s and is one of the hardest materials available. It is manufactured by using high temperature and pressure to bond the cubic boron crystals together with a ceramic or metal binder. CBN is chemically inert to iron and nickel and has high resistance to oxidation. CBN inserts are excellent for finishing and close tolerance work.

DIAMOND

Cutting tools made from industrial grade, mined single-crystal diamonds have been used for many years. However, many applications use polycrystalline diamond tools. *Polycrystalline diamond tools* consist of fine diamond crystals compacted and bonded together under high pressure and temperature (sintering). Both natural and synthetic diamond crystals can be sintered this way. Increased use of polycrystalline diamond cutting tools is due primarily to the greater demand for increased precision and smoother finishes in modern manufacturing, the proliferation of lighter weight materials in today's products, and the need to reduce downtime for tool changing and adjustments to increase productivity.

Polycrystalline diamond cutting tools are generally recommended only for machining nonferrous metals and nonmetallic materials, and not for cutting ferrous metals. In addition to the lower cost, an important advantage of polycrystalline diamond cutting tools over single-crystal diamond tools is that the crystals are randomly oriented. As a result, hardness and abrasion resistance are uniformly high in all directions (Drozda and Wick 1983).

20.5 CUTTING FLUIDS

Fluids are used extensively in cutting operations to reduce costs and enhance workpiece characteristics. Cutting fluid technology has expanded to include the formulation and use of mineral, vegetable, and fatty oils to impart an extended range of desirable properties such as corrosion protection, resistance to bacterial attack, improved lubricity, greater chemical stability, improved emulsibility, and decreased misting and airborne contaminants.

Cutting fluids typically perform numerous functions simultaneously, including cooling the workpiece/tool interface, lubricating, minimizing the effects of built-up edge (BUE), protecting the workpiece from corrosion, reduce cutting forces, and flushing away chips. The relative significance of these functions of cutting fluids for a particular application is dependent upon a combination of interacting parameters, such as cutting fluid formulation, workpiece material, tool material and geometry, surrounding atmosphere, and cutting speed. The major problem with using cutting fluids is their biological and environmental effects, and costs associated with cleaning processes.

Although hundreds of cutting fluids and special formulations exist for cooling and lubricating metal cutting operations, all cutting fluids can be classified according to one of four types. Each of the four basic types, straight cutting oils, emulsifiable oils, chemical fluids, and gaseous products, has distinctive features, benefits to the user, and limitations. An understanding of the similarities and differences among the various types of cutting fluids is necessary to obtain optimum cutting-fluid performance through proper fluid selection.

CUTTING OILS

Cutting oils are made from mineral oil and may be used straight (uncompounded) or compounded (with additives). Applications of compounded cutting oils are generally limited to low-speed, low-feed, chip-crowding conditions on difficult-to-machine metals or when form grinding. High cost, danger from smoke and fire, and operator health problems generally limit application to those machines not designed to use a water-miscible cutting fluid or to those operations in which water-miscible fluid does not provide satisfactory performance.

EMULSIFIABLE OILS

Emulsifiable oils, commonly called *soluble oils*, are oil droplets suspended in water by blending the oil with emulsifying agents and other materials. Emulsifiable oils form mixtures ranging in appearance from milky to translucent. They provide the combined cooling and lubrication required by metal removal operations conducted at high speeds and low pressures with considerable heat generation.

Emulsifiable oils offer several advantages when compared to straight cutting oils. They provide a greater reduction of heat, allowing higher cutting speeds in some applications. Emulsified oils provide potentially cleaner working conditions and better operator acceptance (cooler, cleaner parts). They also provide improved health and safety benefits such as a reduced fire hazard and reduction of oil misting and fogging (hydrocarbon emissions).

CHEMICAL AND SEMICHEMICAL FLUIDS

Chemical or *synthetic fluids* are generally defined as cutting fluids containing no petroleum oil. They may form clear solutions, colloidal dispersions, or translucent emulsions.

GASEOUS FLUIDS

Air is the most commonly used gaseous fluid. It is the sole fluid constituent in dry cutting and is also present, of course, when liquid fluids are used. The cooling and lubricating action of air is taken for granted because it is always present.

Air also can be used as a compressed gas to provide better cooling. A stream of compressed "shop air" directed at the cutting zone removes more heat by forced convection than would be removed by natural convection. In addition, compressed air can be used to blow chips away.

Other gases such as argon, helium, and nitrogen have been used to prevent the oxidation of workpiece and chip, but their high cost generally makes them not economical in production except in very special applications (Drozda and Wick 1983).

REVIEW QUESTIONS

20.1) Which type of back-rake angle requires more cutting force, positive or negative?

20.2) In a turning operation, if $V = 300$ ft/min, $C = 420$, and $n = 0.161$, calculate the tool life.

20.3) What type of wear occurs on the rake face of the tool, crater wear or flank wear?

20.4) Which of the following cutting tool materials will soften below 35 R_C at 1,300° F?

    a) high-speed steels
    b) carbides
    c) ceramics
    d) cast cobalt

20.5) Which type of cutting fluid uses a mixture of oil and water?

REFERENCE

Drozda, Thomas J. and Charles Wick, eds. 1983. *Tool and Manufacturing Engineers Handbook*, Fourth Edition, *Volume 1: Machining*. Dearborn, MI: Society of Manufacturing Engineers.

21.1 TURNING

Lathes and turning machines come in many types and sizes to suit specific application requirements. Engine lathes, turret lathes, and NC/CNC turning machines are just a few of the types in use today.

Engine lathes are generally used for low-volume manufacturing runs. They are capable of performing straight turning, taper turning, facing, parting, boring, thread cutting, and other operations. Generally, engine lathes use single-point tools, parting tools, thread-cutting tools, boring bars, and form tools.

The main parts of the lathe are illustrated in Figure 21-1.

LATHE COMPONENTS

A lathe is composed of a bed, headstock, tailstock, carriage, and a quick-change gearbox.

Bed

The *bed* is made of a heavy metal casting and supports the working parts of the lathe.

Headstock

The *headstock* is the housing for the headstock spindle. The headstock spindle is a hollow shaft supported by bearings. The headstock spindle drives the workholding device, such as a three-jaw chuck, by a motor and series of gears.

Tailstock

The *tailstock* can slide along the ways and lock in different positions. It can serve many functions, such as support for straight turning and taper turning, drilling, and tapping.

Carriage

The *carriage* is made of three parts: the saddle, cross-slide, and apron. It provides the longitudinal movement of the cutting tool along the bed. The saddle is an "H"-shaped part that provides mounting for the cross-slide and apron. It slides on the bed way manually or automatically by being engaged to the feed screw.

The cross-slide is mounted on the top of the saddle, which can be moved manually or automatically to control the transverse movement of the tool. The compound rest that holds the toolholder is fitted on top of the cross-slide.

The apron contains the handwheel and levers that control the carriage and cross-slide movement as illustrated in Figure 21-1. The apron also contains the lever and chasing dial used for thread cutting.

Quick-change Gearbox

The quick-change gearbox connects the carriage to the spindle by means of a system of gears, a feed rod, and a lead screw. The gearbox governs how far the cross-slide and carriage move per revolution of the spindle.

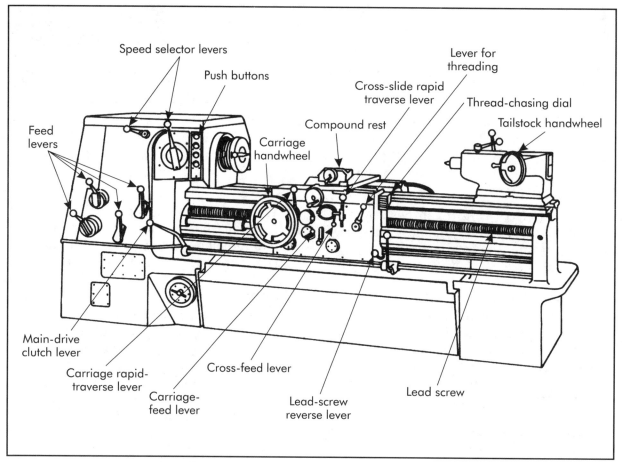

Figure 21-1. Parts of an engine lathe (Schrader and Elshennawy 2000).

The control is convenient when performing most turning operations; however, it is required when thread cutting.

Workholding devices in turning operations consist of three-jaw universal chucks, four-jaw independent chucks, collets, and face-plates. Typically, three-jaw universal chucks are used when tolerances are not high and workpiece geometry is round. Four-jaw independent chucks are used when the workpiece geometry does not allow a three-jaw to be used or when a higher degree of accuracy is needed. Collets provide maximum accuracy but are limited to round workpieces. Face-plates are used to locate a large and/or irregularly shaped workpiece.

TURNING CALCULATIONS

$$N = \frac{V_c \times 12}{\pi \times D} \text{ (English)} \qquad (21\text{-}1)$$

$$N = \frac{V_c \times 1,000}{\pi \times D} \text{ (Metric)} \qquad (21\text{-}2)$$

$$Q = 12 \times d \times f_r \times V_c \text{ (English)} \qquad (21\text{-}3)$$

$$Q = 1,000 \times d \times f_r \times V_c \text{ (Metric)} \qquad (21\text{-}4)$$

$$P_m = \frac{P_s}{E} \qquad (21\text{-}5)$$

$$U = \frac{P_s}{Q} \qquad (21\text{-}6)$$

where:

N = spindle rpm
V_c = cutting speed (ft/min [m/min])
D = workpiece diameter (in. [mm])
Q = metal removal rate (in.^{3}/min [mm^3/min])
d = depth of cut (in. [mm])
f_r = feed rate (in./rev [mm/rev])
P_m = power at motor (hp [W])
P_s = power at spindle (hp [W])
E = efficiency of spindle drive
U = unit power (hp/in.^{3}/min [W/mm^3/min])

Example 21.1.1. What rpm should be used for turning a piece of low-carbon steel with a 25.4 mm diameter at a cutting speed of 30.5 m/min?

Solution.

$$N = \frac{V_c \times 1,000}{\pi \times D} \text{ (Eq. 21-2)}$$

where:

N = spindle rpm
V_c = 30.5 m/min
D = 25.4 mm

so:

$$N = \frac{30.5 \times 1,000}{\pi \times 25.4} = 382 \text{ rpm}$$

Example 21.1.2. Calculate the motor horsepower requirements for machining 2 in. round 1020 steel with a depth of cut of 0.060 in., feed rate of 0.0072 in./rev, 75% efficiency, 100 ft/min cutting speed, and unit horsepower of 1.

Solution.

$$Q = 12 \times d \times f_r \times V_c \text{ (Eq. 21-3)}$$

where:

Q = metal removal rate (in.^{3}/min)
d = depth of cut (in.)
f_r = feed (in./rev)
V_c = cutting speed (ft/min)

so:

$Q = 12 \times 0.060$ in. $\times 0.0072$ in./rev $\times 100$ ft/min

$Q = 0.52$ in.^{3}/min

$$U = \frac{P_s}{Q} \text{ (Eq. 21-6)}$$

where:

U = unit power (hp/in.^{3}/min)
P_s = power at spindle (hp)

so:

$P_s = Q \times U$

$P_s = 0.52$ in.^{3}/min $\times 1$ hp/in.^{3}/min
$P_s = 0.52$ hp

$$P_m = \frac{P_s}{E} \text{ (Eq. 21-5)}$$

where:

P_m = power at motor (hp)
E = efficiency of spindle drive

so:

$$P_m = \frac{0.52 \text{ hp}}{0.75} = 0.7 \text{ hp}$$

21.2 DRILLING

Drilling is the production of holes by the relative motion of a rotating cutting tool and the workpiece. Drilling machine types include vertical, multiple spindle (gang), radial, and turret.

Twist drills are a common type of cutting tool used for drilling. Figure 21-2 illustrates the parts of a twist drill. The size of a drill designates the nominal diameter of its body and hole it is intended to produce. Standard drills are available in numbered, lettered, and fractional inch and millimeter sizes. Fractional-size drills come in 1/64 in. (0.40 mm) steps up to 1¾ in. (44.45 mm) and larger steps above that to over 3 in. (76.20 mm) in diameter. Number and letter drills range from 0.0059–0.4130 in. (0.15–10.49 mm) in diameter in between the fractional sizes so there is only a few thousandths difference between drill sizes in that range.

Figure 21-3 illustrates a variety of other types of drills. *Core drilling*, also known as counter drilling, enlarges existing holes. When a hole of two or more diameters is cut with the same drill, the operation is called *step drilling*. Enlarging a hole to a specific depth is called *counterboring*. *Countersinking* produces an angular opening at the end of a hole. Counterboring and countersinking are typically used to accommodate screw and bolt heads. *Reaming* is typically used to produce an accurate hole (size and roundness) with a good surface finish. A *center drill* is used to produce a tapered hole at the end of a workpiece to accommodate a center in the tailstock or headstock of a lathe. Center drills can also be used to accurately mark the location of a hole to prevent a twist drill from wandering (Schrader and Elshennawy 2000).

DRILLING CALCULATIONS

$$N = \frac{V_c \times 12}{\pi \times D} \text{ (English)} \qquad (21\text{-}7)$$

$$N = \frac{V_c \times 1,000}{\pi \times D} \text{ (Metric)} \qquad (21\text{-}8)$$

$$Q = \frac{\pi}{4} \times D^2 \times f_r \times N \qquad (21\text{-}9)$$

$$P_m = \frac{P_s}{E} \qquad (21\text{-}10)$$

$$U = \frac{P_s}{Q} \qquad (21\text{-}11)$$

where:

N = drill rpm
V_c = cutting speed (ft/min [m/min])
D = drill diameter (in. [mm])
Q = metal removal rate (in.^{3}/min [mm^3/min])

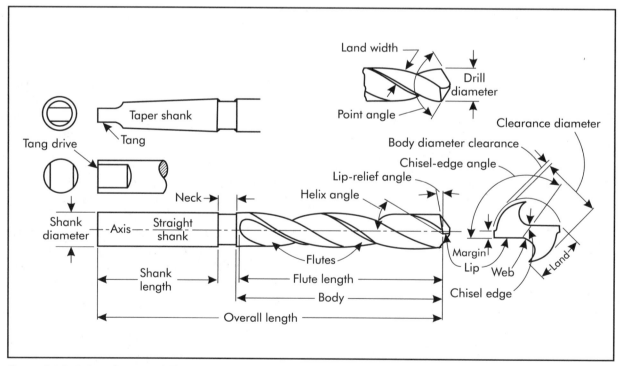

Figure 21-2. Parts of a twist drill.

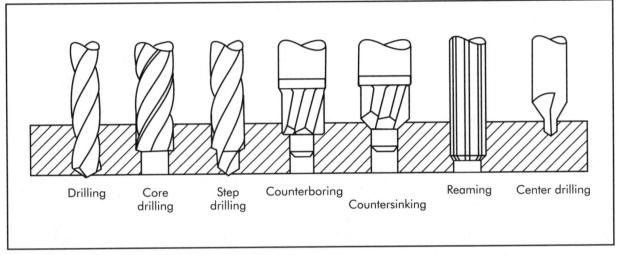

Figure 21-3. Common drilling operations (Schrader and Elshennawy 2000).

f_r = feed rate (in./rev [mm/rev])
P_m = power at motor (hp [W])
P_s = power at spindle (hp [W])
E = efficiency of spindle drive
U = unit power (hp/in.^{3}/min [W/mm^3/min])

Example 21.2.1. Calculate the rpm for a 0.5 in. drill cutting through a 1 in. aluminum plate with a cutting speed of 300 ft/min.

$$N = \frac{V_c \times 12}{\pi \times D} \text{ (Eq. 21-7)}$$

where:

N = drill rpm
V_c = 300 ft/min
D = 0.5 in.

Solution.

$$N = \frac{300 \times 12}{\pi \times 0.500} = 2,292 \text{ rpm}$$

Example 21.2.2. Calculate the motor horsepower requirements for drilling a 1 in. hole in low-carbon steel at 100 ft/min cutting speed, 0.00052 in./rev feed rate, 75% efficiency, and unit horsepower of 1 at 700 rpm.

Solution.

$$Q = \frac{\pi}{4} \times D^2 \times f_r \times N \text{ (Eq. 21-9)}$$

where:

Q = metal removal rate (in.^{3}/min)
D = drill diameter (in.)
f_r = feed (in./rev)

so:

$$Q = \frac{\pi}{4} \times 1 \text{ in.}^2 \times 0.00052 \text{ in./rev} \times 700 \text{ rpm}$$

$$Q = 0.286 \text{ in.}^3/\text{min}$$

$$U = \frac{P_s}{Q} \text{ (Eq. 21-11)}$$

where:

U = unit power (hp/in.^{3}/min)
P_s = power at spindle (hp)

so:

$P_s = Q \times U$
$P_s = 0.286 \text{ in.}^3/\text{min} \times 1 \text{ hp/in.}^3/\text{min}$
$P_s = 0.286 \text{ hp}$

$$P_m = \frac{P_s}{E} \text{ (Eq. 21-10)}$$

where:

P_m = power at motor (hp)
E = efficiency

so:

$$P_m = \frac{0.286 \text{ hp}}{0.75} = 0.38 \text{ hp}$$

21.3 MILLING

Milling is a machining process for removing material by relative motion between a workpiece and a rotating cutter having multiple cutting edges. In some applications, the workpiece is held stationary while the rotating cutter is moved past it. In other situations, the rotating cutter is held stationary while the workpiece is moved into it. The types of milling machines consist of standard vertical or horizontal knee-and-column, computer numerical control (CNC), and machining centers.

General milling methods consist of slab milling, face milling, and end milling as illustrated in Figure 21-4. There are two possible styles of milling, *conventional* or *up milling* and *climb* or *down milling* as shown in Figure 21-5. In conventional or up milling, the cutter is opposed by the feed of the workpiece. Each tooth tends to rub the workpiece upon entry and then produce a thick chip when exiting the workpiece. This style of milling requires more feeding force, generates higher cutting temperatures, produces a rougher finish, and tends to lift the workpiece out of the vise or fixture. Conversely, climb or down milling tends to pull the workpiece along, reducing the feeding force. Each tooth enters the work with a substantial bite resulting in a lower cutting temperature, longer tool life, and a smoother finish. Depending on the setup, the direction of the cutter may tend to force the workpiece against the table or fixture creating a more rigid setup. Figure 21-5 also shows an example of the two milling styles combined. When the center of the cutter overlaps the workpiece, the result is a combination of conventional and climb milling.

MILLING CALCULATIONS

$$N = \frac{V_c \times 12}{\pi \times D} \text{ (English)} \qquad (21\text{-}12)$$

$$N = \frac{V_c \times 1,000}{\pi \times D} \text{ (Metric)} \qquad (21\text{-}13)$$

$$F = f_t \times n \times N \qquad (21\text{-}14)$$

$$Q = w \times d \times f_t \times n \times N \qquad (21\text{-}15)$$

$$P_m = \frac{P_s}{E} \qquad (21\text{-}16)$$

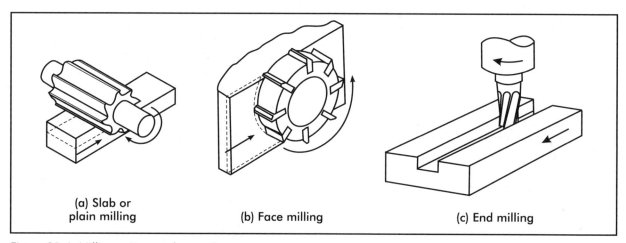

| (a) Slab or plain milling | (b) Face milling | (c) End milling |

Figure 21-4. Milling cutters and operations.

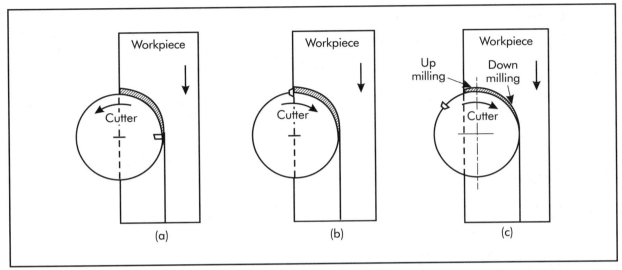

Figure 21-5. (a) Conventional up milling, (b) down (climb) milling, and (c) combination up milling and down milling.

$$U = \frac{P_s}{Q} \qquad (21\text{-}17)$$

where:

N = cutter rpm
V_c = cutting speed (ft/min [m/min])
D = cutter diameter (in. [mm])
F = table feed rate (in./min [mm/min])
f_t = feed per tooth (in./tooth [mm/tooth])
n = number of teeth
Q = metal removal rate (in.^{3}/min [mm^3/ min])
w = width of cut (in. [mm])
d = depth of cut (in. [mm])
P_m = power at motor (hp [W])
P_s = power at spindle (hp [W])
E = efficiency of spindle drive
U = unit power (hp/in.^{3}/min [W/mm^3/min])

Example 21.3.1. Determine the cutting speed of an 8 in. cutter turning at 100 rpm.

$$N = \frac{V_c \times 12}{\pi \times D} \text{ (Eq. 21-12)}$$

where:

N = 100 rpm
D = 8 in.
V_c = cutting speed (ft/m)

Solution.

$$V_c = \frac{8 \times \pi \times 100}{12} = 209 \text{ ft/min}$$

Example 21.3.2. Determine the spindle horsepower needed for a horizontal mill if a 3 × 1 in. plain milling cutter with eight teeth is making a 0.250 in. deep cut at 120 rpm, with a feed rate of 0.050 in./tooth and unit horsepower of 1.

Solution.

$$Q = w \times d \times f_t \times n \times N \text{ (Eq. 21-15)}$$

where:

Q = metal removal rate (in.^{3}/min)
w = width of cut (in.)
d = depth of cut (in.)
f_t = feed (in./tooth)
n = number of teeth

so:

Q = 1 in. × 0.250 in. × 0.050 in./tooth
   × 8 teeth × 120 rpm

Q = 12 in.^{3}/min

$$U = \frac{P_s}{Q} \quad \text{(Eq. 21-17)}$$

where:

U = unit power (hp)
P_s = power at spindle (hp)

so:

$P_s = Q \times U$
$P_s = 12 \text{ in.}^3/\text{min} \times 1 \text{ hp/in.}^3/\text{min}$
$P_s = 12 \text{ hp}$

21.4 BANDSAWING

Power bandsawing uses a long endless band with many small teeth traveling over two or more wheels (one is a driven wheel and the others are idlers) in one direction. The cutting action of bandsawing differs from other sawing methods because its continuous, single-direction cutting action, combined with blade guiding and tensioning, gives it the ability to follow a path that cannot be duplicated by power hacksawing or circular sawing. Band teeth cut with a shearing action and tend to take a full, uniform chip.

Toothed bands with different tooth geometries and harnesses for specific applications are used for conventional bandsawing tasks. Terminology generally accepted for saw bands is presented in Figure 21-6.

Three major types of tooth geometries, generally classified as standard, skip, and hook teeth, are illustrated in Figure 21-7.

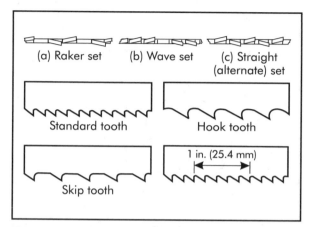

Figure 21-7. Three major types of tooth geometries.

Pitch, the number of teeth per inch, is determined primarily by the thickness of the material to be cut. General recommendations of band pitches for saw materials of different thicknesses are given in Table 21-1.

Other factors, such as workpiece material and surface finish required, must be taken into account in selecting the optimum pitch for a band. Optimum pitch is ensured if at least two teeth are in contact with the workpiece at all times during sawing.

Tooth set is the projection of the teeth from the sides of the band to provide cutting clearance and prevent binding. *Overall set* is the total distance between the outer corners of oppositely set teeth, which determines the kerf. The three most common types of set, as illustrated in Figure 21-7, are: (a)

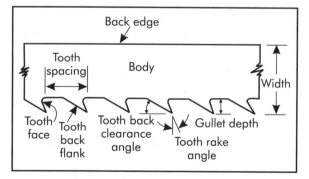

Figure 21-6. Bandsaw terminology.

Table 21-1. Recommended band pitches for saw materials of different thicknesses

Material Thickness	Band Pitch
Less than 1 in. (25.4 mm)	10 or 14
1–3 in. (25.4–76.2 mm)	6–8
3–6 in. (76.2–152.4 mm)	4–6
6–12 in. (152.4–304.8 mm)	2 or 3
Over 12 in. (304.8 mm)	1-1/2–3

(Courtesy DoAll Co.)

raker set; (b) wave set; and (c) straight (alternate) set.

21.5 GRINDING

Grinding is a process used when high surface finish and high dimensional accuracy are needed. Grinding also can be used when standard chip-type forming operations cannot cut harder materials. There are several types of grinders, including surface grinders, cylindrical and centerless grinders, internal grinders, and universal cutter and tool grinders.

Surface grinders, as illustrated in Figure 21-8, can have either a horizontal or vertical spindle with either a traverse or rotary table.

Cylindrical grinders and *centerless grinders* are used for grinding round workpieces. In a center-type cylindrical grinder, the workpiece is generally held between two centers or a chuck and a center. In centerless grinders, the workpiece is held by a grinding wheel, regulating wheel, and work rest blade as illustrated in Figure 21-9.

Internal grinding is the accurate finishing of holes. Internal grinding machines are used for this operation. In production, the wheel is automatically fed into a hole until the hole reaches the required size.

The primary function of the *universal cutter and tool grinder* is to grind cutting tools, such as milling cutters, reamers, and taps.

WHEEL SELECTION

Selecting the appropriate wheel for a specific operation and material is a critical decision. Five distinct elements must be considered: type of abrasive, grain size, bond, grade, and structure.

The *abrasive* is the grinding agent used in the wheel. Chemical composition, physical properties, and particle shape affect performance. The most common natural abrasive used is diamond, and the most common manufactured abrasives used are silicon carbide and aluminum oxide.

Grain size is the particle size of the abrasive grains, which influences the stock removal rate and surface finish generated. Fine-grain sizes are normally used for finishing and medium sizes are used for operations that require both stock removal and finish. Generally, hard materials require fine-grit sizes and soft materials require coarse-grit sizes.

The *bond* is the material that holds the abrasive grains together to form a grinding wheel. Chemical composition affects strength, resilience, and other physical properties of the wheel. Common types of bonds include vitrified, resinoid, and rubber.

The *wheel grade* refers to the strength of the grinding wheel, usually controlled by varying the amount of bonding material. This is frequently referred to as the *hardness of the wheel*. Hard grades of wheels are used to remove large amounts of stock at rapid rates, grind small areas of contact, remove stock from soft materials, and hold form on precise operations. Soft grades of wheels are used for large areas of contact, light stock removal, to remove stock from hard materials, and when grinding conditions are relatively light.

The *wheel structure* refers to the proportion and arrangement of the abrasive grains and bond. The porosity of the grinding wheel is affected by the structure and the grade. Open-structure wheels are used in the removal of stock when chip clearance is a limiting factor. Closed-structure wheels are used for holding form.

Regardless of the type of grinding operation used, the wheel identification system defined by ANSI is used by all grinding wheel manufacturers (ANSI 1977). This system uses letters or numbers in each of the seven positions, as detailed in Figure 21-10. Another ANSI standard covers the specifications of shapes and sizes of grinding wheels and mounted wheels.

In general, before mounting a grinding wheel, the *ring test* should be performed to

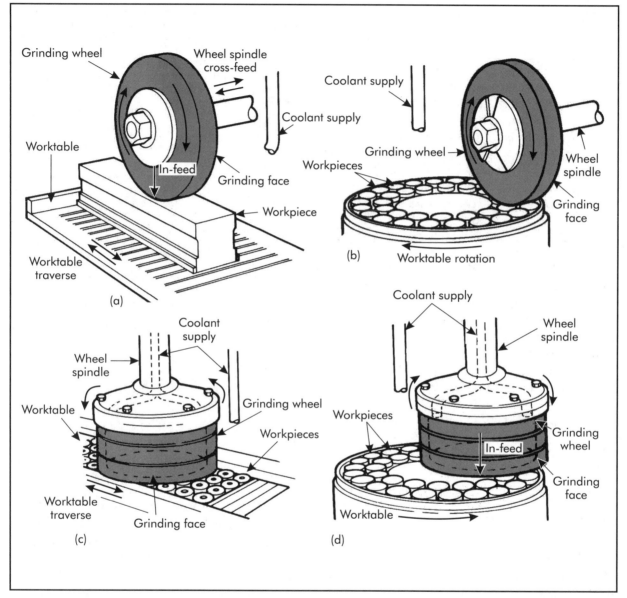

Figure 21-8. (a) Horizontal-spindle grinding with a traverse table; (b) horizontal-spindle grinding with a rotary table; (c) vertical-spindle grinding with a traverse table; and (d) vertical-spindle grinding with a rotary table (Drozda and Wick 1983).

check for cracks by tapping the wheel with a wooden mallet, which should produce a clear ring. A cracked wheel will not produce a ring. *Wheel dressers* are used to clean and true the wheel after it is mounted or after certain periods of usage (Drozda and Wick 1983).

21.6 NONTRADITIONAL MACHINING

The designation "nontraditional machining" is applied to many mechanical, electrical, thermal, and chemical material-removal processes.

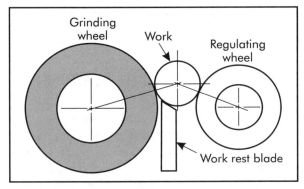

Figure 21-9. Centerless grinding (Drozda and Wick 1983).

Nontraditional machining processes are typically employed when conventional methods are incapable, impractical, or uneconomical because of special material properties, workpiece complexities, or lack of inherent rigidity. In general, nontraditional machining processes are characterized by higher power consumption as a function of material removal rate when compared with traditional machining processes. Although notable exceptions exist, the stock removal rate of nontraditional machining processes

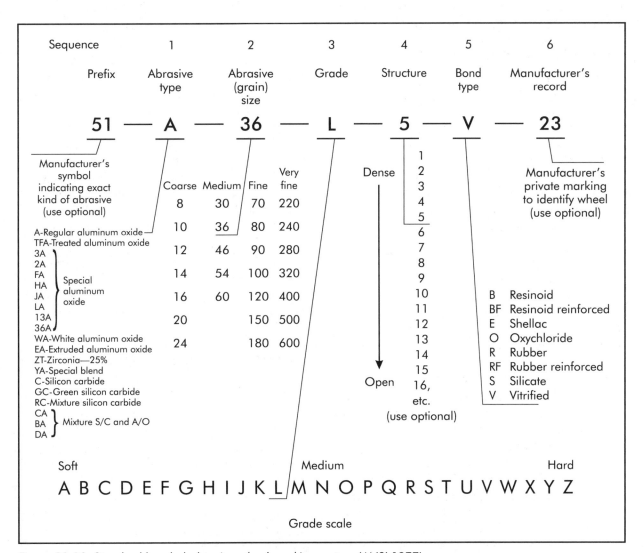

Figure 21-10. Standard bonded-abrasive wheel marking system (ANSI 1977).

is usually less than that attainable with conventional machining techniques.

WATERJET MACHINING

Waterjet machining, also known as *hydrodynamic machining*, removes material and produces a narrow kerf by the cutting action of a fine, high-pressure, high-velocity stream of water or water-based fluid with additives. The fluid pressure can range from 10,000–60,000 psi (69–414 MPa) and produce kerfs as fine as 0.004 in. (101.6 μm). The process can be used to cut items such as meat, fish, frozen food, and acoustical tile.

ABRASIVE WATERJET MACHINING

In abrasive waterjet machining, the waterjet contains abrasive particles such as aluminum oxide or silicon carbide. The abrasive particles increase the material remove rate as compared to waterjet machining. The fluid pressure can range from 30,000–50,000 psi (207–345 MPa) and produce kerfs as fine as 0.010 in. (254.0 μm). The process can be used to cut materials such as aluminum, glass, and stainless steel.

ELECTROCHEMICAL MACHINING

The term "electrochemical machining" (ECM) is often used to describe a broad classification of nontraditional machining and finishing metal-removal processes that employ electrolytic action. In this chapter, coverage is limited to "cavity-type" ECM operations. *Electrochemical machining* is a widely employed method of removing metal without the use of mechanical or thermal energy. Electric energy is combined with a chemical to form a reaction of reverse plating. Direct current at relatively high amperage and low voltage is continuously passed between the anodic workpiece and cathodic tool (electrode) through a conductive electrolyte. At the anode surface, metal is removed from the surface as metal ions, which are dissolved into the electrolyte. Dissolved material is removed from the gap between the work and tool by the flow of the electrolyte.

ELECTRICAL DISCHARGE MACHINING

The removal of material in electrical discharge machining (EDM) is based upon the erosion effect of electric sparks occurring between two electrodes. *Electrical discharge machining*, sometimes referred to as *spark machining*, is a nontraditional method of removing metal by a series of rapidly recurring electrical discharges between an electrode (the cutting tool) and the workpiece in the presence of a dielectric fluid. Minute particles of metal or chips are melted and expelled where the spark strikes the workpiece. They are washed from the gap by the dielectric fluid that is continuously flushed between the tool and workpiece as shown in Figure 21-11. Electrodes can be machined to intricate shapes and then "burned" into the workpiece. For example, tool and die sets for forging, stamping, and extrusion are typically made by EDM.

A type of EDM, called wire EDM, is also popular for cutting very hard metals such as tool steels. Wire EDM works similar to a bandsaw except the blade is a brass or copper wire 0.001–0.012 in. (0.025–0.305 mm) in diameter. Figure 21-12 illustrates the wire EDM process.

LASER BEAM MACHINING

Lasers can be used in many applications, such as drilling, cutting, heat treating, scribing, and welding. Lasers produce (emit) an intense, coherent, highly collimated beam of single-wavelength light. In material processing applications, this narrow beam is focused by an optical lens to produce a small, intense spot of light on the workpiece surface. Optical energy is converted into heat energy upon impact. Temperatures generated can be high enough to melt and/or vaporize any mate-

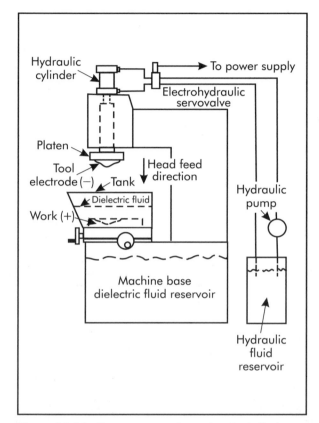

Figure 21-11. Components of an electrical discharge machine (Drozda and Wick 1983).

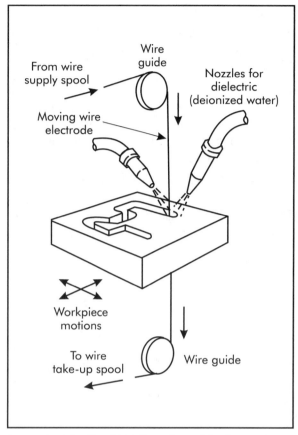

Figure 21-12. Wire EDM (Drozda and Wick 1983).

rial. Advantages include: (a) the ability to machine areas not readily accessible and extremely small holes; (b) no direct contact exists between the tool (laser) and the workpiece; (c) small heat-affected zones; and (d) easy control of beam configuration and size of exposed area.

REVIEW QUESTIONS

21.1) What rpm should be used for turning a piece of low-carbon steel of 1 in. diameter with a cutting speed of 100 ft/min?

21.2) Calculate the maximum depth of cut for a 3 in. round 1020 steel on a lathe with a 3 hp motor, feed rate of 0.0052 in./rev, 100 ft/min cutting speed, 80% efficiency, and unit horsepower of 1.

21.3) Calculate the cutting speed of a material if a 0.5 in. drill is rotating at 1,500 rpm.

21.4) What are the spindle horsepower requirements for drilling a 1 in. hole in aluminum with 300 ft/min cutting speed, 0.00078 in./rev feed rate, 75% efficiency, and unit horsepower of 1?

21.5) Determine the feed rate per tooth of a 4 in. diameter face mill with 20 teeth, cutting aluminum at 300 ft/min cutting speed, and a table feed rate of 4 in./min.

21.6) Calculate the motor horsepower if a 2 × 2 in. plain milling cutter with 15 teeth is making a 0.250 in. deep cut 2 in. wide at 120 rpm, with a feed rate of 0.00055 in./tooth, unit horsepower of 1, and 75% efficiency.

REFERENCES

ANSI Standard B74.13. 1977. Washington D.C.: American National Standards Institute (ANSI).

Drozda, Thomas J. and Charles Wick, eds. 1983. *Tool and Manufacturing Engineers Handbook*, Fourth Edition, *Volume 1: Machining*. Dearborn, MI: Society of Manufacturing Engineers.

Schrader, George F., and Ahmad K. Elshennawy. 2000. *Manufacturing Processes and Materials*, Fourth Edition. Dearborn, MI: Society of Manufacturing Engineers, p. 444.

22.1 FUNDAMENTALS

Metal forming relies on metal's ability to flow plastically in the solid state without a significant change in its properties. Metal forming can be divided into two main areas, bulk metal forming and sheet metal forming. Bulk metal forming processes include rolling, extrusion, forging, and drawing. Sheet metal forming includes shearing, bending, and drawing.

Bulk metal forming operations can be classified as hot forming, cold forming, and warm forming. *Hot forming* is defined as any metal forming operation done above the metal's recrystallization temperature. *Recrystallization* is the heat treating process by which the grains of a strain-hardened or work-hardened metal reform or recrystallize into an unstrained condition. This process eliminates the strain-hardening effects.

Cold forming is defined as any metal forming operation done below the metal's recrystallization temperature. Cold-formed parts will, therefore, exhibit strain-hardening effects. For example, if a cold-rolled and hot-rolled piece of steel with the same chemical composition are tested for hardness, the cold-rolled steel will be harder and, consequently, stronger. However, the drawback is that the cold-rolled steel will have some residual stress and will corrode faster if not protected.

Warm forming is a cross between hot forming and cold forming. Warm forming requires less heating than hot forming and less forming energy than cold forming. Other characteristics include better dimensional accuracy and surface finish than hot forming, but not as good as cold forming. Table 22-1 compares the characteristics of hot forming, warm forming, and cold forming.

22.2 ROLLING

The *rolling* process requires metal to be passed through and squeezed by two revolving rollers as shown in Figure 22-1. Depending on the rollers' shape and orientation, a variety of products can be produced as shown in Figure 22-2.

22.3 HOT EXTRUSION

Extrusion is the plastic deformation process in which material is forced under pressure through one or more die orifices. In hot extrusion, heated billets are reduced in size and forced to flow through dies to form products of uniform cross sections along their continuous lengths.

Extrusions are made using one of two methods: direct or indirect. *Direct* or *forward extrusion* is shown in Figure 22-3. Metal flow from the die is in the same direction as the forward movement of the ram.

With *indirect* or *backward extrusion*, the billet remains stationary relative to the container wall while the punch is pushed into the billet as illustrated in Figure 22-4. As the ram forces the punch into the billet, the

Table 22-1. Forming categories and characteristics

Characteristic	Hot Forming	Warm Forming	Cold Forming
Starting temperature	Above the recrystallization temperature	Approximately 30–59% of the melting temperature	Below the recrystallization temperature
	Approximately 60–90% of the melting temperature		Approximately 1–29% of the melting temperature
Surface finish	Poor	Average	Good
Dimensional accuracy	Poor	Average	Good
Strain hardening	No	Possibly	Yes
Forming force	Low	Medium	High

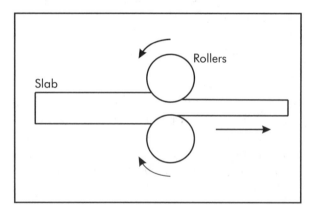

Figure 22-1. Hot-rolling process.

metal is forced to extrude back around the punch.

22.4 FORGING

Forging is defined as the controlled plastic deformation or working of metals into predetermined shapes by means of pressure or impact blows, or a combination of both. Forging aligns the grain to the contour of the part, thus increasing its strength as illustrated in Figure 22-5.

There are several types of forging processes, such as open-die forging used to make simple shapes such as discs, rings, or shafts;

impression-die forging; precision forging; and upsetting. Figure 22-6 illustrates the open-die forging process.

With *impression-die forging*, also known as *closed-die forging*, the workpiece is placed between two dies containing the impression of the shape to be forged as illustrated in Figure 22-7. Excess metal called *flash* squeezes out between the die halves. The flash forms the parting line of the part.

Precision forging or *flashless forging* does not depend on flash to achieve complete die filling. The material is formed in a cavity that does not allow material to flow outside. A specific type of flashless forging called *coining* can provide fine detail in both the top and bottom surfaces of the part with a small amount of deformation. Coining is done cold and is typically used to provide good surface finish and dimensional accuracy. Coining also can be used to enhance localized features. Figure 22-8 depicts the coining process.

Upsetting also known as *heading*, illustrated in Figure 22-9, increases the diameter of a round workpiece by decreasing its length. Upsetting is often referred to as heading since it used to form the heads on bolts.

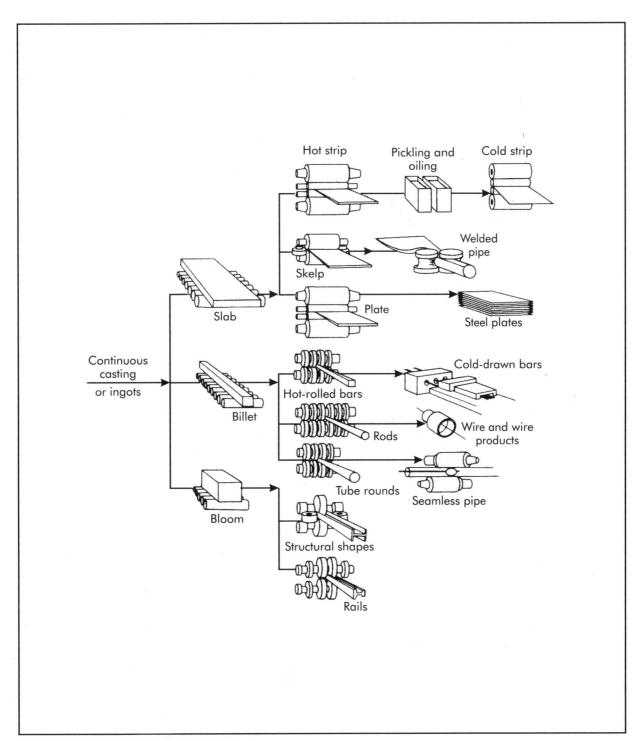

Figure 22-2. Rolled products (American Iron and Steel Institute).

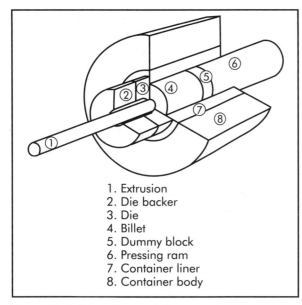

1. Extrusion
2. Die backer
3. Die
4. Billet
5. Dummy block
6. Pressing ram
7. Container liner
8. Container body

Figure 22-3. Direct (forward) hot extrusion.

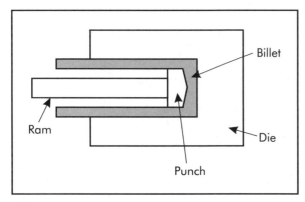

Figure 22-4. Indirect (backward) extrusion.

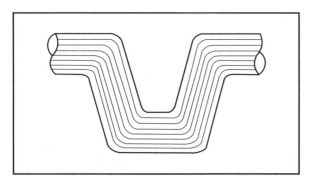

Figure 22-5. Forging grain pattern (Wick, Benedict, and Veilleux 1984).

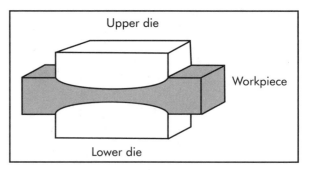

Figure 22-6. Open-die forging.

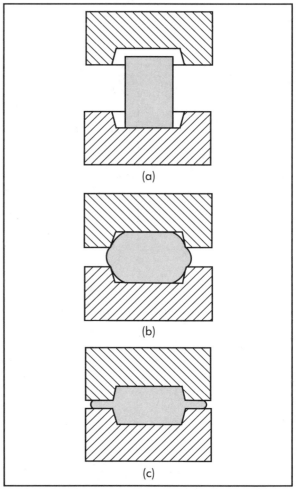

Figure 22-7. Impression or closed-die forging: (a) the workpiece is inserted between the dies; (b) the dies are brought together deforming the workpiece until the sides come in contact with the walls; and (c) the thin flash assists the flow of material and completes die filling (Wick, Benedict, and Veilleux 1984).

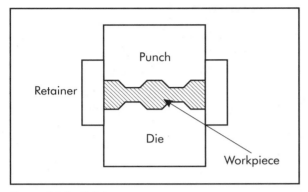

Figure 22-8. Coining process.

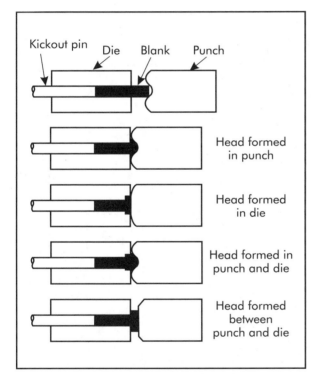

Figure 22-9. Upsetting or heading (Wick, Benedict, and Veilleux 1984).

22.5 WIRE AND BAR DRAWING

Wire and *bar drawing* means reducing the cross section of a wire or bar by pulling it through a die. Wire and bar drawing are similar to extrusion, except that in drawing, the metal is pulled through a die rather than pushed. Figure 22-10 illustrates the draw-

ing process. The amount of deformation drawing causes is referred to as *percent reduction in area*. The formula for percent reduction in area is as follows:

$$\% \text{ reduction in area} = \frac{A_o - A_f}{A_o} \times 100$$

$$(22\text{-}1)$$

where:

A_o = original cross-sectional area (in.^{2} [mm^2])

A_f = final cross-sectional area (in.^{2} [mm^2])

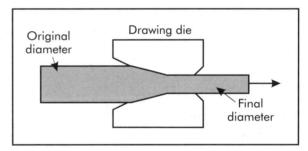

Figure 22-10. Wire and bar drawing.

Example 22.5.1. Determine the percent reduction in area if a 26 mm diameter bar is drawn down to a final diameter of 20 mm.

$$\% \text{ reduction in area} = \frac{A_o - A_f}{A_o} \times 100$$
(Eq. 22-1)

where:

A_o = 26 mm
A_f = 20 mm

Solution.

$\% \text{ reduction in area} =$

$$\frac{\left(\dfrac{\pi(26 \text{ mm})^2}{4}\right) - \left(\dfrac{\pi(20 \text{ mm})^2}{4}\right)}{\left(\dfrac{\pi(26 \text{ mm})^2}{4}\right)} \times 100 = 40.8\%$$

REVIEW QUESTIONS

22.1) Does cold forming produce any strain hardening?

22.2) Does hot forming require more or less forming force than warm forming?

22.3) What is another name for direct extrusion?

22.4) Which forging process creates fine detail in both the top and bottom surfaces of the part with only a small amount of deformation?

22.5) A round billet of copper is drawn from a 1 in. diameter to a 0.750 in. diameter. Calculate the percent reduction in area.

REFERENCES

Schematic Outline of Various Flat- and Shape-rolling Processes. Washington, D.C.: American Iron and Steel Institute.

Wick, Charles, John Benedict, and Raymond Veilleux, eds. 1984. *Tool and Manufacturing Engineers Handbook*, Fourth Edition, Volume 2: *Forming*. Dearborn, MI: Society of Manufacturing Engineers.

Chapter 23

Sheet Metalworking

23.1 SHEARING

Shearing is the process of mechanically cutting sheet metal with the application of shear force. When the cutting blades are straight, the process is called *shearing*. When the cutting blades are curved, the process can be known by different names such as punching, blanking, notching, and trimming. The total force required to cut the metal is comprised of equal and opposite forces spaced a small distance apart on the metal as shown in Figure 23-1.

The capability of a material to resist shearing force is called *shear strength*. The shear strength of a material is directly proportional to its tensile strength and hardness. The shear strength increases as the tensile strength and hardness of a material increases. The force necessary to shear metal can be calculated by:

$$F = SLT \qquad (23\text{-}1)$$

where:

F = blanking or punching force (lb [N])
S = shear strength of material (psi [Pa])
L = sheared length (in. [m])
T = material thickness (in. [m])

For round holes:

$$F = S\pi DT \qquad (23\text{-}2)$$

where:

D = diameter (in. [m])

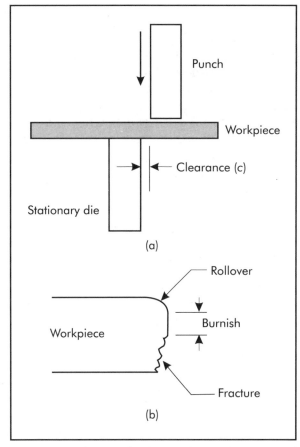

Figure 23-1. Shearing fundamentals: (a) clearance and (b) sheared edge.

Example 23.1.1. Determine the force required to punch a 3 in. diameter blank from 0.50 in.-thick steel plate when the shear strength of the steel is 40,000 psi.

Solution.

$F = S\pi DT$ (Eq. 23-2)

where:

F = punching force (lb)
S = 40,000 psi
D = 3 in.
T = 0.50 in.

$F = S\pi DT = 40{,}000$ psi $(\pi)(3$ in.$)(0.50$ in.$)$

$F = 188{,}496$ lb

The clearance between the punch and die is very important. If the clearance is correct, fracture lines should form at the punch and die. If the clearance is excessive, plastic deformation will occur because the punch will pull the material into the clearance. The following formula can be used to calculate the clearance (one side):

$c = at$ \hfill (23-3)

where:

c = clearance (one side) (in. [mm])
a = allowance (%)
t = material thickness (in. [mm])

Example 23.1.2. Determine the clearance for blanking 2 in. round blanks in 0.250 in. thick steel plate with a 5% allowance.

$c = at$ (Eq. 23-3)

where:

a = 5%
t = 0.250 in.

Solution.

$c = at = 0.05(0.250$ in.$) = 0.012$ in.

The following is a list of various shearing operations and their respective descriptions.

- In *punching*, the sheared slug is discarded. Punching is also known as *piercing* and is used primarily for making holes as shown in Figure 23-2.

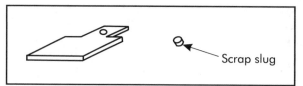

Figure 23-2. Punching (piercing) (Wick, Benedict, and Veilleux 1984).

- In *blanking*, the sheared slug is saved and the remainder is scrap. Blanking produces slugs or blanks that undergo further processing as illustrated in Figure 23-3.

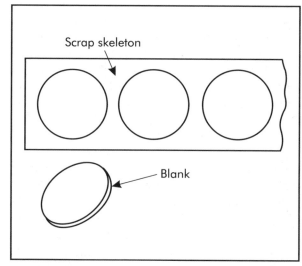

Figure 23-3. Blanking (Wick, Benedict, and Veilleux 1984).

- *Notching* involves removing metal from the edges of a part. Notching is similar to punching except it must be done around the perimeter of the part.
- *Lancing* combines cutting and forming in one step. It creates a hole without completely separating the metal, as illustrated in Figure 23-4.
- *Fine blanking* produces very smooth and square edges. Clearance is less than 1% as compared to the 5–20% clearance of other shearing operations.

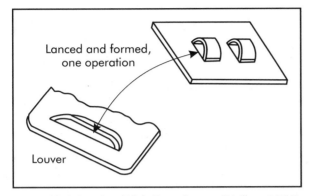

Figure 23-4. Lancing (Wick, Benedict, and Veilleux 1984).

- *Nibbling* punches out a series of overlapping holes to produce an elongated slot.
- *Dinking* is used for materials, such as soft metals, leather, paper, and rubber, which are difficult to cut with conventional shearing operations. Dinking uses a steel die, similar to a cookie cutter, to cut out parts such as gaskets. The die cuts through the material and into a wooden block as illustrated in Figure 23-5.

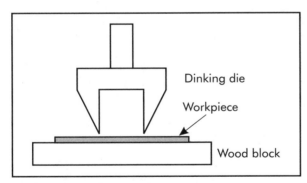

Figure 23-5. Dinking.

23.2 BENDING

Bends are made in sheet metal to gain rigidity and produce a part of desired shape to perform a particular function. Bending is commonly used to produce structural stampings such as braces, brackets, sup-

ports, hinges, angles, and channels. Bending in several directions can produce parts that otherwise would require a drawing operation. Bending is usually done to a 90° angle, but other angles are sometimes produced. The terminology for straight bending or angle bending is illustrated in Figure 23-6. Straight bending is normally accomplished using a press brake as shown in Figure 23-7. Various types of bends can be made by using dies with different contours as illustrated in Figure 23-8.

One important factor to be considered in straight and other types of bending is springback. *Springback* is when a part tries to regain its original shape after the forming pressure is removed. Typically, parts are overbent to account for springback. Spring-back can also be controlled by bottoming the punch, which plastically deforms the bend area.

FLANGING

Flange bending or *flanging* is a forming operation in which a narrow strip at the edge of a sheet is bent down along a straight or curved line. Flanges can be open, at 90°, or at an acute angle. A flange is used for appearance, rigidity, edge strengthening, and removal of a sheared edge, as well as for an accurately positioned fastening surface.

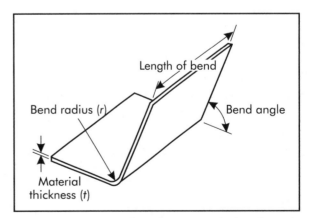

Figure 23-6. Terminology for a straight bend (Wick, Benedict, and Veilleux 1984).

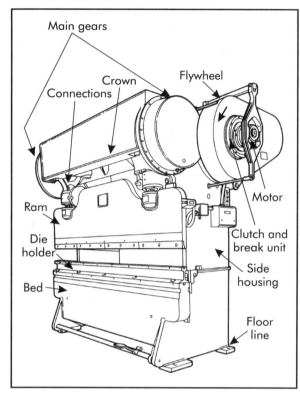

Figure 23-7. Typical mechanical press brake (Wick, Benedict, and Veilleux 1984).

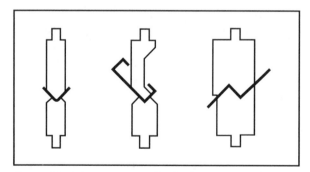

Figure 23-8. Various press brake bending and forming dies (Wick, Benedict, and Veilleux 1984).

Figure 23-9 illustrates a common straight flange.

HEMMING

A *hem* is a flange that has been bent 180° or more. Hems are primarily used for ap-

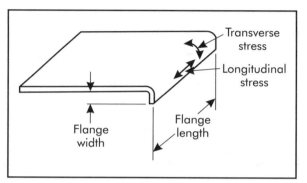

Figure 23-9. Straight flange (Wick, Benedict, and Veilleux 1984).

pearance and for the attachment of one sheet metal part to another. They are not as rigid or accurate as a flange; but they very effectively remove a dangerous sheared edge. Two common types of hems are illustrated in Figure 23-10.

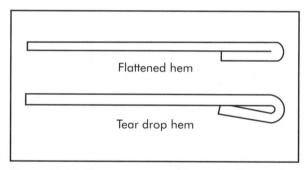

Figure 23-10. Common types of hems (Wick, Benedict, and Veilleux 1984).

ROLL BENDING

Roll bending or curving metal into cylinders or cylindrical segments is carried out on machines that use two or more rolls that rotate and bend the metal as it passes between them. Figure 23-11 illustrates a three-roll, roll-bending machine.

23.3 DRAWING

Sheet metal *drawing* is a process of cold forming a flat precut metal blank into a

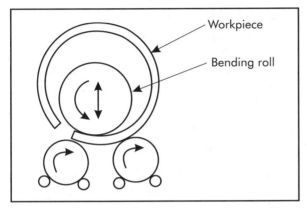

Figure 23-11. Pyramid-type roll-bending machine (Wick, Benedict, and Veilleux 1984).

hollow vessel without excessive wrinkling, thinning, or fracturing. The various forms produced may be cylindrical or box shaped, with straight or tapered sides, or a combination of straight, tapered, and curved sides. Examples of drawn parts include transmission oil pans and cookware pots. Figure 23-12 illustrates the basic drawing process.

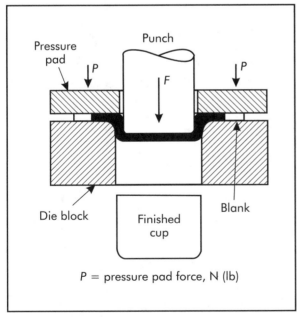

P = pressure pad force, N (lb)

Figure 23-12. The way a cup is drawn (Schrader and Elshennawy 2000).

The punch draws the metal over the edge of the die opening and into the die. The blank holder prevents the blank from wrinkling as it is pulled into the die.

23.4 PRESSES AND DIES

Presses are classified by one or a combination of characteristics that include the source of power and the number of slides. A *slide* is the main reciprocating member of a press, guided in the press frame, to which the punch or upper die is fastened. The slide is also sometimes called the *ram*. Other classifications are based on the types of frames and construction.

The most common sources of power for press operation are manual, mechanical, and hydraulic.

MANUAL PRESSES

Manual presses are either hand- or foot-powered through levers, screws, or gears. The most common press of this type is the arbor press used for various assembly operations.

MECHANICAL PRESSES

Mechanical presses utilize flywheel energy, which is transferred to the workpiece by gears, cranks, eccentrics, or levers.

HYDRAULIC PRESSES

Hydraulic presses provide working force through the application of fluid pressure on a piston by means of pumps, valves, intensifiers, and accumulators.

PRESS TOOLING

Press tooling consists of several components as illustrated in Figure 23-13. They are defined as the following:

- The *punch holder* is a fixture used for mounting the punch.
- The *punch* is the male member of the punch and die configuration.

- A *stripper* is a plate designed to surround the punch. Its purpose is to strip the sheet metal stock from the punch during the withdrawal cycle.
- The *die* is the female member of the punch and die configuration.
- The *die shoe* is a plate or block upon which the die is mounted, functioning primarily as a base for the complete die assembly. It is bolted or clamped to the bolster plate.
- The *bolster* is a plate attached to the top of the bed of the press. The bolster plate contains numerous drilled holes and/or T-slots for attaching the die shoe.
- The *guide pins* connect the punch holder and die shoe and help align the punch with the die.
- The *bushings* are attached to the punch holder and serve as an interface between the punch holder and guide pins.
- The *blank* is the desired shape cut from the strip stock by the punch and die.

Figure 23-13 illustrates a simple die for blanking. Other types of dies, such as compound dies and progressive dies, can perform multiple operations.

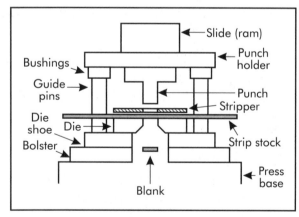

Figure 23-13. Press tooling.

REVIEW QUESTIONS

23.1) Determine the maximum thickness of material that can be punched with a 2 in. diameter punch, 50 ton press, working a material with a shear strength of 35,000 psi.

23.2) Determine the clearance for blanking 3 in. square blanks in 0.500 in. steel with a 10% allowance.

23.3) What type of shearing operation punches out a series of overlapping holes to produce a slot?

23.4) Which bending operation provides an accurate fastening surface?

23.5) Which part of the press tooling prevents the material being cut from sticking to the punch?

REFERENCE

Wick, Charles, John Benedict, and Raymond Veilleux, eds. 1984. *Tool and Manufacturing Engineers Handbook*, Fourth Edition, *Volume 2: Forming*. Dearborn, MI: Society of Manufacturing Engineers.

Schrader, George F. and Ahmad K. Elshennawy, 2000. *Manufacturing Processes and Materials,* Fourth Edition. Dearborn, MI: Society of Manufacturing Engineers.

Chapter 24

Powdered Metals

24.1 APPLICATIONS

Powder metallurgy (PM in this text, although P/M is also widely used in the industry) is a metalworking process for forming near-net shape, precision metal components, and shapes from metal powders. One accepted definition describes *powder metallurgy* as "the material processing technique used to consolidate particulate matter, both metals and/or nonmetals, into discrete shapes." Although the scope of this chapter is confined to metallic materials, the principles of the process apply to ceramics and other types of nonmetallic materials. Complex composite materials that combine metallic and nonmetallic powders are also fabricated by this technique, especially to provide the properties required in certain aerospace, electronic, and nuclear applications.

Modern powder metallurgy began in the early 1900s when incandescent lamp filaments were fabricated from tungsten powder—the same way they are made today. Other important products followed, such as cemented-carbide cutting tools, and self-lubricating bearings. Today, structural PM parts and products are used widely in automobiles, trucks, farm machinery, diesel engines, home appliances, power tools, aircraft engines, lawn and garden equipment, and business machines.

It is instructive to ask: Why would it be desirable to produce a metal product with a given shape starting with metal powders rather than molten metal? One important reason has an economic basis. The cost of producing a product of a particular shape and the required dimensional tolerances by powder metallurgy may be lower than the cost of casting or making it as a wrought product, because of scrap reduction and the fewer secondary processing steps that are needed.

When desired, parts can be sized, coined, or repressed to close tolerances. They can be impregnated with oil or plastic, or infiltrated with a lower melting metal. They can be heat-treated, plated, and when necessary, machined. Production rates range from several hundred to several thousand parts per hour. Shapes that can be fabricated in conventional PM equipment can weigh up to about 35 lb (16 kg) and have a thickness up to approximately 2 in. (50.8 mm) (Wick, Benedict, and Veilleux 1984).

24.2 PROCESS FUNDAMENTALS

There are four basic steps in the widely used conventional powder metallurgy process. These steps are powder manufacturing, blending, compacting, and sintering. The term "conventional" separates this process from isostatic pressing and hot isostatic pressing (HIP), which are not discussed.

POWDER MANUFACTURING

One common method of producing metal powder is called *melt atomization* as shown in Figure 24-1. The process begins by melting the desired metal and pouring it into a tundish (reservoir). As the liquid metal leaves the tundish, it is atomized by a series of argon jets or waterjets. The jets convert the liquid metal into small droplets that solidify as powder particles. Particles range in size from 4 μin. to 0.04 in. (0.1 to 1,000 μm).

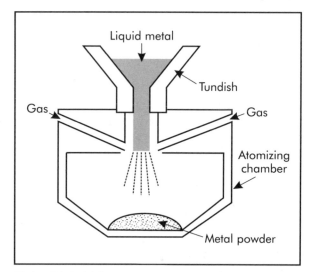

Figure 24-1. Melt atomization.

BLENDING

In the second step, *blending*, oversize and fine particles are filtered out. The metal powder and alloy powder (if desired) are mixed together with lubricants and binders to produce a homogeneous mix of ingredients. Lubricants are added to help the powder fill the die cavity without any air pockets. Binders are added to increase the strength of the green or unsintered part. Alloy powders can be added to improve the final properties of the PM part.

COMPACTING

Compacting is the third step of the conventional PM process. In it, a controlled amount of mixed powder is automatically fed into a precision die and compacted or pressed, usually at room temperature, at pressures as low as 20,000 psi (138 MPa) or as high as 120,000

psi (827 MPa) or more. Compacting consolidates and densifies the loose powder into a shape called a *green compact*. With conventional pressing techniques, the compact has the size and shape of the finished product when ejected from the die. It has sufficient strength for in-process handling and transport to the sintering furnace.

Dies and tools, made of either hardened steel and/or carbides, consist of at least a die body or mold, an upper punch, a lower punch and, in some cases, one or more core rods to provide for holes parallel to the pressing direction. A typical set of tools for producing a straight cylindrical part, such as a sleeve bearing, is shown in Figure 24-2. The pressing cycle for this simple part is illustrated in Figure 24-3.

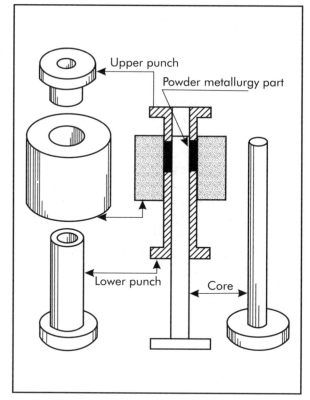

Figure 24-2. Powdered metal tooling (Cubberly and Bakerjian 1989).

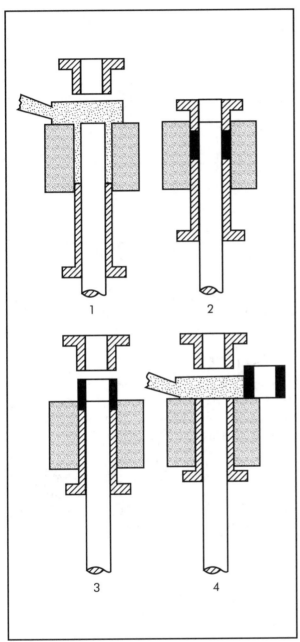

Figure 24-3. Powdered metal compaction cycle: (1) the empty die cavity is filled with mixed powder; (2) both top and bottom punches simultaneously press the metal powder in the die; (3) the top punch is withdrawn and the green compact is ejected from the die by the bottom punch; and (4) the green compact is pushed out of the pressing area to make ready for another operating cycle (Cubberly and Bakerjian 1989).

In general, the compacting cycle is essentially the same for all parts. However, when more than one pressing level is needed, for example in producing flanged shapes, multiple punches are used and separate pressing action may be required (Cubberly and Bakerjian 1989).

SINTERING

The fourth step of the conventional PM process is sintering. *Sintering*, which is mainly a solid-state process, develops metallurgical bonds among the powder particles and thus produces the PM part's mechanical and physical properties. The sintering process is performed in a three-stage continuous furnace, a temperature profile for which is illustrated in Figure 24-4. The first stage burns off the binders and lubricants at a low temperature. This stage is performed at approximately 30% of the metal's melting temperature. During the second stage of sintering, the green compact is heated to approximately 80% of the metal's melting temperature, causing the metal particles to fuse together. After this high-temperature stage, the compact moves to the cool-down stage where it is cooled to a low enough temperature to prevent any significant surface oxidation. All three stages are performed in an inert atmosphere, usually argon.

24.3 SECONDARY OPERATIONS

For many applications, PM parts are ready for use after sintering. However, any one of several secondary operations can be performed to provide specific or special properties. Parts can be repressed, infiltrated, or impregnated. The controlled porosity of PM parts makes it possible to infiltrate them with another metal or impregnate them with oil or a resin to either improve mechanical properties or provide additional performance characteristics such as self-lubrication. Parts

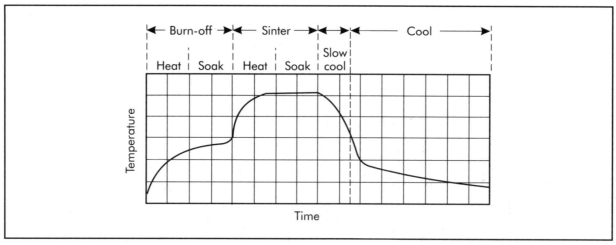

Figure 24-4. Temperature profile in a continuous sintering furnace (Wick, Benedict, and Veilleux 1984).

can be further modified by coining, sizing, machining, tumbling, plating, and heat-treating.

REVIEW QUESTIONS

24.1) Can PM produce parts with less than 100% density?

24.2) Why are lubricants added to the powder prior to compaction?

24.3) After compacting the powder, the part is called a _____ compact.

24.4) Which step in the powdered metal process fuses the metal particles together after compaction?

24.5) In PM, what secondary operation would be used to make a bushing "self lubricating?"

REFERENCES

Cubberly, William and Ramon Bakerjian, eds. 1989. *Tool and Manufacturing Engineers Handbook*, Desk Edition. Dearborn, MI: Society of Manufacturing Engineers.

Wick, Charles, John Benedict, and Raymond Veilleux, eds. 1984. *Tool and Manufacturing Engineers Handbook*, Fourth Edition, *Volume 2: Forming*. Dearborn, MI: Society of Manufacturing Engineers.

Chapter 25

Casting

25.1 CASTING FUNDAMENTALS

Casting is a process in which molten metal is poured or injected into a cavity and allowed to solidify taking on the shape of the cavity. After solidification, the part is removed from the mold and then processed for delivery. Casting processes vary from simple to complex. Material and process selection depends on the part's complexity, function, quality specifications, and the projected cost level. Table 25-1 illustrates the range of materials for casting processes.

Casting offers the following advantages when compared to other processes:

- Castings allow the manufacture of parts from alloys that are difficult to machine or weld.
- Complex shapes are easier to produce by casting than by other processes.
- Parts with internal cavities are easier and more economical to produce by casting than by other processes.

Conversely, castings generally exhibit non-directional properties that make them weaker than wrought metals that are anisotropic. *Anisotropic* means they are stronger and tougher in one direction versus another. Cast parts can also exhibit defects such as porosity, poor surface finish, and poor dimensional accuracy as compared to machined parts.

Figure 25-1 illustrates a typical green-sand mold section with the basic elements common to most casting processes.

Molds are generally made by surrounding a pattern with a mixture of granular refractory and binder mixture. This mixture can be wet or dry depending on the casting process. The choice of mold material depends

Table 25-1. Commercial capability of casting processes

Casting Process	Ductile Iron	Steel	Stainless Steel	Aluminum, Magnesium	Bronze, Brass	Gray Iron	Malleable Iron	Zinc, Lead
Die				•	•			•
Continuous	•				•	•		•
Investment	•	•	•	•	•			
Ceramic cope and drag	•	•	•	•	•	•		•
Permanent mold				•	•	•		•
Plaster mold				•	•			•
Centrifugal	•	•	•		•	•		•
Resin shell	•	•	•	•	•	•	•	•
Sand	•	•	•	•	•	•	•	•

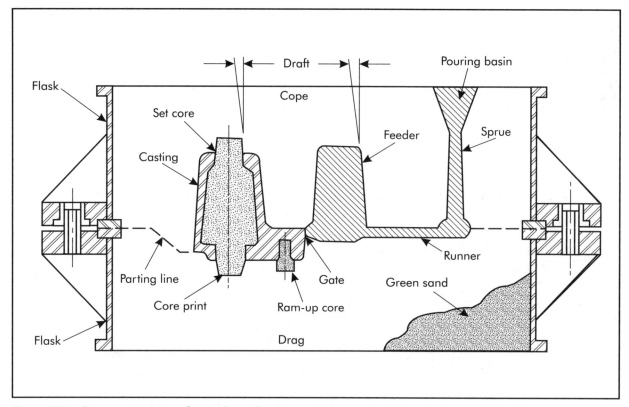

Figure 25-1. Cross-section view of typical cored casting and the sand mold in which it is produced. (Courtesy American Foundry Society)

on the casting quality and quantity as well as the type of metal to be used.

In most processes, the upper half of the mold is called the *cope* and the lower half is referred to as the *drag*. Cores, made of sand or metal, depending on the process, are placed into the cavity to form the inner surfaces of the casting. The mold requires a gating system to distribute metal in the mold, and risers (liquid reservoirs) to feed the casting as it solidifies. The *sprue* is the channel through which the metal enters the mold. A *runner* leads the metal through the mold. *Gates* attach the runner(s) to the mold cavity. A *riser* is a reservoir connected to the mold cavity to feed liquid metal to the casting to prevent shrinkage voids in the casting as it solidifies.

Casting processes can be divided into three categories: (1) multiple-use pattern and single-

use mold; (2) single-use pattern and single-use mold; and (3) multiple-use mold.

25.2 MULTIPLE-USE PATTERN/ SINGLE-USE MOLD PROCESSES

Green-sand casting and shell molding are two processes where patterns can be used repeatedly. However, a new mold is required for each casting, since the molds are destroyed during the casting process.

GREEN-SAND CASTING

In *green-sand molding*, a mold is compacted around a pattern with a sand-clay-water mixtures that may contain other additives. The clay and water act as binders for the sand. When the pattern is removed, the compacted mass retains a reverse image of the pattern's shape. Figure 25-2 shows the typical steps involved in making a casting from a green-sand mold.

SHELL MOLDING

Shell molding offers a higher degree of accuracy and surface finish than sand casting, although it cannot match the accuracy of the permanent-mold process or the precision of investment-casting methods. Shell molding is appropriate for cast iron where a permanent mold is not applicable and investment casting is too expensive and time consuming. The shell-molding process is illustrated in Figure 25-3.

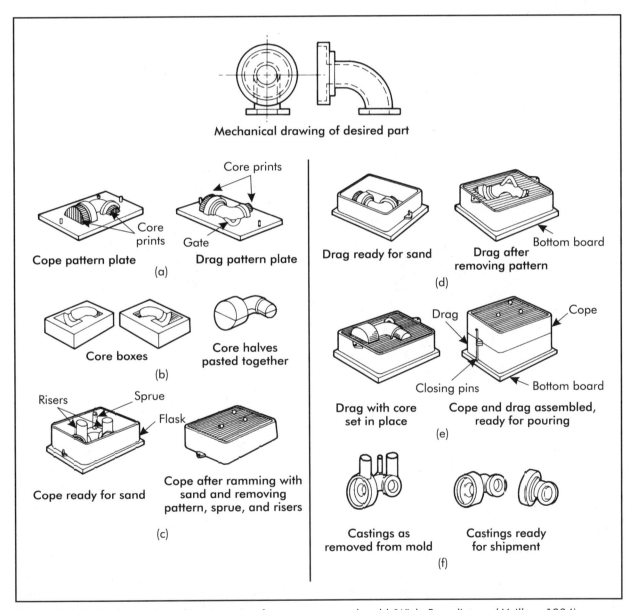

Figure 25-2. Typical steps in making a casting from a green-sand mold (Wick, Benedict, and Veilleux 1984).

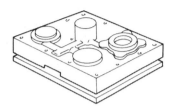

1. Metal pattern is required for shell molding. Surfaces must be smoother and dimensions closer than those used by sand casting.

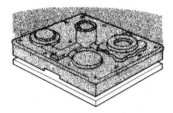

2. Sand and resin mixture is dumped freely onto the heated metal pattern to make the shells.

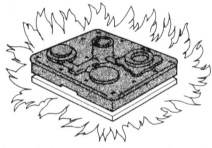

3. Heat is applied to cure the resin-sand mixture and makes a rigid, firm, easily handled shell. Each shell mold consists of two united halves—cope and drag.

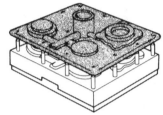

4. Cured mold is ejected from the pattern plate and is ready to be assembled for casting, or can be stored for long periods without deterioration.

5. Ready for casting. The two halves of the mold (cope and drag) are bonded together, and the completed molds are ready for pouring. This is accomplished by placing the molds in a horizontal position on trays that are suspended from a moving conveyor.

6. Casting. As the molds pass by a pouring station, which also is on a moving belt, they are filled with molten iron (poured).

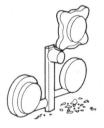

7. Gate of castings emerges from the expendable resin-sand shells.

Figure 25-3. Shell molding process sequence of steps. (Courtesy Foundry Division, Eaton Corporation)

25.3 SINGLE-USE PATTERN/SINGLE-USE MOLD PROCESSES

There are some processes where both the pattern and mold can only be used once. Two of these are investment casting and evaporative (lost foam) casting.

INVESTMENT CASTING

In investment casting, also known as precision casting, a wax pattern is dipped into a ceramic slurry that hardens into a ceramic shell around the pattern. The pattern can then be coated a second time with coarser dry refractory material for strength. When the mold hardens, the wax pattern is melted out. The mold is typically heated before pouring to avoid cracking the shell. After pouring, and the molten metal has solidified, the ceramic shell is broken off. The investment casting steps are shown in Figure 25-4.

Investment casting typically produces porosity-free castings with superior dimensional accuracy and surface finish, however, with low productivity. Investment castings typically are made of high-temperature and/or corrosion-resistant alloys. Since the pattern is melted out of the mold, the need for cores and core boxes is eliminated.

EVAPORATIVE (LOST FOAM) CASTING

Evaporative or *lost foam casting* is a method of making metal castings by the use of expanded polystyrene foam patterns that eliminate the need for traditional mold cavities. The process consists of applying a thin refractory coating to the foam pattern for strength. Next, the foam patterns are embedded in dry sand and then molten metal is poured directly onto the foam. This vaporizes the polystyrene and leaves a casting that duplicates the original pattern as illustrated in Figure 25-5. Evaporative casting also eliminates the need for cores and core boxes.

25.4 MULTIPLE-USE MOLD PROCESSES

Processes such as permanent mold casting and die casting use molds that can be reused many times.

PERMANENT MOLD CASTING

Permanent mold castings are produced by pouring molten metal, under pressure of a gravity head or a low-pressure feed system, into a static mold. Various metals can be cast in permanent molds, but the process is most common for the lighter nonferrous metals.

The sequence of operations in permanent-mold casting is shown in Figure 25-6.

The permanent mold method is used to produce many commercial castings because of the price advantage, superior as-cast dimensional tolerance and surface finish, and improved mechanical properties obtainable in comparison to the sand-casting method. The initial cost of permanent molds is higher than for sand casting. However, the lower cost of casting results in net savings over other casting methods for high-volume parts.

DIE CASTING

In *die casting*, molten metal is forced under pressure into metal molds or dies. Die casting is limited to low-melting-temperature alloys such as aluminum, zinc, and magnesium. Necessary equipment consists of the molds or dies and a die-casting machine that holds, opens, and closes the molds or dies. The process is economical for producing castings with complex contours, thin cross sections and holes and contours that would be costly to produce by machining operations. Holes can be cast to tolerances that often compare with those of drilled, or counterbored holes. Surfaces and dimensions of die castings usually require little or no machining or finishing. However, thick sections may be porous upon solidification.

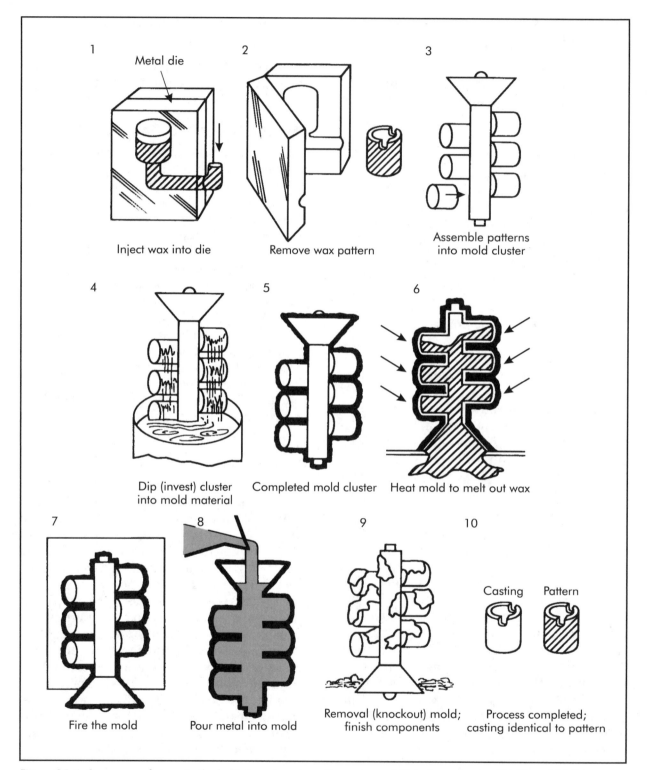

1 — Inject wax into die (Metal die)
2 — Remove wax pattern
3 — Assemble patterns into mold cluster
4 — Dip (invest) cluster into mold material
5 — Completed mold cluster
6 — Heat mold to melt out wax
7 — Fire the mold
8 — Pour metal into mold
9 — Removal (knockout) mold; finish components
10 — Process completed; casting identical to pattern (Casting, Pattern)

Figure 25-4. Sequence of steps in the basic investment-casting process (Wick, Benedict, and Veilleux 1984).

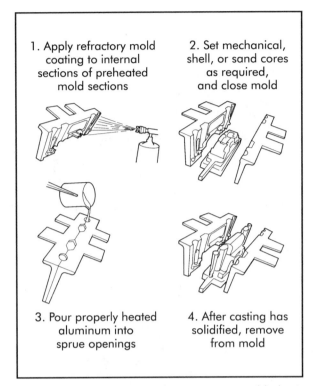

1. Apply refractory mold coating to internal sections of preheated mold sections

2. Set mechanical, shell, or sand cores as required, and close mold

3. Pour properly heated aluminum into sprue openings

4. After casting has solidified, remove from mold

Figure 25-6. Basic steps in the permanent-mold aluminum-casting process (Wick, Benedict, and Veilleux 1984).

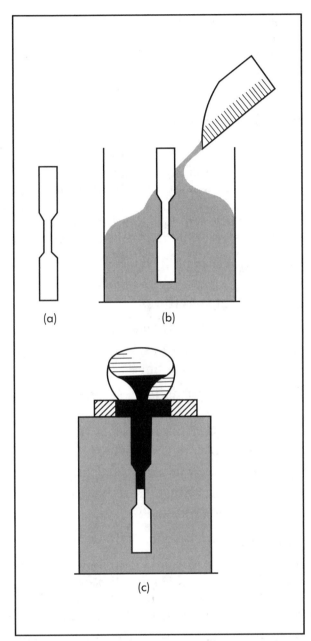

Figure 25-5. Steps in the full-mold (evaporative pattern or "lost foam") casting process: (a) the expandable polystyrene pattern, (b) is buried in sand and (c) vaporized by molten metal (Wick, Benedict, and Veilleux 1984).

Two general types of metal injection mechanisms for die-casting machines are the hot-chamber type and the cold-chamber type.

Hot-chamber Machines

The submerged-plunger, *hot-chamber machine* illustrated in Figure 25-7a is commonly used to produce zinc and some magnesium castings. While the die is open and the plunger is retracted, the molten casting metal flows into the pressure chamber through the filling inlet. After the die closes, the hydraulic cylinder is actuated and the plunger forces the casting metal into the die. This type of injection is generally limited to pressures of 2,000–4,000 psi (14–28 MPa) and cannot be used either with an alloy having a solvent action on the melting pot or pressure chamber, or with an alloy at a temperature high enough to affect the fit of the plunger and cylinder. The submerged-plunger machine is not suitable for use with aluminum, and copper alloys (Wick, Benedict, and Veilleux 1984).

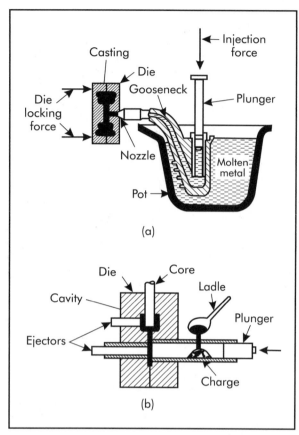

Figure 25-7. Die casting machines: (a) hot-chamber die-casting machine and (b) cold-chamber die-casting machine (Schrader and Elshennawy 2000).

Cold-chamber Machines

In *cold-chamber machines*, the pressure chamber is separate from the melting pot and is not heated. The pressure chamber, therefore, is not exposed directly to the erosive and thermal characteristics of molten metal. The cold-chamber machine is constructed and operated as shown in Figure 25-7b. Molten metal from a separate holding furnace is ladled into the cold-chamber sleeve after the die is closed and all cores are locked into position. The hydraulic cyl-

inder ram forces the metal into the die. After solidification, the die is opened and the cores are withdrawn. The ejector mechanism then removes the casting from the movable, or ejector, half of the die.

Injection pressures in this type of machine range from 2,500–20,000 psi (17–138 MPa), but most castings are made at pressures of 4,000–6,000 psi (28–41 MPa). Machines of the cold-chamber type are chiefly used for making castings in aluminum, brass, and magnesium alloys. Lower-melting-point alloys can be cast in these machines, but these alloys are generally more economically cast in the faster operating hot-chamber machines (Wick, Benedict, and Veilleux 1984).

REVIEW QUESTIONS

25.1) What defect do risers prevent?

25.2) What is used to produce holes or internal cavities in castings?

25.3) Which casting process uses a single-use wax pattern?

25.4) Are cores used in evaporative casting to produce holes in the casting?

25.5) Which casting process would be used to produce intricate, thin-walled aluminum castings in large numbers?

REFERENCES

Schrader, George F. and Ahmad K. Elshennawy, 2000. *Manufacturing Processes & Materials*, Fourth Edition. Dearborn, MI: Society of Manufacturing Engineers.

Wick, Charles, John Benedict, and Raymond Veilleux, eds. 1984. *Tool and Manufacturing Engineers Handbook*, Fourth Edition, Volume 2: *Forming*. Dearborn, MI: Society of Manufacturing Engineers.

Chapter 26

Welding/Joining

Welding is defined as the permanent joining of two materials by coalescence. Coalescence is produced by heat and/or pressure. The amount of heat and/or pressure is dependent on the welding processes. As defined by the American Welding Society (AWS), there are five welding categories: (a) oxyfuel gas welding; (b) arc welding; (c) electric resistance welding; (d) solid state; and (e) unique processes. Oxyfuel gas welding, arc welding, electric resistance welding, and unique processes also can be categorized as fusion welding processes. Fusing welding implies that the parent materials and possibly a filler material melt together to form the welded joint (DeGarmo, Black, and Kohser 1997).

Joining processes are a low-temperature alternative to welding. When materials possess poor weldability or when the effect of high temperature is a concern, joining processes such as brazing, soldering, adhesive bonding, and mechanical fasteners can be used. In this chapter, the joining processes discussed are brazing, soldering, and adhesive bonding.

26.1 OXYFUEL GAS WELDING AND CUTTING

OXYFUEL GAS WELDING

Oxyfuel gas welding generally uses combustion of oxygen and acetylene, which burns at around 6,300° F (3,482° C), to provide heat. Known as *oxyacetylene welding*, it may be performed with or without a filler material.

An example of oxyacetylene welding can be seen in Figure 26-1. Oxygen and acetylene are stored in tanks under high pressure. Regulators are used to adjust the tank pressure down to a working pressure. The gases are mixed inside the torch body and burn at the end of the torch tip. The tips are interchangeable and come with different-sized orifices. Figure 26-2 illustrates the different types of flames. A neutral flame contains the correct proportion of oxygen and acetylene so that all of the gases are consumed. An oxidizing flame has excess oxygen that can oxidize the weld and parent metal during welding. A carburizing flame has too much acetylene, which can add carbon to the weld pool during welding. The addition of carbon will increase the hardness and brittleness of the weld.

OXYFUEL GAS CUTTING

Oxyfuel gas cutting is a widely used thermal cutting process. It is a versatile process that can be used to cut straight or varying lines in steel 2 in. (50.8 mm) thick or less. Cuts can be started at the edges of workpieces or piercing can be used to start a cut at any point on the work surface. Heat-affected zones can be large with oxyfuel gas cutting, and workpieces can be distorted, especially if they are made from thin metals.

Oxyfuel gas cutting is based on one fundamental process—the rapid burning or oxidation of iron in the presence of high-purity oxygen. A torch equipped with a cutting tip

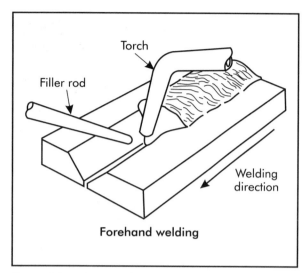

Figure 26-1. Oxyacetylene welding (Wick and Veilleux 1987).

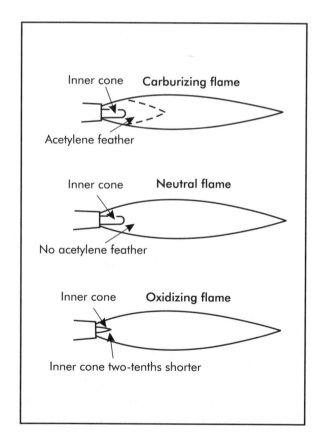

Figure 26-2. Types of oxyacetylene flames. (Wick and Veilleux 1987).

is used to control the operation. When iron is heated to a temperature of 1,600–1,700° F (871–927° C) and then exposed to a stream of high-purity oxygen, the iron oxidizes (burns) rapidly and produces a stream of molten-iron oxides and iron called *slag*. The space from which the iron has been removed is called the *kerf* as shown in Figure 26-3.

26.2 ARC WELDING

In arc welding, an electric arc extends from an electrode to a grounded workpiece. The electric arc generally creates welding temperatures of around 12,000° F (6,649° C). Arc-welding processes are numerous. The more popular are shielded-metal-arc welding (SMAW), gas-metal-arc welding (GMAW), and gas-tungsten-arc welding (GTAW).

SHIELDED-METAL-ARC WELDING

Shielded-metal-arc welding (SMAW), commonly referred to as *stick-electrode welding*, is an arc-welding process that joins metals by heating them with an electric arc between a consumable, flux-coated electrode and workpiece as illustrated in Figure 26-4. Shielding is provided by decomposition of the electrode flux. Part of the electrode flux burns off and forms a protective gas shield around the liquid weld pool. Another part of the flux rises to the top of the weld pool, forming a protective slag. Pressure is not used, and filler metal is obtained from the electrode.

GAS-METAL-ARC WELDING

Gas-metal-arc welding (GMAW), also known as *MIG welding* or *wire welding*, is an arc-welding process that joins metals by heating them with an electric arc between a continuous solid wire and workpiece as illustrated in Figure 26-5. The wire is consumable and becomes part of the weld pool. Shielding is provided by an externally supplied

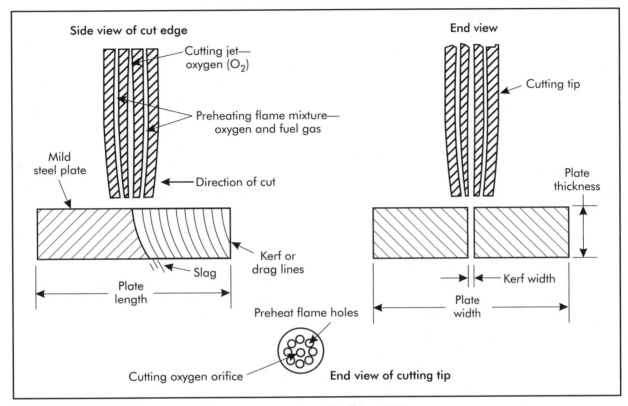

Figure 26-3. *Nomenclature of oxyfuel-gas cutting (Wick and Veilleux 1987).*

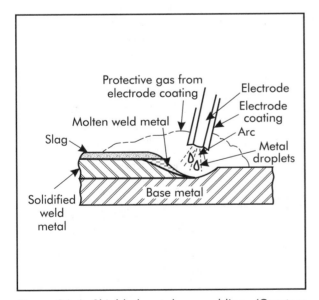

Figure 26-4. *Shielded-metal-arc welding. (Courtesy Hobart Institute of Welding)*

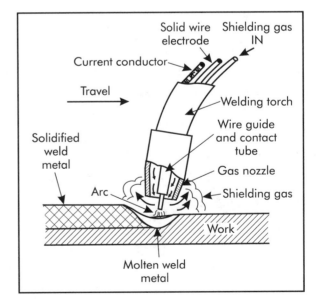

Figure 26-5. *Gas-metal-arc welding. (Courtesy Lincoln Electric Co.)*

gas or gas mixture, usually an argon or argon/CO_2 mix.

GAS-TUNGSTEN-ARC WELDING

Gas-tungsten-arc welding (GTAW), also known as *TIG welding* or *heliarc*, is an arc-welding process that joins metals by heating them with an electric arc between a nonconsumable tungsten electrode and workpiece as illustrated in Figure 26-6. Shielding is obtained by an inert gas envelope, usually argon. Typically, a filler metal is used depending on the application.

26.3 ELECTRIC RESISTANCE WELDING

Resistance welding refers to a group of welding processes that produce a coalescence of metals from the heat obtained by the resistance to electric current and by the application of pressure. No flux, filler metal, or shielding of any type is used. Although there are many resistance-welding types, resistance spot-welding is perhaps most common

and the same methodology applies to all resistance-welding operations.

Resistance spot-welding produces coalescence at the faying surfaces in one spot. Faying surfaces are the contact surfaces of the two pieces being joined. The size and shape of the individually formed welds (called *nuggets*) are influenced primarily by the size and contour of the electrodes. Most spot welding is done by clamping the workpieces between a pair of electrodes and passing a low-voltage, high-amperage current through the electrodes and workpieces for a short cycle. Resistance heating at the joint contacting surfaces forms a fused nugget of weld material as illustrated in Figure 26-7. The amount of heat generated in resistance welding obeys the following equation:

$$H = I^2 RT \qquad (26\text{-}1)$$

where:

H = heat (J)
I = current (A)
R = resistance (Ω)
T = time (seconds)

The amount of electrical resistance is determined by: (a) resistance of the electrodes; (b) resistance of the workpieces; and (c) distance between the faying surfaces.

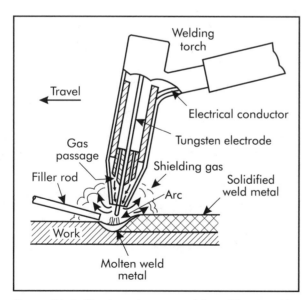

Figure 26-6. Gas-tungsten-arc welding. (Courtesy Lincoln Electric Co.)

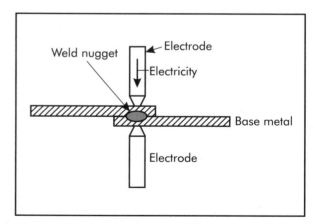

Figure 26-7. Resistance spot-welding.

26.4 SOLID-STATE WELDING

When a welded joint is produced without melting the parent material or filler material, the process is considered to be solid-state welding. There are many solid-state welding processes, such as forge welding, inertia welding, and diffusion welding. However, only ultrasonic welding is discussed in this section.

Ultrasonic welding (USW) is the joining of materials by clamping the components together and applying high-frequency (10,000–100,000 Hz), oscillating shear stresses parallel to the part interface as illustrated in Figure 26-8. The combined static and vibratory forces cause bonding of the component surfaces.

Most metals can be welded ultrasonically, but aluminum and copper alloys are the easiest and most practical to weld. Ultrasonic welding can join dissimilar metals. However, they must be thin and form a lap joint. Plastics also can be ultrasonically welded. The more rigid the parent plastic is, the better the weld.

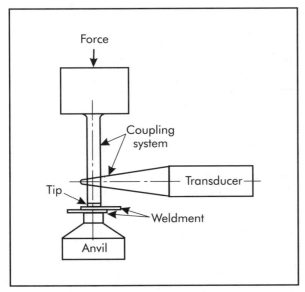

Figure 26-8. Ultrasonic-welding machine (Wick, Benedict, and Veilleux 1984).

26.5 UNIQUE PROCESSES

Unique welding processes are fusion welding processes that do not easily fit into one of the other welding categories listed in the beginning of this chapter. There are many, such as laser-beam welding, electron-beam welding, thermit welding, and flash welding. However, only laser-beam welding is discussed in this section.

Laser-beam welding (LBW) is a fusion joining process that produces coalescence of metals with the heat generated by the absorption of a concentrated, coherent light beam impinging on the components to be joined. In the LBW process, the laser beam is focused to a small spot for high power density and directed by optical elements such as mirrors and lenses or fiber-optic cable, depending on the type of laser used. It is a noncontact process, with no pressure applied. Inert gas shielding is generally employed to reduce oxidation, but filler metal is rarely used. It creates a very small heat-affected zone and does not emit harmful radiation. Figure 26-9 illustrates the cross section of a typical laser-beam weld.

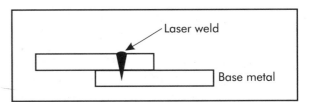

Figure 26-9. Cross-section of laser weld.

26.6 BRAZING AND SOLDERING BRAZING

Brazing is defined by the American Welding Society (AWS) as "A group of welding processes that produces coalescence of materials by heating them in the presence of a filler metal having a liquidus *above* 840° F (449° C) and below the solidus of the base metal. *Liquidus* is the lowest temperature at which a metal or alloy is completely liquid, and *solidus* is the highest temperature at which a metal or alloy is completely solid." The filler metal is distributed between the closely fitted faying surfaces of the joint by capillary action. In brazing, flux generally prevents oxidation and promotes wetting, flow, and the formation of a soundly brazed joint. Since the parent metal is not melted, brazing can join dissimilar metals (Schrader and Elshennawy 2000).

SOLDERING

Soldering is defined by the American Welding Society as "A group of welding processes that produces coalescence of materials by heating them to a suitable temperature and using a filler metal having a liquidus *below* 840° F (449° C) and below the solidus of the base material." The filler metal is distributed between the closely fitted surfaces by capillary attraction. In soldering, flux promotes wetting and the formation of a sound solder joint (Schrader and Elshennawy 2000).

26.7 ADHESIVE BONDING

In *adhesive bonding*, one surface is the adhesive while the other is the adherend. The *adhesive* is a substance capable of holding materials together by surface attachment. The *adherend* is a body that is held to another body by an adhesive. Structural (engineering) adhesives are bonding agents used for transferring required loads between adherends exposed to service environments.

Curing is the changing of the physical properties of an adhesive by chemical reaction, which may be condensation, polymerization, or vulcanization. It is often accomplished by the action of heat and/or a catalyst, and with or without pressure.

Advantages of adhesive bonding include:

- Stresses are distributed uniformly over a large area, significantly reducing stress concentrations that cause fatigue and failure.
- A wide variety of similar and dissimilar materials, as well as combinations of materials, can be joined, including those with vastly different thermal coefficients of expansion.
- Very thin and fragile materials not suitable for mechanical fasteners or welding can be joined.
- The weight of assemblies can be significantly reduced.
- Some adhesives form flexible bonds that are tolerant of repeated cycling, resulting in improved fatigue life.

Adhesives can be classified as natural, inorganic, and synthetic organic. Synthetic-organic adhesives are the most important in manufacturing due to their high strength. Various types of synthetic-organic adhesives, also considered to be structural adhesives, are listed in Table 26-1.

REVIEW QUESTIONS

26.1) What type of oxyfuel flame contains excess carbon?

26.2) Which arc-welding process uses a bare metal consumable electrode?

26.3) SMAW is commonly referred to as what type of welding?

26.4) Is brazing performed at a higher or lower temperature than soldering?

26.5) What welding process discussed in this chapter relies on high-frequency vibrational energy?

26.6) Which category do water-based adhesives belong to?

Table 26-1. Structural adhesives

Adhesive Category	Characteristics	Specific Adhesives
Chemically reactive	Undergo a curing or cross-linking reaction within the adhesive	Epoxies Polyurethanes Phenolics Silicones Anaerobics Cyanoacrylates
Evaporative	Curing occurs with the loss of solvent or water Water-based adhesives are more environmentally friendly than other adhesives	Vinyls Acrylics Polyurethanes
Hot melt	Bond forms rapidly and can join most materials Variable joint gaps can be filled	Polyolefins Polyamides Polyesters
Delayed tack	Nontacky solids are heat-activated to produce a state of tackiness that is retained upon cooling for periods of up to several days	Polystyrenes Polyvinyl acetates Polyimides
Film	Must be supplied on a flexible cloth or tape They have a controlled glue-line thickness Easy to apply	Nylon epoxies Vinyl phenolics Elastomer epoxies
Pressure sensitive	Bond formation occurs by the brief application of pressure	Natural rubber Styrene-butadiene rubber Butyl rubber

REFERENCES

DeGarmo, Paul E., J.T. Black, and Ronald A. Kohser, 1997. *Materials and Processes in Manufacturing*, Eighth Edition. Upper Saddle River, NJ: Prentice Hall.

Schrader, George F. and Ahmad K. Elshennawy, 2000. *Manufacturing Processes and Materials*, Fourth Edition. Dearborn, MI: Society of Manufacturing Engineers.

Wick, Charles and Raymond Veilleux, eds. 1987. *Tool and Manufacturing Engineers Handbook*, Fourth Edition, *Volume 4: Quality Control and Assembly*. Dearborn, MI: Society of Manufacturing Engineers.

Chapter 27

Finishing

27.1 SPRAY FINISHING

In conventional air spraying, the material is usually supplied from a container in one of two ways. The container may be under pressure of up to 100 psi (690 kPa) or the spraying device can pull material from the container to the atomizing area (suction feed).

A typical air-atomizing system consists of: (a) air pressure source; (b) air regulator; (c) air line; (d) material supply; and (e) spray device.

A type of spray gun that controls only the fluid flow is known as a *bleeder-type* because the air constantly bleeds from the gun as it is being used. The other type of spray gun, known as the *nonbleeder-type*, controls the air and the fluid by the action of the trigger. These guns ensure that the air comes on before the fluid begins to flow, known as *lead-lag*.

The air nozzles, referred to as air caps, are the most important part of the air spray gun. They direct the air to the material and cause atomization and pattern development. The two basic types of air nozzles are external-mixing and internal-mixing. *External-mixing systems* mix the air and the fluid outside the air cap. This type of cap is used on both bleeder and nonbleeder types of spray guns and can be either siphon or pressure-fed. External-mixing systems are the most common type used in production.

Internal-mixing systems mix the air and the fluid inside the air cap before being released. The air cap's exit-hole shape controls the pattern of the material spray, which cannot be varied with the gun controls. Internal-mixing systems must be pressure-fed and the air and fluid balance must be closely maintained (Wick and Veilleux 1985).

27.2 ELECTROSTATIC SPRAYING

In the *electrostatic spraying* finishing process, the application of electrostatic charges to the material particles causes them to act like small magnets when placed in the vicinity of a grounded object. During the spraying process, the painted part is grounded. As the material is sprayed toward the part, the magnetic action of the charged particles causes the particles, normally lost due to bounce-back or blow-by, to be attracted back to the part. The phenomenon is known as *"wrap."* By applying an electrostatic charge to the material particles, transfer efficiencies of 60–90% are possible. Electrostatic spraying is illustrated in Figure 27-1 (Wick and Veilleux 1985).

27.3 ELECTROPLATING

In *electroplating*, the workpiece is made cathodic in a solution containing the ions of the metal being deposited. Direct current is passed between the anode and the workpiece (cathode). The anode is usually constructed of the same material as the metal being plated. As the current flows, the metal ions gain electrons at the cathodic workpiece and transform into a metal coating. Figure 27-2 illustrates the electroplating process.

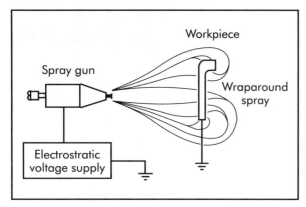

Figure 27-1. Electrostatic spraying (Schrader and Elshennawy 2000).

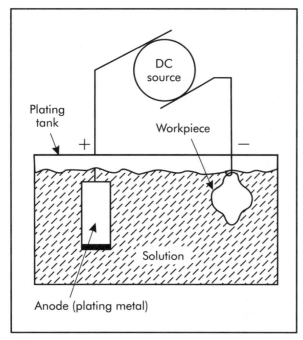

Figure 27-2. Electroplating process (Schrader and Elshennawy 2000).

Proprietary additives are usually incorporated in the plating solution to alter the deposit in a desirable fashion. These additives brighten or level the deposit as well as improve the uniformity of the deposit's thickness over the entire workpiece. The additives also may be used to alter physical properties such as hardness, ductility, internal stress, and corrosion resistance.

Many different metals can be successfully electroplated, such as nickel, copper, chromium, zinc, tin, cadmium, and lead. Alloys and precious metals also can be deposited (Wick and Veilleux 1985).

REVIEW QUESTIONS

27.1) In spray finishing, what type of mixing system is most commonly used for production?

27.2) In electrostatic spraying, does the part to be painted or the paint have an electrostatic charge?

27.3) In electroplating, is the part to be plated the anode or cathode?

REFERENCE

Schrader, George F. and Ahmad K. Elshennawy, 2000. *Manufacturing Processes and Materials*, Fourth Edition. Dearborn, MI: Society of Manufacturing Engineers.

Wick, Charles and Raymond Veilleux, eds. 1985. *Tool and Manufacturing Engineers Handbook*, Fourth Edition. *Volume 3: Materials, Finishing, and Coating*. Dearborn, MI: Society of Manufactruting Engineers.

Selecting a process appropriate for both the material and part geometry is complicated. Most manufacturing equipment can use many types of material and some designs function well made of differing materials. Table 28-1 shows some of these possibilities for thermoplastics. Table 28-2 indicates processes compatible with selected thermoset materials.

28.1 EXTRUSION

The extrusion process is a continuous operation that forces hot plasticized material through a die opening to produce the desired shape. The material coming out of an extruder is called the *extrudate*. Extrusion processes consume more plastics materials than any other process, since large, high-speed extruders run continuously.

A typical extruder consists of a barrel, heaters, and coolers to control the temperature of the barrel, screw, die, and drive motor. Temperature is an important factor for maintaining the part's shape while cooling. Figure 28-1 shows a configuration of an extruder.

Extruders are sized by the diameter of the screw and the horsepower of the drive motor. The basic screw description includes the length-to-diameter ratio of the screw. For example, a short screw might have a 16:1 ratio. A long screw might be up to 40:1. A small-diameter screw is 0.75 in. (19 mm) in diameter, and a large screw may be 12 in. (305 mm) in diameter. Because of these large variations in equipment size, the output of extruders also varies from a low output of 5 lb (2.3 kg) per hour to a high output of 12,000 lb (5,443 kg) per hour.

There are several categories of extruder screws. The most common type is the general-purpose screw, which can handle a wide range of differing materials. When a process is dedicated to only one type of material, then a special-purpose screw may be more efficient. A general-purpose screw has additional special mixing devices. The mixing devices are generally attached to the front end of the screw. The simplest are mixing pins, which are inserted into the screw. The special screw design includes various types of barrier screws. These are screws that have two channels, one containing unmelted pellets and the other with only fully melted plastic. At the rear end of the screw, the solids channel dominates, but it diminishes over the length of the screw. At the front end, the melt channel dominates.

Extrusion processes are categorized by the general shape of the products. These processes are profile extrusion, pipe extrusion, sheet extrusion, film extrusion, filament extrusion, and wire coating. In some cases, the same basic extruder could serve for all these processes, but the dies and secondary equipment would be unique.

Extrusion die design has to account for the shrinkage of the material as it cools. Extrusion dies are not the same size or shape as the desired product. The difficulty of designing a die increases as the product profile becomes more complex.

Table 28-1. Thermoplastics parts manufacturing processes

Thermoplastics	Compression Molding	Transfer Molding	Injection Molding	Extrusion	Rotational Molding	Blow Molding	Thermoforming	Reaction Injection Molding	Casting	Forging	Foam Molding	Reinforced Plastic Molding	Vacuum Molding	Pultrusion	Calendering
Acetal			•	•	•	•	•				•	•			•
Acrylonitrile-butadiene-styrene (ABS)			•	•	•	•	•			•					•
Acrylic	•		•	•		•	•		•						•
Cellulose acetate	•		•	•			•								•
Cellulose acetatebutyrate	•		•	•	•		•								•
Cellulose nitrate	•		•	•			•								•
Cellulose propionate	•		•	•			•								•
Ethyl cellulose			•	•			•					•			•
Chlorinated polyether			•	•	•	•	•								
Chlorotrifluoroethylene (CTFE)	•	•	•	•			•								•
Tetra-fluoroethylene (TFE)	•	•	•	•											•
Fluorinated ethylene-propylene (FEP)	•	•	•	•			•								•
CTFE-VF$_2$	•	•	•	•			•								•
Nylon			•	•	•	•		•	•	•		•			•
Phenoxy			•	•		•									
Polyimide			•												
Polycarbonate			•	•		•	•								•
Polyethylene			•	•	•	•	•				•	•			•
Polyphenylene oxide (PPO)			•	•		•						•			
Polypropylene (PP)	•		•	•	•	•	•		•	•		•			•
Polystyrene			•	•	•	•	•				•	•			•
Polysulfone			•	•		•	•					•		•	
Polyurethane			•	•	•						•	•	•		•
Styrene-acrylonitrile copolymer (SAN)			•	•		•									
Polyvinyl chloride (PVC)	•	•	•	•	•	•	•				•	•	•		•
Polyvinyl acetate	•	•	•	•	•	•	•				•				•
Polyvinylidene chloride			•												

Table 28-2. Thermoset plastics parts manufacturing processes

Thermosetting Plastics	Compression Molding	Transfer Molding	Injection Molding	Rotational Molding	Thermoforming	Reaction Injection Molding	Casting	Foam Molding	Reinforced Plastics Molding	Laminating
Alkyd	•	•	•				•		•	
Allyd					•		•		•	•
Epoxy				•		•	•	•	•	•
Melamine	•	•	•				•		•	•
Phenolic	•	•	•				•	•		•
Polyester (unsaturated)	•					•	•	•	•	
Polyurethane						•				
Silicone							•	•	•	
Urea	•	•	•					•		

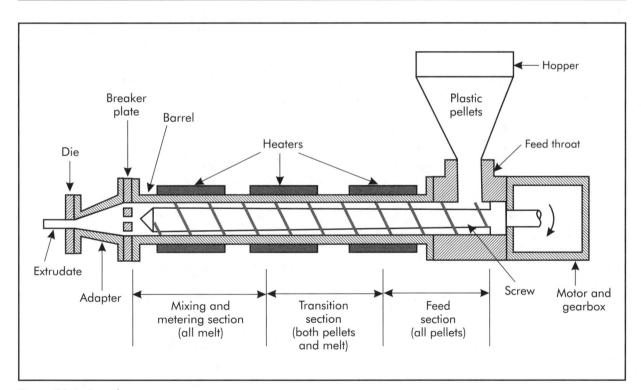

Figure 28-1. Extruder components.

The most commonly extruded materials are rigid and flexible vinyl, ABS, polystyrene, polypropylene, and polyethylene. Nylon, polycarbonate, polysulfone, acetal, and polyphenylene are included among other plastics that can be extruded.

28.2 BLOW MOLDING

Blow molding is a process for shaping thermoplastic materials into one-piece, hollow articles by heat and air pressure. The two principal methods are extrusion blow molding and injection blow molding.

EXTRUSION BLOW MOLDING

In *extrusion blow molding*, an extruder creates a thick tube called a *parison*. A mold then closes on the parison, pinching the bottom shut. At the top of the mold, the mold closes around a blow pin, which introduces pressurized air into the parison. The parison then inflates until it fills the mold. When the plastic is cool enough to be rigid, the mold opens and the container is ejected. Figure 28-2 shows the basic steps in the extrusion blow-molding process.

Milk bottles, shampoo bottles, pill bottles, and squeeze bottles for condiments are produced with extrusion blow-molding processes. The process can be identified by the line across the bottom of the container, which shows where the parison was pinched-off.

INJECTION BLOW MOLDING

In *injection blow molding*, a parison is created by injection molding. The parison can be immediately transferred to a blowing station and inflated into a desired container. Figure 28-3 shows a three-station process for injection blow molding. The parison also can be cooled and stored for subsequent blowing. The biggest use for injection blow molding is the creation of containers for carbonated soft drinks. Extrusion blow molding cannot produce bottle top

screw threads that are strong enough and accurate enough to hold the pressure exerted by the carbonation. Precision, strong threads are injection molded into the parison, and then the blowing process creates the major shape of the bottle.

Injection blow-molded bottles exhibit a single blemish in the center of the bottom of the bottle. That is the mark left by the gate in the injection mold.

28.3 INJECTION MOLDING

Injection molding is a versatile process for forming thermoplastic and thermoset materials into molded products of intricate shapes, at high production rates, with good dimensional accuracy. Injection molding generally makes use of the heat-softening characteristics of thermoplastics materials. These materials soften when heated and reharden when cooled. No chemical changes take place when the material is heated or cooled; the change is entirely physical, allowing the softening and rehardening cycle to be repeated several times.

The basic injection molding process uses high pressure to deliver a metered quantity of heated and plasticized material into a relatively cool mold, which solidifies the plastics material. Figure 28-4 illustrates the components of an injection molding machine.

The single-stage reciprocating screw system prepares the plastic thoroughly for the mold. As the screw turns, it is pushed backward and forces the charge of plastic bead from the hopper into the heating cylinder. When enough plastic has been prepared, the screw stops turning and is driven forward as a plunger to inject the charge into the die.

Injection molding machines are described by the shot size and the clamp tonnage. The *shot size* is the maximum amount of material the machine can inject per cycle. A small machine may inject only 1 oz (28 g), while a large machine can shoot about 20 lb (9 kg).

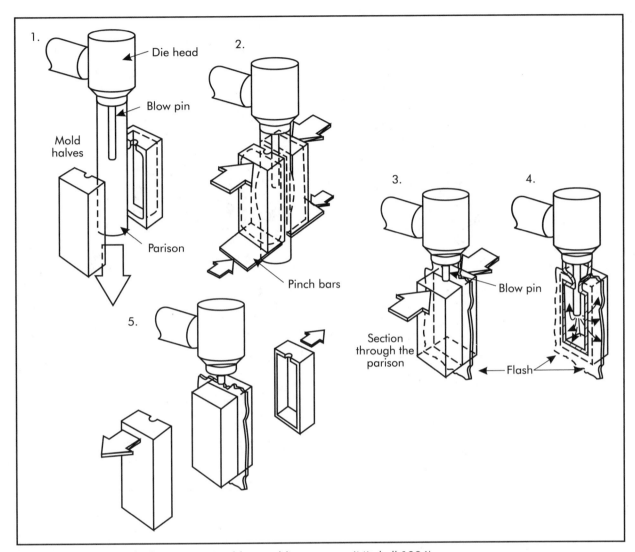

Figure 28-2. Steps in the basic extrusion blow-molding process (Mitchell 1996).

Because plastics vary in density, a standard is required to measure shot size. The accepted standard for shot size is for the material polystyrene. Consequently, a 12 oz (340 g) machine can prepare 12 oz (340 g) of polystyrene, but cannot deliver 12 oz (340 g) of polypropylene, because the polypropylene is considerably less dense than the polystyrene.

Clamp tonnage is the amount of force the machine can generate to squeeze a mold together. Small machines are 100 tons (889 kN) or less. Medium-sized machines are 100–2,000 tons (889 kN–18 MN). Large clamp tonnage is 2,000 tons (18 MN) and up. Clamp size determines the size of parts that can be manufactured. Many easily molded plastics require about 2.5 tons (22 kN) of clamp force per square inch of projected part area. To mold a flat plaque 8 × 10 in. (203 × 254 mm), a 200-ton (1.8 MN) clamp would be required. Plastics such as

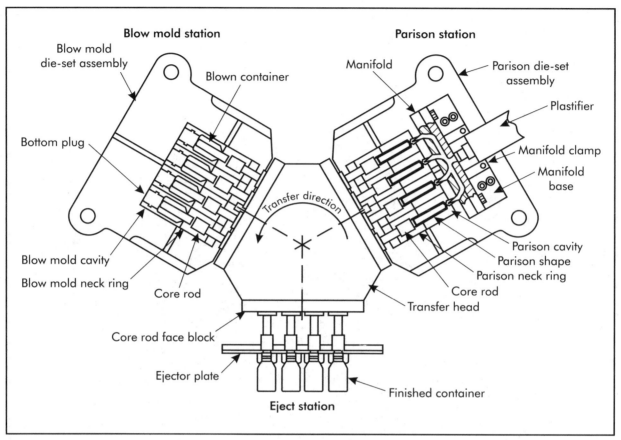

Figure 28-3. Three-station injection blow-molding (Mitchell 1996).

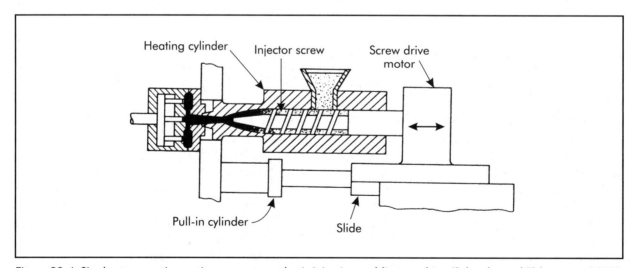

Figure 28-4. Single-stage, reciprocating-screw-type plastic injection molding machine (Schrader and Elshennawy 2000).

polycarbonate and nylon require much greater tonnage to mold. If the clamp force is not great enough, the mold will open slightly when the plastic is injected, creating *flash* around the parting line.

The temperature of the melted plastics and the temperature of the mold are critical process parameters in injection molding. Material manufacturing companies recommend melt and mold temperatures for their materials.

REACTION INJECTION MOLDING

Reaction injection molding (RIM) is a form of injection molding that brings temperature and ratio-controlled, liquid reactant streams together under high-pressure impingement mixing to form a polymer directly in the mold. Two liquid reactants (monomers) are mixed together as they enter the mold. A chemical reaction produces the plastic as it forms the part.

When compared to other molding systems, RIM offers more design flexibility, lower energy requirements, lower pressures, lower tooling costs, and lower capital investment. Significant advantages in design and production are gained from the RIM fabricating capability for incorporating a load-bearing, structural skin and a lightweight, rigid, cellular core into a part in one processing operation.

28.4 THERMOFORMING PLASTIC SHEET AND FILM

Thermoforming consists of heating a thermoplastic sheet to its processing temperature and forcing the hot, flexible material against the contours of a mold. This pliable material is rapidly moved either mechanically with tools, plugs, matched molds etc., or pneumatically with differentials in pressure created by a vacuum or by compressed air.

The most simple and common thermoforming process is *vacuum forming*. This process involves a mold that can be connected to a vacuum tank. When the heated plastic sheet contacts the mold and creates a seal, the vacuum is applied to the mold. The atmospheric pressure above the sheet forces it into the mold, where the sheet rapidly cools.

Thermoforming has several advantages:

- low costs for machinery and tooling because of low processing pressures;
- low internal stresses and good physical properties in finished parts;
- capability of being predecorated, laminated, or coextruded to obtain different finishes, properties, etc.;
- capability of forming light, thin, and strong parts for packaging and other uses; and
- capability of making large, one-piece parts with relatively inexpensive machinery and tooling.

The main disadvantages are:

- higher cost of using sheet or film instead of plastic pellets; and
- necessity of trimming the finished part.

The greatest problem in thermoforming is controlling the thinning of the sheet. The greater the draw into or over a mold, the thinner the sheet becomes. Corners are particularly susceptible to thinning. Numerous techniques are used to reduce or control this thinning. Some of them are: plug-assist forming, pressure bubble forming, and snap-back forming. All of these techniques stretch the sheet as evenly as possible. Figure 28-5 shows vacuum forming into a female mold with a plug assist.

Most thermoplastic materials are appropriate for thermoforming. However, amorphous materials are easier to control than the semicrystalline materials. This means polystyrene is more convenient to thermoform than polyethylene.

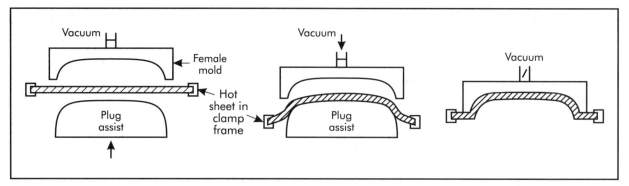

Figure 28-5. Plug-assist vacuum forming (Mitchell 1996).

28.5 ROTATIONAL MOLDING

Rotational molding is a process for forming hollow plastics parts. The process uses the principle that finely divided plastic material becomes molten in contact with a hot metal surface and then takes the shape of that surface. When the polymer is cooled while in contact with the metal, a reproduction of the mold's interior surface is produced.

Rotational molding uses an oven to heat the mold enough to melt the plastic powder. Cooling stations generally use blowers or water spray to reduce the cooling time. Since low pressures are generated inside the mold, rotational molds can be made of thin metals, often aluminum. The mold-making process for rotational molds is much less expensive than for injection molds, which have to withstand tremendous pressures. Figure 28-6 shows the configuration of a turret-type rotational molding machine.

28.6 CASTING

Casting processes are applicable to some thermoplastics and thermosets. These materials can be cast at atmospheric pressure while using inexpensive molds to form large parts with section thicknesses that would be impractical by other manufacturing processes. Casting resins are molded on a production basis in lead, plaster, rubber, and glass molds.

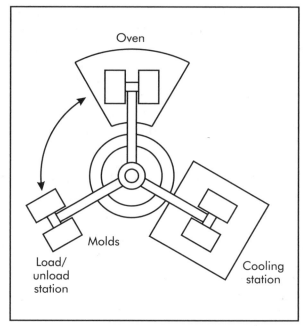

Figure 28-6. Turret-type rotational molding machine (Mitchell 1996).

One of the common plastics materials in wide-scale use is transparent acrylic sheet. The thick acrylic plates used for security in banks are cast. These sheets are called *cell cast*, because they are manufactured by pouring liquid plastic resin into a mold made with thick glass plates. After the polymerization is complete, the mold is removed and the edges of the thick acrylic are cut and polished. The high cost of these forms of plastics indicate the long times required to complete the process.

28.7 COMPRESSION AND TRANSFER MOLDING

In compression molding, *thermoset* molding compounds placed in a mold (generally hardened steel) are first heated to plasticize and cure the material, then placed under pressure to form the desired shape. The mold is held closed under pressure for a sufficiently long period to polymerize or cure the material into a hard mass. Compression molds are available in flash-type molds, semi-positive molds, and positive molds. The differences have to do with the provisions for letting excess material escape from the mold. Figure 28-7 shows a flash-type compression mold. When the mold closes, excess

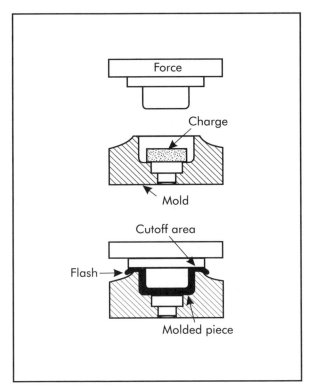

Figure 28-7. Flash-type compression mold (Schrader and Elshennawy 2000).

material (flash) is forced out around the sides of the parts.

Phenolic, urea, melamine, melamine-phenolic, diallyl phthalate, alkyd, polyester, epoxy, and the silicones are thermoset materials capable of being compression molded. Thermosetting molding compounds processed from the individual heat-reactive resin systems are available in a wide range of formulations to satisfy specific end-use requirements. Depending upon the type of material, products may be supplied in granular, nodular, flaked, diced, or pelletized form. Polyester materials are supplied in granular, bulk, log, rope, or sheet form, and polyurethanes are made in many forms, ranging from flexible and rigid foams to rigid solids and abrasion-resistant coatings.

Transfer molding is an extension of compression molding. In transfer molding, unpolymerized material is placed in a transfer pot and melted. A plunger forces the molten plastic into a die cavity as shown in Figure 28-8. Temperature and pressure are maintained until the resin has cured. This process produces thin-walled, intricate shapes similar to injection molding. Resins also can be reinforced to improve electrical and mechanical properties (Schrader and Elshennawy 2000).

REVIEW QUESTIONS

28.1) How are extruders sized?

28.2) What are the two major categories of blow molding?

28.3) Before it is inflated, what is the starting blank for blow molding called?

28.4) What plastics material is the standard for the measurement of the shot size of injection molding machines?

28.5) What defect is caused by insufficient clamping force in injection molding?

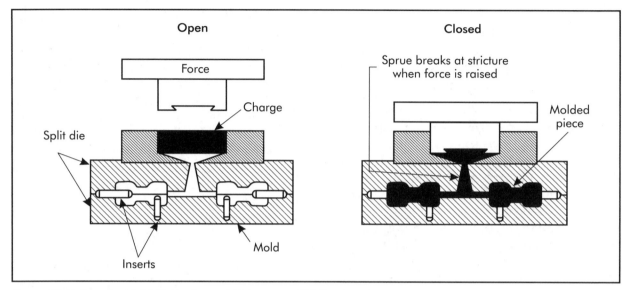

Figure 28-8. Transfer Mold (Schrader and Elshennawy 2000).

28.6) What is the purpose of a plug assist in thermoforming?

REFERENCES

Mitchell, Philip, ed. 1996. *Tool and Manufacturing Engineers Handbook*, Fourth Edition. *Volume 8: Plastic Part Manufacturing.* Dearborn, MI: Society of Manufacturing Engineers.

Schrader, George F. and Ahmad K. Elshennawy, 2000. *Manufacturing Processes & Materials*, Fourth Edition. Dearborn, MI: Society of Manufacturing Engineers.

Chapter 29

Composite Processes

Composite fabrication has many processes. Some of the most important of these processes are hand and automated tape lay-up, resin injection, compression molding, pultrusion, and filament winding. The most commonly used processes can be divided into two categories: high- and low-volume.

The low-volume processes are manual and low-pressure spray lay-up in low-cost molds with a high labor cost. High-volume processes, such as lamination, filament winding, pultrusion, and resin transfer molding (RTM), have an initial high cost for tooling and equipment but the labor intensity is low. Some processes can fit in both the low-volume and high-volume categories. For example, lamination may be a hand lay-up process or it may be automated using sheet-molding compounds.

Lamination, filament winding, pultrusion, and resin transfer molding are particularly important in the production of continuous-fiber composites with closely controlled properties. The shape, size, and type of the part and the quantity to be manufactured determine construction techniques. The lamination method is used for comparatively flat pieces. Filament winding is a powerful and potentially high-speed process for making tubes and other cylindrical structures. Pultrusion can be used for parts with constant cross-sectional shapes. Resin transfer molding shares some similarities with injection molding.

29.1 LAMINATING

Advanced composites are typically used as *laminates*. They are processed by starting with a prepreg material (partially cured composite with the fibers aligned parallel to each other). A pattern of the product's shape is cut out, and the prepreg material is then stacked in layers into the desired laminate geometry.

A final product is obtained by curing the stacked plies under pressure and heat in an autoclave. Graphite-epoxy composites are cured at approximately 350° F (177° C) at a pressure of 100 psi (690 kPa). The new high-temperature composites, such as bismaleimides, are cured at 600° F (316° C). The tooling is essentially a mold that follows a part through the lay-up and autoclaving processes. Tooling materials commonly used for manufacturing composite parts include aluminum, steel, electroplated nickel, a high-temperature epoxy-resin system casting, and fabricated graphite composite tools (Mitchell 1996).

29.2 FILAMENT WINDING

In the *filament-winding* process, *roving* (a form of glass fibers made of filaments or strands gathered together to form a bundle) or tape is drawn through a resin bath and wound onto a rotating mandrel. Filament winding is a relatively slow process, but the fiber direction can be controlled and the diameter can be varied along the length of the piece. In some versions of the process, the fiber bundle, which may be made up of several thousand carbon fibers, is first coated with the matrix material to make a prepreg tape. The tape width may vary from an inch to a yard (several centimeters to a meter). With both the fiber and tape-winding processes, the finished part is cured in an autoclave and later removed from the mandrel. Figure 29-1 shows the filament-winding process (Mitchell 1996).

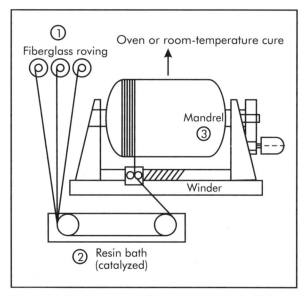

Figure 29-1. Filament winding process (Mitchell 1996).

For strength-critical aerospace structures, carbon fibers are usually wound with epoxy-based resin systems. The polyesters, phenolics, and bismaleimides are limited to special applications. Filament winding is used to produce round or cylindrical objects such as pressure bottles, missile canisters, and industrial storage tanks.

29.3 PULTRUSION

In composites technology, pultrusion is the equivalent of metals extrusion. *Pultrusion* (also called *pultruding*) consists of transporting continuous fiber bundles through a resin matrix bath and then pulling them through a heated die. Figure 29-2 illustrates the basic components of a pultrusion machine. The pultrusion process combines longitudinal reinforcements (roving doffs in the figure) and transverse reinforcements (mat creels). Roving resembles a glass rope, while mat resembles a glass sheet. The reinforcements are pulled through a guide plate that helps to locate the reinforcing materials correctly in the final pultruded part. The aligned materials are then passed through a resin impregnation chamber, which contains the polymer solution. The polymer solution impregnating the reinforcements acts as a glue connecting the various components of the reinforcement. Surfacing material is generally added to pultruded structural shapes after the impregnation step. The curing of the product (changing from a wet, saturated reinforcement to a solid part) occurs in the heated curing die. After exiting the die, the part passes through a cut-off system. Unlike extrusion, which pushes the part from the entrance end of the die, pultrusion pulls the part from the exit end of the die.

The process can be used to make complex shapes, however, it typically is limited to items of constant cross section such as tubing, channels, I-beams, Z-sections, and flat bars (Mitchell 1996).

29.4 RESIN TRANSFER MOLDING

Filling a niche between hand manufacturing lay-up or spray-up of parts and compression molding in matched metal molds is *resin transfer molding* (RTM).

In the conventional RTM process, two-piece matched-cavity molds are used with one or multiple injection points and breather holes. The reinforcing material, either chopped or continuous strand mat, is cut to shape (preform) and draped in the mold cav-

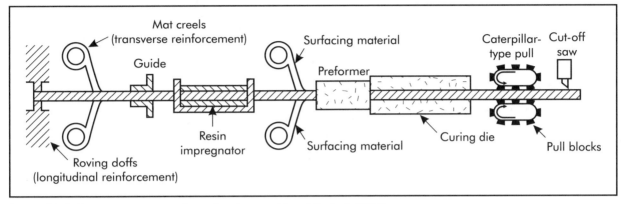

Figure 29-2. Basic components of a pultrusion machine (Mitchell 1996).

ity. The mold halves are clamped together, and a polyester resin is pumped through an injection port in the mold.

Compared with the spray-up method, RTM permits faster cycle times and usually requires less labor. The RTM cycle times are longer than for compression molding, but the low cost of RTM tooling often compensates for the differential when the production run is low enough (Mitchell 1996).

REVIEW QUESTIONS

29.1) In the laminating of composites, what is a prepreg?

29.2) Which composite manufacturing process discussed resembles plastic injection molding?

29.3) Which composite manufacturing process discussed resembles metal extrusion?

29.4) What is the term for a series of glass fibers gathered to form a bundle?

REFERENCE

Mitchell, Philip, ed. 1996. *Tool and Manufacturing Engineers Handbook*, Fourth Edition. *Volume 8: Plastic Part Manufacturing*. Dearborn, MI: Society of Manufacturing Engineers.

Chapter 30

Ceramic Processes

The processing techniques for ceramics greatly depend on the characteristics of the raw materials. To organize a discussion of techniques, three categories of materials will be used: glasses, clays, and crystalline ceramic powders.

30.1 GLASS PROCESSES

Glass manufacturing begins with molten glass at approximately 2,200° F (1,204° C). Then, a variety of techniques, such as the ones described next, can be used for shaping the viscous mass.

Glass blowing can be done as a craft process to produce unique and artistic works. The same process has been thoroughly mechanized in the manufacture of light bulbs. The viscous blob of glass is inflated with air. The final shape may be determined by a mold or it may be shaped by hand with various fixtures and tools.

Pressing of viscous glass may involve mechanical forces and centrifugal forces. Mechanical shaping usually involves matching molds that press a blob of viscous glass into a desired shape. If the viscous glass is shaped by centrifugal forces, a spinning mold forces the glass to conform to its shape.

Flat sheets of glass may be shaped using water-cooled rollers. One problem associated with rolling glass is that surface imperfections are difficult to eliminate. An extremely smooth glass plate can be manufactured by floating a sheet of viscous glass onto a bath of liquid tin. This type of glass is frequently called *float-glass*.

Glass fibers, such as the fibers found in fiberglass insulation, are produced by forcing the molten glass through tiny openings in a metal die.

Conventional heat-treating processes increase the strength of glass. For example, for tempered glass the surface of the glass is rapidly cooled after it has been formed. After the surface has cooled, the inside cools. As the inside cools, it also contracts, which causes the surface to be compressed, as illustrated in Figure 30-1. The residual surface compression prevents the glass from shattering when nicked. A common example of tempered glass is an automobile windshield.

Glass also can be annealed to remove any unwanted residual stress, which may cause the glass to fail in service. This type of annealing is similar to the stress relieving of metals.

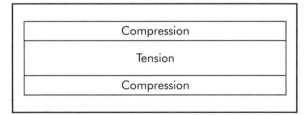

Figure 30-1. Tempered glass cross section.

30.2 CLAY PROCESSES

Manufacturing clay products involves processes such as casting, plastic forming, and dry powder pressing.

CASTING

Casting requires the clay to be prepared as *slip*, which is a suspension of clay in water. In addition to the clay and water, chemicals are added to the slip to keep the clay particles from settling to the bottom of the container. Often these chemicals are deflocculents, which prevent the clay particles from adhering to each other. When properly prepared, the slip will have the consistency of heavy cream and will demonstrate a uniform viscosity.

Slip casting is the pouring or pumping of slip into a porous mold, most commonly made of plaster. The plaster molds rapidly draw the water out of the slip, leaving a uniform layer of clay on the surface of the mold. For large, hollow shapes, the slip is emptied out of the mold once the desired wall thickness has been achieved. When the clay has dried to a leathery consistency, the mold is removed and the product is finished. A common product made by slip casting is a toilet tank.

Slip-cast products that are not hollow require additional slip to keep the mold full as water is being removed from the mold. In metal casting, the additional liquid metal flows into the part from a riser. However, in slip casting, the riser is called a *spare*. Coffee mug handles are typically slip cast using plaster molds with a spare attached.

PLASTIC FORMING

Traditional methods of forming clay in a pliable state include pressing, throwing, jiggering, and extrusion. The pressing method uses hydraulic presses to form clay between two dense plaster molds. These molds contain air lines so that when the mold opens, pressurized air releases the part from the

mold. Considerable force is required since the clay does not flow easily.

Throwing requires the use of a potter's wheel. While some thrown products are hand-thrown, mechanical devices have partially automated this process. *Jiggering* is a process that forms one side of a clay product, such as a plate, with a plaster mold and the other side using a metal template. As the blank of clay rotates on the mold, the profile is formed by the template. The process is illustrated in Figure 30-2.

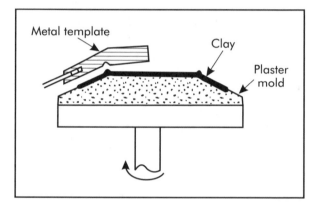

Figure 30-2. Jiggering.

Extrusion is a process used in the manufacture of clay pipe and drainage tiles. It is similar to the extrusion of other materials. An auger or ram forces the clay through a tubing die. The extruded pipe must be handled carefully in the green state to preserve its dimensions. Pipes are usually fired in vertical position to avoid bending during firing.

DRY POWDER PRESSING

Similar to powdered metals, dry powder pressing compacts clay powder with a very low moisture content (4%) between two dies. Dry-powder pressing works very well for the continuous production of dimensionally accurate products. In some cases, dry powder compressing may have a lower cycle time and higher quality than jiggering. Dinner plates are made by dry powder pressing for this reason.

30.3 CRYSTALLINE CERAMIC POWDER PROCESSING

Crystalline ceramics are very hard and brittle and have very high melting points. For these reasons, they can not be formed with plastic or casting techniques. They are compacted as powder into the desired shape. The pressing can be dry pressing with a ram, isostatic pressing, or hot-isostatic pressing. *Isostatic pressing* uses a flexible cover and pressurized hydraulic oil. It has the advantage of pressure compacting the powder in all directions. In contrast, ram pressing tends to compact the powder near the ram more than the powder at some distance from the ram. This leads to non-uniform density in the final product. Automotive spark plugs are an example of parts produced by isostatic pressing.

30.4 DRYING, FIRING, AND FINISHING

After a ceramic part has been formed, it needs to be dried prior to firing. Drying removes enough moisture to prevent the ceramic part from cracking in the firing kiln. The loss of moisture causes the part to shrink and, in some cases, warp if the moisture gradient is too large.

Firing heats the ceramic part to an elevated temperature, which causes the oxide particles in the parts to bond, and reduces the porosity. Firing provides strength and hardness to the final part.

After firing, many finishing operations can be performed. One of the most widely used finishing techniques is called *glazing*. Glazing improves appearance and strength and makes the ceramic part impermeable. The glaze forms a smooth, glassy coating after it is fired.

Decorations such as flowers can be painted on with colored glazing or applied as decals prior to glazing. For example, decorations on coffee mugs are decals underneath the clear glazing. After glazing, the part is fired a second time to harden the glaze.

REVIEW QUESTIONS

30.1) Name two methods for producing glass plate.

30.2) What type of glass contains residual compressive surface stress to prevent it from shattering?

30.3) Slip casting uses a suspension of clay in _____.

30.4) What plastic forming process uses a metal template and a rotating plaster mold?

30.5) What material or process is used to make ceramic parts impermeable?

Chapter 31

Printed Circuit Board Fabrication and Assembly

31.1 PRINTED CIRCUIT BOARD FABRICATION

Creation of a printed circuit board usually begins with a schematic capture of an electrical or electronic design that meets the specifications of the original circuit design. The schematic with the component selection list is then transformed into a circuit layout, usually with the use of a computer-aided design (CAD) program. The board layout includes component placements and conductor pathways or traces.

Printed circuit boards are usually made from copper that is laminated to a fiberglass substrate. Circuit traces are typically produced by selectively etching the copper. Printed circuit boards can be fabricated as a single-sided, double-sided, or multi-layer configuration. Figure 31-1 illustrates a multi-layer board where a semi-cured glass/epoxy substrate joins the copper laminated boards together permanently after being fully cured.

For multi-layer configurations, some of the inner layers serve as power, ground, or electrical isolation planes. Inner layers are connected to the outer layers with the use of plated through holes (PTH) as shown in Figure 31-2.

31.2 THROUGH-HOLE TECHNOLOGY ASSEMBLY

As its name implies, through hole technology assembly indicates that the component

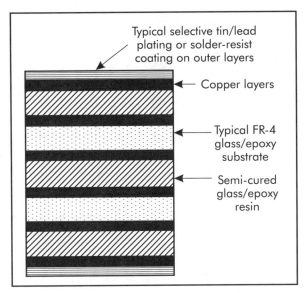

Figure 31-1. Typical six-layer printed circuit board cross section.

leads are placed through holes in the board and soldered on the other side. There are three basic types of components used in through-hole technology (THT) assembly: (a) axial-lead components; (b) radial-lead components; and (c) single (SIP) or dual (DIP) in-line packages. Figure 31-3 illustrates some of the various through-hole components.

The insertion of axial-lead components is also called variable center distance (VCD) insertion. VCD refers to axial-lead components such as resistors, capacitors, and diodes. Axial-lead components require their leads to be bent at right angles prior to insertion. The final distance between the leads

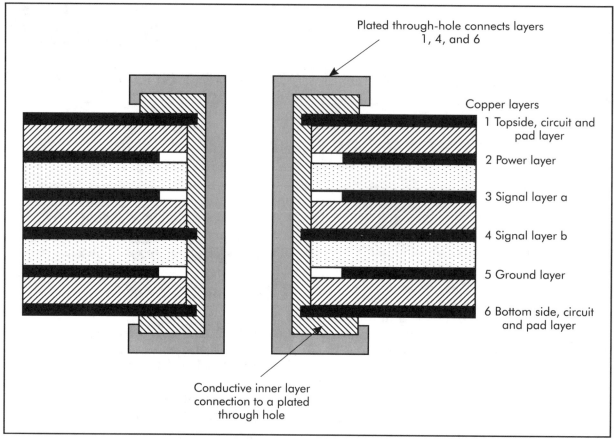

Figure 31-2. Plated through-hole connection also known as a "via."

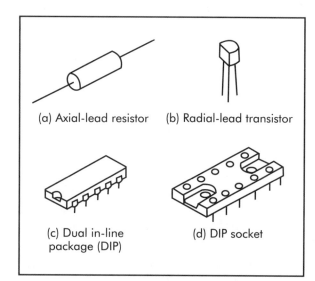

(a) Axial-lead resistor

(b) Radial-lead transistor

(c) Dual in-line package (DIP)

(d) DIP socket

Figure 31-3. Sample through-hole electronic components.

after being bent to 90° is called the *center distance*. The center distance changes depending on the size and type of component. Prior to automatic insertion, a component sequencer automatically places the required components on a tape in the order that they are to be inserted. The automatic axial-lead insertion machine then cuts the component from the tape, forms the leads at 90°, inserts the component into its programmed location, and then cuts and clinches the leads on the opposite side as illustrated in Figure 31-4. Sometimes the automatic component sequencing and insertion steps can be combined on one large machine.

Auto-insertion machines, whether they be for axial-lead or DIP-type components, have

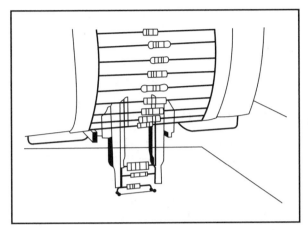

Figure 31-4. Axial-lead components on tape at insertion head (Boothroyd and Dewhurst 1994).

an insertion head that grips the components and supports the component leads while a ram moves in the vertical direction to push down and insert the component. The circuit board is usually mounted on a tooling plate, which can rotate in 90° increments and move in the *x* and *y* directions according to the program. The leads are usually cut and clinched in a continuous action at the time of component insertion.

The insertion method for radial-lead components is similar to the method for axial-lead components, except for the head that grips the component. The same is true for single in-line package (SIP) as compared to dual in-line package (DIP) insertion.

After component insertions are completed, the component leads are soldered to the underside of the board using a process called *wave soldering*. The circuit board assembly is placed on a conveyor using spring-tension fingers or a pallet to hold the circuit assembly. Prior to wave soldering, the underside of the board is coated with flux to help remove oxides and improve the wetting of the solder to ensure the quality of the solder connection. The boards then continue along the conveyor through pre-heaters and finally over a cascading fountain of molten solder.

After taking the assembly from the conveyor or pallet, some solder removal may be necessary to eliminate solder bridges or icicles, which can cause circuit shorts. This may be done by using a hand-held soldering iron. The assemblies are then cleaned and dried to remove any flux residue.

31.3 SURFACE MOUNT TECHNOLOGY ASSEMBLY

Surface mount devices (SMDs), illustrated in Figure 31-5, have leads or pads that are mounted directly to the board surface. In surface mount technology (SMT) assembly, holes are not required for securing the component. The surface area of both sides provides increased density for component population as compared to that for through-hole technology (THT). Prior to placing the components, the surface mount component pads on the board are coated with solder paste using a stencil printing operation. The SMDs are positioned on the board usually by a pick-and-place component placement machine. The surface tension of the solder paste temporarily secures the component. After all of the

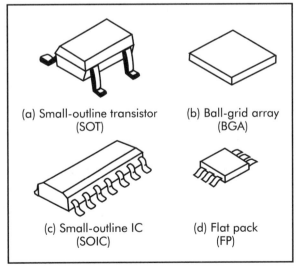

(a) Small-outline transistor (SOT) (b) Ball-grid array (BGA)

(c) Small-outline IC (SOIC) (d) Flat pack (FP)

Figure 31-5. Sample surface mount devices (Boothroyd and Dewhurst 1994).

SMD components are placed for one side, they are soldered using a process called *reflow soldering*. Reflow soldering requires heating the surface and the components until the solder paste flows and wets into a consistent solder fillet between the SMD leg and the circuit pad of the board. This produces a permanent mechanical and electrical connection of the SMD component to the printed circuit board.

For increased density of component population, both sides of the board may be used for SMD components. The second side is completed similarly to the first for those assemblies that do not have THT components. For those hybrid assemblies that require THT in addition to SMT, the bottom or circuit side may have the components glued on the board. This is accomplished by stenciling glue dots on the board between the circuit pads, placing the components, and then curing the glue side in a reflow process. Finally, the THT components are placed and the assembly is wave soldered. The glue secures the bottom-side components during the wave operation. At this time, the SMD as well as the THT components are soldered. After wave soldering, it may be necessary to perform some solder removal to remove solder bridges or icicles, which can cause circuit shorts. This may be done using a hand-held soldering iron. The assemblies are then cleaned and dried to remove any flux residue.

REVIEW QUESTIONS

31.1) Which type of printed circuit board contains circuit pathways on both sides of the board?

31.2) What is the insertion of axial-lead components referred to as?

31.3) What type of wave soldering defects cause short circuits?

31.4) What soldering process is used with surface mount devices?

31.5) What process is used to apply the solder paste to the circuit board when surface mount assembly is used?

REFERENCE

Boothroyd, Geoffrey and Peter Dewhurst. 1983. *Product Design for Assembly*. Amherst, MA: Department of Mechanical Engineering, University of Massachusetts.

Chapter 32

Traditional Production Planning and Control

Manufacturing companies gain a competitive advantage whenever they satisfy customers by producing products reliably, swiftly, and economically. In turn, this requires highly effective planning and scheduling processes to synchronize the availability of resources, material, labor, equipment, tooling, engineering specifications, space, and money. Misaligning any one resource creates a serious problem. While the other expensive resources wait, costly expediting chases the shortages.

This chapter discusses production environments, forecasting, aggregate planning, master scheduling, requirements and capacity planning, scheduling and production control, material planning, and manufacturing resource planning (MRP).

32.1 PRODUCTION ENVIRONMENTS

There are four basic production environments to choose from: (1) manufacture-to-stock; (2) assemble-to-order; (3) manufacture-to-order; and (4) engineer-to-order. Choosing one of these environments is a fundamental strategic decision and is heavily influenced by competitive pressures (Mitchell 1998).

MANUFACTURE-TO-STOCK

Manufacture-to-stock, also known as *make-to-stock*, is a production environment where products can be, and usually are, finished before receipt of a customer order. Customer orders are typically filled from existing stock and production orders are used to replenish stock. Examples of manufacture-to-stock products are consumer goods such as televisions, power hand tools, lunch boxes, and thousands of other off-the-shelf items. Since the manufacturer must quickly ship these products in response to customer orders, the products must be manufactured ahead of need and in quantities based on forecasted demand.

ASSEMBLE-TO-ORDER

Assemble-to-order is an environment where a product can be assembled after receipt of a customer's order. The key components used in the assembly or finishing process are planned, and possibly stocked, in anticipation of a customer order. Receipt of an order initiates assembly of the customized product. This strategy is useful where a large number of end products can be assembled from common components. Examples of assemble-to-order products are automobiles, office furniture, retail display units, and any product where color, fabric, or similar choices can be incorporated late in the manufacturing process. Like manufacture-to-stock environments, assemble-to-order environments plan production and inventory on the basis of a forecast. However, where the manufacture-to-stock environment forecasts the demand for completed end items, the assemble-to-order environment forecasts the demand for key components that typically have a large reserve production capacity to accommodate widely varying tasks and work load levels.

MANUFACTURE-TO-ORDER

Manufacture-to-order, also known as *make-to-order*, is a production environment where a product can be made after receipt of a customer's order. As a rule, this environment relies heavily on standard components and often on simple, custom variations of similar parts. Industrial punch presses, vehicle chassis, and standard conveyor systems are typically made-to-order.

Forecasts may be used to plan for raw materials with long lead times and the capacity that will be needed. Detailed material planning and production are performed after receiving an order. This results in longer customer lead times than in manufacture-to-stock or assemble-to-order environments.

ENGINEER-TO-ORDER

An *engineer-to-order* environment is one with products whose customer specifications require unique engineering design or significant customization. Each customer order results in a unique set of part numbers, bills of material, and routings. Examples include products such as custom-designed capital equipment, stamping dies, and space vehicles.

Forecasts, if done at all, are used only to plan capacity and predict raw material usage. Product and process engineering are completed after receipt of a customer order, as are detailed planning and manufacturing. Some engineering may be completed prior to receiving the order for developing cost and delivery estimates, or to ensure form, fit, and function.

32.2 FORECASTING

The production and inventory planning process begins with forecasting. All techniques of production and inventory control require some calculation of quantities, which represent future demand. The specific needs of each application are determined by the lead times inherent in the manufacturing processes being supported. Short lead-time processes, including material procurement, may be well supported utilizing current open orders and only a few weeks' history of estimated demand. Very long process requirements (12 months or longer) are most likely supported by a contractual order process.

The basis of all forecasts may be described as an extrapolation of a demand pattern over some future period. The final forecast developed will often be the result of a combination of methods; the most likely is one based on statistical interpretation of intrinsic data modified by expert opinion.

There are several general principles regarding forecasts, regardless of their origin. It is important that both marketing and manufacturing staffs understand the importance of these principles and the impact they should have on routine decision processes. Four key concepts and principles describing forecasts are as follows:

1. Accuracy of the forecast is indirectly proportional to the length of time in the forecasted period; the shorter the forecast period, the more accurate the forecast.
2. Accuracy of the forecast is directly proportional to the number of items in the forecast group. The total company forecast can be expected to be more accurate than the corresponding forecast for a given product line, which, in turn, will be more accurate than the corresponding forecast for a single part number in that product line.
3. Forecast error is always present and should be estimated and measured on all forecasts.
4. No single forecast method is best; alternate methods should be tested periodi-

cally to determine if another method would result in a smaller forecast error.

32.3 AGGREGATE PLANNING

Companies typically plan at three levels: (1) long term; (2) intermediate term; and (3) short term. Long-term planning determines what products to manufacture, facility location and size, etc. Long-term decisions influence intermediate planning or aggregate planning. Aggregate planning impacts employment, inventory, output, immediate-term planning, and short-term planning.

The purpose of aggregate planning, also known as production, sales, and inventory (PSI) planning, is to provide an overall framework for reconciling the demands of the marketplace through forecasting based on the capabilities of the manufacturing place. The senior management team is responsible for producing two aggregate plans: the business plan, and the sales and operations plan. Together, these plans provide the direction and limitations for the operators of the detailed processes.

All manufacturing companies have a business plan projecting at least a year into the future. In monetary terms, it projects what is expected to happen, specifying gross revenues, profits, and cash flows. From the approved business plan, budgets are developed for the individual departments. Generally, the business plan remains fixed for the fiscal year because it is used as a benchmark for judging performance.

The sales and operations plan has many important differences from the business plan. The planning horizon normally extends beyond the fiscal year to provide guidance for activities requiring long lead times, such as acquisition of capital equipment, negotiations with suppliers, and finding new channels of distribution. Broad categories or "families" of products are reviewed in the planning process (Mitchell 1998).

32.4 MASTER SCHEDULING

With the completion of the aggregate plan, top-level management authorizes the production-planning department to develop a master production schedule (MPS). The MPS translates the aggregate plan into a separate plan for individual items and operates at a part-number level. The schedule provides weekly requirements over a 6–12-month period. Figure 32-1 shows an example of a master production schedule. The MPS is an input into a material requirements planning (MRP) system.

32.5 REQUIREMENTS AND CAPACITY PLANNING

After the master production schedule has been formulated, rough-cut capacity planning (requirement planning) is done to determine its feasibility and where bottlenecks will occur. Limitations in machine capacity, labor capacity, and supplier capacity may require changes in the master production schedule.

A much more detailed capacity plan can be generated using capacity requirements planning (CRP). CRP differs from rough-cut capacity planning because it uses time-phased information from the MRP system. CRP considers work-in-process when calculating work center capacities. CRP also includes the demand not accounted for in the MPS, such as replacement parts.

The process of production planning involves tradeoffs between changes in production and inventory investment. Production plans must consider the economics and feasibility of the alternatives as they relate to inventory investment, storage capacity, purchased component availability, personnel availability, and machine capacity. The longer the total manufacturing process time and corresponding lead time, the more complex the problem. Production scheduling alternatives are always limited to some

Part number	Periods . . . 1	2	3	4	5	6	7	8	9	10	11	12	13
A1	35	40	45	55	45	35	30	25	30	30	30	30	30
A2	50	45	35	30	35	45	45	50	50	50	50	50	50
Totals	85	85	80	85	80	80	75	75	80	80	80	80	80
	| Released || . . . . Firm . . . . || . . . . Planned . . . . |												

Figure 32-1. *Example of master production schedule. (Courtesy K.W. Tunnell Company, Inc.)*

degree by the lead times required to obtain parts and materials from suppliers. In some cases, the final restriction comes from the possibility of exceeding the capacity of a key material supplier.

32.6 SCHEDULING AND PRODUCTION CONTROL

Based on the master production schedule, the production scheduler and the production and inventory control department establish the "right" sequence of jobs to be run in the shop. The requirements of a good priority system should:

- specify the jobs to be done first, second, third, and so on;
- allow for quick updating of the main concerns as priorities and actual conditions quickly change, and
- be objective. If jobs are overstated, an "informal" system determines which jobs are really needed.

Some of the commonly used priority schemes are: first in/first out, start date, due date, and critical ratio. Other priority schemes commonly used, such as slack time ratio and queue ratio, are not discussed here (Veilleux and Petro 1988).

FIRST-IN/FIRST-OUT PRIORITY

The *first-in/first-out* (FIFO) method is the simplest priority rule. It assumes that the first

shop order to enter a work center is the first shop order to be worked on. A *work center* is defined as a group of operators with similar skills or equipment with similar capabilities. The major advantage of this rule is that it does not require a computer or other sophisticated system to determine priorities. The major disadvantage is that it assumes that all jobs have the same relative priority. It normally does not allow for the redistribution of priorities, nor does it permit an order that was released late to be moved ahead of other orders in the schedule.

START DATE PRIORITY

The *start date* priority rule is really a subset of the FIFO rule because the shop order with the earliest start date is the first job to be worked on. This scheme assumes that all shop orders are released on time. The start date can be calculated from a backward rather than a forward scheduling technique.

DUE DATE PRIORITY

The *due date* is the time period when the material is needed to be available. The due-date priority rule is a very popular priority technique used in manufacturing industry, particularly with the use of MRP-type systems. When properly used and kept up-to-date, the due-date rule can be very effective. If the master schedule is kept up-to-date with actual conditions from the shop floor, the due-date technique is a simple tool to determine shop priorities for planning and scheduling.

CRITICAL RATIO

The *critical ratio* priority considers the total standard lead time remaining to complete the job relative to the total time remaining to the due date of the order. The critical ratio can be found by:

$$C_r = \frac{D_d - T_d}{L_t} \qquad (32\text{-}1)$$

where:

C_r = critical ratio
D_d = due date
T_d = today's date
L_t = lead time remaining

Lead time is defined as the sum of the processing time, setup time, move time, and queue time. Any order with a critical ratio of less than 1.0 is behind schedule, while an order with a critical ratio of more than 1.0 is ahead of schedule. An order with a critical ratio of 1.0 is right on schedule. Using this technique, shop orders with the lowest ratio have the highest priority. Conversely, the orders with the higher ratios have the lowest priority.

Based on the prioritized schedule, work is authorized and the shop floor receives a shop order. Production and control of each shop order is tracked by collecting and analyzing the data from the work centers through which each shop order must pass. The goal is to identify any production problems as soon as possible, so that action can be taken to correct the problem and get production back on schedule.

32.7 MATERIAL PLANNING

There are two general types of material planning, rate-based planning and time-phased planning. *Rate-based material planning* is generally limited to a small range of products that are not revised very often and are produced in high volumes. Rate-based planning decreases overhead and work-in-process costs. However, it decreases capacity utilization. Examples of rate-based systems are assembly lines and just-in-time (JIT) systems.

Time-phased planning, usually thought of as "batch" manufacturing, results in higher capacity utilization. However, it generates high overhead and work-in-process costs. Time-phased planning is typically used for many products that are produced in low volumes. MRP is an example of a time-phased planning system.

The purpose of material planning is to answer these questions:

• What do we need?
• How much do we need?
• When do we need it?

There are two approaches for determining these answers. One is quantity based and the techniques used are reorder points and the two-bin system. The other is time based and uses material requirements planning (MRP).

Reorder points are determined by calculating the average demand during the replenishment lead time, plus safety stock. The resulting figure is compared against available daily inventory, which is the sum of stock-on-hand plus existing schedules. Whenever the reorder point is equal to or greater than the available inventory, a message to replenish is generated. *Safety stock* is used as protection against two types of uncertainties: forecast inaccuracy (representing uncertainty of demand) and unreliable completion of schedules (representing uncertainty of supply). Users should always put greater emphasis on correcting the causes of these uncertainties, rather than accepting the extra costs of safety stocks.

Although the two-bin system and reorder points operate similarly, the *two-bin system* does not require daily inventory transactions to be recorded. Rather, it separates inventory into two locations, and whenever one becomes empty, it triggers a reorder for more material. The second bin must contain adequate inventory to satisfy the average demand during the replenishment lead time, plus safety stock.

MRP is a set of procedures, decision rules, and policies that govern many of the routine decisions required in setting the manufacturing schedule. As such, it provides a highly disciplined approach for arranging lower-level factory schedules. Its exception-action orientation is not a clerical system in nature, although when out of control, an MRP system can become a tremendous clerical burden. One critical aspect of the definition is that it is a highly disciplined management process. MRP depends on shop events happening just as they were simulated by the computer. The simulation is based on the plans entered in the master production schedule (MPS) and the policies and operations data loaded in its databases.

Given the rules and procedures implemented for a given company, MRP determines the time and quantity for order releases and part-manufacture requirements in support of the finished product schedules. MRP is not for controlling finished goods. MRP systems are driven by a master schedule to show the top-level demands that will be supported by MRP's subsequent arithmetic calculations.

Initially, demands are converted into time-period requirements for lower-level subassemblies and components. Demands are netted against available orders and committed replenishments (both shop orders and purchase orders) to calculate the actions required to support the master schedule. Two types of messages with associated quantity calculations result: (1) new order require-

ments and (2) changes required to existing orders. Order change messages may indicate either data change needs only, quantity change requirements, or both.

The basis for improving operations through an MRP system requires that the functions related to scheduling be integrated and that it be driven by a valid master production schedule (MPS). Those who operate and manage the variables of the MRP system also must be qualified. This means they are educated and trained in not only the techniques of a given system, but also in the principles they are dealing with.

Procedures and controls for data accuracy are primarily operating discipline issues. The single largest failing in most MRP systems is the lack of discipline in the day-to-day activities that maintain data integrity within the system. A system attempting to emulate the total production environment within the computer depends on accurate information about the elements shown in Figure 32-2.

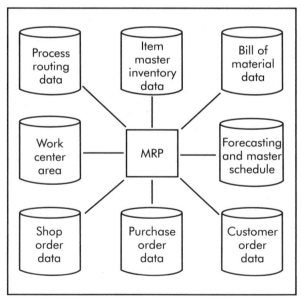

Figure 32-2. Elements in an MRP database. (Courtesy K.W. Tunnel Company, Inc.)

MRP does not, in and of itself, reduce inventory or cause a reduction in inventory, nor can it improve customer service or productivity or reduce costs. However, as a tool, it can provide the means for management to gain those benefits.

MRP is sometimes considered to be a "push" system. A "push" system means that individual work centers can "push" material to a downstream work center regardless of its status (that is, off-line, operation below capacity, etc.) (Mitchell 1998).

32.8 MANUFACTURING RESOURCE PLANNING

For many manufacturing companies it is mandatory to do aggregate planning, master scheduling, material planning, capacity planning, shop scheduling, and supplier scheduling. One approach to integrate these activities is shown in Figure 32-3. This operating system is called manufacturing resource planning (MRPII). It is an accepted approach for planning and scheduling all of the resources that manufacturing companies need.

A key feature of MRPII is that, given accurate data, it plans in matched sets of resources. Only when labor, material, equipment, tooling, specifications, space, and money are available at the right place and time can a company quickly and economically convert raw materials to products and deliver them in a competitive manner. Missing any resource stops the flow. Until the missing resource is provided, having all of the others waiting adds unnecessary costs.

The arrows in the MRPII schematic in Figure 32-3 point in both directions. Unfortunately, some companies use it only in the top-down direction, communicating plans from the front office down to the factory floor. Unavoidable problems will cause some schedules to be unattainable. If the users cannot possibly execute the plans, they must come up with the best possible alternative and advise other users of the situation. Without an equally strong upward flow of information, valid plans cannot be maintained. For example, if a supplier cannot deliver on time, purchasing must swing into "damage control":

- Can the supplier deliver a partial shipment on time?
- Should overtime and premium transportation be authorized?
- Is there an alternative supplier who can help?, etc.

If no practical alternative can be found, then the factory schedulers must react:

- Is there any safety stock that can be used?
- Can lead times be compressed?
- Are there any interchangeable parts that could be used?, etc. (Mitchell 1998).

REVIEW QUESTIONS

32.1) Which type of production environment manufactures products in anticipation of customer orders?

32.2) Will the forecast for a longer period of time be more accurate than the forecast for a shorter period of time?

32.3) The master production schedule converts the _____ plan into a separate plan for individual parts.

32.4) Which scheduling method or priority assumes the first job to enter a work center is the first shop order to be worked on?

32.5) Is MRP time-phased planning or rate-based planning?

32.6) What does MRP II stand for?

REFERENCES

Mitchell, Philip, ed. 1998. *Tool and Manufacturing Engineers Handbook*, Fourth Edition. *Volume 9: Material and Part Handling*

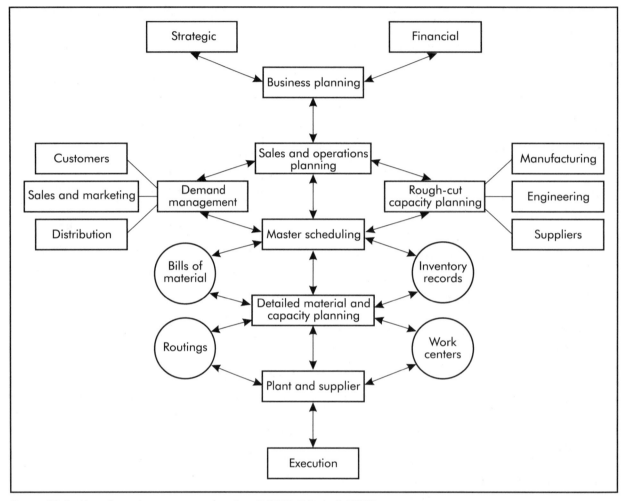

Figure 32-3. Manufacturing resource planning (MRPII) (Mitchell 1998).

in Manufacturing. Dearborn, MI: Society of Manufacturing Engineers.

Veilleux, Raymond F. and Louis W. Petro, eds. 1988. *Tool and Manufacturing Engineers Handbook*, Fourth Edition. *Volume 5: Manufacturing Management*. Dearborn, MI: Society of Manufacturing Engineers.

Chapter 33

Lean Production

33.1 MASS PRODUCTION

The making of goods by one-of-a-kind craft production has a long history. In contrast, the volume production of goods has a much shorter history.

The Industrial Revolution in England during the mid-1750s produced high volumes of textiles and metal goods, but without interchangeable parts. The American, Eli Whitney, made musket locks with interchangeable parts for the War of 1812, but each part had to be manually filed to shape by skilled craftsmen.

Volume production, which did not realize economies of scale, is not true mass production. *Mass production* is a system in which the more goods are produced, the lower the cost of the good or true economies of scale. Mass production uses semi-skilled workers to make and assemble product while skilled workers set up machines and maintain them. True mass production does not rely on "fitters" who shape and fit individual parts. Rather, mass production is dependent on statistically capable manufacturing processes, which yield parts that are mostly within tolerance.

The first widely known mass-production system was functioning by about 1910 to produce automobile magnetos at Ford Motor Company in Detroit. By 1914, Ford was mass producing the entire Model T on the now famous moving assembly line. This transition from volume (but fitter-dependent) production to true mass production by Ford reduced direct labor by 88% and revolutionized manufacturing. Economies of scale were soon realized and consumers enjoyed successive reductions in price while Ford workers soon earned the fabulous sum of five dollars a day.

However revolutionary, Ford's mass-production system carried the seeds of its own destruction. The changeover from the Model T to another vehicle was not contemplated in the creation of the system. When consumers demanded improved features (like windows that rolled up and down), Ford's system was slow to respond.

By the 1920s, Alfred Sloan at General Motors supported the creation of a mass-production system that could accommodate frequent product changes and even annual model changeovers. Sloan realized that there were many kinds of customers and a single, unchanging product could not meet all of their needs. Modern mass production is a combination of Ford's realization of economies of scale by eliminating fitters and Sloan's customer focus. Thus defined, mass production made the United States the undisputed global manufacturing leader from World War I until the mid-1970s.

33.2 TOYOTA PRODUCTION SYSTEM

Ford's assembly line first challenged, then replaced the craft-built automobile industry. Since the 1980s, the Toyota production system (TPS), or lean production, has been widely acknowledged as a revolutionary challenger to conventional mass production. By the mid-1980s, this threat to U.S. preeminence in manufacturing gave rise to a major research effort at the Massachusetts Institute of Technology (MIT): the International Motor Vehicle Project (IMVP). The term "lean production" was coined to describe the Toyota production system (Womack 1990).

According to IMVP, *lean* (as opposed to mass) production uses less of everything: half the human effort in the factory, half the manufacturing space, half the investment in tools, half the engineering hours to develop the product, and inventory levels far lower as well as low defect rates. Furthermore, "lean" inventory levels are continually reduced to deliberately reveal flaws in the system.

Lean production employs teams of multiskilled workers at all levels of the organization and uses highly flexible machines to produce high volumes and high variety. In contrast, mass production uses narrowly skilled professionals to design products made by semiskilled workers tending expensive, single-purpose machines at high volumes. Changes are expensive and infrequent and production buffers are needed to smooth production. Mass production also yields low costs to consumers for standard designs. It sets an "acceptable" level for defects, while lean systems concentrate on perfection. Mass-production systems are relatively static once launched, while lean systems are dynamic and intent on continuous improvement.

Since the advantages of lean production systems were documented by the IMVP, many U.S. mass-production systems (especially in the automotive industry) have been moving in the "lean" direction; yet substantial differences persist. At this time, all the major automobile and many other manufacturers in the U.S. are pursing major "lean manufacturing" initiatives. Lean implementations have been successful when: (a) the whole lean system is embraced, not just a few elements, and (b) everyone in the organization sees a clear-cut advantage to doing business the "lean" way. This usually means a high level of management commitment to job security for the workforce.

33.3 ESSENTIAL COMPONENTS OF LEAN PRODUCTION

Lean production uses many techniques for successful implementation. They include value stream analysis, Takt time, kanban, Kaizen, visual control, total productive maintenance, one-piece flow, error proofing, standardization, autonomation, production leveling, problem-solving circles, and 5S.

VALUE STREAM ANALYSIS

Value stream analysis is the set of all the specific actions required to bring a specific product through the three critical management tasks.

1. Problem solving: running from concept through detailed design and engineering to production.
2. Information management: running from order taking through detailed scheduling to delivery.
3. Physical transformation: proceeding from raw materials to a finished product in the hands of the customer.

Value stream analysis will help to identify: (a) unambiguous value-adding steps; (b) steps that do not add value but that are unavoidable; and (c) steps that create no value and are immediately avoidable.

TAKT TIME

Takt (Takt = rhythm or beat in German) *time* is used to determine how often a product should be produced based on the rate of sales to customers.

$$T_t = \frac{A_t}{D_r} \qquad (33\text{-}1)$$

where:

T_t = Takt time
A_t = available work time per shift
D_r = customer demand rate per shift

KANBAN

With *kanban* (card system), the type and quantity of units are written on a tag-like card that is sent from workers of one process to workers of the preceding process. When all the parts in a lot have been used, the card becomes the mechanism for reorder. The kanban system manages the JIT production method.

KAIZEN

Kaizen refers to ongoing improvement involving everyone—managers and workers. Kaizen refers to aggressive, proactive improvement activities. Lean organizations value and support Kaizen as having equal value to production and maintenance activities.

VISUAL CONTROL

With *visual control*, a worker uses his/her eyes to monitor the state of the line and the flow of production. The operator either seeks help or "closes the loop" if an abnormality appears. Examples include visible inventory/kanban tickets, foolproofing by paint color or light, and/or call lights.

TOTAL PRODUCTIVE MAINTENANCE

Machines must be in safe operating condition and have predictable process capability and uptime. Proactive, preventive (total) maintenance programs use operators and skilled trades to achieve these goals.

ONE-PIECE FLOW

In *one-piece flow* systems, a worker completes a job within a specified cycle time; the introduction of one unit is balanced by the completion of another unit of finished product. This flow reduces inventory, reduces lead time, and attunes production mix and volume to sales. Figure 33-1 illustrates a typical plant layout. Figure 33-2 illustrates the one-piece flow arrangement.

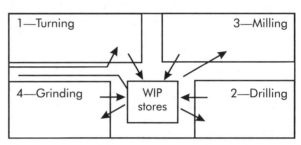

Figure 33-1. Traditional functional layout of a manufacturing company (Veilleux and Petro 1988).

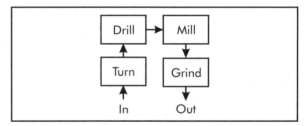

Figure 33-2. One-piece flow layout (Veilleux and Petro 1988).

ERROR PROOFING

Multifunctional workers move from job to job, making quick acclimatization to a new job mandatory. One-piece flow and autonomation in response to kanban pull require that the system prevent errors. *Error proofing* attempts to eliminate mistakes by making it impossible to do a job incorrectly. *Mistake proofing* attempts to ensure that a mistake is caught before the next operation or shipment to the customer.

STANDARDIZATION

The standard operation shows the sequential routine of various operations performed by multi-functional workers who handle multiple kinds of machines. Jobs are standardized across operators and shifts. Lean systems attempt to improve, then standardize the improvement.

AUTONOMATION

To realize perfect just-in-time (JIT) delivery schedules, 100% defect free units must flow to the subsequent process and this flow must be rhythmic and without interruption. *Autonomation* means to build in a mechanism to prevent mass production of defective work. It is the autonomous check of the abnormal occurrences in the process.

PRODUCTION LEVELING

Producing too much is waste; producing too little does not meet customer needs. Overtime and fatigue cause waste. *Production leveling* assures a constant flow from suppliers and appropriate utilization of workers.

PROBLEM-SOLVING CIRCLES

Lean work is team-based. Work groups run cells or work areas. In addition, *problem-solving circles* are made up of work groups and/or anyone who can help solve the problem. Problem-solving circles meet outside of production time to solve specific problems identified by circle members or management. Many suggestions eminate from problem-solving circles. The very best lean systems elicit 50–100 suggestions per employee per year with a 90% implementation rate, and 90% of employees contribute at least one suggestion.

5S

The 5S strategy covers the basic principles of industrial housekeeping translated from Japanese as: sort (clutter-free work area), straighten (orderly work area), shine (clean work area), standardize (standard best practices), sustain (discipline to maintain 5S strategy).

33.4 JUST-IN-TIME

An example of functional lean production is *just-in-time* (JIT). Just-in-time is a philosophy that has the elimination of waste as its objective. Waste may appear in the form of rejected parts, excessive inventory levels, interoperation queues, excessive material handling, long setup and changeover times, and a number of other forms. Just-in-time highlights the need to match production rate to actual demand and eliminate non-value-adding activities.

The major features of JIT include:

- change from batch production to one-piece flow;
- level capacity loads;
- reduction of work-in-process;
- fewer changeovers;
- quicker setup times;
- versatile processes;
- visual cues for shop-floor workers;
- direct links with suppliers;
- process improvement;
- preventive maintenance;
- error proofing and mistake proofing (poka-yoke); and
- a pull system.

Changeover and setup are non-value-adding activities. JIT philosophy requires a minimal number of changeovers with a minimal setup time. JIT philosophy requires manufacturing processes be designed to accommodate a fairly mixed set of products without building inventory to level the capacity requirements.

JIT is a very visual process. Remembering sets of instructions and procedures is difficult. Additionally, JIT requires workers to be cross-trained in a variety of jobs to accommodate production surges. Visual cues can reduce the number of innocent mistakes (Veilleux and Petro 1988).

PULL SYSTEMS

The pull system is the next logical step in a JIT program when uniform plant loading and process flow revisions have been implemented. The pull system has dramatic effects on inventory levels because it does not provide for production of any inventory until it is needed. Pull systems do not allow parts to be produced until an "authorization" (pull signal) is received from the subsequent operation.

Pull systems generally take one of two possible forms, overlapped or linked. *Overlapped pull systems* utilize empty space as the pull signal or communication device between production operations. This technique is best applied when operations are in close physical proximity. One example is a simple square marked off with tape or painted lines that, when empty, indicates the following operation is ready for additional material. No material is produced until the square is emptied by the subsequent operation.

Linked pull systems are typically utilized when parts compete for the same resource and cannot be made on a one-for-one basis with end-item demand, or when they have to travel significant distances between operations in a lot (batch) mode. In these situations, it is typical to utilize a pull signal, or kanban, to trigger the production of components from operation to previous operation. The kanban is the only authorization for additional material to be produced at the previous operation. When no kanban is issued, no additional components are made. Kanbans may be cards, colored golf balls, or even empty containers. They may be moved by hand, slotted slide, or pneumatic tube (Veilleux and Petro 1988).

REVIEW QUESTIONS

33.1) Toyota's production system also can be called _____ production.

33.2) What Japanese term is used for ongoing improvement involving everyone—managers and workers?

33.3) What type of system is being used when the introduction of one unit is balanced by the completion of another unit of finished product?

33.4) _____ time is the available work time per shift divided by the customer demand rate per shift.

33.5) What type of system (push or pull) does not allow parts to be produced until authorization is received from the subsequent operation?

33.6) What is the Japanese term for the signal used to trigger the production of components in JIT manufacturing?

REFERENCES

Veilleux, Raymond F. and Louis W. Petro. 1988. *Tool and Manufacturing Engineers Handbook*, Fourth Edition. Volume 5, *Manufacturing Management*. Dearborn, MI: Society of Manufacturing Engineers.

Womack, James P. 1990. *The Machine that Changed the World*. New York: Rawson Associates.

Chapter 34

Process Engineering

34.1 PROCESS PLANNING

During product design and once a part design is finalized, the production processes must be planned. Process planning requires:

- determining the processes to be used;
- the development of operation flow charts;
- production layouts;
- routings and operation (process) sheets;
- setup charts and machine tool layouts;
- equipment selection and sequence;
- material handling details;
- tooling requirements;
- inspection plans for quality assurance and quality control; and
- much more.

Due to the broad nature of process planning, only a few steps will be discussed.

In process planning, the general characteristics of the part, such as the general part configuration, material, surface finish, and tolerances, must be determined first. These characteristics will affect part handling, the type of tooling and machines, the sequence of operations, assembly, and rate of production.

Another step in process planning is tolerance analysis. Due to workpiece variation, interchangeability requires that acceptable workpiece variations (tolerances) be specified. Process planning ensures that tolerances are neither too tight nor too loose and that tolerance stacks do not occur. A *tolerance stack* occurs when acceptable tolerances on individual dimensions combine in such a way as to create an unacceptable part or assembly. *Design tolerance stacks* are created by the designer and found on the part print. *Process tolerance stacks* are the result of improper processing (Early and Johnson 1962).

PROCESS SELECTION

Process selection is dependent on many criteria such as wall thickness, symmetry, draft, cavities, surface finish, tolerances, and material. Depending on the criteria, some processes may be excluded. From the remaining process alternatives, the best process must be selected. Fundamentally, the *best process* is the one that meets the requirements with the least cost. In reality, many other constraints such as capability, versatility, maintenance, etc., confound the issue.

EQUIPMENT SELECTION

Equipment selection is another issue that may affect process selection. The need to select equipment can occur:

- for a part not previously produced;
- for a part previously made by hand;
- to replace old equipment;
- to lower production costs; and/or
- to extend production.

There are two types of machines to choose from: general purpose (standard) and special purpose. *General-purpose machines*, such as drill presses and milling machines, are less expensive, more flexible, require less maintenance, and require less debugging time than special-purpose machines.

Special-purpose machines, although more expensive, offer several advantages when compared to general-purpose machines. They can create unique part geometries faster and with higher quality than general-purpose machines (Early and Johnson 1962).

34.2 COMPUTER-AIDED PROCESS PLANNING

Computer-aided process planning (CAPP) systems are expert computer systems that collect and store the knowledge of a specific manufacturing situation, as well as general manufacturing engineering principles. This information is used to create the optimum plan for manufacturing a new part. The CAPP system specifies the machinery to be used for production, the sequence of operations, the tooling, required speeds and feeds, and other necessary data.

With CAPP, the part is designed on a CAD/CAM system. The part file is transferred into the CAPP system and the part characteristics are matched to the machines and processes available on the shop floor. The CAPP system then prints out the process and routing sheets that make up the process plan.

Two main types of CAPP systems, variant and generative, are in use today. The *variant system* modifies the process plan for a similar, previously produced part to produce a plan for the new part. The *generative system* starts from scratch when developing a process plan, and therefore needs a large database containing manufacturing logic, the capabilities of existing machinery, standards, and specifications (Veilleux and Petro 1988).

34.3 JIGS/FIXTURES/LOCATING

A *jig* is a device used to locate and hold a workpiece while guiding or controlling a cutting tool. A *fixture* is simply a locating and holding device. It has nothing to do with tool guidance or control.

In good design, the fixture must confine the workpiece through six degrees of freedom: three linear and three rotational. This idea leads to the 3-2-1 principle, which states that a workpiece will be confined when placed against three points in one plane, two points in another plane, and one point in a third plane, if the planes are perpendicular to each other (see Figure 34-1).

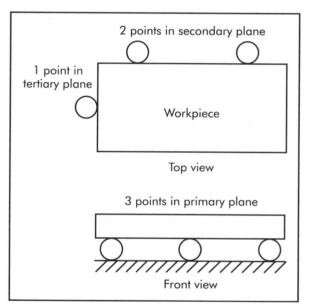

Figure 34-1. The 3-2-1 principle.

LOCATING DEVICES

Generally, *locating devices* can be either a machined surface on the fixture to support the workpiece, pins aligned to locate finished holes, or V-blocks. Typically, rest buttons are used in place of machining a pad on the fixture. These buttons have hardened heads and tempered shafts.

Locating pins can sometimes cause part jamming. To reduce the amount of jamming, several parameters can be changed, such as the length of fit and alignment groove depth.

Cutting three equal flats on the length of the pin (diamond locator) also reduces jamming.

CLAMPING

There are many guidelines for designing or choosing clamps. Clamps come in several types, including screw, cam, level, toggle, wedge, and latch. In general, clamps should hold the workpiece against a locating surface with the force transmitted through a fixed support point without distorting the workpiece. Fixed locators should oppose the force of the cutting tool, not the clamps. Clamping forces can vary based on depth of cut, the dulling of cutting tools, changes in material hardness, and cutting rate changes.

34.4 ASSEMBLY METHODS

The five basic types of assembly systems in use today are single-station assembly, synchronous assembly, nonsynchronous assembly, continuous-motion assembly, and dial (rotary) assembly.

SINGLE-STATION ASSEMBLY

Machines with a single workstation are used most extensively when a specific operation is performed many times on one or a few parts. These machines are incorporated into multistation assembly systems and may be used when different operations are performed and if the required tooling is not too complicated.

SYNCHRONOUS ASSEMBLY

Synchronous (indexing) assembly systems are available in dial, in-line, and carousel varieties. With these systems, all pallets or workpieces are moved at the same time and the same distance. Synchronous systems are used primarily for high-speed and high-volume applications on small lightweight assemblies where the various operations have relatively equal cycle times.

NONSYNCHRONOUS ASSEMBLY

Nonsynchronous transfer (accumulative or power-and-free) assembly systems, with free or floating pallets or workpieces and independently operated individual stations, are widely used where the times required to perform different operations vary greatly. The systems also are applied for larger products with many components. One major advantage of these so-called "power-and-free systems" is increased versatility.

CONTINUOUS-MOTION ASSEMBLY

In continuous-motion systems, assembly operations are performed while the workpieces or pallets move at a constant speed and the workheads reciprocate. High production rates are possible because indexing time is eliminated. However, the cost and complexity of these systems are high, because workheads must synchronize and move with the product being assembled.

DIAL (ROTARY) ASSEMBLY

Dial or rotary index machines of synchronous design were one of the first types used for assembly. They are still used for many applications. Workstations and tooling can be mounted on a central column or around the periphery of the indexing table. These machines are generally limited to small- and medium-sized lightweight assemblies requiring a relatively low number of operations that are not too complicated.

34.5 FACILITY LAYOUT

Facility layout may be defined as the planning and integration of the paths of the component parts of a product to obtain the most effective and economical interrelationship between employees, equipment, and the movement of materials from receiving, through fabrication, to the shipment of the finished product.

Facility layout is critical to the productivity of a plant. If facility layout is not optimal, it affects the non-operation time for the part, the level of manpower required to move the part, and the capital investment in material handling equipment. First, it increases the non-operation time, which is a component of manufacturing lead time. This, in turn, lengthens manufacturing lead time, increases work-in-process inventory, and increases the capital investment in work-in-process. Second, the increase in non-value-adding material handling adds labor hours to the cost of the product without adding any value to the product. Finally, the capital investment in material handling equipment is increased commensurate with the greater material handling activity without generating any more income from the sale of the product.

Facility layouts are of the process, product-process (cellular), or fixed (station) types.

PROCESS LAYOUT

The facility layout may be designed according to function or process. The process-oriented plant layout is most common in manufacturing today. This arrangement groups together all similar functions such as milling, turning, grinding, etc., resulting in an arrangement that requires less capital, achieves higher machine utilization, and is easier to automate. However, the process layout requires increased material handling. A typical process facility layout is shown in Figure 34-2.

PRODUCT-PROCESS (CELLULAR) LAYOUT

In the product-process arrangement, one product family is produced in a cell using group technology. This arrangement, as shown in Figure 34-3, produces greater volumes of the part family with shorter manufacturing lead times because the batch of parts is not waiting to be moved to the next process and the next setup. The equipment

for the product family is arranged either linearly or radially according to the sequence of processes. The process cell has the least material handling and work-in-process inventory. Continuous operation of the product process is easiest to automate with robots and other material handling equipment.

FIXED (STATION) LAYOUT

The fixed (station) type of production, shown in Figure 34-4, has a fixed or stationary product with the manufacturing and assembly going on around it. This layout is typical of large, low-volume products such as machine tools and aircraft. This layout is highly flexible. However, it requires greater skills for personnel.

LAYOUT OPTIMIZATION

New machines should be positioned on the floor in such a way as to minimize production costs and ensure quality levels. The facility layout should maximize the time spent in adding value to the part.

Many major criteria should shape the equipment acquisition and installation process as it pertains to plant layout. The position of the machine on the plant floor should facilitate the manufacturing process and maximize machine utilization. Material handling should be minimized, including work handling to change positions for machining. Some flexibility of arrangement and operation should be maintained. Work-in-process should be minimized through a high turnover rate. Equipment investment should be minimized through effective use of floor space. Direct and indirect labor should be minimized and a safe and convenient workspace should be created. Many production components are typically affected by plant layout:

- Are parts arriving by truck or rail?
- What is the form of packaging of incoming stock?

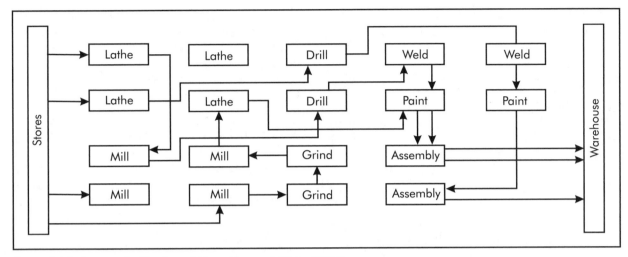

Figure 34-2. Process facility layout (Tompkins and White 1984).

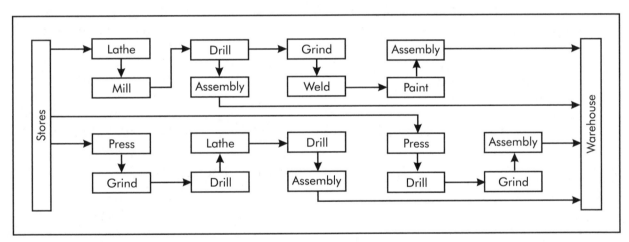

Figure 34-3. Product-process (cellular) layout (Tompkins and White 1984).

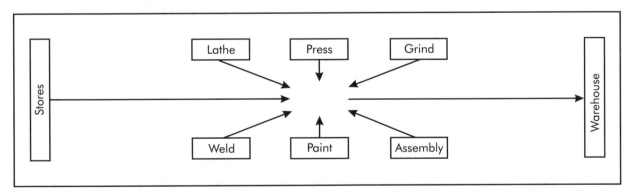

Figure 34-4. Fixed (station) production layout (Tompkins and White 1984).

- Are there intermediate steps between external transportation and the planned operation such as unpacking, inspection, or storage?

Production activities must be defined and established as well as their location. The position of service and auxiliary activities also must be considered. For example, the location of extra tools and maintenance stations should be evaluated. The location of the new machine and gaging or other inspection stations must be carefully planned. An optimal location should be planned for buffer storage or shipping on the output side of the process. Basic guidelines for effective plant layout include:

- a planned materials flow pattern;
- adequate, straight aisles;
- minimal backtracking;
- minimal work-in-process;
- some built-in flexibility;
- maximum ratio of processing time to overall time;
- minimum travel distances for material handling;
- optimal quality practices;
- ergonomics within the workplace;
- smooth and adequate materials flow;
- good housekeeping; and
- access to maintenance.

34.6 MAINTENANCE

There are three approaches to the maintenance of production equipment: (1) corrective maintenance; (2) preventive maintenance (PM); and (3) predictive maintenance.

CORRECTIVE MAINTENANCE

Corrective maintenance is simply fixing equipment when it breaks down. This type of maintenance can be very expensive depending on the type of breakdown and when it occurs. When a machine, such as a stamp-ing press, breaks down unexpectedly, subsequent presses may be idled and production may have to be shifted to other, possibly slower presses.

PREVENTIVE MAINTENANCE

Preventive maintenance (PM) will not prevent all breakdowns, but it can dramatically reduce the amount of production time lost waiting for equipment to be repaired. The main activities of PM are lubrication, parts replacement, machine adjustments, and overall inspections. PM may also include regularly scheduled input by machine operators to describe potential problems. With PM:

- machines will last longer;
- maintenance time and cost will be cut;
- severity and frequency of breakdowns will be reduced;
- safety levels will rise;
- product quality will be maintained; and
- production costs will be cut by increasing asset utilization time and decreasing time lost by idle operators.

A well-designed preventive maintenance program includes:

- adequate record keeping;
- a regular schedule of inspection to determine optimal intervals between inspections;
- use of checklists;
- well-qualified tradespeople as inspectors;
- appropriate budget allocation;
- administrative procedures to ensure compliance and follow-up; and
- input by machine operators who know the machine and/or process the best.

Preventive maintenance can begin at the first stage of machine design when features that reduce the need for maintenance can be integrated. Machine design can include ease of access for maintenance. In the process of machine specification and acquisition, the concept of preventive maintenance should be a prominent factor. Proper location of lubrication points or reservoirs, design of guards, access to motors and fluid-power components, ease of cleaning, proper chip disposal, design of lockouts, ease of visual inspection of critical areas, and accessibility of adjustment points are just some of the many elements enabling successful PM.

Good preventive maintenance procedures should reduce the likelihood that assignable causes of excessive process variation are due to poor equipment condition. Some SPC auditing authorities require documentation of such procedures to be certified as a parts supplier.

PREDICTIVE MAINTENANCE

A more sophisticated form of preventive maintenance is *predictive maintenance* that uses various types of sensors to predict breakdowns. Monitoring vibration signatures is a common practice of predictive maintenance. A baseline vibration signature, using a fast fourier transform (FFT), is recorded when the machine is set up so that variation from this signature signals malfunction. The widespread use of sophisticated sensors, programmable controllers, and other computers has made predictive maintenance easier to execute.

34.7 METHODS ENGINEERING AND WORK MEASUREMENT

Methods engineering and work measurement form another component of process engineering. *Methods engineering* focuses on analyzing methods and equipment used in performing a task, on either existing processes or future jobs.

Several tools are available for methods engineering such as process charts, micromotion, and memomotion. Process charts are a graphical representation of the step-by-step sequence taking place in the manufacturing cycle. With the emergence of motion pictures and video recorders, filming workers performing their tasks became a popular method of analyzing job performance. Micromotion uses motion pictures taken at constant and known speeds. It is applicable for analyzing processes with short cycle times and rapid movements. Memomotion, on the other hand, uses a slower film speed and is quite useful to analyze jobs with long cycle times or those involving many interrelationships.

Work measurement is another process design tool. By standardizing or allowing times for specific tasks, engineers plan and schedule production and conduct cost estimating and line balancing. While doing a time study, the operator may work faster or slower than what the analyst considers to be normal. To compensate, it is necessary for the analyst to rate the operator. Essentially, this means that the analyst compares the performance of the operator with the analyst's opinion of normal performance. The rating factor is expressed as a percentage of normal performance (normal performance = 100%). Normal time can be calculated by:

$$N_t = \frac{A_t \times P_r}{100} \qquad (34\text{-}1)$$

where:

N_t = normal time
A_t = average time
P_r = percent rating

With machine downtime, material delays, and other interruptions, the normal time is not completely accurate. To compensate for delays and interruptions, a standard time is calculated by increasing the normal time by an allowance. The standard time is calculated by:

$$S_t = \frac{N_t(100 + P_a)}{100} \qquad (34\text{-}2)$$

where:

S_t = standard time
N_t = normal time
P_a = allowance percentage

Example 34.7.1. After 15 trials, the average time for a worker to assemble a cable clamp is 10.3 seconds. If the rating factor is 95%, what is the normal time?

Solution.

$$N_t = \frac{A_t \times P_r}{100} \quad \text{(Eq. 34-1)}$$

where:

A_t = 10.3 seconds
P_r = 95%

$$N_t = \frac{10.3 \times 95}{100}$$

$$N_t = 9.8 \text{ seconds}$$

Example 34.7.2. Due to assembly fatigue and humid conditions, an allowance of 10% is necessary. Calculate the standard time for the process in example 34.7.1.

Solution.

$$S_t = \frac{N_t(100 + P_a)}{100} \quad \text{(Eq. 34-2)}$$

where:

N_t = 9.8 seconds
P_a = 10%

$$S_t = \frac{9.8(100 + 10)}{100}$$

$$S_t = 10.8 \text{ seconds}$$

REVIEW QUESTIONS

34.1) Although more expensive, _____ -purpose machines can provide faster production rates and high quality for some parts.

34.2) A good fixture must confine the part through how many degrees of freedom?

34.3) What type of assembly method is performed when all the workpieces move at the same time?

34.4) What type of facility layout produces one product family in a given cell?

34.5) Which type of maintenance replaces machine components at specified time intervals?

34.6) Find the rating factor if the normal time is 15 seconds and the average time is 20 seconds.

34.7) Calculate the standard time if the normal time is 10 seconds and an allowance of 10% is given due to assembly fatigue.

REFERENCES

Early, Donald F. and Gerald E. Johnson, 1962. *Process Engineering for Manfuacturing*. Englewood Cliffs, NJ: Prentice-Hall, Inc.

Tompkins, James A. and John A. White. 1984. *Facilities Planning*. New York: John Wiley & Sons, Inc.

Veilleux, Raymond F. and Louis W. Petro, eds. 1988. *Tool and Manufacturing Engineers Handbook*, Fourth Edition. *Volume 5: Manufacturing Management*. Dearborn, MI: Society of Manufacturing Engineers.

Chapter 35

Materials Management

35.1 INVENTORY MANAGEMENT

Inventory management is a varied collection of many disciplines. In its simplest forms, the *inventory management* responsibilities may include the establishment of policies and procedures as well as the maintenance of manually posted card records. Thousands of materials managers depend heavily on computerized forecasting and manufacturing resource planning (MRP II) systems to control the flow of inventories. In the most competitive and innovative manufacturing companies today, newer methods utilizing the pull concepts of just-in-time (JIT) and frequent supplier communications orchestrate the management of inventories that may be turning over 20, 40, or more times per year.

Inventory is one of the most important financial assets present in manufacturing companies. Stocks of raw materials, work-in-process inventory, and finished goods constitute the focus of control for the time they are held before being converted into sales dollars. The shorter the period that inventory is held, the more productive the asset. Inventory affects the financial health of a company in the following ways:

- it is an asset representing stored value that, when sold, will produce income and, hopefully, a profit; and
- it is a major investment that is financed by equity or debt.

Types of inventories usually include the following:

- work-in-process and in-transit inventories;
- raw material;
- finished goods or semifinished products, manufactured to cover anticipated demand and prone to significant forecast error;
- inventory buildup in anticipation of a new product introduction or special promotion;
- purchase of a stockpile inventory in anticipation of a supply interruption such as an impending strike, or in anticipation of a substantial price increase; and/or
- manufactured products to cover seasonal demands that exceed near-level production requirements (Veilleux and Petro 1988).

35.2 DEMAND

Item demand is considered to be an *independent demand* when that demand is unrelated to the demand for other items. Product demand arriving through orders is the principal element of this type of demand. This form of demand is usually associated with the manufacturer's primary revenue source and is the subject of most of the forecasting effort. Items that will be consumed in destructive testing and service parts requirements are likewise independent demands.

Demands for parts or raw materials are considered to be *dependent demands* when they are derived directly from the demands for other items. The usual source of these requirements is the output of a bill of material "explosion." These demands are then accumulated as component and material requirements by time period. Such demands are therefore calculated and should not be forecasted independently. Some items are subject to both independent and dependent demands.

Demand for products, parts, components, and materials is rarely stable over time. Forecasting addresses the trends and variations of demand, but since forecasting is an estimate of demand, inventory management must accommodate forecasting error. Response to this demand variability may be dealt with either by inventory buffers or by improvement in the capability and flexibility of the manufacturing processes (Veilleux and Petro 1988).

35.3 INVENTORY REPLENISHMENT

Inventory is replenished according to some set of rules or policies, either formal or informal. The objective of inventory rules or policies must be to balance the cost of carrying inventory with the service level required. The principal measure related to this activity is called *inventory turns*. The equation for calculating the inventory turn ratio is:

$$I_t = \frac{A_y}{A_i} \qquad (35\text{-}1)$$

where:

I_t = inventory turns
A_y = annual inventory usage at cost ($)
A_i = average inventory at cost ($)

Conventional/traditional manufacturers typically experience turn ratios in the range of 2–10, while companies using just-in-time

(JIT) techniques have ratios of 10–50 or more. Stock in inventory costs money, so more companies are using JIT to have as little in inventory as possible, and to achieve as high a turn ratio as possible. The use of *safety stock* to reduce the risk of an out-of-stock occurrence will lower the turn ratio. Companies using JIT also reduce or eliminate safety stock.

The economic order quantity (EOQ) has been the most common statistical calculation used in inventory control for several decades. The standard EOQ formula is based on the model shown in Figure 35-1.

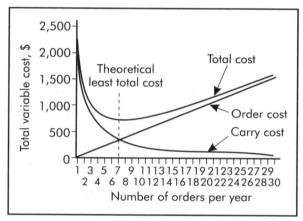

Figure 35-1. Order cost versus inventory carry cost curve. (Courtesy K.W. Tunnell Company, Inc.)

EOQ attempts to balance inventory carrying costs with ordering costs. Annual usage in pieces is required as the first estimate in the calculation. The approximation of ordering costs must include setup costs if the part is a manufactured item's cost rather than a purchased one. Inventory carrying costs result from the multiplication of one item by the management policy variable. This last factor describes the interest rate percentage believed to be a forecast of appropriate costs, including the cost of money, cost of storage, cost of handling, cost of storage loss, and costs associated with inventory obsolescence (Veilleux and Petro 1988). While the calculation of EOQ is an estimate based upon estimates, it is useful in preliminary analyses. The formula for EOQ is:

$$EOQ = \sqrt{\frac{2AS}{ic}} \qquad (35\text{-}2)$$

where:

EOQ = economic order quantity (units)
 A = annual usage (units)
 S = setup and order costs per order ($)
 i = interest and storage costs (%)
 c = unit cost of one part ($)

Example 35.2.1 Calculate the EOQ for a product that has an annual usage of 20,000 units, setup and order costs of $50, a unit cost of $20, and an interest and storage cost of 12%.

Solution.

$$EOQ = \sqrt{\frac{2AS}{ic}}$$

where:

A = 20,000
S = $50
I = 0.12
c = $20

$$EOQ = \sqrt{\frac{2(20,000)(50)}{0.12(20)}}$$

EOQ = 913

35.4 ABC ANALYSIS

A popular technique that lends itself to good management of the inventory asset dollar is classical "ABC" analysis, which results in the coding of items by categories called A, B, and C. This technique requires sorting items by the amount of dollar demand (at cost) recorded over some past period, as illustrated in Table 35-1, or from the output of an MRP system projected over some future period. Based on Pareto analysis, it is

Table 35-1. ABC analysis of $1,000,000 annual inventory usage at cost

Number of Parts	Cost	Percent	Inventory Category
6	680,000	68	A
16	200,000	20	B
80	120,000	12	C

(Veilleux and Petro 1988)

usually observed that only about 20% of the items in inventory will be involved in 80% of the usage measured in dollars. If this top 20% is managed carefully, the lower-dollar items can be handled less often with little effect on the total dollar investment. Therefore, it is appropriate to set inventory policy based on ABC analysis as a method of establishing an inventory plan. Basing inventory policies on the ABC analysis results in items being given replenishment rules like the following:

- Review A items weekly and order one week's supply when less than a lead time plus one week's supply remains.
- Review B items biweekly and order four weeks' supply when less than a lead time plus two weeks' supply remains.
- Review C items monthly and order 12 weeks' supply when less than a lead time plus three weeks' supply remains.

The result of such policies and procedures is that the high-dollar volume items get the most attention. In this example, the "A" items will be individually reviewed four times as frequently as the "B" items and 12 times as frequently as the "C" items (Veilleux and Petro 1988).

35.5 JUST-IN-TIME (JIT) INVENTORY

Just-in-time (JIT) inventory is usually referred to as *zero inventory* (ZI) by the American Production and Inventory Control Society

(APICS). The popular beliefs about the methods, the conditions of its success, and the potential in American manufacturing remain diverse. The most popular misconception is probably the one that says "... it is a method based on someone else holding inventory for you until you need it."

In a manufacturing environment, inventory exists for two reasons:

1. to compensate for the uncertainties associated with material flow related to lead times; and
2. to cover the risks associated with the failure of prior processes to deliver quality materials.

Therefore, to eliminate the inventories, the reasons for their existence must be eliminated.

The first cause is approached through a continuous reduction of lot size requirements. Because of the impact of economic job sizing, the factors contributing to order costs must be eliminated. Even in the standard economic order quantity (EOQ) formula (Eq. 35-2), it can be seen that as setup or order costs approach zero, the calculated economic lot size approaches the practical lowest limit, one. This leads to setup reduction efforts—a part of the continuous improvement process.

The second cause is addressed by using methods that allow the manufacturer to gain process control and make its output statistically predictable as "good" parts. This requires the use of statistical process control (SPC) techniques in the manufacturing workplace. It further requires the involvement of all employees striving for a common goal of production that is free of all defects and waste costs.

To achieve near-zero inventories on purchased parts, suppliers must use the same statistical quality management techniques in their operations as does the manufacturer.

Defects or missed delivery dates on vendor-supplied parts and materials can very quickly shut down a production activity that is not buffered by inventory.

There are several steps that can improve the opportunity for near-zero inventory on purchased materials:

- reduce the overall quantity of suppliers;
- design long-term partnership programs to make both vendor and customer more profitable;
- devote human resources in the purchasing department to long-term cost and quality gains, not adversarial negotiating and expediting;
- concentrate the supplier base near the manufacturing facility; and
- order small lots, demand short lead times, and accept no defects (Veilleux and Petro 1988).

35.6 SUPPLY CHAIN MANAGEMENT

Supply chain management extends the linkage from the company upward to the customers' customers and downward to the suppliers' suppliers. It coordinates and tunes the chain of business entities to accept and fulfill customers' orders. As illustrated in Figure 35-2, information, money, and materials flow in the supply chain.

In general, physical material (product) flows from left to right. In some cases, such as recycled packaging and damaged products, material flows from right to left. Information must flow bidirectionally and be ready for all trading partners. Client orders, for example, move from right to left. Information about orders moves from left to right. In addition to transactions, information about product requirements and specifications flows in the supply chain. Money in the form of payments flows from right to left. However, money from rebates and returns flows from left to right.

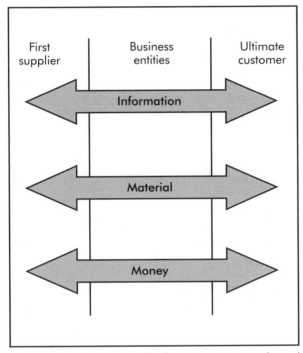

Figure 35-2. The flow of information, material, and money in the supply chain.

The emphasis or focus of the supply chain varies between industries. Industries such as automotive and aerospace place a premium on factory capacity and production scheduling. The need to be responsive to customer orders means effective scheduling and execution.

The supply chain for consumer electronics, semiconductors, and appliances is purchasing oriented. Procurement costs are a significant component of product cost, in contrast to heavier industry where manufacturing and labor content is a more significant portion of product cost.

The third type of focus is a distribution-oriented supply chain. Consumer nondurables and some products, such as gas and oil, focus on replenishment and transportation of finished goods. The emphasis is on market share and shelf space in the retail stores.

Better customer information helps the suppliers improve their operations. The extension of this in both directions constitutes a major competitive advantage.

Before companies can build effective partnerships with customers and suppliers, they must demonstrate the capability of controlling their operations. Well-managed companies know the consequences of a weak link in the chain. They want partners that can convert better information into significant benefits for them. In the same manner, a company without control cannot possibly provide valid plans to its suppliers, even if it announces its intentions of being a good partner (Rowen 1999).

REVIEW QUESTIONS

35.1) _____ demands are derived from the demand for other items.

35.2) The principal measure related to balancing the cost of carrying inventory with the service level required is known as _____ .

35.3) Calculate the EOQ for a product that has an annual usage of 100,000 units, setup and order costs of $50, a unit cost of $10, and an interest and storage cost of 20%.

35.4) On what basis does ABC inventory analysis categorize items?

35.5) To achieve zero inventory on purchased materials, what is the maximum acceptable defect rate from suppliers?

35.6) In which direction does money from customer rebates flow in the supply chain?

REFERENCE

Rowen, Robert B. 1999. *A Manufacturing Engineer's Introduction to Supply Chain Management*. CASA/Blue Book Series, September. Dearborn, MI: Society of Manufacturing Engineers.

Veilleux, Raymond F. and Louis W. Petro, eds. 1988. *Tool and Manufacturing Engineers Handbook*, Fourth Edition. Volume 5, *Manufacturing Management*. Dearborn, MI: Society of Manufacturing Engineers.

Part 7
Automated Systems and Control

Chapter 36

Computer Applications/Automation

36.1 APPLICATION CRITERIA

Computer and automation applications exist in manufacturing in the form of computer-aided design (CAD) to islands of automation to computer-integrated manufacturing (CIM) to hard automation. Any computer or automation application must be a justifiable investment. To justify the purchase and installation of a computer or automation application, including hard automation, it must improve:

- the quality of the product;
- the productivity in manufacturing the product (this typically includes labor in the calculation);
- the quality of the work environment in manufacturing the product, and/or
- the development time for a new product or new model of a product.

Improving the quality of the product increases customer satisfaction and market share in addition to reducing rework (commonly called the "factory within a factory"). Improving productivity in manufacturing is linked to the net costs of labor, material, facilities, equipment, etc., to produce a product. However, labor cost is only 5–15% of the total cost of a product. Therefore, improving the quality of the work environment is often a better criterion for justifying automation. The work environment needs to be improved to reduce medical insurance, health, labor replacement, legal, safety, and environmental costs.

Product development time can be reduced through the application of CAD, computer-aided engineering (CAE), computer-aided manufacturing (CAM), and other applications. Integration of CAD through CAM and business functions can lead to CIM and manufacturing execution systems. CIM is the concept of integrating the design, engineering, manufacturing, and business functions of the enterprise to better serve the customer.

36.2 MANUFACTURING ENTERPRISE INTEGRATION

The theory of CIM is that all the activities involved in the manufacturing of a product are related and require computers for their organization and integration. While the tasks can be completed more effectively and efficiently with computers, the people in an organization are an integral component and the customer is at the core. The activities include not only the manufacturing processes but also the data used in defining and managing the manufacturing activities. The Manufacturing Enterprise Integration (MEI) wheel, shown in Figure 36-1, shows the significance of the shared information and the integrated databases required for CIM or MEI.

The MEI wheel focuses on computer technology and people (Marks 1994). At the heart of the MEI wheel, level 1, is the customer. People, teamwork, and organization comprise level 2 and encircle the customer both

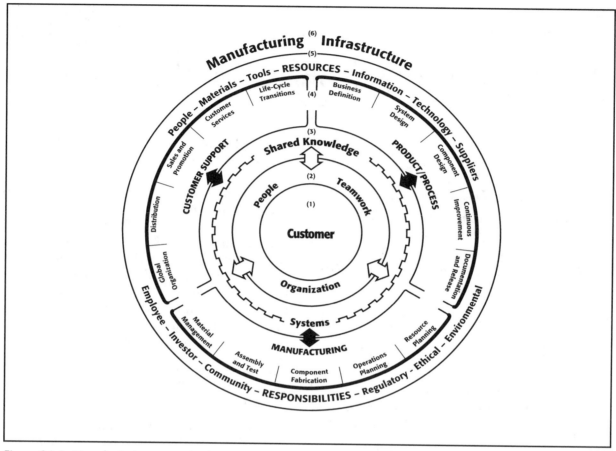

Figure 36-1. Manufacturing enterprise integration (MEI) wheel (CASA 1994).

conceptually and in practice. Level 3 introduces the computer-based technology in the supporting shared knowledge system: the integrated manufacturing databases. This level manages the data common to manufacturing and is concerned with information resource management and communications found in levels 2 and 4. The radial sections in level 4 include the product/process design data, manufacturing planning, fabrication, control, factory automation, automatic data collection and procedures, and customer support activities and data. Level 5 is composed of the organizational resources and responsibilities. The outside covering, level 6, is the manufacturing infrastructure that would include manufacturing networks, engineering, and management.

CIM technologies include computer-aided design (CAD), computer-aided engineering (CAE), computer-aided process planning (CAPP), computer-aided manufacturing (CAM), computer numerical control (CNC), distributed numerical control (DNC), flexible manufacturing systems (FMS), robotics, automatic guided vehicle systems (AGVS), and automatic storage and retrieval systems (AS/RS). The benefits of CIM are:

- reduction in engineering design cost,
- reduction in overall lead time,
- increased product quality,
- increased capability of engineers,

- increased productivity of production operations,
- reduction of work-in-process, and
- reduction of personnel costs.

REVIEW QUESTIONS

36.1) Name one justification for purchasing and installing automation.

36.2) CIM is the integration of design, engineering, manufacturing, and _____ functions.

36.3) What is MEI an acronym for?

36.4) Which level of the MEI wheel represents the customer?

REFERENCES

Manufacturing Enterprise Integration (MEI) Wheel. 1994. Computer and Automated Systems Association (CASA). Dearborn, MI: Society of Manufacturing Engineers.

Marks, P. 1994. *Process Reengineering and the New Manufacturing Enterprise Wheel: 15 Processes for Competitive Advantage.* Dearborn, MI: Society of Manufacturing Engineers.

Chapter 37

Manufacturing Networks

37.1 NETWORK APPLICATIONS

Manufacturing networks provide the infrastructure to transmit manufacturing and management data used to define and control computer-integrated manufacturing systems or components of computer-aided design (CAD) and computer-aided manufacturing (CAM). These data consist of CAD drawings, production schedules, inventory information, production information, production programs (for example, computer-numerical control [CNC] and programmable logic control [PLC] programs), production order releases, operation sheets, routing sheets, production order releases, inventory levels, and maintenance information. These data need to be transmitted to and from the production floor and within the corporate enterprise. The computer networks consist primarily of local area networks (LANs). LANs also can be joined to form enterprise-wide computing (EWC) or corporate intranets. An *intranet* is similar to the Internet except it can only be accessed by people within the company or organization.

Computer networks are specified by bandwidth architecture, access protocol, cable, distance, and cost. As computer network technology changes, the specifications for these terms will change, but the industry will continue to use them to describe the various networks for the foreseeable future. *Bandwidth* has become the focus for the computer communications industry with intranets and the internet becoming common information sources for manufacturing and corporations. Bandwidth refers to the number of signals that can be carried simultaneously on the same conductor.

There have been numerous types of LANs but ethernet is the primary network architecture for both office and plant floor. (*Architecture* refers to an organized combination of protocols and standards.)

37.2 NETWORK COMPONENTS

The four components of a network are:

1. servers (file, client, communications, print, and web);
2. transmission medium (cable or wireless);
3. network interface card (NIC), and
4. network operating system.

Application constraints, changes in networking technology, and costs affect the appropriate choices of the different types of available products. The use of different types of components has specific advantages and disadvantages in manufacturing environments. The migration from LANs to intranets also changes the types and numbers of servers and the network operating systems. The connectivity (cabling or wireless) technology is in most cases a very significant issue because manufacturing facilities are often much larger than office complexes. These longer distances require

---

more careful planning of the connectivity system. The higher levels of electromagnetic radiation also need to be considered when planning the layout and choosing the type of conductor.

SERVERS

The file, client, and web servers are the most common servers and are important components for LANs and intranets. With the growth and implementation of technology that support the internet and intranets, web and communications servers will become more prevalent. However, print servers are becoming less common due to the availability of network boxes that interface printers to the network, and the lower cost of high-quality printers that connect directly to local computer ports.

The *file server*, the centerpiece of networks, stores program or data files for shared use. It also stores the network operating system, controls user access and security, provides redundancy in file or directory tables or registries, and performs periodic backup of data and program files. The *client server* (also called a *database server*) is important for real-time access by multiple users to any file, but most commonly databases or CAD documents. The major difference between file servers and client servers is in a user's access to a file. When a user requests a file from a file server, the entire file is downloaded to the client's workstation and only that user has access to it at that time. However, client servers retain the files and allow multiple users to access portions of the file simultaneously. This difference in access and control of files prohibits the file server from providing real-time access for multiple users. Enterprise resource planning (ERP) databases and CAD files are two examples of manufacturing files that engineers and production operations managers need to have access to in real time. Web servers, required for intranet or internet posting of an organization's web files, are a specific type of client server.

TRANSMISSION MEDIUM

Cabling was, and still is, the most common transmission medium, but wireless technology is available and appropriate for specific applications. Cabling has been made from a variety of copper conductors such as thick coaxial cable, thin coaxial cable, unshielded twisted pair (UTP) cable, and shielded twisted pair (STP) cable. Fiber-optic cable and wireless systems have been developed and have replaced some of the copper conductors. Fiber optics is the most secure medium, since the light does not have the electromagnetic fields inherent with wire or wireless communications, and the medium is the least susceptible to electromagnetic interference (EMI). UTP is the common media for local area networks in environments that are relatively free of EMI that comes from motors, transformers, and fluorescent lights. Fiber-optic or shielded cables are better for areas with high EMI. When describing the cabling for a network, the frequency is listed first as 10 or 100 baseband (unmodulated signal). For example, 10BaseT indicates a 10 megabit per second transmission rate, a twisted pair, and baseband transmission. Some devices may be used with dual frequencies and are listed as 10/100BaseT.

Twisted-pair cable capability is specified by the category of the cable. The category determines the bandwidth and distance the cable is capable of transmitting in addition to the number of twists per foot, capacitance, frequency, attenuation, and pair-to-pair near-end cross talk. *Cross talk* occurs when the signal from one wire in the twisted pair cable induces a random signal in an adjacent wire.

NETWORK INTERFACE CARD

The network interface card (NIC) connects the computer motherboard to the cabling.

Internal network interface cards are used with desktop computers while laptops use an NIC that connects to the laptop by the PCMCIA port. PCMCIA stands for Personal Computer Memory Card International Association, which promotes standards on integrated circuit cards for mobile computers. NICs have specific word lengths (16, 32, or 64 bits) and need to operate at the frequency designated by the network operating system and hardware. The network throughput increases proportionately to changes in the NIC word length and network frequency.

Network interface cards are not the only way to connect the motherboard to the cabling. Some laptops have built-in network capability. Also available are adapters that work on the universal serial bus (USB), parallel, or serial ports.

DATA TRANSMISSION

When a corporation wants remote access to its network, enterprise-wide computing, or to be connected to the internet, the local area networks need the ability to communicate beyond the network. At the least expensive and lowest performance level, plain old telephone system (POTS) lines and modems are used. This is still a prevalent technology for individual users contacting a network. While POTS lines may be used between networks or with the internet, the bandwidth is low.

Companies that use enterprise-wide computing often rely on T1 lines for data transmission. A *T1 line*, consisting of 24 channels, can transmit data at 1.544 Mbps (1.544×10^6 bits per second). While these lines are leased and costly, they provide the opportunity for greater exchanges of data, voice, and video conferencing. As corporations increase in size, have multiple geographical locations, and centralize their data processing, they tend to lease multiple T1 lines. While the T1 line is copper wire, the *T3 line* is fiber-optic cable and can support

a transmission rate of 44.736 Mbps. T1 and T3 lines are expensive because of the cost of installation of cabling to the corporation by the telephone company and leasing 24-hour access. There are also less well known E1 and E3 lines, which are capable of sending data at 2.048 Mbps and 34.368 Mbps respectively.

Integrated services digital network lines (ISDN) were developed to provide an intermediate solution to the high performance and high cost of the T1 line and low performance of the modem on a POTS line. While T1 has been available wherever there were phone lines, ISDN lines have been available only in selected areas.

ISDN has never been universally available and its performance has been questioned. The standard calls for a switched line that uses a three-channel configuration of two full duplex 64 Kbps (64×10^3 bits per second) channels and one 16 Kbps channel for a total of 144 Kbps (basic rate interface or BRI). In reality, the channels are usually regulated by the providers to 56 Kbps and 16 Kbps. Divisions within the ISDN standard are BRI at 144 Kbps, primary rate interface (PRI) at 1.536 Mbps, and broadband ISDN (B-ISDN), which allows simultaneous transmission of voice, video, and data over fiber-optic lines at 155 Mbps. Dial-up ISDN voice calls, data transfer, and video conferencing are all possible over BRI with increasing capabilities available with PRI and B-ISDN. The lack of availability of the lines in many communities, their high line and supporting equipment costs, and the lower transmission rate of BRI and PRI, which has restricted their use for LAN-to-LAN connections, have minimized their implementation (Goldman 1995).

Digital subscriber lines (DSL) and digital data service (DDS) use conventional four-wire telephone lines in a digital mode. Since it is digital, a modem is not necessary. DSLs were intended to transmit data at high speed over low-cost telephone lines. DSL and DDS support speeds of 64 Kbps to 1.544 Mbps depending on the distance between the user and the provider.

Issues that determine the performance of a DSL include: (a) the distance from the telephone company's communications equipment to the user's local office or manufacturing plant; (b) the type of cable used between the communications equipment and the manufacturing plant; and (c) the services that have been sold to other subscribers running on adjacent lines.

Regardless of the technology, the central issues of how to transmit data reliably over a distance at the highest appropriate speed (bits per second or bps) and at an economical cost (communications lines, hardware, software, and support personnel) remain constant. As the technology changes from POTS to ISDN to DSL to T1 to T3 to the next levels, the central issues of communicating remotely with networks, between networks, and with the internet will also remain constant.

NETWORK OPERATING SYSTEM

An *operating system* is the software that interfaces the user with the network and its components. Common operating systems that support ethernet architecture include Novell Netware, Windows NT, and Unix. Since each has different characteristics and applications, it is common to find at least two of them used in the same manufacturing facility.

37.3 OPEN-SYSTEMS INTERCONNECT MODEL

The open systems interconnect (OSI) seven-layer computer network model is an ideal model that provides a logical description of the various functions in computer networking. For any user, the layers should be transparent. However, a fundamental knowledge is helpful. The OSI model is illustrated in Figure 37-1.

The *physical layer* processes digital information into a form transmitted by the physical medium (wires, radio waves, or fibers). The EIA-232 C or D (RS-232C), which are cable standards, operate at the physical layer as does the network interface card when it generates the voltages and sends them over the transmission medium (cable, fiber, or radio wave). Ethernet uses baseband with the digital signal transmitted one signal at a time over the conductors. A second method, broadband, modulates the signal into a radio frequency and can handle multiplexed signals.

The *data-link layer* arranges the raw data bits of the physical layer into frames. These discrete frames are coded and form the building blocks for sending large volumes of data over the network. This level includes the access protocol such as token passing, polling, and carrier-sense multiple access with collision detection (CSMA/CD). The data-link layer provides error detection, transmits its frames to the physical layer for transmission, and receives data from the physical layer.

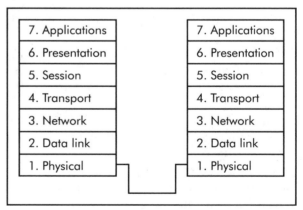

Figure 37-1. Open-systems interconnect (OSI) seven-layer model.

The *network layer* identifies the destination address of the frames and requests network facilities and priorities. This layer provides switching and routing. Addressing is of importance for computers on a network and for communication between multiple networks.

The *transport layer* verifies that data are sent and received correctly and in the correct order. A message may be routed over different paths when being transmitted across two or more networks. A portion of a message can arrive at a destination after a later portion arrives. The transport layer reads the code inserted on the frame by the data-link layer and reassembles the message in the correct order.

The *session layer* determines how two networks communicate, establishes communication, and monitors that communication.

The *presentation layer* is the interface between the application layer and the session layer. This layer has the capability to translate between different formats or codes. An example is sending a message from an IBM mainframe and receiving it on a PC over ethernet.

The *applications layer*, the level seen by users, exchanges information between the programs and the user interface.

37.4 REPEATERS, BRIDGES, ROUTERS, AND GATEWAYS

Repeaters, bridges, routers, and gateways all work at different levels of the OSI model to add capability to local area networks. *Repeaters* operate at level 1, the physical level, by receiving a signal and transmitting the same signal (repeating it). Repeaters are used to increase the overall transmission distance for the different conductors in a given network. They typically do not do error control, flow control, or address correction. Repeaters are reasonably fast because

they do not process the signal. Repeaters and bridges are similar because they cannot change data or the form of the data.

Bridges enable computers on two similar but different networks to communicate with each other. Bridges transmit similar data from one network to another and filter out information that is not addressed for the other network. Bridges are used to link identical LANs to increase the range of user access. This linkage generally increases user access to file servers and application software, number of users, e-mail communications, and printing resources. Bridges store and forward frames at the data-link level (layer 2) of the OSI model.

Routers are protocol-sensitive units that support communication between dissimilar LANs (architectures) using the same protocol. Novell's SPX/IPX® or DEC's DECnet® are examples of common protocols for ethernet architecture. Routers operate at the third level of the OSI model (network layer) and communicate in packets. Routers are capable of modifying the network-specific information so that they can route a message from one type of network (for example, ethernet) to another (for example, token ring) if both are based on a common network operating system. If there are redundant routes for the flow of data from one network to another, a router is capable of selecting an appropriate path.

Gateways connect networks of different network operating systems, architectures, and protocols by translating the protocol from one to the other. They process bits at the physical layer all through error detection, framing, routing, flow control, etc., at the appropriate level from the physical through the application layers. The advantage of being able to translate and connect a network to any other network has the disadvantage of a time delay in the propagation of the message.

37.5 TOPOLOGIES

Network architecture also includes the topology of the network. LANs have both physical and logical topologies. The physical topology is the method of attaching PCs to a LAN. The three fundamental LAN physical topologies are star, ring, and bus as illustrated in Figure 37-2. The star layout is often preferred because it is often the easiest to troubleshoot if there is a failure in a cable.

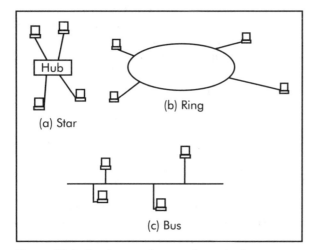

Figure 37-2. Fundamental network topologies.

Most networks today are a hybrid of at least two of the three fundamental topologies. Figure 37-3 illustrates two different hybrid topologies. Others topologies such as ring-star or bus-ring are also possible. The ease of network modification, cable installation, and cable troubleshooting makes the star-star or bus-star common configurations. A fundamental constraint of network cabling is that each type of cable has a maximum length for a given network system. While unshielded twisted pair may be used to connect hubs or hubs and a bus, greater distances can be gained by using fiber-optic cable, thinnet, or thicknet coaxial cables. Since manufacturing facilities are often very large, the design of the hybrid topology is very important for a cost-efficient installation.

37.6 PROTOCOLS

A *protocol* is the predefined manner or set of rules that a function or service is provided. Protocols regulate the data format for moving data between levels of the open-systems interconnect (OSI) model. Common protocols include network access, carrier-sense multiple access/collision detection, token passing, token-ring passing, and polling. Carrier-sense multiple access/collision detection (CSMA/CD) is used by ethernet.

The CSMA/CD protocol requires each user to wait until the line of channel is clear (idle) before he or she begins transmitting. If a data collision from two users is detected, the protocol requires that each user cease transmitting and wait a randomly determined period of time before checking for a clear line and transmitting again.

Token passing allows a workstation to transmit data (for example, save a file on the server) when the workstation holds the token. The token can be directed to the specific addresses of specific workstations more frequently than others. Token-ring messages pass through the multiple workstations, being received and re-transmitted, until the message or data arrive at the designated workstation.

Polling is the least common protocol. In polling, a central computer or host polls each specific workstation in some predetermined manner. Polling is most frequently used with host or mainframe-based systems.

The internet and intranet both require the transmission-control protocol/internet protocol (TCP/IP) suite. *Intranets* use the same technologies as the internet except they are restricted to a specific set of users. TCP/IP was originally developed by the Department of Defense (DoD) to allow different computing hardware and software to

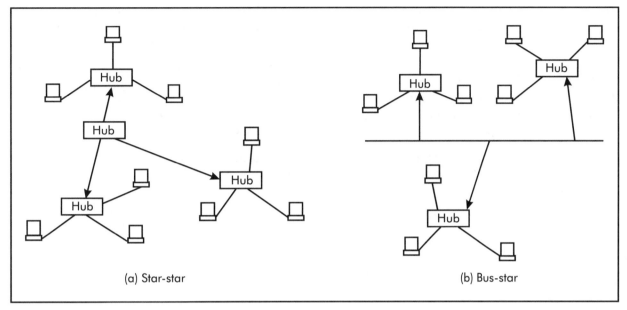

Figure 37-3. Common hybrid topologies.

communicate with each other and the DoD. TCP is used to transfer data between two internet devices. Virtual ports are used to make these connections and TCP monitors the flow of data. The *internet protocol* (IP) addresses the data and directs it to the appropriate destination. Each internet device has an IP number composed of four segments of one to three digits separated by decimal points (for example, 198.109.68.194). The *domain name system* (DNS) permits names to be coupled to the IP address. For example, www.sme.org may be used instead of 198.109.68.194 to locate the web page for the Society of Manufacturing Engineers. Since the internet has grown so rapidly, static IP addresses for specific computers are becoming a luxury. Dynamic IP addresses that are captured by a user at login to the network or internet reduce the total number of addresses required at a specific time. Dynamic IP addresses are managed by a dynamic host configuration protocol (DHCP) server. If the user wishes to upload a specific file to or from a server, file transfer protocol (FTP) is used.

Hypertext transfer protocol (HTTP) is used to transfer information from web servers to web browsers.

Intranet software is required to operate an intranet. Common intranet suites are Novell® Intranetware®, Microsoft® Back Office®, and Lotus® Domino® (formerly Lotus® Notes®). The advantage of using an intranet instead of a LAN is multiple-user real-time access of multimedia, personal appointment data, e-mail, enterprise-wide computing information that is both text and graphic, access from the internet, and video conferencing. Intranets help share the corporate information in formats similar to the web. Groupware software on both the internet and intranets allow groups of people to work together.

The internet and intranets are key components in MEI wheel level 3 "shared knowledge systems (refer to Figure 36-1)." Each is instrumental in joining the customer (level 1) to the organization, to the people of the organization, and to enhance the teamwork within an organization (level 2). They are also significant in providing design and manufacturing information to level 4 for product design, manufacturing, and customer service.

REVIEW QUESTIONS

37.1) What term is used to describe the number of signals that can be carried simultaneously on the same conductor?

37.2) Which network component provides real-time access to database and CAD files?

37.3) Which type of cabling is least sensitive to electromagnetic radiation?

37.4) What piece of network hardware allows two similar but different networks to communicate with each other?

37.5) What type of fundamental LAN topology uses a central hub that each computer is connected to?

37.6) What protocol is used to transfer information from a web server to a web browser?

REFERENCE

Goldman, J.E. 1995. *Applied Data Communications*. New York: John Wiley & Sons, Inc.

Chapter 38

Computer Numerical Control Machining

38.1 MACHINE COORDINATE AXES

CNC machines machine parts by moving a tool along a predetermined or programmed path based on the workpiece geometry. Defining the tool path and part geometry requires a coordinate and axis identification system.

A CNC machine tool's linear axes are X, Y (if a three-axis machine), and Z. The X axis is the major axis of movement perpendicular to the spindle. The Y axis is mutually perpendicular to the X axis and the spindle. However, it has a shorter range of travel than the X axis. The Z axis generally coincides with the spindle and is perpendicular to the X and Y axes. Figure 38-1 illustrates the axes for a three-axis vertical milling machine. Figure 38-2 illustrates the axes for a two-axis lathe.

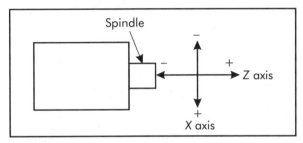

Figure 38-2. Two-axis lathe coordinate system.

The *Right-hand Rule*, illustrated in Figure 38-3, is helpful for keeping the axes in the correct orientation. The thumb points toward $+X$, the index finger is perpendicular to the thumb and points toward $+Y$, and the second finger is perpendicular to both the thumb and the index finger and points toward the $+Z$ axis.

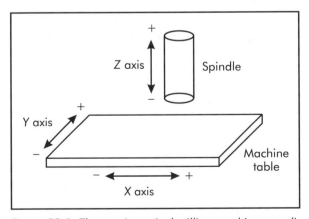

Figure 38-1. Three-axis vertical milling machine coordinate system.

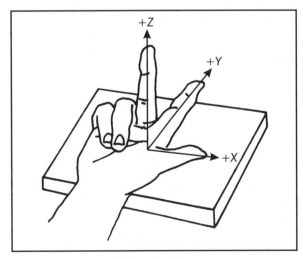

Figure 38-3. The Right-hand Rule.

If a CNC machine has additional linear axes of movement, such as the turret on a turret lathe, the axes need a separate identification system. The axes U, V, and W are parallel to the X, Y, and Z axes, respectively. When a machine has rotation of the workpiece or tool about the X, Y, and Z axes, the rotation is designated by A, B, and C, respectively.

38.2 COMPUTER NUMERICAL CONTROL/NUMERICAL CONTROL PROGRAMMING

A computer numerical control (CNC) machine consists of computer instructions (software or program), the machine control unit, and the processing machine. The standard programming includes the tool path, turning the spindle on and off, the coolant on and off, tool changes, and machine feeds and speeds. Programs may be entered manually or with surface modeling software and post-processed into conventional G-code programs. Programs are transmitted electronically from the computer via RS-232 or ethernet network connections to the machine control unit.

Preparatory functions, often referred to as *G codes*, and miscellaneous functions (*M functions*) for CNC are listed in Appendix B of this book. The syntax or sequence for the code is: block number (optional); G instruction(s) and the X, Y, Z, etc., parameters with numerical values; and decimal points for the instruction. These are followed by the spindle speed (S) and feed rate (F) if the speed or feed is changed from the value in the previous block. Spindle operation, coolant operation, tool changes for machining centers or chuck operation, and tailstock operations for lathes or turning center lathes are programmed with M functions. Most current controllers have an M function for changing the machine movements from code written either in SI units (mm) or U.S. customary units (inches). Controllers from different manufacturers may have some differences in syntax for executing the program.

Programs may be run in single-step or continuous modes. The *single-step mode* executes a single block per operator action and is used for checking or editing a program. The *continuous mode* is used for production with proven programs. Sample turning and milling programs with explanations are shown in Figures 38-4 and 38-5 respectively.

In most companies, the preparation of CNC programs for all but the simplest of geometric parts is done with graphical computer-aided manufacturing (CAM) software. CAM systems have linear and circular interpolations built into the CNC operating system and the software may incorporate helical, parabolic, and cubic interpolations.

Other than manual programming, the earliest numerical control (NC) language was automatic programming of tools (APT). This text-based language is still popular with companies doing four- or five-axes CNC operations, especially in the airframe and machine-tool-building industries. The 3-D graphical CAM programs are currently the choice for constructing complex three-dimensional surfaces.

Computer-assisted part programming elements include the operating system specified to each proprietary language, the compiler, the NC processor, and the post-processor. The NC processor generates an intermediate file, called a *cutter location file*, which contains cutter location data. The postprocessor is specified for each brand of machine control unit and converts the cutter location data into a file (G codes and M functions) for each specific machine tool.

38.3 CNC OPERATIONS

All early NC machines were point-to-point units that move either the tool (lathe/turning center) or table/workpiece (milling) to a given location. The control unit in these

Line #	CNC Turning Program	Explanation of Codes
N0740	G50 S1000	Maximum speed setting of spindle to 1,000 rpm
N0750	G20 G96 S1000 M04	Inch data input Constant surface speed control at 1,000 sf/m Start spindle CCW
N0760	G00 Z3.487 T1	Rapid traverse to Z value of 3.487 in. for tool #1 (in this example a button turning tool) Note: The turret is rotated before the rapid traverse of the X axis to insure completion of the rotation so other tools with larger footprints do not strike the workpiece or chuck
N0765	G00 X.600	Rapid traverse to X value of 0.600 in.
N0770	G42 G00 W–.746	Tool nose radius compensation turned on Rapid traverse to W –0.746 in. from reference point (parallel to Z axis)
N0780	G20 G98 F3.0	Inch data input, feed rate of 3.0 in./min
N0790	G01 X.370	Feed to X value of 0.370 in.
N0800	G01 W–.240	Feed to W value of –0.240 in. (parallel to Z axis)
N0810	G01 X.570 W–.300	Feed to X value of 0.570 in. and length of –0.300 in.
N0820	G00 X.7	Rapid traverse away from workpiece to X value of 0.700 in.
N0830	G28 U0.0 W0.0 T1	Return to reference point
N0840	T8 M06	Change turret to position (tool) #8

Figure 38-4. Sample turning program.

machines attempts to move each axis independently of the other and the tool path can only approximate a straight line or arc. Current control system technology for turning and machining centers has both linear and circular interpolation. In a literal sense, CNC drilling and tapping machines do not require more than point-to-point operation because that is the function of the tool.

Linear and circular interpolations are standard features on most CNC machines. These features require the capability of simultaneous control of multiple axes to generate a two- or three-dimensional (2 or 3D) line or a 2D circle (in a principal plane). The interpolator may be considered a small, fixed macro. It receives from active storage the

slide direction and measurement calculations that dictate how fast the cut of the path is to be made. Then it calculates the data and directs the movement of each slide at the correct time/distance constants.

Linear interpolations can achieve interpolations in increments as small as 0.0001 in. (0.00254 mm). A linear interpolation can be programmed as short as the tolerances the machine will allow. With CAM software, complex and free-form curves can be accurately estimated by the computer, generating a very large number of circular interpolated points to estimate the curve. *Circular interpolation* is the most common higher order interpolation. It is used to approximate circles in the principal plane (2D) of the machine. *Parabolic*

Line #	CNC Milling Program	Explanation of Codes
N160	G00 X-3. Y-3. T4 M06	Rapid traverse away from workpiece so tools can be changed without interference from the workpiece or workholding devices Tool #4 is loaded into the spindle
N170	G00 G90 X-1.75 Y-1.062 Z-.075 M03 M08	Rapid traverse toward workpiece, maintaining tool and workpiece clearance; select absolute coordinate system; tool is lowered to 0.075 in. below the top of the workpiece Start spindle CW Start coolant
N180	G01 Z-.188 F160 S4000	Tool is moved at 16.0 in./min (feed rate) to a depth of 0.188 in., tool is rotating at 4,000 rpm
N190	G01 X1.755	Workpiece has a shoulder milled from -1.75 to +1.755 in. parallel to the X axis
N210	G03 X1.937 Y-.88 I1.755 J-.88 F160 S4000	CCW arc interpolation with a radius of 0.182 in. and centered on the I and J coordinates
N220	G01 Y.88	Feed in +Y direction from -0.881 to 0.88
N230	G03 X1.755 Y1.062 I1.755 J.88 F160 S4000	CCW arc interpolation with a radius of 0.182 in. and centered on the I and J coordinates
N240	G01 X-1.75	Feed in -X direction from 1.755 to -1.755
N250	G03 X1.755 Y-.88 I1.755 J-.88 F160 S4000	CCW arc interpolation with a radius of 0.182 in. and centered on the I and J coordinates
N260	G01 Y-.88 F160 S4000	Feed in -Y direction from +.88 to .88
N270	G03 X1.755 Y-1.062 I-1.755 J-.88 F160 S4000	CCW arc interpolation with a radius of 0.182 in. and centered on the I and J coordinates
N280	G00 Z-.07 M05 M09	Rapid traverse in the Z axis to clear the workpiece Stop spindle Coolant off
N290	G90 G00 X-3 Y-3 T1 M06	In the absolute coordinate system, rapid traverse to X -3.0 and Y -3.0 (so the tool clears the workpiece for the tool change); remove tool #4 and load tool #1

Figure 38-5. Sample milling program.

interpolation is a second higher order interpolation. Though it is not as effective with circles as circular interpolation, it is generally more efficient with other curves.

Limited contouring machine control systems have been built with circular interpolation capability but without buffer storage. These machines were built to provide lower-cost CNC machine tools. Without the buffer storage, the control unit causes the machine tool to accelerate, machine, decelerate, and read in a new block. During the read time, the feed rate is greatly reduced, resulting in an average feed rate that is less than programmed. The reduced feed rate may also result in pulsating and undercuts.

Full contouring machines have both interpolation and *buffer storage*. The buffer storage permits the controller to read the next block(s) and store the new data in the buffer. When the machine has reached the coordinates specified in the current block, the active storage data is dumped, the buffer downloads its data to active storage, and the machine continues its interpolated motion at the specified feed. The controller reads in a new block(s) and stores data for the next block in the buffer, while active storage in the control unit executes the current interpolation. These data transfers require only microseconds, and the inertia of the mechanical system is sufficient to continue at the same velocity for the transfer time.

38.4 CNC CONTROLLERS

The primary elements of a CNC machine control unit are an operator interface, machine control unit, and machine interface. Common *operator interfaces* are computers or keyboards with monitors. Part programs may be input or output via paper-tape punch/ readers, magnetic-tape readers, communication with computers, and networks. The *machine control unit* has all the characteristics of a microcomputer: both read only memory (ROM) and random access memory

(RAM); an arithmetic unit; and a control unit.

The *machine interface* passes outputs and inputs between the control unit and the processing machine. The machine interface transforms the digital output signal of the control into an amplified analog alternating current (AC) or direct current (DC) signal or an amplified pulse-width modulated DC signal to drive the motors on the processing machine. It also transforms closed-loop feedback generated by resolvers and encoders from the motors or ball lead screws. *Resolvers* are analog devices that read machine movements and then convert the information to digital in contrast to encoders that are strictly digital. Resolvers are less sensitive to vibration and temperature than encoders. Other outputs include discrete signals for coolant pump operation, powered tools mounted in turrets on turning centers, and hydraulic valve operation for power clamping, indexing tables, power chucks, and power tailstocks. Input from the machine to the control unit to give closed-loop feedback is generated by resolvers or encoders mounted on the servomotors or ball lead screws that indicate the commanded position has been achieved. Additional discrete inputs include:

- proximity switches indicating extreme limit and "home" locations for each axis;
- safety mechanical switches for cabinet and enclosure doors;
- a pressure switch or oil level switch for lubrication of the spindle and ways;
- an air-pressure switch for machine-tool change operation; and
- temperature-sensitive switches for cabinet, oil, and motor temperatures.

Most control interfaces have additional discrete input/output (I/O) for linking the CNC machine to pallet changers, programmable logic controllers, or cell controllers.

The motion control for CNC is open-loop stepping motor or closed-loop servo control. In general, *open-loop control systems* generate commands based on time, discrete on and off control, or stages for stepping motors. Motion control systems receive no feedback information or signals to indicate if the motion command was completed. Open-loop control is like the design of some older garage door openers, plotters, most printers, and most stepper-motor drives. Its obvious weakness is its inability to detect if the motion control caused the mechanism to reach the desired objective. Open-loop control is typically found on lower-cost equipment.

Closed-loop control is used with discrete systems as well as servo systems. It generates information called *feedback* to the control unit that the controller compares with the motion command to determine if the motion command was achieved. CNC equipment, robots, and cruise control on automobiles are common closed-loop systems.

Distributive numerical control (DNC) systems are overlays on a network operating system such as Novell Netware®, Windows® NT, Windows®, TCP/IP (Unix), or some other proprietary system to link CNC machines into an integrated system of communications and file management. DNC has the ability to download entire part programs to the CNC machine controllers connected to the network.

Communications with individual CNC machines have been by tape readers and RS-232 serial connections. Most installations now are based on TCP/IP or ethernet. Complete communication of programs and data for CNC programs is vital. Missed bits in a program may be disastrous. Therefore, DNC operating systems typically include more robust error-checking schema than do the conventional local area networks (LAN). DNC systems can support file management, input from bar code or statistical process control systems, and communications with programmable logic controllers and enterprise computing systems.

The future trend in CNC controllers is open-architecture system control. The advantages of an open-architecture system include network connectivity, data sharing, and operator familiarity (Laduzinsky 1999). Network connectivity brings ethernet capability to the computer/controller without an intermediate computer. Data sharing and processing is enhanced by the integration of a database program and spreadsheet into the controller. Most operators familiar with a graphical-user-interface operating system find the CNC less formidable.

A disadvantage of open-architecture system controls is that they are defined differently. One vendor may use a PC as the processor. A second may use the PC as the controller and servo cards to interface with the CNC machine. A third interpretation may have the PC interface with the CNC circuit boards via a bus.

REVIEW QUESTIONS

38.1) What M function is used to start the spindle of a CNC milling machine clockwise?

38.2) What manual programming language is popular for doing four- or five-axes CNC operations?

38.3) The spindle of a three-axis or two-axis CNC machine is generally designated as which axis?

38.4) Which type of control contains no feed back?

38.5) Which feedback device, a resolver or encoder, is less sensitive to vibration and temperature changes?

38.6) What letter will the following milling program generate?

```
N010 G00 X0.0 Y0.0 T4M06
N020 G00 X1.0 Y1.0
N030 G01 Z–.1 F3 S1000
N040 G01 X4.0 Y4.0
N050 G00 Z1.0
N060 G00 X1.0 Y4.0
N070 G01 Z–.1
N080 G01 X4.0 Y1.0
N090 G00 Z1.0
```

REFERENCE

Laduzinsky, A. 1999. "Open Minded." *Cutting Tool Engineering*. September: 51.

Chapter 39

Programmable Logic Controllers

39.1 INTRODUCTION

Programmable logic controllers (PLCs) are one of the primary forms of manufacturing automation. They are used to replace relays, control analog and digital open- and closed-loop systems, and control manufacturing cells in islands of programmable automation, flexible manufacturing, and computer-integrated manufacturing.

The use of PLCs as relay replacement is one of their major functions. This application results in PLCs of all sizes being used to replace existing relay control panels or to control new equipment. Advantages of relay replacement include ease of program modification at later dates, capability of collecting data relevant to the process under control, communication with other equipment at the bit input/output (I/O) level, communication with other computer equipment at either serial or network levels, and troubleshooting the control system. However, if PLCs without data communication capability are selected for an application, the result is an "island of automation." An island of automation is an automated system with minimal capability of communicating with the remainder of the manufacturing operations.

PLCs used in analog and digital closed-loop control systems are quite common with the migration of PLCs to more powerful central-processing units. Historically, the analog inputs and outputs were cumbersome to program. Because of the increase in variety and sophistication of programming languages and embedded commands, the difficulty in programming analog functions has been reduced. PLC outputs commonly have a maximum current-carrying capability of one or two amperes. It is common to find one or even two relays between a PLC and a large motor starter because of current capacities.

When control commands are executed without indication that the command has been appropriately executed, then the control is *open-loop*. Timer-based control systems are often open loop, for example, pneumatic cylinders controlled by the time cycle. Stepper-motor drives that are driven by electrical pulses are often open-loop without feedback. As a result, the mechanical system is moved in proportion to the number of steps that the stepper-motor controller sent to the motor without any indication of the actual movement.

Closed-loop systems include feedback that a command has been executed and may be non-servo as well as servo. For example, non-servo systems may include limit switches that must be activated by a closed safety gate before a press will operate or a lathe will turn. All practical servo-driven automated equipment has closed-loop feedback. Many PLC systems use closed-loop feedback to insure that specific motions have been accomplished prior to energizing the next output in a sequential or combinational logic program.

39.2 APPLICATIONS

The original PLCs were designed in 1968 as programmable replacements for hard-wired relays. By then both the computer and solid-state electronics were over 20 years old, but still in the early stages of their development. The development of the PLC was one of the earlier applications of computers to the factory floor. The PLC of today can perform relay replacement, Boolean algebra functions of logical AND, OR, and NOT, count programmed actions, execute the various types of time delays, and perform sequence operations. It can also manipulate data, do arithmetic functions, and communicate with other PLCs or computers via networks. The primary application of programmable logic controllers is still discrete (on-off) control. However, PLCs are now used to control servo operations, proportional-integral-derivative (PID) systems, drive-stepper motors, and automatic data collection. Some higher level PLCs are even capable of fuzzy logic control. The PLC and its primary language excel at discrete control whether it is combinational logic to ensure all logical conditions have been met before a machine executes a cycle, or sequential control that executes a specific set of operations in a given pattern, cycle after cycle. The most complex control can integrate multiple discrete functions with computer numerical control systems, robot systems, or PID control systems and report data via a network to an enterprise control system. PLCs used for cell control are an efficient application that frees the CNC or robot controller to execute its servo control functions while the PLC moves parts, controls the other activities in the cell, and communicates manufacturing and statistical process control data to the enterprise-wide computing system.

Cell control can be accomplished by a computer-based cell controller but PLCs are more common for this function. Even when a piece of automated equipment has the capability of performing cell control (for example, a robot controller), engineers should consider using PLCs to interface with the robot to:

- increase control capability and flexibility (approximating co-processing);
- get faster processing of the robotic program without the additional cell control statements; and
- develop simpler robotic programs.

If the robot system is not functioning, the material handling or process functions of the robot may be performed in some other manner and the cell will still be controlled by the PLC. Likewise, if the PLC has a failure, the diagnosis is easier and the time to repair is reduced.

39.3 COMPONENTS

The PLC, regardless of size, speed, and memory, has components similar to any computer, that is, input modules, central processing unit (CPU), memory, and output modules. The CPU is composed of a processor, memory, and power supply. The I/O modules are the interface between the physical inputs and outputs and the CPU. The operating system for the PLC is designed to permit the programmer to easily access the input/output units in a timely manner. The PLC is designed to control operations in real-time by scanning or reading the input module, executing the program, and setting or writing the outputs in the output memory to the appropriate states. The input and output cards identify terminals so they have the same state as the binary input or output memory table (ON, 1, or TRUE; OFF, 0, or FALSE).

While PLCs have the same systems as personal computers, they are designed to operate in a harsh electrical environment, and execute a single program. The single-purpose operating system has in the past provided the speed and dedication needed for real-time control. Personal computers have been used to program and communicate data with PLCs. Each year, more control functions are being performed by modified personal computers.

PLCs are sized according to the number of inputs and outputs and have five general classifications. Micro PLCs have up to 32 I/O, small PLCs have 32-128 I/O, medium PLCs have 64-1024 I/O, large PLCs have 512-4096 I/O, and very large PLCs have 2048-8192 I/O. Obviously, there is overlap between small and medium, medium and large, and large and very large. Other distinctions are based on size of memory and other features provided with the increasingly larger sizes.

Due to the nature of the hardware of PLC controls, safety considerations mandate local control of a system for startup, emergency shutdown, and lockout. Further, safety considerations require that emergency stops be hard-wired to stop the machine and the PLC. When a PC fails, data is lost and production stops. More importantly, when a PLC fails, operators can be injured, sometimes fatally. Despite the efforts of PLC manufacturers, it is impossible to accurately predict how a PLC will behave if the CPU, memory, or I/O cards fail. The follow-up to this safety issue is to identify the component and system conditions necessary for a safe restart.

39.4 PROGRAMMING

Historically, the programming language common to PLCs has been relay ladder logic (RLL), the language used with relay control systems. The basic elements in a relay ladder logic program are:

RAILS
RUNGS
BRANCHES

INPUTS EXAMINE ON   --| |--
           EXAMINE OFF   --| / |--
TIMERS   --[T]--
OUTPUTS   --( )--
COUNTERS   --CNT]--

Rails are vertical lines serving as the voltage source for relay circuits and logic for the PLC. *Rungs* are horizontal lines and contain the branches, inputs, and outputs. A *branch* starts and ends an OR function. The input, EXAMINE ON, is true only when the input is high or on. EXAMINE OFF performs a NOT logic function. The input, EXAMINE OFF, is true only when the input is low or off. The output, a logic bit in memory as well as on the output card, is sometimes called a "coil" reference to its predecessor the "relay coil." It is generally on the right-hand side of the rung. Figure 39-1 illustrates the AND, OR, and NOT functions in PLC programming.

A common hard-wired magnetic motor starter has a relay ladder logic control circuit as shown in Figure 39-2. When the start switch is depressed, the first rung is true. Closing the start switch completes the circuit and activates output C1. Output C1 can be thought of as a relay with two contacts, C1-1 and C1-2. When C1 is energized, C1-2 is on (contacts closed), thus activating the motor starter M1 in rung two. When the start switch is released, the motor remains on because output C1 remains energized. C1 remains energized because C1-1 is on (closed contact). C1-1 is sometimes referred to as a "holding contact." The only way to stop the motor (M1) is to de-energize C1 by depressing the hard-wired stop switch. Since the stop switch is normally closed, depressing it will open the circuit between the rails, thus de-energizing C1 and then M1.

Relay ladder logic was chosen as the programming language for PLCs because the electricians understood that language from working with relay control. RLL works well

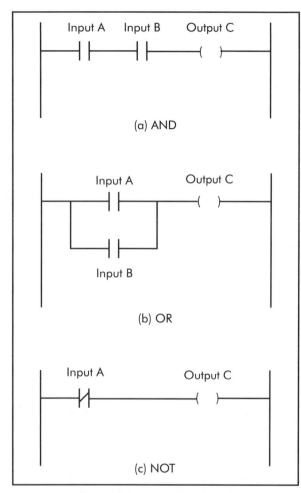

Figure 39-1. Basic relay ladder logic: (a) AND; (b) OR; and (c) NOT.

for discrete control. However, it does not provide the grammar or tools for higher level programming of today's PLCs. These tools have been developed along with newer programming languages. Even though RLL has been the standard language, each PLC manufacturer had a proprietary programming system. The goal of a common PLC instruction set for PLCs was the objective of the International Electrotechnical Commission (IEC) SC65B-WG7 committee. The committee achieved its theoretical objective with the approval of the IEC 1131 standard in 1992.

REVIEW QUESTIONS

39.1) What electrical component were PLCs designed to replace?

39.2) PLCs without data communication result in _____ of automation.

39.3) How are PLCs sized?

39.4) Historically, what has been the programming language for PLCs?

39.5) In Figure Q39-1, what will be the state (ON or OFF) of output D if all the inputs are low (OFF)?

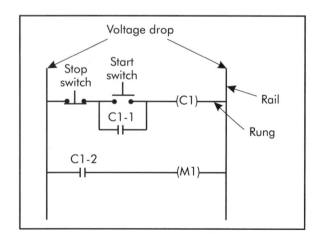

Figure 39-2. Motor-starter ladder diagram.

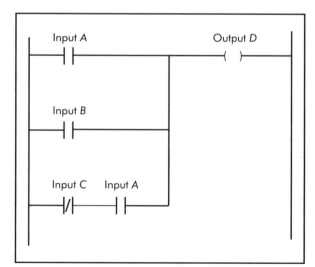

Figure Q39-1. Review Question 39-5.

Robots are programmable multifunctional tools. A robot has four subsystems consisting of the power system, the control system, the mechanical system, and the mechanical-world interface system. The power system drives the robot arm (mechanical system), the control system directs the power system to move the robot arm or end-of-arm tooling, and the end-of-arm tooling interfaces the mechanical system (robot arm) with the world (the parts to be manipulated or processed).

40.1 POWER SYSTEMS

The power system for robot arms may be electrical, hydraulic, or pneumatic. Electricity is the power system of choice for robots with closed-loop servo control and is more robust than hydraulically powered units. Electrical servo control is a well-understood technology with high accuracy, repeatability, and speed. However, hydraulic power is used for robots that work with large heavy loads, and pneumatics are used for small, fast, non-servo-controlled robot arms. Today, positive pressurized servomotors permit them to be used in a flammable environment. In the earlier years of robotics, flammable environments required hydraulic or pneumatic power systems.

40.2 CONTROL SYSTEMS

Robot control systems may be categorized according to the type of control (non-servo and servo), the type of feedback (open loop or closed loop), the resolution and accuracy, and the communications capability. Robot control systems, like computer numerical control (CNC) systems, are incorporating network interfaces in their controllers.

Programmable controllers are commonly used as control systems for non-servo robot systems. Servo controllers may be point to point, continuous path, or adaptive. The non-servo controllers may have the same number of degrees of freedom (joints of motion) as a servo robot but will have only a limited number of programmable positions. Velocities of the various links are also limited to a small finite number. Many small non-servo controlled robots use a pneumatic power system for the movement of parts. While they meet the technical definition of a robot, these devices are often called pick-and-place machines.

Servo control offers the programmer as many positions as the controller will accept in memory. The finite limit is the minimum movement of the robot arm in any one of the degrees of freedom. Point-to-point control is programmed by identifying and storing specific points that the arm will either "pass through" or "stop at." The path between those points is determined by the controller, not the programmer. More sophisticated controllers may be capable of linear and circular interpolation that allows the programmer to determine the path between end points according to some limited algorithms. The number of axes a controller can control simultaneously determines if the controller can cause a robot arm to do linear or circular interpolation or continuous path control. A true continuous path allows the programmer to define irregular or regular paths, often by lead-through programming. Lead-through programming requires the programmer to physically move the end-of-arm tooling through the desired path. The robot controller records all the points during the lead-through. Adaptive control requires outside sensing to modify the robot program. In a simple form of adaptive control, machine vision identifies new coordinates for a tool path and downloads the new coordinates to the robot controller. The controller can execute the appropriate changes in program coordinates.

Three common coordinate systems used with robotics are the world, tool, and part coordinate systems. The ability to do linear interpolation is a fundamental requirement for a controller to move the robot arm in world, tool, or part coordinate systems. The *world coordinate system* uses an X, Y, Z coordinate system with 0,0,0 located at the center of the base of the robot. The world coordinate system is similar to that for CNC machine tools. X is the primary axis, Y is perpendicular to X and is the minor axis, and the Z axis is perpendicular to X and Y and is concentric with the rotation of the first joint above the robot base or the extension from the base. This coordinate system is used for programming in either the on-line mode with a *teach pendant* or the off-line mode with a computer.

The *tool coordinate system* has its center on the tool flange. X and Y axes are parallel to the tool flange surface and Z is perpendicular to the flange. This coordinate system is used in programming a robot arm to approach parts or pick parts out of fixtures. The advantage to this system is that the tool flange can be oriented parallel to an oblique surface and then it can be easily moved parallel or perpendicular to that surface.

The *part coordinate system* has the coordinate center oriented according to the dimensions of the part. This system permits the robot tool, a MIG welding gun for example, to move according to the geometry of the part.

40.3 MECHANICAL SYSTEMS

The mechanical systems being controlled are composed of links and joints. *Links* are the solid members and *joints* provide for movement between the links. While links can be of many shapes, the joints are one of four types: linear transverse joint (Figure 40-1a), linear telescoping joint (Figure 40-1b), rotary hinge joint (Figure 40-1c), and rotary pivot joint (Figure 40-1d). The *hinge joint* has the axis of rotation perpendicular to the primary dimension of the links while the *rotary pivot* has the axis of rotation parallel to the primary axes of the links. Each joint is a degree of freedom (DOF). Most robots in the USA have four to six DOF, three in the arm and one to three in the wrist between the arm and the end-of-arm tooling.

Figures 40-2 through 40-6 illustrate many robot configurations and their respective work envelopes.

40.4 ROBOT ARM/WORLD INTERFACE

The mechanical-world interface is the link between the robot arm and its environment. That is, the end-of-arm tooling moves or processes parts. If part manipulation is required, grasping with two, three, or four mechanical fingers is most common. Other grasping systems may use hooks, vacuum suckers, or electromagnetism. Processing tooling may include spray finish guns, resistance welding guns, and MIG welding guns.

Any irregular part requires four degrees of freedom in a gripper to grasp it securely.

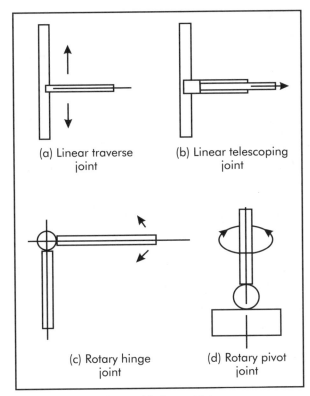

(a) Linear traverse joint

(b) Linear telescoping joint

(c) Rotary hinge joint

(d) Rotary pivot joint

Figure 40-1. Mechanical links and joints.

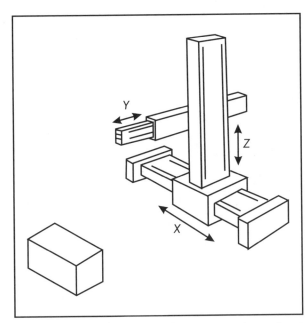

Figure 40-2. Cartesian arm (Cartesian work envelope) (Cubberly and Bakerjian 1989).

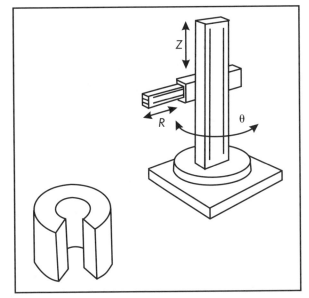

Figure 40-3. Cylindrical arm (cylindrical work envelope) (Cubberly and Bakerjian 1989).

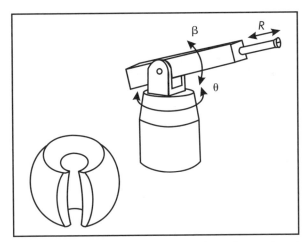

Figure 40-4. Polar arm (spherical work envelope) (Cubberly and Bakerjian 1989).

This can be accomplished with four rigid fingers or three or more articulated fingers. When using vacuum or electromagnetics on sheet stock, the sheet should be kept horizontal. When the sheets or loads are vertical, the required holding force is four times that of the force required when the workpieces are in the horizontal position.

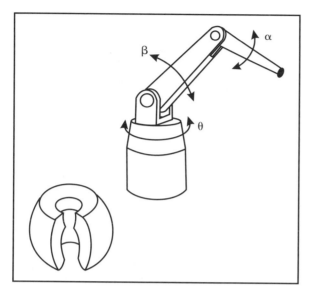

Figure 40-5. Articulated arm (spherical work envelope) (Cubberly and Bakerjian 1989).

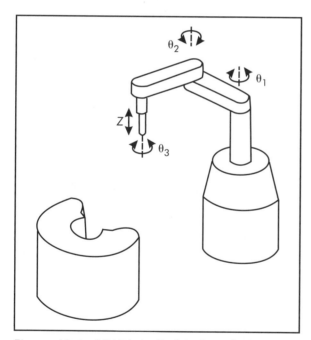

Figure 40-6. SCARA (cylindrical work envelope) (Cubberly and Bakerjian 1989).

Robotic assembly is within the capability of robotic systems. With vision and force-sensing systems providing closed loop feedback to the control system, robot arms are capable of precision placement of components at the stated locations.

The advantages of robots doing part handling are their repeatability and reliability. However, the disadvantage is that part handling does not add much, if any, value to the part. It is difficult for engineers to justify an expensive machine unless it improves product quality, productivity, or the quality of work life.

Any process that involves skill in the execution of it (for example, sealant dispensing or spray painting) may be a good candidate for a robotic or automated operation.

REVIEW QUESTIONS

40.1) What robotic power system is typically used for heavy loads?

40.2) The robotic joints of motion are called _____ of freedom.

40.3) _____ control requires outside sensing to modify the robot program.

40.4) What coordinate system has its center on the tool flange?

40.5) What is the shape of the work envelope created by a polar-arm robot?

REFERENCE

Cubberly, William and Ramon Bakerjian, eds. 1989. *Tool and Manufacturing Engineers Handboook*, Desk Edition. Dearborn, MI: Society of Manufacturing Engineers.

Chapter 41

Automated Material Handling and Identification

Material handling equipment can move either unit loads or bulk loads. *Unit loads* are either large single pieces or parts or products that may be grouped onto a pallet or into a tote. *Bulk loads* are liquids or semi-solids (for example, granulated solids that take the shape of their container) often moved by conveyor or pipeline and stored in bins or silos. This chapter will focus on the unit load.

41.1 AUTOMATED MATERIAL HANDLING SYSTEMS

Two very common forms of automated material handling systems are automated guided vehicle systems and automated storage and retrieval systems. They are capable of moving material required for push or pull manufacturing and providing data needed for manufacturing management.

Automated guided vehicle (AGV) systems are divided into four different configurations: train, forklift, unit load, and assembly. Until the 1990s, many AGVs used a wire in the floor with electromagnetic signals or a painted stripe. One newer guidance system includes fixed bar codes mounted at a specific height throughout the area used by the AGVs and read by a rotating laser mounted on the AGV. Another guidance system uses radio frequency to read fixed transmitters. Both of these systems use triangulation to determine the location of the AGV. The type of guidance system should be appropriate for the

application, and the required reliability, flexibility, and cost effectiveness. Most wire-in-the-floor systems are not easy to reconfigure and are costly to modify.

Orders to move material are transmitted to automated guided vehicles by radio control. The control system tracks the movement of the vehicle and knows when the assignment is completed. The controller can also provide data on the location, movement, and quantity of parts being moved. These data can be transmitted to the manufacturing management system via the manufacturing network for inventory control.

Each of the different configurations of AGVs has a primary application. The AGV train is used to move carts of parts, often from storage to manufacturing. The forklift and unit load AGVs are appropriate for moving pallets and totes on the manufacturing floor, respectively. The assembly AGV moves a part being assembled or a part to the assembly process.

Automated storage and retrieval systems (AS/RS) have evolved from their initial application of warehousing raw materials to storing work-in-process or assemble-to-order inventory, finished product inventory, and tool and fixture inventory. AS/RS are classed by the size of the unit load: micro load, mini load, or unit load. The mini and micro loads typically use totes, while the larger systems use pallets or are unit loads. Since AS/RS systems provide high-bay storage with a smaller footprint than conventional storage, they can improve the manufacturing productivity of an enterprise as well as move parts efficiently through the manufacturing process.

41.2 AUTOMATIC IDENTIFICATION SYSTEMS

Automatic identification improves both the accuracy (quality) and speed (production efficiency) of data entry for inventory, work-in-process, and final products. Bar code, radio-frequency data transmission, radio-frequency identification, magnetic stripe, voice recognition, and machine vision are the common forms of automatic identification used on the manufacturing floor.

BAR CODES

Bar coding is one of the most robust and reliable forms of automatic identification. Bar codes come in multiple symbols and densities. They are also available in linear, two-dimensional, and three-dimensional or matrix formats.

The most common linear bar codes are Universal Product Code (UPC), Code 39, Interleaved 3 of 5, and Code 128. The different bar codes offer different numeric or alphanumeric schemes. UPC is strictly numeric, while Code 39 is alphanumeric. The density of the bar code, defined by the width of the narrowest bar, can be high, medium, or low. The narrower the bar, the higher the density. Regardless of the density and the wide/narrow ratio, widths must be uniform throughout the code. In addition, there is a nine-segment start and a nine-segment stop bit on each end of the code. Each bar code must also have a plain (quiet) zone on each end of the code. The American Automotive Industry Group (AAIG), a trade group for manufacturers of domestic automobiles, has defined not only which bar codes are used, but also their size and location on cartons and pallets.

A bar code is read starting at either end and the software adjusts for the direction of reading. The code is read by contact wands, noncontact lasers, and fixed laser scanners. Contact scanners require the operator to move the wand across the bar code at both an appropriate angle and velocity. This is an operation requiring some skill and operators are therefore commonly required to make multiple passes with contact scanners. As the price of noncontact scanners has dropped, they have become more common because of the improved productivity over the contact wand. Rotating scanners are capable of making many scans per second.

Bar codes are used in shipping and receiving to identify the contents of pallets, boxes, or stock items entering or leaving a warehouse. Within manufacturing operations, bar codes are used on pallets, carriers, or parts to track the work-in-progress. When the manufacturing operations are completed, resulting in a final product, a bar code is placed on the product, container, wrap, or pallet. The bar code data from receiving, manufacturing, and shipping can be transmitted to the various computer systems for enterprise resource planning, shipping, accounts payable, etc.

Bar code data can be transmitted by radio-frequency terminals to a host computer system. The radio-frequency transmitter provides mobile real-time input of bar code data to the host computer and is under the control of the computer. The mobility is valuable around shipping/receiving docks, AGVs, warehouses, work-in-process storage, and AS/RS. Advantages of this type of system include: direct, real-time transmission of data; broad access to information on any products in the host computer; and labor savings stemming from real-time access to data. The range of about a mile is the major limitation of radio-frequency transmission.

RADIO FREQUENCY IDENTIFICATION

Radio-frequency identification (RFI) utilizes an electronic, battery-powered unit called a "transponder" (tag) attached to a pallet or part. The tag transmits information about the pallet number, parts, and status of the manufacturing operations performed on the parts or on the parts on the pallet. When the part or pallet has completed the operations and is unloaded, the tag is reprogrammed for its next trip through the manufacturing processes with the new part or pallet. The responder (antenna) receives the data and communicates it to the computer system and the software. The data contained on the tag are hardened to withstand vibration, liquids common in manufacturing, and temperature extremes of –40° to 400° F (–40° C to 204° C). The electronic power of a tag ranges from milliwatts to 10 watts. As with all electronics, the tags are becoming smaller, more economical, and capable of transmitting and receiving more data. Since RFI is more costly than bar codes, its application must justify the additional cost. RFI is typically used in applications where a variety of parts with different manufacturing routings or processes may cover or destroy a bar code (for example, painting).

MAGNETIC STRIPE

Magnetic stripes, similar to those on bank and credit cards, may be attached to pallets or parts. They are more expensive than bar codes, cannot be read remotely, and are not as resistant to mechanical damage. Magnetic stripes are not as popular on the factory floor as bar code or radio-frequency identification.

VOICE RECOGNITION

Voice recognition systems operate by either dictation or command and control. *Dictation* is used to enter data via voice rather than keyboard or one of the other types of data entry. Dictation software is used by people with limited typing ability, repetitive strain injury (for example, carpal tunnel syndrome), or those who believe it improves their productivity.

Computer voice recognition software is now capable of continuous speech versus speaking discrete words. This is a result of the increased memory and faster processing time of current computers. Command-and-control software allows the user to control a computer or a computer-based system via voice commands. Both dictation and command and control require training of the software by each user. However, the limited vocabulary of a command-and-control system requires less training than dictation software that may be searching for 50,000–100,000 words. Command-and-control or voice command software that can navigate operating system software, productivity software, and the Internet is commercially available. Justification of voice recognition for command and control of factory automation is a function of demand and cost benefits to the user. As control systems move to a PC or workstation, voice recognition hardware and software will more easily and economically be integrated into programmable automation.

MACHINE VISION

Typical industrial applications of machine vision include inspection, identification, and machine guidance. Machine vision systems must be capable of:

- forming an image and converting the image into appropriate electrical signals;
- organizing the signals into a form that may be processed by a computer;
- analyzing and measuring various features or characteristics of the signals generated by the image, and

- interpreting the data so that useful decisions can be made about the image.

A complete machine vision system is composed of machine vision hardware and software, the lighting system, and the optical system. A basic machine vision system has one or more cameras, a camera controller, a camera vision processing unit interface, a vision system central-processing unit, and a display unit. Machine vision in manufacturing settings requires an interface between the output of the machine vision central-processing unit and manufacturing hardware, such as robots and programmable logic controllers (PLCs). The integration of machine vision with robot systems can improve the positional accuracy of robot arms.

The basic unit of machine vision display is the *pixel*. Less expensive systems have 256 × 256 picture elements (pixels) on the display. Higher quality systems at greater cost and requiring greater computing power for the same speed of data image processing have more pixels. Machine vision may be monochrome or gray scale, and gray scale systems may be either two dimensional or three dimensional (2D or 3D). Monochrome systems are less expensive, faster with comparable hardware, and simpler than gray scale systems.

Lighting is a very significant component of machine vision systems. If appropriate lighting techniques are not used, the image formation subsystem may not be able to see the parts or it may present an incorrect image to the system. Three types of common lighting techniques are front lighting, back lighting, and structured lighting. *Front lighting* has the camera and the light source on the same side of the part. *Back lighting* has the light source and camera on opposite sides of the part and generates a silhouette. *Structured lighting* is similar to front lighting with the light beam controlled with lenses, apertures, coherent light sources, or lasers. Structured light is used to identify specific features of a part or specific parts.

The optics determine the area that the camera can see and, for a given camera, the resolution of the display. The most common camera is the charge-coupled device (CCD). Resolution of the CCD camera is determined by the size of the array of photosensitive elements. An image is scanned 30 or 60 times a second in the U.S. (25 times a second in Europe). Each set of pixels is a frame and may be stored in the frame buffer as part of preprocessing that also includes analog to digital conversion. Processing results in the output of an image that is then interpreted for decision analysis. The software processes the image from the cameras and performs image recognition by template matching or feature weighing. The higher the resolution, the longer time a given processor requires to process the image.

REVIEW QUESTIONS

41.1) What method is used to determine the exact location of an AGV?

41.2) Is the footprint of an AS/RS system larger or smaller than that of conventional storage?

41.3) How is the density of a bar code defined?

41.4) Which automatic identification system uses a transponder attached to a pallet or part?

41.5) Which automatic identification system forms an image of the part?

Part 8
Quality

Chapter 42

Quality Assurance

42.1 QUALITY ASSURANCE

Quality assurance in the manufacturing enterprise ensures that the quality function is appropriately executed. Its activities extend far beyond the quality department. Quality assurance (QA) is different from quality control (QC) because QC primarily identifies and responds to nonconformities, such as defects, and is reactive in nature. In contrast, QA is proactive in its approach to quality planning, instituting system improvements, such as defect prevention and reliability, while maintaining the after-the-fact QC and audit functions.

Essential to an understanding of *total quality management* (TQM) is a definition of quality. Prior to the 1970s, the quality function in a manufacturing organization was charged with detecting defects by checking and sorting parts. In a TQM organization, the quality system is employed to prevent defects, not detect them. The quality function is proactively linked to customer satisfaction by ensuring that the enterprise's products and services exceed customer expectations. *Quality* is then defined as those product and/or service features that meet or exceed customer expectations. TQM is the system that ensures that this is the enterprise's constant focus and that continuous improvement never stops.

The phrase "total quality management" represents a philosophy or world view with implicit definitions of how a TQM enterprise will be organized and run. The central goal of TQM is to achieve increasingly higher levels of customer satisfaction while continuously improving processes linked to business measurables such as cost and productivity. TQM also includes a set of facilitating technical and organizational tools designed to link observable phenomena and measurable data to problem resolution. Tools such as statistical process control (SPC) and structured problem solving assign problem definition and solution to everyone in the organization; not just technical specialists. A TQM organization is driven by customer needs and maintains a constant sense of urgency to improve.

TQM emerged in the early 1980s in response to increasing competition from Japanese products in the U.S. market. At that time, there was a widespread realization among American managers that many Japanese products, especially automobiles and consumer electronics, were superior to U.S. goods across a variety of dimensions. After World War II, Japan's industrial recovery was accelerated by using American quality techniques taught by W. Edwards Deming and Joseph Juran. By the mid-1970s, after two decades of development, Japanese manufacturers were exporting products that were less expensive, contained fewer defects, and were closer to customer requirements than their American counterparts. Additionally, the imported products were designed and produced in far less time than those domestically produced. Many Japanese companies had institutionalized successful programs of continuous improvement. In response to market share eroded by highly efficient foreign competitors, most major U.S. manufacturers initiated some form of TQM during the 1980s. Global competition for U.S. manufacturers will continue to increase and those enterprises mastering the tools of TQM will survive. The acronym "TQM" may or may not remain in fashion. However, the core concepts of continuously enhancing customer satisfaction and the endless pursuit of perfection will live on.

42.2 COST OF QUALITY

The cost of poor quality ranges from 20–40% of sales in most companies. This percentage usually exceeds the profit margin. Quality costs can be grouped into four categories: internal failure, external failure, appraisal, and prevention.

INTERNAL FAILURE COSTS

Internal failure costs include the costs of defects identified prior to the customer's receipt of the product (or service). Examples include unrepairable scrap, rework, and the cost of analyzing nonconforming product to determine cause(s), sorting bad lots, sorting nonconforming product from suppliers, avoidable process loss, and decreasing selling price due to poor quality.

EXTERNAL FAILURE COSTS

A monetary value is assigned to defects found after the product leaves the company. External failure costs include warranty charges, complaint adjustments, cost to return material, and a reduction in the price paid by the customer for less-than-acceptable product.

APPRAISAL COSTS

Appraisal costs include expenditures related to determine the degree of conformance to product requirements. Examples include: incoming inspection and testing, in-process inspection and testing, final inspection and testing, quality audits of in-process and finished products, calibration of instruments, and measuring devices.

PREVENTION COSTS

Prevention costs are incurred to reduce expenditure on failure and appraisal costs. These include quality planning, process planning, process control, evaluating suppliers, and training. These categories can all be measured, although accurate numbers may be buried or hidden. Important costs that are difficult or impossible to measure are customer dissatisfaction and lost customers. Determining optimum quality costs also is usually difficult. Many of the cost of quality categories are not tracked by companies. The manufacturing company's accounting system may require gathering data beyond what is normally collected, logged, and tracked.

Many mathematical tools exist for determining the optimum cost of quality. They assume a cost-benefit relation between the cost of prevention and appraisal compared to the benefit of reduced internal and external failure costs. Cost-of-quality initiatives can provide very important feedback on a manufacturing system's performance. However, cost-of-quality initiatives often fail because they result in blaming someone for failure instead of yielding a prioritized list of opportunities for improvement.

42.3 ISO 9000

The International Organization for Standardization (ISO) was founded in 1946 in Geneva, Switzerland. The organization's primary function was (and is) the development of international standards to facilitate international trade. In the United States, the ISO representative is the American National Standards Institute (ANSI). The ISO standard for quality is the 9000 series first published in 1987. The standards, 9000-9004, are advisory in nature and were designed for use in two-party contractual arrangements and for internal auditing. It is now more common that ISO 9000 be used with third-party audits. More than 60 countries have adopted the ISO 9000 series. The standards are published in the U.S. as the ANSI/ASQ Q9000 series. An industry-specific version of ISO 9000, known as QS 9000, has been adopted by the U.S. automotive industry.

The ISO 9000 standard can be used to assess the quality system of any organization. Manufacturers, hospitals, police departments, and universities can be certified compliant with ISO 9000. However, standards such as ISO and QS 9000 are more often employed as criteria for third-party audits between a supplier of production parts, components, or equipment, and an original equipment manufacturer (OEM). In a third-party registration system, a certified registrar audits to the ISO or QS standard. This relieves the OEM (or second party) from incurring the cost of performing their own audits. Furthermore, the supplier does not have to be audited to the standards of each and every customer.

It is important to emphasize that having a certified quality system in place does not guarantee the quality of the system's outcome. For example, ISO 9000 certification can be extended to a factory producing concrete life jackets. The existence of a quality system does not guarantee that all the rules and structures will be followed every day. However, ISO 9000 certification does mean that a quality system is in place. An effective quality system is initially certified by third-party audits to ISO 9000 and is periodically (usually every six months) revisited by the registrar as well as monitored by internal auditors and occasionally a second party.

42.4 MALCOLM BALDRIGE AWARD

Congress passed Public Law 100-107 in 1987 creating the Malcolm Baldrige National Quality Award (MBNQA) to encourage improved quality and competitiveness from American companies. The National Institute of Standards and Technology (NIST), part of the Department of Commerce, manages the award. The MBNQA was instituted by the federal government in reaction to serious foreign encroachment in the domestic market, especially in manufactured goods.

The Baldrige Award is granted annually to up to six winners in three categories: large manufacturing companies, large service companies, and small businesses. Companies must prepare an application and submit to assessment by approved examiners. MBNQA criteria and relative emphasis include:

1. leadership (9.5%);
2. information and analysis (7.5%);
3. strategic quality planning (6%);
4. human resources development and management (15%);
5. management of process quality (14%);
6. quality and operational results (18%), and
7. customer focus and satisfaction (30%).

An important difference between ISO 9000 and the MBNQA is the latter's emphasis on system outcomes, improvement, and customer satisfaction—elements that are missing from the ISO 9000 standard. Many companies use the MBNQA criteria for internal audits to promote continuous improvement.

The MBNQA criteria are widely accepted as effective measures of a customer-focused quality system. Also, many states have adopted

MBNQA-like quality awards to promote quality within their borders.

REVIEW QUESTIONS

42.1) What distinguishes quality assurance from quality control?

42.2) TQM is driven by whose needs?

42.3) Which of the four costs of quality would include final inspection?

42.4) What is the primary function of the ISO standards?

42.5) If a company is ISO 9000 certified, does this guarantee that all parts they produce are "good?"

42.6) Who created the Malcolm Baldrige Award?

42.7) Which of the seven Baldrige Award criteria is emphasized most?

Chapter 43

Statistical Methods for Quality Control

43.1 INSPECTION

Inspection is the process of checking the conformance of a final product to its specifications. In most cases, 100% inspection of a process is too costly. Therefore, there are established methods of sampling a product or process to characterize its correspondence to its specifications. Inspection must be a continuous activity because raw material, machines, and operators are all subject to variability.

Two types of inspection are typically employed in a quality assurance activity. *Inspection of variables* requires the quantitative measurement of characteristics such as dimensions, surface finish, and other physical or mechanical properties. Such measurements are made with instruments that produce a variable result. A micrometer and a thermometer are typical tools used for inspection of variables. The resulting measurements are compared against specifications and conformance assessments are made. The other type of inspection is *attribute*. This approach involves the observation of a quality characteristic with a device such as a go/no-go gage. Attribute inspection offers the direct comparison of a dimension to a specification. The presence or absence of a flaw, such as a visible scratch in a painted panel, is another direct observation of a quality characteristic.

Modern approaches to quality assurance place emphasis on preventing rather than detecting defects. Inspection may be necessary, but it is a non-value-added activity, which draws resources from the enterprise that could be more profitably employed elsewhere. Many current practices diminish reliance on inspection to sort good product from bad. These include:

- reducing the impact of variation through robust design;
- anticipating problems through design for manufacturability and assembly;
- the use of mistake and error proofing, and
- attacking common-cause variation to push process-capability indices high enough to eliminate the need for inspection.

While some inspection is unavoidable, every effort should be exercised upstream from the inspection process to reduce it to a minimum.

43.2 STATISTICAL METHODS

Statistical methods are used to extract the significant information from large amounts of numerical information. These approaches are important in quality control since large quantities of material or product may be involved. Statistical methods are also employed when dealing with variable data, such as that from manufacturing processes. No two products are ever manufactured exactly alike. There are always variations in

---

the dimensions or properties of raw materials, and in the operation of machines and operator performance. Statistics are important tools for quality assurance because they offer a way of characterizing a *population* (all of the individual parts) by means of a *sample* (a small group of parts studied).

STATISTICAL QUALITY CONTROL

One of the most important uses of statistical quality control (SQC) is to detect variation in the process. There are two types of variation occurring in a process: natural and assignable. *Natural variability* in a manufacturing process is the inherent, uncontrolled changes that occur in the composition of material, the performance of the operator, and the operation of machines. These variations occur randomly with no particular pattern or trend. In contrast, *assignable variability* can be traced to a specific, controllable cause. SQC methods are intended to distinguish between natural and assignable variability. Ideally, if the assignable causes of variability can be identified, the process can be better controlled and defects can be prevented.

STATISTICAL PROCESS CONTROL

The systematic method of detecting assignable variability in a process is known as *statistical process control* (SPC). To use SPC tools, certain concepts from statistics must be employed. For example, assume that a series of several dozen shafts are being turned on a lathe. A micrometer will be used to measure the diameter. After a short period, it becomes evident that the diameters vary. If they were listed in order from smallest to largest, it could be seen that very few diameters are close to the two extremes. Most would lie between the two extremes with fewer diameters found near the extreme small or large size.

If the diameters were collected into groups defined by a minimum and maximum size, the size of these groups would indicate how many shafts had diameters close to a particular dimension. If these groups were plotted on a bar graph with the diameter on the horizontal axis and the size of the group on the vertical axis, a distribution of the shaft diameters would be revealed as shown in Figure 43-1. The distribution describes how often a particular diameter occurs.

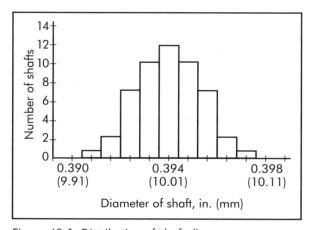

Figure 43-1. Distribution of shaft diameters.

If a very large number of measurements are made and the width of the bars in the graph are made very thin, the frequency of occurrence of a diameter would follow a characteristic "bell-shaped" distribution as shown in Figure 43-2. Data from many manufacturing processes (and a large number of other naturally occurring processes) has this characteristic distribution. This distribution corresponds well to a theoretical distribution known as the *normal distribution* (also called *gaussian distribution*). The shape of this distribution is repeatable; there are only two parameters needed to completely characterize it. These two parameters are the mean (or average value) and the dispersion. Figure 43-3 shows several

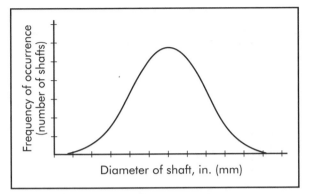

Figure 43-2. Continuous distribution of shaft diameters.

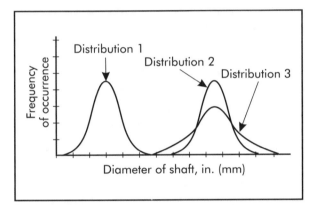

Figure 43-3. Normal distributions with different means and dispersions.

different normal distributions with different means and dispersions.

The distributions illustrated in Figure 43-3 show the significance of the mean and dispersion. Distribution 1 has the same dispersion as Distribution 2. However, their measurements are clustered around different mean values. Distribution 2 has the same mean as Distribution 3, but the dispersion of Distribution 3 is much greater, indicating that the measurements tended to vary more from the mean value.

The mean shows the value that the measurements tend to cluster around. The arithmetic mean of a sample is called the average value $\overline{x}$ (called "x bar") and can be calculated using the following familiar formula:

$$\overline{x} = \frac{x_1 + x_2 + x_3 \ldots + x_n}{n} \qquad (43\text{-}1)$$

where:

$\overline{x}$ = average value
x = sum of all measurements
n = number of measurements

The dispersion is the width of the normal curve and indicates how much variability is present in a set of measurements. Many different measures of dispersion can be used. One of the simplest is the range, R, which is the difference between the largest and smallest measured value:

$$R = x_{max} - x_{min} \qquad (43\text{-}2)$$

where:

R = range
x_{max} = largest measured value
x_{min} = smallest measured value

Another measure of dispersion is the *sample standard deviation, s,* which is given by:

$$s = \sqrt{\frac{(x_1 - \overline{x})^2 + (x_2 - \overline{x})^2 + (x_3 - \overline{x})^2 \ldots + (x_n - \overline{x})^2}{n - 1}}$$

$$(43\text{-}3)$$

where:

s = sample standard deviation

The units used to find the standard deviation are the same as the units of the original measurements.

Since it is rarely possible or practical to count or measure all items in a population, the sample average ($\overline{x}$) and sample standard deviation (s) can be used as estimates of the population mean (μ) and the population standard deviation (σ), respectively. The accuracy of the estimate depends on various factors such as sample size and sampling method.

Example 43.2.1. Calculate the mean and sample standard deviation of the group of shaft diameters shown in Table 43-1.

Table 43-1. Observed shaft diameters
(Example 43.2.1)

Observation	Diameter (mm)
1	1.05
2	0.96
3	0.99
4	1.04
5	1.03
6	1.02
7	0.99
8	1.01

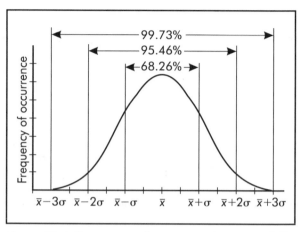

Figure 43-4. Percentage of occurrence in a normal distribution.

Solution. The mean is found by summing the measurements and dividing by the number of measurements:

$$\bar{x} = \frac{1.05 + 0.96 + 0.99 + 1.04 + 1.03 + 1.02 + 0.99 + 1.01}{8} = 1.01$$

The sample standard deviation is found by taking the square root of the sum of the squares of the difference between each measurement and mean and dividing by the number of measurements minus one:

$$s = \sqrt{\frac{(1.05 - 1.01)^2 + (0.96 - 1.01)^2 \ldots + (1.01 - 1.01)^2}{8 - 1}} = 0.03$$

One of the most important uses for the mean and standard deviation in a normal distribution is predicting the percentage of measurements that will fall into a certain range. Figure 43-4 shows the percentage of measurements that fall into ranges defined by distance measured in number of standard deviations for a normal distribution. For example, 68.26% of all observations will fall within plus or minus one standard deviation from the mean.

Example 43.2.2. The mean diameter of a part is 25.00 mm and the standard deviation is 0.02 mm. The process is normally distributed. Estimate the percentage of parts that will have a diameter greater than 25.04 mm.

Solution. The diameter 25.04 mm is two standard deviations greater than the mean:

$$25.04 = \bar{x} + 2\sigma = 25.00 + 2(0.02)$$

The percentage of parts in question is shown as the area under the bell-shaped curve in Figure 43-5. The percentage of parts less than $\bar{x} - 2\sigma$ and greater than $\bar{x} + 2\sigma$ can be found by:

$$100\% - 95.46\% = 4.54\%$$

The number of diameters greater than $\bar{x} + 2\sigma$ is half this amount or 2.27% due to the symmetry of the normal curve about the mean.

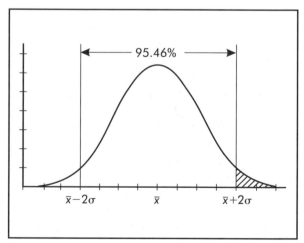

Figure 43-5. Percentages of occurrences with dimension greater than the mean plus two standard deviations.

43.3 CONTROL CHARTING

One of the principal tools used in SPC is the control chart. *Control charts* are a plot of a quality characteristic (such as the average diameter of a sample of parts or the number of defects in a sample) with respect to time. The quality characteristic is compared to control limits. The basic purpose for the chart is to determine whether the quality characteristic is varying within acceptable limits for natural variability or whether the process is "out of control." Typical control charts display limits for the natural variability of the process and the quality characteristic calculated at various times. Table 43-2 defines several common control charts.

The two most common control charts in use for variables are the $\bar{x}$ and R charts. (There are other types of charts used for attributes, but the basic concept is the same.) These charts are used to show the statistics of samples of measurements made on the process. The $\bar{x}$ chart shows the quality characteristic of the average of the sample. The R chart shows the quality characteristic of the range of the sample. The $\bar{x}$ and R charts are typically plotted and used together to interpret the performance of a process. A set of typical $\bar{x}$ and R charts is shown in Figure 43-6.

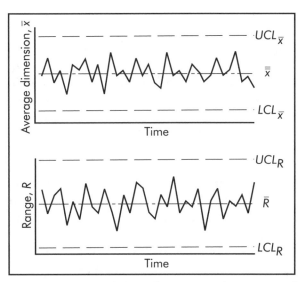

Figure 43-6. Control charts for average dimension and range.

The concept of sampling is used to efficiently represent the overall performance of the process with a limited number of observations. A sample (subgroup) size of four or five is typically used for $\bar{x}$ and R charts. This means that a fixed quantity of randomly selected parts is used to estimate the quality characteristics corresponding to a particular period of time. For example, five shafts might be selected every hour for generating the control chart data. The diameters of the

Table 43-2. Commonly used control charts

Data Type	Chart Name	Value Charted
Variables	$\bar{x}$ and R chart	Sample averages and ranges
	$\bar{x}$ and s chart	Sample averages and standard deviations
	X and moving R chart	Individual observations and moving ranges
	Median and R chart	Sample medians and ranges
Attributes	p chart	Proportion or percent of units nonconforming (defective) per sample
	np chart	Number of units nonconforming (defective) per sample
	c chart	Number of nonconformities (defects) per inspection unit
	u chart	Average number of nonconformities (defects) per production unit

(Wick and Veilleux 1987)

five shafts are averaged to obtain the $\bar{x}$ characteristic for that hour and the difference between the largest and smallest diameter is used to obtain the R characteristic. In general terms, $\bar{x}$ characterizes the typical measurement and R characterizes the variability of the measurement. If the process is in statistical control, the typical measurement and the variability of the measurement will change somewhat over time, but these changes should be random and limited in their magnitude. If the changes in $\bar{x}$ and R occur in a pattern or have excessive magnitude, it is assumed to be due to an assignable cause. Such pronounced changes are not typically part of the inherent variability in the process. Figure 43-7 shows an $\bar{x}$ chart that exhibits control for the first 10 samples, but then shows a marked shift in magnitude. This type of change is almost always assigned to a cause such as changing a tool, adjusting a machine, etc. Such assignable causes can be controlled, thus the performance of a process can be improved by some type of intervention.

A control chart needs some limits that define the maximum acceptable deviations of the quality characteristic for a process in statistical control. These control limits are established when the process is under close observation and known to be operating properly. The control limits are used as a standard to compare future performance. Both $\bar{x}$ and R have average values that normal variances in the process fluctuate about. Figure 43-8(a) shows a horizontal line labeled $\bar{\bar{x}}$. This is the average of averages or *grand average*. It represents the average of the typical values for a measurement and the population mean. Figure 43-8(b) shows a horizontal line labeled $\bar{R}$. This represents the typical variance in the process. These two parameters provide the basis for determining the control limits on a control chart.

Example 43.3.1. A shaft diameter is measured as part of an SPC plan. Four observations of the diameter are recorded in each subgroup (labeled x_1 to x_4, as shown in Table 43-3). Calculate $\bar{\bar{x}}$ and $\bar{R}$.

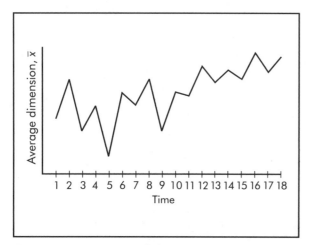

Figure 43-7. Deviation of the average dimension in a control chart.

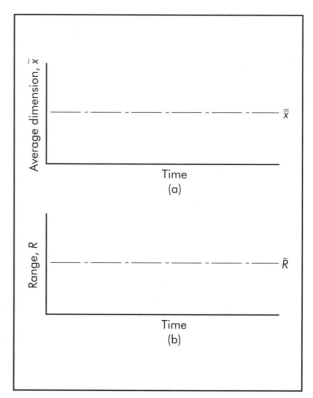

Figure 43-8. Mean lines in control charts.

Table 43-3. Shaft diameters (inches) (Example 43.3.1)

Subgroup	Measurements				$\bar{x}$	R
	x_1	x_2	x_3	x_4		
1	5.005	4.994	5.002	5.004	5.001	0.011
2	4.998	4.999	5.005	5.001	5.001	0.007
3	5.002	5.006	5.000	4.999	5.002	0.007
4	5.003	5.005	5.000	4.997	5.001	0.008
5	5.001	4.996	4.995	5.005	4.999	0.010
				Sum	25.004	0.043

Solution. The quantity $\bar{x}$ is found by averaging the four measurements in each subgroup. The quantity R is found by computing the difference between the largest and smallest measurement in each subgroup. The sum of each $\bar{x}$ is used to compute $\bar{\bar{x}}$:

$$\bar{\bar{x}} = \frac{25.004}{5} = 5.0008 \approx 5.001$$

The sum of each R is used to compute $\bar{R}$:

$$\bar{R} = \frac{0.043}{5} = 0.0086 \approx 0.009$$

The quality characteristics $\bar{x}$ and R tend to be normally distributed (for reasons related to an idea from statistics known as the Central Limit Theorem). Consequently, most of the variation in $\bar{x}$ and R can be characterized by three standard deviations of the quality characteristic from the average quality characteristic. The upper control limit on the $\bar{x}$ chart, $UCL_{\bar{x}}$, is given by:

$$UCL_{\bar{x}} = \bar{\bar{x}} + 3\sigma_{\bar{x}} \quad (43\text{-}4)$$

where:

$\bar{\bar{x}}$ = average of the subgroup averages
$\sigma_{\bar{x}}$ = standard deviation of the subgroup averages

Note that the standard deviation used is for $\bar{x}$, not simply for x. The control limit characterizes the variability of the typical performance of the process, not the variability in the population. Similarly, the lower control limit is given by:

$$LCL_{\bar{x}} = \bar{\bar{x}} - 3\sigma_{\bar{x}} \quad (43\text{-}5)$$

The computation of the standard deviation of $\bar{x}$ is sometimes a time-consuming and error-prone operation. In production operations, a simplified means of estimating the control limits on an $\bar{x}$ chart are typically used:

$$UCL_{\bar{x}} = \bar{\bar{x}} + 3\sigma_{\bar{x}} = \bar{\bar{x}} + A_2\bar{R} \quad (43\text{-}6)$$

$$LCL_{\bar{x}} = \bar{\bar{x}} - 3\sigma_{\bar{x}} = \bar{\bar{x}} - A_2\bar{R} \quad (43\text{-}7)$$

where:

A_2 = a variable based only on subgroup size (also known as sample size)

This means of estimating control limits is accurate enough for virtually all applications. The approach has been proven to be less error prone than one that calls for calculating $\sigma_{\bar{x}}$ directly. The constant A_2 is given for various subgroup sizes in Table 43-4.

The second control chart, seen in Figure 43-6, shows the range in each subgroup of observations. As stated earlier, this chart characterizes the variability of the measurements. The line in the center of the chart, $\bar{R}$, is actually a measure of the variability in the process. The upper and lower control limits should bound the natural deviations in the range in each subgroup. Since the

Table 43-4. Constants for control charts

Subgroup Size	A_2	D_4	D_3	d_2
2	1.880	3.267	0	1.128
3	1.023	2.575	0	1.693
4	0.729	2.282	0	2.059
5	0.577	2.115	0	2.326
6	0.483	2.004	0	2.534
7	0.419	1.924	0.076	2.704
8	0.373	1.864	0.136	2.847
9	0.337	1.816	0.184	2.970
10	0.308	1.777	0.223	3.078

range can be treated as a normally distributed phenomena (according to the Central Limit Theorem), the control limits can be formed as:

$$UCL_R = \bar{R} + 3\sigma_R \qquad (43\text{-}8)$$

$$LCL_R = \bar{R} - 3\sigma_R \qquad (43\text{-}9)$$

where:

$\bar{R}$ = average of the subgroup ranges
σ_R = standard deviation of the subgroup ranges

For simplicity, the control limits can be estimated by:

$$UCL_R = D_4\bar{R} \qquad (43\text{-}10)$$

$$LCL_R = D_3\bar{R} \qquad (43\text{-}11)$$

where:

constants D_3 and D_4 = functions of the subgroup size and are given in Table 43-4

Example 43.3.2. Find the control limits for the $\bar{x}$ and R charts using the data from Example 43.3.1.

Solution. Since the subgroup size is four, the following constants are found in Table 43-4:

$$A_2 = 0.729, D_3 = 0, \text{ and } D_4 = 2.282$$

The results of Example 43.3.1 can be applied to determine the control limits for the $\bar{x}$ chart:

$$UCL_{\bar{x}} = \bar{\bar{x}} + A_2\bar{R} = 5.001 + (0.729)(0.009) = 5.008$$

$$UCL_{\bar{x}} = \bar{\bar{x}} - A_2\bar{R} = 5.001 - (0.729)(0.009) = 4.994$$

Similarly, the control limits on the R chart can be found as:

$$UCL_R = D_4\bar{R} = (2.282)(0.009) = 0.021$$

$$LCL_R = D_3\bar{R} = (0)(0.009) = 0$$

The most important use for control charts is to track down assignable causes for changes in process performance as part of a process improvement activity. Figure 43-9(a) shows an $\bar{x}$ control chart that exhibits good statistical control. There is no obvious trend in the data. The subgroup averages are random with time and all points are contained within control limits. An obvious case where an assignable cause might be identified is illustrated in Figure 43-9(b) where subgroup averages exceed the upper control limit. An investigation into the circumstances that surrounded the process at the time of the control limit excursion might reveal that a cutting tool was changed. A shift in level, even one that does not exceed the control limit, can be an indicator of nonrandom behavior, as shown in Figure 43-9(c). This type of change might be attributable to changing the supplier for the incoming material used in the process. Finally, a repeated pattern is another form of nonrandom behavior. Figure 43-9(d) shows a cyclic pattern in the subgroup average. This type of performance may be related to shop temperature (cold in the morning and warm in the afternoon). Possibly, the low and high points are caused by a machine or operator that behaves differently when the temperature is high or low.

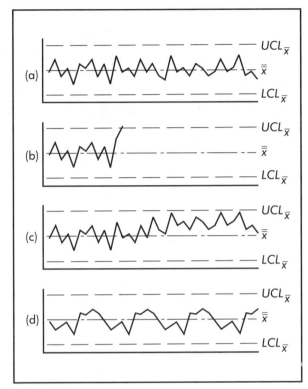

Figure 43-9. Various conditions monitored on an $\bar{x}$ control chart.

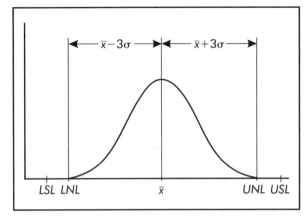

Figure 43-10. Relationship of specified limits and natural limits for a capable process.

43.4 PROCESS CAPABILITY ANALYSIS

Process capability analysis is a method of determining or assuring that a process can meet specifications. A process is said to be capable if it is able to consistently produce parts within specification. The capability of a process can be viewed as the relationship between the specified limits for a dimension and the limits of the natural variability of the dimension. Figure 43-10 shows a frequency distribution for a dimension. The upper specified limit and the lower specified limit (possibly taken from an engineering drawing) are designated as the *USL* and *LSL*, respectively. There are two additional limits shown: the lower natural limit (*LNL*) and the upper natural limit (*UNL*). These limits reflect 3σ variation on either side of the mean dimension. If the process is capable, the natural limits, which describe the typical range of variation for a measurement, will fall within the specified limits.

The extent that the natural limits fall within the specified limits is a variable measure of process capability. The process capability ratio (often designated as C_p) is one measure that is frequently used for processes that have natural limits centered within the specified limits. The process capability ratio can be calculated by dividing the difference in the specified limits by the total amount of variation expected in the process:

$$C_p = \frac{USL - LSL}{6\hat{\sigma}} \qquad (43\text{-}12)$$

where:

USL = upper specified limit
LSL = lower specified limit
$\hat{\sigma}$ = estimate of process standard deviation

$$\hat{\sigma} = \frac{\bar{R}}{d_2} \qquad (43\text{-}13)$$

where:

$\bar{R}$ = average of the subgroup ranges
d_2 = constant based on subgroup size

Clearly, C_p should be greater than or equal to one or else a significant percentage of defective parts will be produced. If C_p is less than one, as shown in Figure 43-11, the process is generally considered incapable of producing good parts. A larger value of C_p is preferable. Ratios above 1.33 are considered acceptable. This ratio can be used to quantify and compare process capability. Most major manufacturers insist that their suppliers provide a report of the C_p for a process. This variable is often used as an indicator of a good supplier.

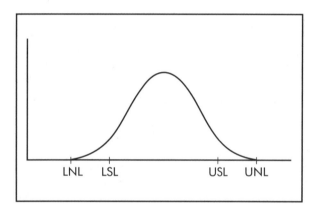

Figure 43-11. Incapable process.

Example 43.4.1. If the specifications on the dimension being monitored in Example 43.3.1 are:

$$5.000 \, {}^{+0.020}_{-0.020}$$

find the C_p ratio.

Solution. The process standard deviation needs to be found. The average range of the process is used in conjunction with the constant d_2 from Table 43-4 for a subgroup size of four to find:

$$\hat{\sigma} = \frac{\overline{R}}{d_2} = \frac{0.009}{2.059} = 0.004$$

Then C_p can be found as follows:

$$C_p = \frac{USL - LSL}{6\hat{\sigma}} = \frac{5.020 - 4.980}{6(0.004)} = 1.67$$

One limitation of C_p as a measure of process capability is that it does not reflect the process distribution relative to the center of the tolerance. A process may have a high C_p but produce parts outside of the specification because it is not at the center of the tolerance. C_{pk} is the measure of process capability that considers process centering and variability. If a process is centered, then $C_p = C_{pk}$. C_{pk} is defined as:

$$C_{pk} = \frac{\text{nearest specification} - \overline{\overline{X}}}{3\hat{\sigma}} \quad (43\text{-}14)$$

Example 43.4.2. Find the C_{pk} for the process in example 43.4.1.

Solution.

$$C_{pk} = \frac{USL - \overline{\overline{X}}}{3\hat{\sigma}} = \frac{5.020 - 5.001}{3(0.004)} = 1.58$$

43.5 ACCEPTANCE SAMPLING

Acceptance sampling is used to determine if parts that have already been produced are acceptable. The difference between statistical process control (SPC) and acceptance sampling is that SPC is used to control the process so that all parts are acceptable. Acceptance sampling requires less than 100% inspection and thus fewer inspectors. It also is very applicable when destructive testing is required. However, acceptance sampling creates the risk of rejecting good lots and accepting bad ones. Acceptance sampling does not guarantee that all the parts in an accepted lot are good.

Two types of sampling plans include the lot tolerance percent defective (LTPD) plan and the acceptable quality level (AQL) plan. The LTPD plan specifies a certain quality level with respect to a percent defective at a given risk of being accepted by the customer. The AQL plan expresses the quality level in terms of the percentage of acceptance of the lots at a given quality level.

Acceptance sampling plans contain two types of risks: producer's risk and consumer's risk. The *producer's risk* is the probability that a good lot will be rejected. The risk is typically given in conjunction with the maximum quality level the plan will accept (AQL). The *consumer's risk* is the probability that a bad lot will be accepted.

Acceptance sampling plans have decreased in popularity for several reasons. First, by definition, acceptance sampling indicates that a manufacturer will accept some bad parts from a supplier, which is not the case for medium- and large-sized companies. Secondly, sampling lots is a non-value-added activity. Larger manufacturers place the burden of supplying only good parts (0% defective) on the supplier. Many companies rely on the process capability of the supplier rather than acceptance sampling. However, some smaller companies may continue to use acceptance sampling techniques.

REVIEW QUESTIONS

43.1) Does excessive tool wear produce natural variability or assignable variability?

43.2) Give two measures of dispersion.

43.3) The mean diameter of a bored hole is 1.875 in. The standard deviation of the diameter is 0.0005 in. A total of 1,000 parts are to be bored. Estimate the number of parts with diameters smaller than 1.8745 in.

43.4) Calculate the control limits for x bar and range control charts using the data in Table Q43-1.

Table Q43-1. Problem 43.4

Subgroup	Measurements			
	x_1	x_2	x_3	x_4
1	22.0	22.5	22.5	24.0
2	20.5	22.5	22.5	23.0
3	20.0	20.5	23.0	22.0
4	21.0	22.0	22.0	23.0
5	22.5	19.5	22.5	22.0
6	23.0	23.5	21.0	22.0
7	19.0	22.0	22.0	20.5
8	21.5	20.5	19.0	19.5
9	21.5	22.5	20.0	22.0
10	21.5	23.0	22.0	23.0
11	20.0	19.5	21.0	20.0
12	19.0	21.0	21.0	21.0
13	19.5	20.5	21.0	20.5

43.5) The tolerance on the dimension being monitored in Question 43.4 is specified as:

$$21.0^{+2.0}_{-2.0}$$

Find the process capability ratio, C_p. Is the process capable of producing an acceptable percentage of good parts?

43.6) Calculate the C_{pk} for Question 43.5.

REFERENCE

Wick, Charles and Raymond Veilleux, eds. 1987. *Tool and Manufacturing Engineers Handbook*, Fourth Edition. *Volume 4: Quality Control and Assembly*. Dearborn, MI: Society of Manufacturing Engineers.

Chapter 44

Dimensional Metrology

44.1 TERMINOLOGY

Dimensional metrology uses terms such as accuracy, repeatability, and precision, just to name a few. Figure 44-1(a-e) uses the analogy of a marksman shooting at a target to illustrate some of these terms (Wick and Veilleux 1987).

- *Accuracy* is the closeness to the true answer.
- *Precision* refers to the dispersion of measurements or fineness of the readings. According to Figure 44-1, the shooting of marksman "b" is very precise but not very accurate. However, marksman "e" is both precise and accurate.

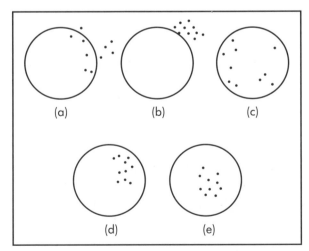

Figure 44-1. Target analogy: precision and accuracy compared (Wick and Veilleux 1987).

- *Reliability* is the probability of achieving a desired outcome. In Figure 44-1, the shots from both marksman "d" and "e" are precise. However, marksman "e" is more reliable than "d." If the wind shifts or another variable changes, marksman "e" has a higher probability of having more shots in the target than marksman "d."
- *Repeatability* of a group of measurements taken with the same instrument on the same part is the extent to which they are in agreement. Repeatability is a test of precision not accuracy.
- *Sensitivity* is the minimum input required to produce a noticeable output.
- *Resolution*, in reference to dial indicators and other similar instruments, is the ratio of one scale division to the width of the dial hand. The finer the resolution of the gage, the smaller the range.
- *Discrimination* refers to the fineness of an instrument's scale divisions. Discrimination is the smallest division of an instrument's scale that can be read reliably.

44.2 LENGTH STANDARDS AND TRACEABILITY

Measurement is a comparison process whereby an unknown quantity is compared with a known quantity or standard. The comparison is made by means of an instrument that indicates the differences between the unknown and the standard. Ideally, all measurements should be made directly in terms of the basic standards that define primary units. However, this is impractical, and consequently, it is necessary to establish a hierarchy of standards similar to the pyramidal organization structure of a large company. The chain of standards ends at the shop floor.

Using a micrometer, a lathe operator checks the diameter of the shaft being turned. The micrometer has a precision thread on the spindle and a scale engraved on the barrel or a digital readout. These combine to form the standard by which the diameter of the shaft is measured. But how accurate is this standard? When the micrometer indicates a value of 0.750 in. (19.05 mm), does it really mean that the dimension it is measuring is actually 0.750 in. (19.05 mm)? The accuracy of the micrometer is checked by using it to measure a known dimension, normally the length of a gage block. The value of the gage block is determined in turn by comparing it with a master block of higher accuracy, and so on, until the basic standard is reached. The process of comparing one standard or measuring device against a higher-order standard of greater accuracy is known as *calibration*. Through the process of calibration, all measurements are related back to the primary standard. In other words, traceability is maintained to ensure that all measurements are consistent. The requirements for traceability go together with the requirements for interchangeability, a feature of modern-day production.

Two basic types of measurement exist: *absolute* or *direct measurement* and *comparative measurement*. Although all measurements are comparative in nature, the term is normally reserved for situations where like or essentially like items are compared. For example, if the length of a gage block is measured with a microme-

ter, the measurement is classified as direct. If the length of the gage block is compared to the length of a known gage block with a dial indicator, the measurement is classified as comparative.

44.3 ABSOLUTE OR DIRECT MEASUREMENT

Examples of absolute or direct measurement instruments include rules, calipers, height gages, and micrometers.

RULES

The *rule* is a basic measuring tool from which many other tools have been developed. Rules are different than scales because a *scale* is graduated in proportion to a unit of length and a rule is the unit of length. Because rules are so frequently used on a variety of work, a wide selection exists to suit the needs of the precision worker. Rules are graduated in the U.S. customary or metric system units and sometimes scales for both systems are provided on a single rule. The graduations can be on each edge of both sides and sometimes on the ends. U.S. customary graduations are commonly as fine as 0.01 in. (in decimals) or 1/64 in. (in fractions). Metric graduations are usually as fine as 0.5 mm.

Rules can be used in combination with some refinements, such as a combination square, to increase their applications. Combination squares combine the rule with a specific head, which may be a square, protractor, or center head.

SLIDE CALIPERS

Slide calipers are a refinement of the steel rule and are capable of more accurate measurements. With these tools, a head or pair of jaws is added to the rule; one jaw is fixed at the end and the other movable along the scale. The movable jaw may be clamped to lock the setting and the slide is graduated to read inside or outside measurements. The scale is graduated in increments of either 1/ 32 in. or 1/64 in. for the U.S. customary system and in increments of 0.5 mm for the metric system.

VERNIER CALIPERS

A typical *vernier caliper* has a stationary bar and a movable vernier slide assembly. It is more precise than a typical slide caliper. The stationary rule is a hardened, graduated bar with a fixed measuring jaw. The stationary rule frequently is graduated in increments of 0.050 in. in the U.S. customary system and 0.5 mm in the metric system. The vernier slide assembly combines a movable jaw, vernier plate, clamp screws, and adjusting nut. It moves as a unit along the graduations of the bar to bring both jaws in contact with the work. The vernier plate is graduated in increments of 0.001 in. in the U.S. customary system and 0.02 mm in the metric system.

CALIPER HEIGHT GAGES

Like the vernier caliper, the *caliper height gage* consists of a stationary bar or beam and a movable slide. The graduated, hardened, and ground beam is combined with a hardened, ground, and lapped base. The vernier slide assembly can be raised or lowered to any position along the bar. It can be adjusted in thousandths of an inch (U.S. customary system) or hundredths of a millimeter (metric system) by means of the vernier slide fine-adjusting knob. The primary uses of caliper height gages are for either layout or measurement. They are commonly used for marking off vertical distances and for measuring height differences between steps at various levels. When marking off distances, scribers are attached to the contact jaw. A dial indicator is typically attached to the height gage for making comparison measurements. However, height gages are notorious for inaccurate measurements due to their large height-to-base length ratio.

DIAL CALIPERS

Similar to vernier calipers, *dial calipers* have a stationary bar and a movable slide assembly. The bar is graduated in increments of 0.1 in. (2 mm) and is available in sizes ranging from 4–12 in. (100–300 mm). The vernier plate is replaced by a caliper dial graduated in increments of 0.001 in. (0.02 mm). A pinion gear actuates the dial hand as it moves along a rack located in the stationary bar. Because the dial caliper is direct reading, there is no need to determine the coincident line on a vernier scale. This feature facilitates the reading of these instruments. Dial heads are also incorporated on caliper height gages and depth gages.

DIGITAL CALIPERS

Because gaging is a vital part of statistical process control (SPC), a new generation of electronic instruments has been produced. These instruments incorporate a liquid crystal display (LCD) and are capable of interfacing with a data collection device. Both inch and metric units are incorporated in one tool. The electronic feature is available on calipers, height gages, depth gages, and micrometers.

MICROMETERS

Many micrometers are available for different applications. The three major types of micrometers are: outside, inside, and depth. All micrometers work on the principle that an accurately made screw will advance a specified distance with each complete turn. Micrometers graduated in the inch system advance 0.025 in. for each turn; those graduated in the metric system advance 0.5 mm for each turn.

Micrometers have both a linear and circumferential scale. The *linear scale* measures the axial advance of the spindle. It is usually graduated in increments identical to the pitch of the micrometer screw. The *circumferential scale* indicates the amount of partial rotation that has occurred since the last complete revolution. For inch-based micrometers, this scale is divided into 25 equal parts, with each division representing 0.001 in. For metric-based micrometers, the circumferential scale is divided into 50 equal parts, with each division representing 0.01 mm. Some micrometers also have a third scale that permits the fractional evaluation of circumferential graduations.

Example 44.3.1. What is the shaft diameter measured by the 1 in. micrometer in Figure 44-2?

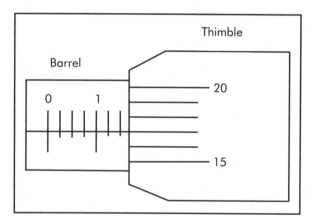

Figure 44-2. One-inch micrometer.

Solution. Each graduation on the barrel of the micrometer is 0.025 in. Therefore, the shaft diameter is at least 0.150 in. but less than 0.175 in. To determine the diameter, the thimble value is added to the barrel value. The thimble is graduated from 0 to 0.025. Therefore, the shaft diameter is 0.150 in. + 0.017 in., which equals 0.167 in.

44.4 COMPARISON MEASUREMENT

Comparative measurements have the advantage of being considerably more accurate than direct measurements. The relative size of two similar gage blocks is known with much greater accuracy than the absolute size of either. The principal reason for this is that in comparative measurement, many systematic errors are eliminated. *Systematic errors* refer to errors that occur consistently in all measurement regardless of repetition. Examples of comparison measurement instruments include dial indicators, test indicators, and optical comparators.

There are three major types of indicators. Type-A indicators have the spindle parallel to the dial face, Type-B indicators have the spindle at right angles to the dial face, and for Type-C indicators, the measuring contact is a lever. The first two types are referred to as dial indicators and the third type is a test indicator. Indicators are available in four different classes based on the bezel diameter and discrimination. Units may be either U.S. customary or metric.

DIAL INDICATORS

The magnification of a dial-type indicator is obtained by means of a gear train. This type of indicator is most commonly used because its magnification accuracy meets the large majority of requirements. A typical dial indicator is shown in Figure 44-3.

The amplification of dial indicators ranges from approximately 40:1 to about 1,500:1. On long-range indicators, revolution counters track the revolutions of the main hand.

The readings on dial indicators may be continuous or balanced as illustrated in Figure 44-4. For *continuous dials*, the graduations are normally numbered clockwise from 0 to the range included in one complete revolution of the pointer. This arrangement is best for measuring linear displacements. *Balanced dials* have the graduations numbered systematically in both directions from the starting 0. This arrangement is best for comparative measurements.

When selecting a dial indicator, generally the highest precision for the range required is chosen. The part feature tolerance should be spread over 10 dial divisions. In other

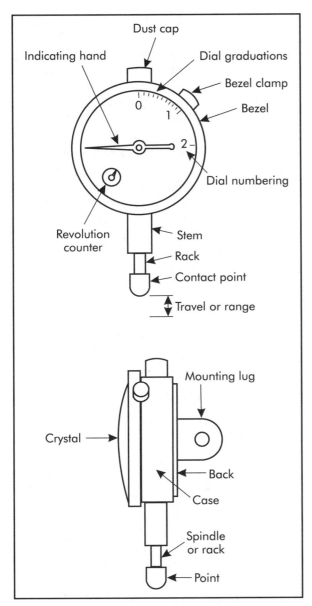

Figure 44-3. Dial indicator (Wick and Veilleux 1987).

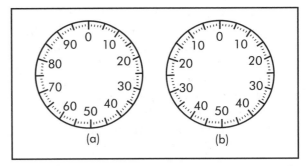

Figure 44-4. Types of indicator dials: (a) continuous, (b) balanced.

TEST INDICATORS

Test indicators sense and measure displacements that occur in a direction perpendicular to the shaft of the contact point as shown in Figure 44-5. Magnification is obtained by gears and levers. Because they are small, test indicators are particularly useful in setup inspection and toolroom work.

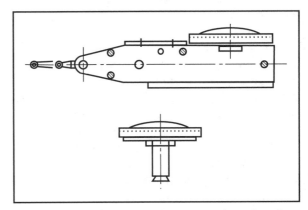

Figure 44-5. Typical test indicator (Wick and Veilleux 1987).

OPTICAL COMPARATORS

An *optical comparator* (sometimes also called an optical or *profile projector*) is a measuring microscope for small parts. It has a stage for mounting parts to be measured and/or inspected, stage transport mechanisms, stage lighting, an optical path that is usually folded by mirrors within the machine

words, the indicator discrimination should be 10% of the part feature tolerance. The tolerance should only consume 10–25% of the indicator's total range. Dial indicators lose accuracy as their range increases, and their sensitivity decreases as the amplification increases (Bush, Harlow, and Thompson 1998).

itself, and a viewing and control area where the operator/inspector works. The image appears on the screen as either an inverted (reversed) or erect image and the part is seen exactly as it is staged. Optical comparators are available with magnifications ranging from 5–500×. Figure 44-6 illustrates a typical horizontal optical comparator (Wick and Veilleux 1987).

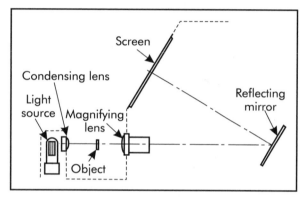

Figure 44-6. Horizontal shadow-lighted optical comparator (Wick and Veilleux 1987).

Both translational measurement and direct measurement can be used with an optical comparator. *Translational measurement* involves using the micrometer barrels to move the stage. Accuracy using this method depends on the accuracy built into the stage movement mechanism and the ability of the operator to align the reference line on the screen with the part feature. If the part feature fits entirely on the screen, direct measurement can be used. Due to the magnification of the comparator, a drafting scale or comparator chart could be used to measure the part feature. The only limitation of direct measurement is the size of the screen.

44.5 COORDINATE MEASURING MACHINES

Coordinate measurement is a two or three-dimensional process that determines

the position of holes, surfaces, centerlines, and slopes. Up to six sides of a cube-shaped part may be inspected without repositioning.

A basic coordinate measuring machine (CMM) consists of four elements: (1) the machine structure, which basically is an *X-Y-Z* positioning device; (2) the probing system used to collect raw data on the part and provide input to the control system; (3) machine control and computer hardware; and (4) the software for three-dimensional geometry analysis. There are several configurations for CMMs, such as the cantilever arm, column, bridge, horizontal arm, and gantry. Figure 44-7 illustrates a typical moving-bridge CMM.

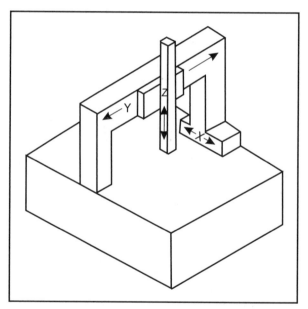

Figure 44-7. Moving-bridge coordinate measuring machine (Wick and Veilleux 1987).

In a typical operation, the part is placed or clamped on the table of the CMM at a random or fixed location. Generally, this is approximately central to the machine axes to access all the part surfaces to be inspected with the probe. The probe is then moved, manually or by machine control, until contact is made with desired part features. Reader heads, traveling on each axis along built-in axis measuring scales, transfer the instantaneous machine position to the computer interface. The dimensional and geometric elements may then be calculated, compared, and evaluated, or stored or printed out as required. In the part-program-assisted mode, the operator positions the machine. Once the initial position has been set, the machine is under the control of a program that eliminates operator choice. In the computer numerically controlled (CNC) mode, motor-driven machines run totally unattended by operators. The advantages of using CMMs when compared to conventional gaging techniques include flexibility, reduced setup time, improved accuracy, reduced operator influence, and improved productivity (Wick and Veilleux 1987).

44.6 MEASUREMENT ERROR

Measurement errors exist regardless of the instrument's precision or the skill of the operator using the instrument. Realizing and quantifying the amount of error in a measurement permits the results to be used more appropriately. Focusing on minimizing the magnitude of measurement error will result in accurate and repeatable measurements. Minimizing measurement error requires using the correct instrument, correct measuring technique, and consistent conditions.

Examples of measurement errors include instrument, parallax, bias, technique, and condition (Bush, Harlow, and Thompson 1998).

INSTRUMENT ERROR

Because of inherent accuracy limitations due to the instrument's construction in addition to calibration issues, *instrument errors* will occur.

PARALLAX ERROR

Parallax error refers to a measurement error due to the position of the operator with respect to the instrument. For example, depending on the position of an observer relative to the face of a dial indicator, different values will be obtained.

BIAS ERROR

Bias indicates that an operator will unconsciously influence a measurement. For example, if a measurement falls between 4.11 and 4.12, the operator may record 4.12 if he or she is biased toward even numbers.

TECHNIQUE ERROR

Technique error, sometimes called *manipulative error*, is due to using the instrument incorrectly. For example, when using a rule, its axis must lie along the line of measurement, not on an angle to it.

CONDITION ERROR

Condition error refers to the conditions the measurement instrument is used in. Temperature fluctuations can cause inaccurate measurements. Most materials expand and contract to some extent when heated and cooled.

44.7 QUALIFYING TOLERANCES WITH GAGES

Quality control of manufactured components often calls for determining if a dimension is within the limits specified by the tolerance. This type of inspection is performed with *gages*, which are special tools designed to determine if a fixed dimension lies within the proper limits. A gage is dedicated to a particular dimension and specific tolerances. If a dimension or the associated tolerances are changed, a new gage must be made.

Two types of gages are commonly used for qualifying parts in mass production: snap gages and plug gages. A *snap gage*, as shown in Figure 44-8(a), is used for external dimensions such as the diameter of a shaft. A *plug gage*, as shown in Figure 44-8(b), is used to qualify an internal dimension, typically an internal diameter. Both of these gages have a go and a no-go feature on them. In the case of a plug gage, one side must be able to "go into" a hole being gaged, while the other side must "not go into" the same hole for the diameter to be within the specified limits.

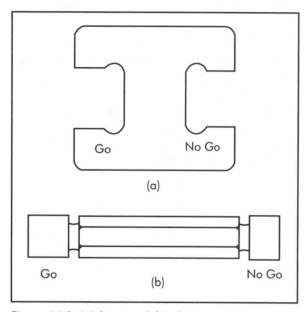

Figure 44-8. (a) Snap and (b) plug gage.

The key principle that is applied in the design of any gages states: it is better to reject a good part than declare a bad part to be within specifications. All gage design decisions are made with this principle in mind. Gages must have tolerances like other manufactured components.

• *Gage tolerance* states the permissible variation in the manufacture of the gage. It is typically 10% or less of the working tolerance.

• *Wear allowance* compensates for the wear of the gage surface as a result of repeated use. Wear allowance is only applied to

the nominal size of the "go" side of the gage since the "no-go" side should seldom see contact with a part surface. It is typically 5% of the working tolerance.

Example 44.7.1. Design a plug gage to qualify the internal diameter shown in Figure 44-9. Use a 10% gage tolerance and a 5% wear allowance.

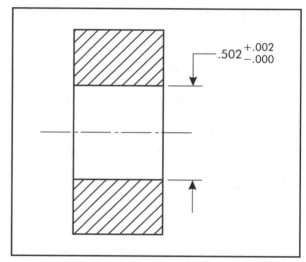

Figure 44-9. Internal diameter to be qualified.

Solution. The gage and wear tolerances are determined first. The total gage tolerance will be 10% of the total tolerance of the dimension.

The gage tolerance is:

0.1 × 0.002 in. = 0.0002 in.

The wear allowance is:

0.05 × 0.002 in. = 0.0001 in.

The gage tolerance is applied on both the go and no-go sides of the gage. Each side of the gage has a 0.0002 in. gage tolerance applied unilaterally. The wear allowance is only applied to the nominal size of the go side, which is typically the only side of the gage subject to wear. The go side has a 0.0001 in. wear allowance applied to the diameter of the "plug" or the diameter used for gaging.

Next, the go and no-go side plug dimensions are determined. The go side must be inserted into the smallest hole that meets specifications (0.502 in.). The gage dimension is based on this diameter and increased by the wear allowance so the gage diameter approaches the smallest specified diameter as the gage wears. Some parts that are within specification will be rejected, but this is consistent with the principle of gage design. The gage tolerance is similarly applied. The 0.0002 in. tolerance is applied unilaterally on the positive side. This permits a gage to be fabricated that will reject a small number of good parts, but this condition is consistent with the design principle.

The no-go side must not be able to be inserted in any hole within specifications. The nominal diameter of this side is equal to the upper limit on the gaged dimension or 0.504 in. The 0.0002 in. gage tolerance is applied unilaterally on the negative side. Consequently, it is possible that the no-go side can be inserted into a small number of holes that are within specification, but this is consistent with the design principle.

The resulting gage design is shown in Figure 44-10.

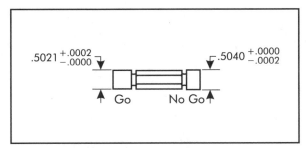

Figure 44-10. Plug gage design.

Example 44.7.2. Design a snap gage to qualify the external diameter on the shaft shown in Figure 44-11. Use a 10% gage tolerance and a 5% wear allowance.

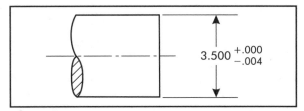

Figure 44-11. External diameter to be qualified.

Solution.

The gage tolerance is:

0.1 × 0.004 in. = 0.0004 in.

The wear allowance is:

0.05 × 0.004 in. = 0.0002 in.

Each side of the gage has a 0.0004 in. gage tolerance applied unilaterally to the distance between the gage surfaces. Since the go side is subject to the most wear, a 0.0002 in. wear allowance is applied to the gap distance on the go side.

The go side must be able to fit over the largest shaft within specifications (3.500 in.). This diameter is decreased by the wear allowance so the gage approaches the largest specified diameter as the gage wears. The 0.0004 in. gage tolerance is applied unilaterally on the negative side.

The no-go side should not be able to fit over any shaft within specifications. The nominal diameter of this side is equal to the lower limit on the gaged dimension or 3.496 in. The 0.0004 in. gage tolerance is applied unilaterally on the positive side.

The resulting gage design is shown in Figure 44-12.

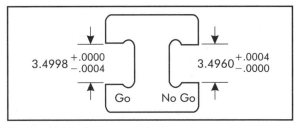

Figure 44-12. Snap gage design.

Another method for determining gage tolerance is by specifying the class of gage to be used. Table 44-1 outlines four common classes of gagemakers' tolerances. Class XX gages are used primarily as master gages and for final close tolerance inspection. Class X gages are used for some types of master gage work, and as close tolerance inspection and working gages. Class Y gages are used as inspection and working gages. Class Z gages are used as working gages where part tolerances are large and the number of pieces to be gaged is small. Going from Class XX to Class Z, tolerances become increasingly greater and the gages are used for inspecting parts having increasingly larger working tolerances. The smaller the gage tolerance, the more expensive the gage (Nee 1998).

Example 44.7.3. Design a class Z go/no-go gage to qualify an internal diameter with the following dimension (in inches). Do not include a wear allowance.

$$.250^{+.002}_{-.002}$$

Solution. Using Table 44-1, a Class Z gage used for inspecting a 0.250 in. diameter hole would have a gage tolerance of 0.00010 in. Without a wear allowance, the plug gage would have the following dimensions.

$$\text{Go: } .2480^{+.0000}_{-.0001} \quad \text{No-go: } .2520^{+.0000}_{-.0001}$$

REVIEW QUESTIONS

44.1) Is repeatability a test of precision or accuracy?

44.2) The process of comparing a measuring device against a higher-order standard of greater accuracy is known as what?

Table 44-1. Standard gagemakers' tolerances

Above in. (mm)	To and including in. (mm)	Class			
		XX in. (mm)	X in. (mm)	Y in. (mm)	Z in. (mm)
0.010 (0.254)	0.825 (20.95)	0.00002 (0.00051)	0.00004 (0.00102)	0.00007 (0.00178)	0.00010 (0.00254)
0.825 (20.95)	1.510 (38.35)	0.00003 (0.00076)	0.00006 (0.00152)	0.00009 (0.00229)	0.00012 (0.00305)
1.510 (38.35)	2.510 (63.75)	0.00004 (0.00102)	0.00008 (0.00203)	0.00012 (0.00305)	0.00016 (0.00406)
2.510 (63.75)	4.510 (114.55)	0.00005 (0.00127)	0.00010 (0.00254)	0.00015 (0.00381)	0.00020 (0.00508)
4.510 (114.55)	6.510 (165.35)	0.000065 (0.00165)	0.00013 (0.00330)	0.00019 (0.00483)	0.00025 (0.00635)
6.510 (165.35)	9.010 (228.85)	0.00008 (0.00203)	0.00016 (0.00406)	0.00024 (0.00610)	0.00032 (0.00813)
9.010 (228.85)	12.010 (305.05)	0.00010 (0.00254)	0.00020 (0.00508)	0.00030 (0.00762)	0.00040 (0.1016)

44.3) Are rules and micrometers absolute or comparison measurement instruments?

44.4) What is the diameter of the shaft measured with the 1 in. micrometer in Figure Q44-1?

44.5) CMM is an acronym for _____?

44.6) Which type of error is generated when an operator uses the correct measurement instrument but the wrong measuring procedure?

44.7) Design a go/no-go gage capable of qualifying a shaft with the following dimension (in inches):

$$2.150^{+.000}_{-.002}$$

Use a 10% gage tolerance and 5% wear allowance.

44.8) Design a Class Z go/no-go gage capable of qualifying the following internal diameter (in inches). Do not include a wear allowance.

$$3.000^{+.004}_{-.000}$$

REFERENCES

Bush, Ted, Roger Harlow, and Richard Thompson. 1998. *Fundamentals of Dimensional Metrology,* Third Edition. Albany NY: Delmar Publishers.

Nee, John G., ed. 1998. *Fundamentals of Tool Design*, Fourth Edition. Dearborn, MI: Society of Manufacturing Engineers.

Wick, Charles and Raymond Veilleux, eds. 1987. *Tool and Manufacturing Engineers Handbook,* Fourth Edition. *Volume 4: Quality Control and Assembly*. Dearborn, MI: Society of Manufacturing Engineers.

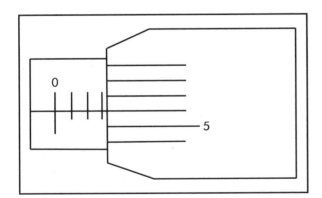

Figure Q44-1. Question 44.8—1 in. micrometer.

Part 9
Manufacturing Management

Chapter 45

Management Introduction

A successful manager must consider many things. This chapter will discuss communication, engineering ethics, the difference between supervision and management, and organizational psychology. Subsequent chapters will discuss labor, safety, human factors, and engineering economics.

45.1 COMMUNICATION

The communication model, shown in Figure 45-1, indicates a fairly simple process. The communicator and receiver are individuals in the organization at any level. The effectiveness of the communication can be evaluated by how well the receiver obtains the message as it was intended to be understood by the sender. However, there are many barriers to communication. People may say one thing and appear to mean another because of nonverbal cues transmitted to the receiver. These might include body movement and facial expression, vocal charac-teristics, physical distance between sender and receiver, and time orientation. Other significant barriers include role perception in the company hierarchy between sender and receiver, selective listening, use of jargon, perceived credibility of the source, and "noise" and filtering based on personal agendas and other factors.

Graphic communication is an important complement to other techniques such as face-to-face oral communication or written communication via newsletters, etc. A person remembers about 10% of what is read, 20% of what is heard, 30% of what is seen, and 50% of what is seen and heard. Charts, slides, cartoons, transparencies, posters, and videotaped presentations are significant means of conveying information to employees. On the manufacturing floor, visual cues for operators, trouble light (andon) boards, and graphically based job aids or operator instructions are all quick and effective means of communication.

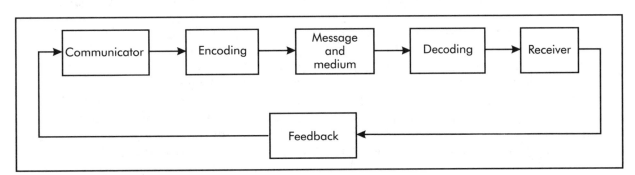

Figure 45-1. A communication model.

45.2 ENGINEERING ETHICS

Ethics refers to the system of moral principles and values established and/or demonstrated by individuals. Ethics is neither very precise nor organized in business, despite the entire field of business law and a large amount of business literature written on relevant moral issues. A high standard of human behavior and the good principles guiding it are the core of civilized life. In many cases, those ethical people who follow good principles are trusted, respected, honored, and favorably viewed by other people and especially by business associates.

Because so much is contractual and promissory in nature, the ethical qualities of participants are critically important. A business must operate through agents and get its job done through people, so this concern extends from the top of the organization, which sets overall policies, to the bottom, which follows the example set by management. Management should: (a) demonstrate and demand ethical behavior; (b) take clear and swift action to correct inappropriate conduct; and (c) place value on the use of ethics in training and performance evaluations.

From a more individual standpoint, a person who is unethical should not be tolerated by a business organization. There are many unethical opportunities in commerce tempting those with weak principles. Therefore, good conduct must be immediate and instinctive.

For example, suppose a flaw exists in a minor part used in a jetliner. This flaw, and its use in the airplane, can result in an extremely costly loss to the fleet, and in human lives and property, if a crash results. Insurance rates would climb, lawsuits mount, and the airline and airframe manufacturer may experience such a crushing loss in reputation that their futures may be in jeopardy. Of course, they go on to sue the parts manufacturer, which would probably have to close

its doors. And all of this can occur if a single worker chooses to act unethically and knowingly uses a bad part rather than be delayed in his or her production activity. The possibility of this happening can be reduced if management expects a high standard and demonstration of ethical behavior.

An ethical problem in business is often a gray area beyond the reach of existing laws. One tool for dealing with gray area matters is for each company, industry, and profession to develop a code of work behavior. Of course, where employees must abide by both professional and company codes, there can be an overlap so long as they do not conflict.

Professional codes may serve two purposes. They can recommend appropriate rulings to the firm as well as help shield the professional from having to carry out inadvisable actions. A single firm might have to deal with codes of varying content and strength from many outside societies that can be local, regional, or national in authority. This is similar to dealing with different unions in which every employee involved is not a member of the authoring body. Further, international firms can experience greater complications as slightly different ideologies try to merge into one. Other complicating factors come into play as well, such as the various cultures, values, and ethical perspectives of countries other than the U.S.

Approximately 75% of U.S. firms have a written code of ethics. It should be recognized that differing conditions in separate firms make it unrealistic to standardize a detailed code of ethics for all organizations. A code of ethics is somewhat specific to an organization, as it aids in defining and guiding real-life practices. The code of ethics for the Society of Manufacturing Engineers (SME), as shown in Figure 45-2, is a good example of a professional code of ethics.

Society of Manufacturing Engineers

PREAMBLE

Practitioners of manufacturing engineering recognize that their professional, civic and personal activities have a direct and vital influence on the quality of life and standard of living for all people. Therefore, manufacturing engineers should exhibit high standards of competence, honesty and impartiality; be fair and equitable; and accept a personal responsibility for adherence to applicable laws, the protection of the public health, and maintenance of safety in their professional actions and behavior. These principles govern professional conduct in serving the interests of the public, clients, employers, colleagues and the profession. Honesty, integrity, loyalty, fairness, impartiality, candor, fidelity to trust, and inviolability of confidence are incumbent upon every member as professional obligations. Each member shall be guided by high standards of business ethics, personal honor, and professional conduct. The words "practitioner," "manufacturing engineer," and "member" as used throughout this Code include all classes of membership in the Society of Manufacturing Engineers.

THE FUNDAMENTAL PRINCIPLE

The manufacturing engineer is dedicated to improving not only the manufacturing process, but manufacturing enterprises worldwide. This includes striving to instill a sense of concern and awareness throughout the manufacturing community of public health, safety, conservation, and environmental issues that are related to the practice of manufacturing and through the application of sound engineering and management principles. Engineers realize that in carrying out this responsibility their individual talents and services can be more effective when funneled through the activities of the Society of Manufacturing Engineers. Therefore, engineers shall strive to support the mission of the Society of Manufacturing Engineers and the activities, products, and events sponsored and produced by them.

CANONS OF PROFESSIONAL CONDUCT

Members offer services in the areas of their competence and experience, affording full disclosure of their qualifications.

Members consider the consequences of their work and societal issues pertinent to it and seek to extend public understanding of those relationships.

Members are honest, truthful, and fair in presenting information and in making public statements reflecting on professional matters and their professional role.

Members engage in professional relationships without bias because of race, religion, sex, age, national origin or impairment.

Members act in professional matters for each employer or client as faithful agents or trustees, disclosing nothing of a proprietary nature concerning the business affairs or technical processes of any present or former client or employer without specific consent.

Members disclose to affected parties known or potential conflicts of interest or other circumstances which might influence—or appear to influence—judgement or impair the fairness or quality of their performance.

Members are personally responsible for enhancing their own professional competence throughout their careers and for encouraging similar actions by their colleagues.

Members accept responsibility for their actions; seek and acknowledge constructive criticism of their work; offer honest constructive criticism of the work of others; properly credit the contributions of others; and do not accept credit for work not theirs.

Members perceiving a consequence of their professional duties to adversely affect the present of future public health and safety shall formally advise their employers or clients and, if warranted, consider further disclosure.

Members of the Society of Manufacturing Engineers act in accordance with all applicable laws and the Constitution & Bylaws of the Society of Manufacturing Engineers and lend support to others who strive to do likewise.

Members of the Society of Manufacturing Engineers shall aid in preventing the election to membership of those who are unqualified or do not meet the standards set forth in this Code of Ethics.

Approved by: Society of Manufacturing Engineers Board of Directors
Date: December 2, 1990
Last modified: January 18, 2001

Figure 45-2. Professional code of ethics adopted by the Society of Manufacturing Engineers.

45.3 MANUFACTURING SUPERVISION AND MANAGEMENT

This section will explain the difference between supervision and management, as well as describe the important elements of management activities.

SUPERVISION

Supervision is the motivation and guidance of subordinates toward goals established by the enterprise. Historically, this role has been the first level of management with direct oversight over factory workers. While the traditional "command-and-control" supervisor still abounds, manufacturing organizations are moving to supplant this role by employing hourly team leaders and supervisors who act as coaches and facilitators rather than autocrats.

Supervision of technical employees is distinct from that of production employees. With technical employees, such as engineering technicians or manufacturing engineers, the supervision is much less direct. These employees exercise much more autonomy and need less direction and more support and liaison work. However, the supervisor is still responsible for the work being done and has additional work not required of first-line supervision such as budgets and personnel evaluation.

Organizational leadership styles may be viewed through the managerial grid of Figure 45-3 where the concern for production is integrated with the concern for people.

Basic people skills make up the vertical axis of the managerial grid. To be an effective coach or motivator, a manager must be effective in relating to individuals and groups. Skills such as one-on-one communication, group facilitation, providing support and feedback for performance, and listening skills are among the most important people skills. The horizontal axis is comprised of manufactur-

ing skills. To be effective, a manager must meet production goals. Managers must know how to combine people and processes to meet productivity goals as efficiently as possible.

MANAGEMENT

Management can be defined as the activity that allocates and utilizes resources to achieve organizational goals. Some common components of management include leadership, planning, budgeting, and control.

Leadership

A leader, as viewed from the "big" picture, is an individual who has brilliant ideas and the capacity to inspire others, or on a more pragmatic level, as a person with the interpersonal influence used in face-to-face dealings with subordinates, superiors, peers, and others who may have an effect on the organization. Measures of leadership must assess both how a job gets done and the effects of that chosen method on others and the organization. The managerial grid shown in Figure 45-3 illustrates some key leadership elements for manufacturing managers.

Planning

Planning has been considered a key responsibility for management for most of the last century, but has taken on more importance in the more recent period of rapid change. Manufacturing managers today must:

- be prepared for problems that develop from bad management decisions or unexpected changes;
- promote flexibility and adapt to market and manufacturing changes;
- identify new business opportunities;
- identify key problem areas and foster motivation to resolve the problems;
- enhance the generation of new ideas;
- communicate top management's expectations down the line;

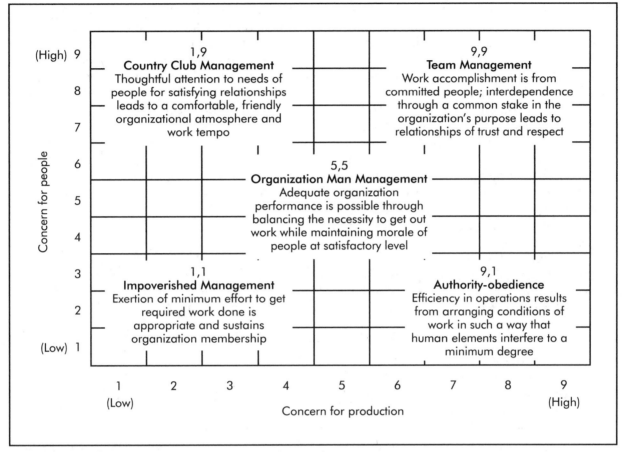

Figure 45-3. The managerial grid.

- foster employee self-control;
- promote organizational learning;
- communicate line managers' concerns to top management;
- integrate diverse functions and operations; and
- enhance innovation.

In a given organizational context, generic planning and control systems consist of several key elements: (a) a plan or desired state; (b) actual performance; and (c) controls that compare the plan with actual performance and suggest changes to promote the desired state. Such a "plan, do, review" sequence is typical in many manufacturing organizations.

Budgeting

A *budget* is a financial plan for an organizational unit. A budget should permit planning, coordinating, and controlling the flow of capital for a given unit in conjunction with divisional or company budgets. The budgeting process in manufacturing involves the planning of costs such as indirect labor, overhead, and general/administrative costs into the future.

Control

Management control is the process by which managers ensure that resources are obtained and used effectively and efficiently in achieving the organization's objectives.

The function of management control is to facilitate reaching organizational goals by implementing strategies identified in the planning process. The control process must be accomplishable through the use of technology and people. While manufacturing converts raw materials and adds value to them through processes and people, the controlling subsystem ensures that the intermediate and end product meet quality standards and schedules. A management control system allows an organization to record, measure, and minimize variability in the business process against predefined goals, objectives, and quality standards.

Some of the major management concepts that have emerged in organizations include centralization-decentralization, line-and-staff, and span of management (also known as span of control).

Centralization-decentralization

Centralization-decentralization has to do with where real authority resides. That is, if authority is not delegated but rather resides in one person, then the organization can be regarded as centralized. Decentralization is the extent to which authority is delegated. Measurements of centralization-decentralization are qualitative rather than quantitative and can be made by assessing decision-making. The more decisions made at the lower levels, the more decentralized the organization. The more important and broader the decisions made at lower ranks, the more decentralized.

Line-and-staff

Line-and-staff refers to relationships within an organization. *Line relationships* are those established by the flow of authority. *Staff relationships* are advisory. Staff departments in a manufacturing plant are those units that contribute financial, legal, or engineering advice. *Line departments* are

those performing activities critical to the smooth operation of the organization. In a production facility, common line positions are plant manager, area managers, superintendents, and first-line supervisors (Veilleux and Petro 1988). Figure 45-4 illustrates a typical line-and-staff organizational chart.

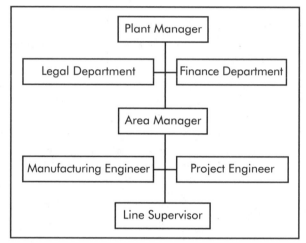

Figure 45-4. Line-and-staff organizational chart.

Span of Management

Span of management, also known as *span-of-control*, refers to the number of subordinates a manager is in charge of. The higher a manager goes in a line-and-staff organization, the larger his or her span of control becomes.

Project Management

A *project* refers to all activities associated with the achievement of a set of specific objectives considered worthy of financial support. It has a finite life and its successful management requires that technical objectives are met, project timelines are adhered to, and that the budget not be exceeded. Project management begins with a good understanding of the product and the environment in which the project will be produced. Knowledge of the technologies involved and of the financial and contractual matters is essential. Strong human relations and communications skills are also critical.

Milestones to check progress are normally executed at logical points in time and some form of cumulative evaluation at the end is usually done. Many project control tools are available to the project manager such as the critical path method (CPM), Gantt charts, and program evaluation and review technique (PERT).

Critical path method. In this method, graphical elements identify the longest path or sequence of events, with regard to time, needed to complete a project. For example, in Figure 45-5, if events 1 through 8 require the same amount of time, then path D-E-F-G is the critical path because it requires the most time. The time interval associated with that path dictates the total project length.

Gantt chart. The Gantt chart is a type of bar chart in which each project task is represented by a horizontal bar, the length of which represents the total time expected for task completion. At project initiation, all bars (tasks) are represented by open or unshaded bars. As time proceeds and work is accomplished on some tasks, the corresponding bars are shaded along the bar in

proportion to how much of the task has been completed. The project manager then can determine at a glance the status of all project tasks. If some tasks are behind schedule, resources from tasks that are ahead of schedule can be reallocated. Figure 45-6 is an example of a simple project represented by a Gantt chart.

PERT. In addition to CPM, PERT is a method best suited to planning and controlling large and complex projects. One practical aspect of this method is that it permits management by exception. The project manager does not have to pay attention to the activities that are on schedule. The technique identifies those tasks that are not being accomplished within the time estimates. Management by emergency is thereby eliminated because emergencies are highlighted and thus can be dealt with (Veilleux and Petro 1988).

Problem-solving. Effective problem-solving techniques allow a manufacturer to get more outputs using the same or less inputs. Productivity improvement, quality, and lower costs can be achieved by harnessing the thinking skills of managers and workers. Improving the quality and precision of problem solving in an organization releases a productive force far greater than that of equipment,

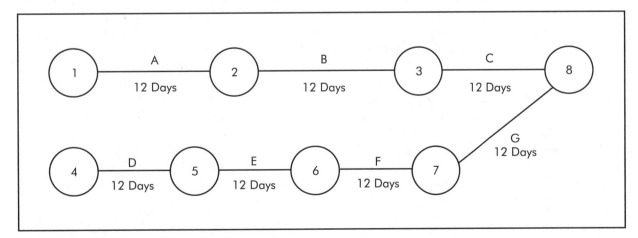

Figure 45-5. Critical path method (CPM).

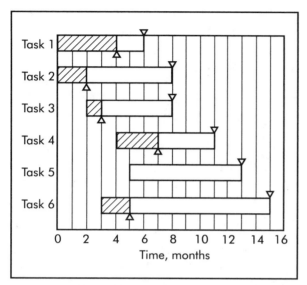

Figure 45-6. Gantt chart (Veilleux and Petro 1988).

tools, software, and more worker effort. The general steps for problem-solving are:

- problem recognition;
- problem definition or specification;
- developing possible causes;
- testing for the most probable causes;
- verifying the problem solution;
- updating documentation; and
- training the personnel.

Many techniques are used, almost always in a group setting. Common problem-solving tools include Ishikawa or fishbone diagrams, Pareto charts, brainstorming, and statistical tools such as histograms and control charts.

The *Ishikawa diagram*, illustrated in Figure 45-7, is a common technique used for *cause-and-effect analysis*. This diagram analyzes the causes of an effect or problem by considering the many diverse and complex relationships that exist. The process is driven by the influences of man, machine, method, material, management, and environment. By identifying the sources of a problem, corrective action can be taken to create an improvement. The weakness of this approach, as well

as other approaches, is that root causes are not distinguishable among all the causes identified (Bakerjian 1993).

Pareto analysis involves identifying the trivial many and the vital few. In other words, there are usually many identifiable problems that cause defects. However, of the problems identified, only a few will cause most of the defects. Pareto analysis helps engineers focus their efforts on the few problems that are generating the majority of the defects.

45.4 ORGANIZATIONAL/ INDUSTRIAL PSYCHOLOGY

Organizational behavior is more complex than a collection of individual behaviors. A manufacturing manager needs to understand how membership in a group affects individuals, how groups define individual roles, how norms are established and controlled, and how decisions are made by groups. Groups are either formal (individuals interacting based on their roles in the company hierarchy) or informal (individuals' interaction based on factors other than their organizational relationship, such as ethnicity, age, religious affiliation, or family). The organizational leader should come to know both informal and formal relationships and other factors such as the relative status of individuals and groups. Group standards of conduct result in what is considered to be acceptable or unacceptable behavior. These norms and standards are frequently derived as a company or plant "culture." The culture may be closely linked to those values needed for company prosperity or it may conflict with enterprise goals. Organizational behavior must be viewed and understood as a result of compliance with the dominant cultural values. Good management works toward developing a company culture that supports values and reinforces behaviors that serve the enterprise as well as the individual.

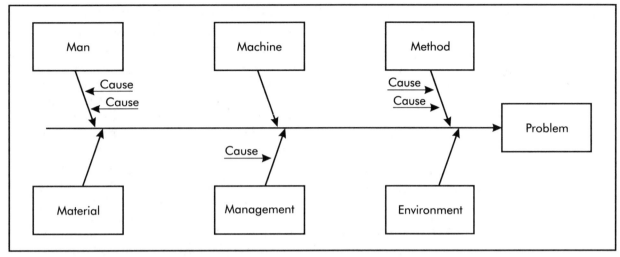

Figure 45-7. Ishikawa diagram (Bakerjian 1993).

Some organizational management techniques include the use of teams, participatory management, goal setting, continuous improvement, and the use of Deming's 14 points.

TEAMS

When personal and enterprise goals are congruent, motivation is unquestionably higher. Employees' participation in decision-making that affects their future instills a sense of belonging and of empowerment. A common and successful vehicle for such meaningful participation is the work team. The team may be temporary or semi-permanent. Team members support one another and can create a synergy for problem-solving, resulting in superior performance. An individual's need for social interaction, for approval and esteem from others, for personal achievement, and for self-realization can all be met in a well-managed, team-oriented environment.

Components of a successful team are:

- clear sense of direction (goal);
- members with diverse and appropriate skills;

- clear and motivating responsibilities and the authority to fulfill them;
- fair operating guidelines and practices;
- supportive relationships between team members;
- positive reinforcement; and
- supportive relationships between team members and nonmembers.

PARTICIPATORY MANAGEMENT

Participatory management techniques are based on power sharing among managers who, in a traditional command-and-control organization, are the sole executors of power. This form of organization is based on the premise that group participatory problem-solving and decision-making contribute to higher-quality problem solutions, while increasing the level of worker commitment. Specific techniques include quality circles, kaizen (continuous improvement) groups, employee-involvement groups, cross-functional problem-solving groups, etc. Organizations effectively utilizing worker participation in problem-solving have a means of passing to higher managers the problems requiring management decisions.

Important characteristics of participatory management systems include:

- unwavering commitment to the process by the highest levels of management;
- effective and constant communication up, down, and sideways throughout the organization;
- trust between management and the work force; and
- true empowerment of employees to implement their decisions.

Participatory management is consistent with the view that workers are important assets of an organization and that most people want to work and get satisfaction from their work by doing a good job. This is in contrast to traditional management techniques, which assume that labor is an interchangeable commodity like any other purchasable resource and that most people find work distasteful and will avoid it, if possible. Participatory management can harness the energy of individuals by allowing their personal achievement to advance simultaneously with the goals of the organization.

GOAL SETTING

Goal-setting theories of motivation suggest that individuals with specific goals are better performers than those with no goals. Within this theory, the behaviorist approach states that individuals want rewards for attaining goals and that managers should see that such rewards are provided for in the organization. A similar view says that when an individual is involved in setting the goals, more effort will be made to reach them. Thus, participation in the creation of the objectives is itself a motivator. Management-by-objectives (MBO), which utilizes individual participation in objective setting, is one example of goal-setting theory.

CONTINUOUS IMPROVEMENT

Incremental or continuous improvement of manufacturing processes is one of the keys to Japanese manufacturing success. Japanese manufacturing companies are likely to spend two-thirds of their R&D budgets on process improvement and one-third on product improvement. For U.S. companies, just the reverse is true. Improving quality, reducing costs, reducing the concept-to-market time, and turning inventories more quickly are all areas for continuous improvement. U.S. companies tend to view a manufacturing process as static after ramping up to production levels, while the Japanese or "continuous improvement" model sees the process as dynamic with the quest for improvement never ending.

DEMING'S 14 POINTS

Dr. W. Edwards Deming has become known for the transformation of management through his "14 points for management." These 14 points are criteria for a company to become successful with management as the primary agent and focus of change (Bakerjian 1993).

1. Create constancy of purpose toward improvement of product and service, with the aim to become competitive, stay in business, and provide jobs.
2. Adopt the new philosophy. We are in a new economic age. Western management must awaken to the challenge, learn their responsibilities, and take on leadership for change.
3. Cease dependence on inspection to achieve quality. Eliminate the need for inspection on a mass basis by building quality into the product in the first place.
4. End the practice of awarding business on the basis of price tag. Instead, minimize total cost. Move toward a single

supplier for any one item, on a long-term relationship of loyalty and trust.

5. Improve constantly and forever the system of production and service, to improve quality and productivity, and thus constantly decrease costs.

6. Institute training on the job.

7. Institute leadership. The aim of supervision should be to help people and machines and gadgets to do a better job. Supervision of management is in need of overhaul, as well as supervision of production workers.

8. Drive out fear, so that everyone may work effectively for the company.

9. Break down barriers between departments.

10. Eliminate slogans, exhortations, and targets for the work force asking for zero defects and new levels of productivity.

11. Eliminate work standards (quotas) on the factory floor. Eliminate management by objective, management by numbers, numerical goals. Substitute leadership.

12. Remove barriers that rob the hourly worker, and people in management and engineering of their right to pride of workmanship.

13. Institute a vigorous program of education and self-improvement.

14. Put everybody in the company to work to accomplish the transformation. It is everybody's job.

REVIEW QUESTIONS

45.1) A person retains how much of what is heard?

a) 10%
b) 20%
c) 30%
d) 50%

45.2) The management concept in which many of the decisions affecting the operation of the plant are made at the lower levels is called _____ .

a) centralization
b) line-and-staff
c) span-of-control
d) decentralization

45.3) What project management tool graphically depicts the progress of various tasks with shaded horizontal bars?

45.4) What type of problem-solving tool identifies the vital few and the trivial many?

45.5) Participatory management views workers as important _____ of the organization.

45.6) Management by objectives is an example of what theory?

REFERENCES

Bakerjian, Ramon, ed. 1993. *Tool and Manufacturing Engineers Handbook*, Fourth Edition. Volume 7, *Continuous Improvement*. Dearborn, MI: Society of Manufacturing Engineers.

Veilleux, Raymond F. and Louis W. Petro, eds. 1988. *Tool and Manufacturing Engineers Handbook*, Fourth Edition. Volume 5, *Manufacturing Management*. Dearborn, MI: Society of Manufacturing Engineers.

Chapter 46

Labor, Safety, and Human Factors

46.1 LABOR RELATIONS

The Industrial Revolution has altered the way the modern world thinks and works. In the United States, the full flow of commerce and full production of the economy is deemed essential to national interest. To prevent or minimize interference with the normal flow of commerce and the full production of articles and commodities for commerce, U.S. Congress enacted the National Labor Relations Act (Wagner Act) in 1935, which was subsequently amended in 1947 by the Taft-Hartley Act, also known as the Labor Management Relations Act (LMRA). In 1957, the law was further amended in part by the Landrum-Griffin Act, also known as the Labor-Management Reporting and Disclosure Act (Veilleux and Petro 1988). For the purpose of this chapter, these assorted acts and amendments will be referred to as the Labor Management Relations Act, the Labor Act, or simply the Act.

The laws were enacted to define the legitimate rights of both employers and employees in their relations affecting commerce, to encourage collective bargaining, and to eliminate certain practices by management and labor that are detrimental to the general welfare. While the Labor Act primarily focuses on union-management relations, it does have an effect on employee-employer relations whether the work environment is union, non-union, blue collar, or white collar.

The rights specifically provided in the Labor Management Relations Act, as amended, do not apply to certain categories of workers such as independent contractors, supervisors, and public employees. An individual is an *employee* if under the direct control of the employer, while an *independent contractor*, although physically working for the employer, is called on to produce a result without the employer controlling or directing the means or methods used to accomplish it. A worker is deemed a *supervisor* if he or she has the authority to recommend and/or cause another employee to be hired, promoted, discharged, rewarded, or disciplined. Additional characteristics of supervisory status include the authority to direct the job duties of rank-and-file employees, authorize overtime, authorize use of sick leave, and schedule work.

The basic rights of employees under the Labor Management Relations Act are defined in Section 7 of the Act: "Employees shall have the right to self-organization to form, join, or assist labor organizations, to bargain collectively through representatives of their own choosing, and to engage in other concerted activities for the purpose of collective bargaining or other mutual aid or protection; and shall also have the right to refrain from any or all such activities except to the extent that such right may be affected by an agreement requiring membership in a labor organization as a condition of employment."

Under Section 7, employees cannot be prevented from:

- forming or attempting to form a union among employees of a company;
- assisting a union in organizing;
- striking to secure better working conditions; or
- refraining from organizing should they so choose.

It is important to recognize that the rights specified in Section 7 are rights granted to individuals who choose to act collectively (Veilleux and Petro 1988).

Although Section 7 of the Labor Management Relations Act grants to employees the right to refrain from activity on behalf of a union, this right is limited. Under certain conditions, an employer and union can make an agreement (union security agreement) that would require all employees to join the union to retain their jobs. A union security agreement cannot require union membership as a condition of hire, but can only require that employees become union members after a certain period. This grace period cannot be less than 30 days, except in the building and construction industry where employees may be required to join the union after 7 full days. This type of company is known as a *union shop* (Veilleux and Petro 1988).

Congress believed that if workers had the right to associate and organize for the purpose of negotiating the terms and conditions of their employment, industrial strife would be minimized. The process of *collective bargaining* as mandated by law requires an employer and the employee's representative to meet at reasonable times to confer in good faith with respect to wages, hours, and other terms or conditions of employment. Under the Labor Management Relations Act, neither management nor labor may refuse to bargain collectively with the other. However, it should be noted that the obligation to bargain collectively does not require either party

to concede or agree to a proposal by the other. Where there exists a valid, enforceable, collective bargaining agreement, certain steps must be taken before the contract can be terminated or modified. First, a party seeking modification or termination must provide the other party with written notification in the form of a proposal for termination or modification 60 days prior to the expiration of the agreement. Second, the party must offer to meet and confer with the other party to negotiate a new collective bargaining contract. Third, after notice to the other party, the Federal Mediation and Conciliation Service must be notified of the existence of a dispute. Finally, neither party can resort to a strike or lockout until 60 days after notice to the other party (Veilleux and Petro 1988).

As noted earlier, Section 7 of the Labor Management Relations Act permits employees to engage in concerted activities for the purpose of collective bargaining. Section 13 of the Act ensures that, except in a few circumstances such as health care institutions, an employee's right to strike may not be impeded or diminished. An *employee's right to strike* assumes the strike is lawful, which will depend on the purpose of the strike, its timing, or on the conduct of the strikers. A strike that has a lawful purpose, such as higher wages or better working conditions, may become unlawful because of the conduct of the strikers, such as blocking the entrance or exit of a plant, threatening violence against non-striking employees, or attacking management representatives. Employees who participate in an unlawful strike or unlawful strike activities may be discharged and are not entitled to reinstatement when the strike ends. Employees striking for economic concessions, such as higher wages or improved working conditions, are economic strikers. Although they cannot be discharged, they can be replaced during the strike. They are not entitled to reinstatement if the employer has hired permanent replacements. However, they may be entitled to recall when an opening occurs. The exact terms will usually be the subject of the collective bargaining between the employer and the union.

The Labor Management Relations Act defines certain practices by an employer as unfair labor practices. Employees who strike to protest a company's unfair labor practice cannot be discharged or permanently replaced. When the strike ends, the strikers are entitled to immediate reinstatement even if replacements hired during the strike have to be discharged (Veilleux and Petro 1988).

46.2 SAFETY

The Occupational Safety and Health Act of 1970 was enacted to assure safe and healthy working conditions for every working man and woman in the nation. The Act applies to every employer in the U.S. or in U.S. possessions who has any number of employees and who engages in a business affecting commerce. Employers covered by the Act have the obligation of complying with the safety and health standards connected with the Act. Also, the act has a "general-duty clause" that obligates employers to provide employees with a workplace free from recognized hazards that are likely to cause death or serious physical harm. This legislation makes on-the-job safety and health a management responsibility. The law places on every employee the duty to comply with safety standards. However, final responsibility for compliance remains with the employer.

The Occupational Safety and Health Administration (OSHA) has the authority to institute and revoke safety and health standards, conduct inspections and investigations, issue citations and penalties, place requirements for record keeping of safety and health data, and petition the courts to act against employers with dangerously hazardous work environments. OSHA also

has the authority to provide employer and employee training, implement voluntary protection programs including injury prevention consultation, grant funds to states for the operation of safety and health training programs, and develop and maintain occupational safety and health statistics programs.

Every organization, no matter what the size, should make a written safety policy statement and follow it. It should publicize the policy to everyone in the organization, from all supervisory levels to employees. All top-level managers must agree with the policy, and each level of management must understand who is responsible for safety.

Regardless of the size of a manufacturing organization, the integration of the safety ethic throughout the business is essential if the safety function is to be effective. If safety is a separate function, its effectiveness is doomed. Safety is not a concern for only the manufacturing personnel; it is a necessity for the engineering, marketing, accounting, shipping, industrial relations, and customer service groups.

There should be an unbroken chain of accountability for safety from the line supervisor to the president or owner. A good system can operate in accordance with the following assignment of safety responsibility:

- The supervisor is accountable for the safety of all subordinates and for the safe condition of the work area under his or her responsibility.
- The department head is responsible for the establishment of good housekeeping practices in the department and for the safety training and development of each supervisor.
- The superintendent's safety commission is to see that the corporation's safety program is administered at the plant level. He or she is responsible for all safety activities in his or her administration.

• The plant manager, who is generally accountable to a vice president at the corporate level, is vested with the responsibility for safety performance at the plant. The plant manager should see that members of the staff complete safety training (Veilleux and Petro 1988).

HAZARD AWARENESS

Hazard awareness is a key element of safety training specifically, and health and safety programs in general. Management must work with safety professionals and the work force to determine locations with a high accident potential as well as to identify severe hazards with a low occurrence likelihood. Hazard analysis precedes hazard awareness and should factor in both the probability of accident occurrence and the severity of injury or property damage. After identification of hazards has been completed, control methods are implemented. Training in hazard awareness should be done after the hazards have been identified, analyzed, and control measures undertaken.

AUTOMATED OPERATIONS

Automated versus manual operations place a greater onus of responsibility on the engineer. In the manual operation, a worker initiates the change of state of equipment and/or a process. In the automated mode, a controller of some sort (often remote from the areas of potential hazard) effects the change of state. Safe automated systems require more effort in the machine design phase and, increasingly, in the nature of communication interfaces within the factory. Also, automated systems require training for the operator, which may include more sophisticated concepts than those for manual operations. To illustrate, Figure 46-1 depicts a fault-tree analysis of hazards created by robots.

LOST-TIME ACCIDENTS

A lost-time accident is any time that a worker loses time from the job. Typically, any injury requires some time lost for treatment, so an injury is usually considered lost-time if a worker fails to return the day after the accident. Records of lost-time injuries also carry some determination of injury severity. Non-lost-time accidents may be designated minor injuries and compensable injuries. By documenting lost-time incidents, a safety record is created.

MATERIAL SAFETY DATA SHEETS (MSDS)

Many states have "right-to-know" laws as part of their health and safety legislation. These laws mandate that employers make material safety data sheets (MSDS) available to employees in a readily accessible manner. Employees cannot be discharged or discriminated against for exercising their rights, including the request for information on hazardous materials. Employees must be notified and given direction for locating material safety data sheets and the receipts of new or revised ones.

All hazardous materials must be labeled in accordance with federal laws. The U.S. Environmental Protection Agency (EPA) has oversight of hazardous materials with regard to use and human exposure, labeling, containment, and disposal. Increasingly, the design-for-manufacture (DFM) process attempts to engineer hazardous materials out of the product and process. While many efforts such as DFM have been undertaken to reduce and/or eliminate these materials from the manufacturing environment, many are still present. Each plant is responsible for the management of hazardous materials and frequently a broad-based hazardous materials committee establishes procedures consistent with EPA regulation, state-level regulation, and company policy. Common procedures include: (a) control of exposure

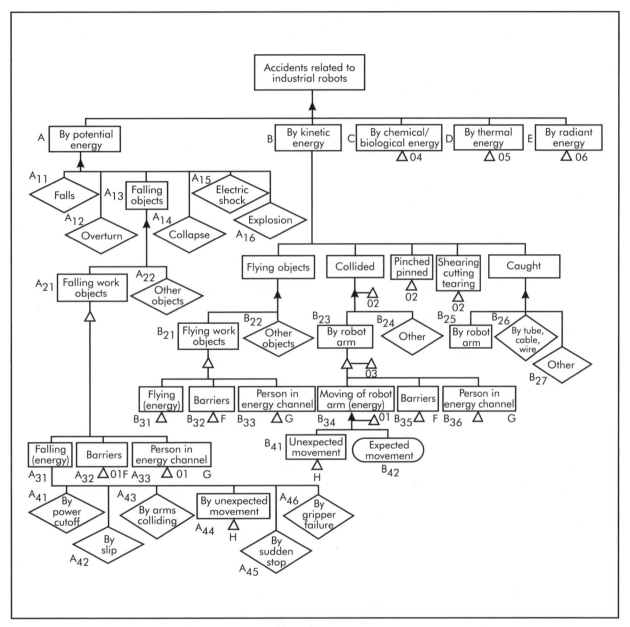

Figure 46-1. Fault-tree analysis of hazards created by robots.

including operator protection such as mist collection systems, gloves, and guards; (b) rules for storage, handling, and disposal; and (c) contingency plans and training for accidental spills and exposure.

ENVIRONMENT

Environmental concerns influence the manufacturing workplace. Manufacturing engineers and managers must make protection of the environment and compliance with regulations a major priority. The task is difficult, but there are no real alternatives to proactive efforts to protect the environment, workers, and the general public. First, the manufacturer must determine which codes must be met and the nature of the process to issue permits and submit reports. Areas of major concern include air and water pollution, hazardous wastes, existing conditions, and noise abatement.

PRODUCT LIABILITY

The U.S. government's product liability laws require that all products comply with appropriate standards and regulations and be free of safety-related defects. Lawsuits against manufacturers have forced companies to anticipate and defend liability claims based on injury or death caused by their products. Civil lawsuits for damages predominate and are aimed at companies. However, criminal liability suits may be directed at corporations and, in a few cases, individuals. For the great majority of industrial managers, the probability of criminal prosecution is remote. Before there can be such liability, the manager must be found guilty of knowingly carrying out illegal actions or being grossly negligent in his or her duties. Manufacturers have been under increasing pressure to exercise care and to document all activity in the design and manufacture of products.

46.3 HUMAN FACTORS

Human factors is often called *ergonomics*. Human factors and safety engineering emerged from the disciplines of industrial engineering and psychology. Work in this area is concerned with the effective and safe application of people as elements of a system. The original emphasis was on controls, consoles, and cockpits in the military. In recent years, this field has expanded to cover virtually all areas where people interact in engineering systems.

Human factors also includes engineering anthropometry, lighting and workplace effectiveness, and exposure to noise, vibration, and repetitive motion.

ENGINEERING ANTHROPOMETRY

Engineering anthropometry is the application of scientific measurement techniques to the human body to improve the interaction between people and machines. Many worker performance problems can be eliminated by properly selecting workplace dimensions based on anthropometric measures.

The goal in such studies is to ensure that the workplace layout can accommodate the physical capabilities of the majority of people. The typical measure is based on the percentage of the population having a particular body dimension or capability (such as overhead reach or gripping strength) equal to or less than a particular value. General design limits are usually based on a range from the 5th percentile female to the 95th percentile male. For any body dimension, the 5th percentile indicates that 5% of the population will be equal to or smaller than that value. A design range from the 5th percentile of women to the 95th percentile of men should cover a large majority of personnel.

In most applications, the important percentile for the selection of workplace dimensions is the 5th percentile. For example, the 5th percentile in women for overhead reach, standing is 73 in. (1,854 mm). Consequently, a workspace designed for both men and women should not require a standing overhead reach over 73 in. (1,854 mm). Table 46-1 gives anthropometric data for common working positions.

LIGHTING AND WORKPLACE EFFECTIVENESS

The illumination level in a workplace can strongly affect worker performance. Proper

Table 46-1. Anthropometric data for common working positions

Feature	Percentile Values							
	5th Percentile				95th Percentile			
	Men		Women		Men		Women	
	(in.)	(mm)	(in.)	(mm)	(in.)	(mm)	(in.)	(mm)
Stature—clothed	66.4	1,687	61.8	1,570	74.4	1,890	70.3	1,786
Functional forward reach	28.3	719	25.2	640	34.0	864	31.1	790
Overhead reach, standing	78.9	2,004	73.0	1,854	90.8	2,306	84.7	2,151
Overhead reach, sitting	50.3	1,278	46.2	1,174	57.9	1,471	54.9	1,395
Functional leg length	43.5	1,105	39.2	996	50.3	1,278	46.7	1,186
Kneeling height	48.0	1,219	45.1	1,146	53.9	1,369	51.3	1,303
Kneeling leg length	25.2	640	23.3	592	29.7	754	27.8	706

lighting is necessary for the safe and efficient execution of tasks.

The quantity of light emitted from a light source per unit time is called *luminous flux*. It is expressed in the units of lumens (lm). *Luminance* is a measure of the light intensity emitted from a light source per unit area normal to the direction of the light flux, and is expressed in candela/ft^2 (candela/m^2) (cd/ft^2 [cd/m^2]). Another important unit of measurement in lighting is *illuminance*, the part of the total light flux that is incident on a given surface. In standard practice, it is the quantity of light that illuminates a work surface. The measure of illuminance is the footcandle or fc (1 fc is equal to 1 lm/ft^2 [10.76 lm/m^2] or 10.76 lux).

The recommended illumination level of a workplace is determined by the type of task that is performed. Inadequate illumination can result in poor efficiency, fatigue, or damage to eyesight. Table 46-2 lists recommended levels of illumination for different workplaces and tasks.

NOISE

Noise is frequently defined as "unwanted sound." Noise or any sound is measured by frequency in Hertz (Hz) and its intensity is defined in decibels (dB). Noise has several undesirable side effects. Continuous exposure to intense noise can cause deafness. Noise also interferes with communication and prevents recognition of warning signals.

Measurements of sound intensity used in human factors engineering are typically made on the A-weighted scale (dBA). This scale is made up of de-emphasized frequencies less than 1,000 Hz (the ear is less sensitive to these frequencies). Extremely intense noise for prolonged periods or impulses of intense noise over 120 dBA can cause permanent damage to hearing. Industrial noise at levels of 90 dBA or above can also cause permanent hearing loss if experienced over a period of months.

Most industrialized countries have legally enforceable maximum noise levels for workers. In 1971, OSHA developed maximum noise exposure standards for all employees. The noise exposures permitted under OSHA are given in Table 46-3.

Personal protective equipment, such as earplugs, earmuffs, and sound-deadening helmets, or a combination thereof, should be

Table 46-2. Recommended ranges of illumination

Type of Activity or Area	Recommended Illumination fc (lux)
Public areas with dark surroundings	2–5 (22–54)
Areas for brief visits	5–10 (54–108)
Working areas where visual tasks are occasionally performed	10–20 (108–215)
Performance of visual tasks of high contrast or large size (reading printed matter or rough assembly)	20–50 (215–538)
Performance of visual tasks of low contrast or small size (reading handwritten text or difficult inspection)	100–200 (1,076–2,153)
Performance of visual tasks of extremely low contrast and small size (surgical procedures or circuit-board repair)	1,000–2,000 (10,764–21,528)

Table 46-3. Noise exposures permitted by OSHA

Duration per Day (hours)	Sound Level (dBA)
8	90
6	92
4	95
3	97
2	100
1.5	102
1	105
0.5	110
0.25 or less	115

(Drozda and Wick 1983)

supplied to employees in areas where noise abatement is difficult or expensive.

VIBRATION

Vibration is characterized in terms of its frequency, amplitude, and direction. It can affect health in a variety of ways. One of the most important is the resonance frequency range of the human body. Vibrations in the range of 4–8 Hz cause internal organs to resonate. Prolonged exposure to vibrations of approximately 1-g (32.2 ft/s^2 [9.81 m/s^2]) acceleration in the resonant range can cause abdominal pain, loss of equilibrium, nausea, and shortness of breath. Sequential vibrations to the hands in the range of 1.5–80-g with frequencies from 8–5,000 Hz are also of concern. Tools may transmit such localized vibrations to the hands. Problems such as stiffness, numbness, pain, and loss of strength may result from prolonged exposure.

REPETITIVE MOTION

Repeated simple motions during the workday can result in a variety of health problems that can have severe consequences. Repetitive-motion disorders or cumulative trauma disorders (CTD) can result from the execution of a simple task, such as raising an arm overhead or using a screwdriver repeatedly. Typical motion patterns that can cause risk are bending of the wrist, grasping or pinching objects, raising an arm overhead, and applying a large amount of force with the hand.

Repetitive-motion injuries occur over months of executing the same motion pattern without an opportunity for the body to recover. Pain and minimized movement can result from a variety of repetitive-motion-related ailments. A repeated motion in an awkward position or requiring a high application of force coupled with a lack of rest cause these types of injuries. Some common forms of repetitive-motion problems include tendinitis, carpal tunnel syndrome, rotary cuff injury, and tenosynovitis. *Tendinitis* causes inflamed and sore tendons, swelling, and weakness. *Carpal tunnel syndrome* results from excessive pressure on the median nerve in the wrist causing numbness, tingling, and pain in the wrist. *Rotator cuff injury* is inflamed tendons in the shoulder accompanied by pain and limited motion. *Tenosynovitis* is the swelling of the tendon and the sheath that covers it, causing tenderness and pain.

Repeated-motion injuries can be prevented by proper tool selection, minimized force-application requirements, and adding variety to the tasks being performed (providing an opportunity for the body to recover).

REVIEW QUESTIONS

46.1) Under what condition may an employee who participates in a union-organized strike be discharged and not be entitled to reinstatement when the strike ends?

46.2) Employee "right-to-know" laws focus on _____ .

   a) dangerous machinery
   b) affirmative action plans
   c) hazardous materials
   d) company policies and procedures

46.3) What should be the minimum standing height for a walk-in freezer?

46.4) What is the maximum sound level that employees can be exposed to during an 8-hour period without hearing protection?

46.5) A truck seat resonates at 5 Hz. What is the potential problem with this design?

46.6) What is the risk associated with repeatedly using a screwdriver throughout the workday?

REFERENCES

Drozda, Thomas J. and Charles Wick, eds. 1983. *Tool and Manufacturing Engineers Handbook*, Fourth Edition. *Volume 1: Machining*. Dearborn, MI: Society of Manufacturing Engineers.

Veilleux, Raymond F. and Louis W. Petro, eds. 1988. *Tool and Manufacturing Engineers Handbook*, Fourth edition. *Volume 5: Manufacturing Management*. Dearborn, MI: Society of Manufacturing Engineers.

Chapter 47

Engineering Economics

Engineering economics is the name given to techniques for evaluating financial decisions in the engineering enterprise. The objective is to provide a means of making economically sound decisions in the execution of engineering projects.

47.1 TIME VALUE OF MONEY

Over a short period of time, sums of money can be treated in the same way as any other algebraic quantity. In the short term, simple addition and subtraction is all that is necessary to evaluate economic alternatives. However, money cannot be treated this way over longer periods of time. Money available today is always worth more than the same amount of money available at some time in the future. Consequently, a thousand dollars today is more valuable than a guarantee of a payment of a thousand dollars a year from now. Someone could deposit the $1,000 in a bank and at the end of a year period, collect both the $1,000 and the interest that was earned. If the annually compounded interest rate is 5%, $1,000 today is really equivalent to $1,050 a year from now. Clearly, economic decision-making requires careful consideration of the value of money over time.

47.2 CASH FLOW PATTERNS

Engineering economics requires the comparison of cash flow patterns. A car loan that requires a down payment and a series of equal monthly payments is an example of a cash flow pattern. This review will consider three patterns of cash flow:

1. P-pattern—a single amount P occurs at the beginning of n periods. P represents the principal or present amount. This quantity might refer to a single deposit in a mutual fund for later use.
2. F-pattern—a single amount F occurs at the end of n periods. F represents the future amount. This quantity might represent the withdrawal from a long-term savings plan for retirement.
3. A-pattern—equal amounts of A occur at the ends of n periods. A represents an annual amount (although the period may be a month or other period). This quantity might represent the payments made on a mortgage.

The solution to most engineering economics problems involves finding a pattern of cash flow equivalent to another pattern of cash flow. For example, how much money must be deposited in a bank at a given interest rate to yield a desired amount in the future? This problem can be thought of as finding the amount in an F-pattern that is equivalent to a P-pattern. These two amounts are proportional with a factor that is dependent on the interest rate per period, i, and the number of interest periods, n. The number of periods depends on the frequency of compounding.

There are symbols for the proportionality factors that have an appearance that suggests algebraic cancellation. This notation is designed to prevent selection of the wrong factor in a given problem. In the case of determining the amount that must be deposited now to yield a desired sum in the future, the proportionality factor is written $(P/F,i,n)$. The factor is applied in the following equation:

$$P = F(P/F,i,n) \qquad (47\text{-}1)$$

This indicates that a present sum of P is required at an interest rate of i for n periods given a desired future sum of F. Table 47-1 illustrates some various constants of proportionality and the formulas used to find them.

The numerical values for the factors in Table 47-1 can also be found in tabular form. Many texts on engineering economics provide these factors in this form as an alternative to manually calculating the values.

Example 47.2.1. A truck is to be purchased for $78,000. The truck dealer offers terms of a $5,000 down payment with 12 monthly payments at an annual interest rate of 12%. What is the monthly payment?

Solution. The problem required finding the "annual sum" A (although in this case the payments are monthly) based on the present sum P of $73,000 (the principal of the loan). The number of periods is 12 with a periodic interest rate of 1% (12%/12). The problem can be represented by the equation:

$$A = P(A/P,i,n)$$
$$A = (78,000 - 5,000)(A/P,0.01,12)$$
$$A = 73,000 \left(\frac{0.01(1+0.01)^{12}}{(1+0.01)^{12} - 1} \right)$$
$$A = 73,000(0.0888) = \$6,482$$

Table 47-1. Proportionality factors for compound-interest formulas

Symbol	To Find	Given	Formula	Name and Example
$(F/P,i,n)$	F	P	$(1 + i)^n$	Single-payment compound amount factor (find the amount that results from leaving a given amount in a bank account)
$(P/F,i,n)$	P	F	$\dfrac{1}{(1+i)^n}$	Single-payment present worth factor (find the amount that must be left in a bank account in order to yield a desired amount)
$(A/P,i,n)$	A	P	$\dfrac{i(1+i)^n}{(1+i)^n - 1}$	Uniform series capital recovery factor (find the payment on a car loan)
$(P/A,i,n)$	P	A	$\dfrac{(1+i)^n - 1}{i(1+i)^n}$	Uniform series present worth factor (find the amount that can be borrowed given a fixed monthly payment)
$(A/F,i,n)$	A	F	$\dfrac{i}{(1+i)^n - 1}$	Uniform series sinking fund factor (find the amount that must be deposited into an individual retirement account each month to yield a desired amount at retirement)
$(F/A,i,n)$	F	A	$\dfrac{(1+i)^n - 1}{i}$	Uniform series compound amount factor (find the amount that results from a series of fixed deposits into a bank account)

Example 47.2.2. The goal of a savings plan is to accumulate $10,000 at the end of 10 years. How much money must be invested now if the savings account offers 4% annual interest compounded quarterly?

Solution. The problem requires finding the present sum based on a known future sum. The periodic interest rate is 1% over 40 periods. This can be expressed as:

$$P = F(P/F,i,n)$$

$$P = 10,000(P/F, 0.01,40)$$

$$P = 10,000\left(\frac{1}{(1+0.01)^{40}}\right)$$

$$P = 10,000\ (0.6717) = \$6,717$$

Example 47.2.3. What amount must be deposited in a bank at 5% annual interest, compounded annually, to provide $1,000 per year for the next 50 years?

Solution. The problem requires finding a present sum based on a known annual sum.

$$P = A\ (P/A,i,n)$$

$$P = 1,000\ (P/A,0.05,50)$$

$$P = 1,000\left(\frac{(1+0.05)^{50}-1}{0.05(1+0.05)^{50}}\right)$$

$$P = 1,000\ (18.2559) = \$18,256$$

47.3 COMPARISONS BASED ON ANNUAL COST

There are many different techniques used in engineering economic analysis to evaluate alternatives. One of the most common is comparison of equivalent uniform annual cost (EUAC). This technique allows the comparison of a non-uniform series of cash flows

to identify the minimum cost alternative. This approach is used to decide between two alternative investments in equipment, property, or some other resource, known as an asset. There are several assumptions made in applying this approach:

- There is a uniform time value or interest rate on all money involved in the problem whether it is borrowed or not. Money that is not invested represents an opportunity cost of lost interest.
- The annual cost of an asset is reduced by the money made from the sale or salvage of an asset at the end of its useful life.
- If two alternatives have different useful service lives, it is assumed the asset with the shorter life will be replaced with an identical item.

The solution to these types of problems requires identifying all the components of the annual cost, including the opportunity cost of not investing the present value of the asset, the operating cost, and the cost reduction associated with the salvage of the asset.

Example 47.3.1. A company is considering purchasing a machine for $10,000. After 12 years of use, there is a projected salvage value of $3,000. The machine will require $150 per year in maintenance. Determine the equivalent uniform annual cost (EUAC) if the annual interest rate is 10%.

Solution. The EUAC has three components: the annual opportunity cost of the purchase price, the maintenance cost, and the equivalent annual benefit of the salvage value of the machine.

$$EUAC = 10,000\ (A/P,0.1,12) + 150$$
$$- 3,000\ (A/F,0.1,12)$$

$$EUAC = 10,000\ (0.1468) + 150$$
$$- 3,000\ (0.0468) = \$1,478$$

Example 47.3.2. A specialized machine tool costs $500,000. It has an estimated life of 20 years with no salvage value. What amount should the company be willing to spend on *extra* maintenance if it would extend the service life to 30 years? Assume a 12% annual interest rate.

Solution. The company should only invest in extra maintenance, E_m, until the EUAC of the 30-year service life program is equal to the EUAC of the 20-year service life program. Therefore, the problem can be expressed as:

EUAC for 30 year service
= EUAC for 20 year service

$$500,000 \,(A/P,0.12,30) + E_m$$
$$= 500,000 \,(A/P,0.12,20)$$

$$500,000 \,(0.1241) + E_m$$
$$= 500,000 \,(0.1339)$$

$$E_m = \$4,900$$

47.4 COST ESTIMATING

Manufacturing cost estimating has been defined as the process of forecasting the "bottom line" cost totals associated with the completion of a set of manufacturing tasks. This forecast is normally made prior to the time the sequence of tasks actually begins. In contrast, *cost control* has been described as the process of updating or refining prior initial cost estimates for a sequence of manufacturing tasks that is currently in process. Cost control is a function related to project performance. It is related to the problem of "living within the budget."

Costs generally fall into the categories of fixed, variable, or semifixed. Among the manufacturing costs are direct labor, direct material, indirect labor, indirect manufacturing costs, general administrative costs, and tooling costs (Veilleux and Petro 1988).

FIXED COSTS

Fixed costs are those that are generally independent of the production quantity being built. Indirect labor and indirect manufacturing costs are generally fixed. Setup costs for machine tools are also fixed costs.

VARIABLE COSTS

Variable costs are those incurred on a per-unit basis of the quantity that is being produced. Variable costs increase with each additional unit that is produced. Per-piece direct labor and direct material costs for assembled or machined parts are examples of variable costs.

SEMIFIXED COSTS

Semifixed costs are sometimes known as *step variable costs*. These costs are somewhat independent of quantity and vary with specific groups of units that are produced. The costs to change cutting tools and the completion of scheduled maintenance operations after a specified number of production units are examples of semifixed costs.

DIRECT LABOR

Direct labor is the cost of all "hands-on" effort associated with the manufacture of a specific product. Typical direct-labor activities include machining, assembly, etc. Direct-labor activities are characterized by the presence of some physical contact between the worker and the workpiece. This contact usually adds value to the product being produced.

DIRECT MATERIAL

Direct material is the cost of all components included in the end product being produced. To be considered direct material, the components or raw materials must be a permanent part of the end product. Examples of material costs that are not direct include raw material from which tooling is fabricated, test equipment, and packaging materials. Direct material is a variable manufacturing cost.

INDIRECT LABOR

Indirect labor is the cost of all labor effort that cannot be directly associated with the manufacture of a product. Examples of indirect labor include the salary costs of workers in the accounting, purchasing, and personnel departments, together with the salary costs of supervisors and managers.

INDIRECT MANUFACTURING COST

Indirect manufacturing cost (IMC) is a term often used synonymously with *overhead costs*. It includes all costs for rent, heat, electricity, water, and expendable factory supplies, together with the annual costs of building and equipment depreciation. Expendable factory supplies are often indirect materials that are consumed during the manufacturing process.

GENERAL AND ADMINISTRATIVE COSTS

General and administrative (G&A) *costs* are those incurred at the plant or interplant level that are not easily associated with a specific work center or department. Examples include the costs of top executives' salaries, plant mainframe computer procurement, operation costs, and technical library facilities. G&A costs are generally fixed.

TOOLING AND TEST EQUIPMENT COSTS

Tooling and test equipment costs are those costs incurred for the fabrication of jigs and fixtures for machining. They also include CNC programming costs and costs for the design and fabrication of special-purpose test equipment. Tooling and test equipment costs are generally fixed.

The cost-estimating procedure relies on the use of performance standards and the separate estimation of labor and material costs.

Separate labor overhead (LOH) rates are used to convert labor hours to labor dollars on each defined cost center. A cost center (CC) is a numerical way of designating different parts of an organization. The estimate total is augmented by both a contingency allowance and a profit margin. To make a detailed and accurate cost estimate, the design configuration of the end product to be built must be complete. A complete bill of materials, showing the assembly relationship between component parts of the final assembly, is required. For each component part, a decision must be made to purchase the part from an outside vendor or fabricate the part in-house. This decision is often made by manufacturing engineers as opposed to design engineers. Make/purchase designations for all line items on the bill of materials must be made prior to beginning the actual estimating process.

Computer-aided process planning (CAPP) can simplify the cost-estimating procedure. For parts previously built, a file will exist that specifies both the process sequence and the related standard times. For parts that have not been previously fabricated, part geometries and tolerances may permit the computer generation of routings and corresponding standard times.

47.5 VALUE ENGINEERING

Value engineering provides a systematic approach to evaluating design alternatives. Value engineering is often very useful and may even point the way to innovative new design approaches or ideas. It is also called *value analysis, value control,* and *value management.* In value engineering, a multidisciplinary team analyzes the functions provided by the product and the cost of each function. Based on the analysis results, creative ways are sought to eliminate unnecessary features and functions and to achieve required functions at the lowest cost while optimizing manufacturability, quality, and delivery.

In value engineering, "value" is defined as a numerical ratio of function (or performance) to cost. Because cost is a measure of effort, the value of a product using this definition is simply the ratio of output (function or performance) to input (cost) commonly used in engineering studies. In a complicated product design or system, every component contributes both to the cost and the performance of the entire system. The ratio of performance to cost of each component indicates the relative value of individual components. Obtaining the maximum performance per unit cost is the basic objective of value engineering.

For any expenditure or cost, two kinds of value are received, functional (use) value and esteem (prestige) value. *Functional value* reflects the properties or qualities of a product or system that accomplish the intended work or service. To achieve maximum functional value is to achieve the lowest possible cost in providing the performance function. *Esteem value* is composed of the properties, features, or attractiveness that make ownership of the product desirable. To achieve maximum esteem value is to achieve the lowest possible cost in providing the necessary appearance, attractiveness, and features the customer wants. Examples of prestige items include surface finish, streamlining, packaging, and decorative trim.

In addition to the two kinds of value received, additional costs come from unnecessary aspects of the design. *Waste* describes features or properties of the design providing neither functional value nor esteem value. Typical scales of value for some common, well-known items are shown in Figure 47-1.

Tie	5% function	90% esteem		5% waste
Hammer	80% function		15% esteem	5% waste
Tie clasp	20% function	75% esteem		5% waste
Button	90% function		10% esteem	

Figure 47-1. Estimated scale of value of some common products. (Courtesy Industrial Technology Institute)

REVIEW QUESTIONS

47.1) If the goal of a savings plan is to accumulate $50,000 after 20 years, how much should be deposited now if an annual interest rate of 6% is available?

47.2) A car is to be purchased for $15,000. A $4,000 down payment is made. The remainder is borrowed at an annual interest rate of 12%. Find the monthly payment for a three-year loan.

47.3) A machine costs $46,000 and has an expected life of five years with no salvage value. A service contract costing $4,000 per year is available, which promises a seven-year service life with no salvage value. If a 9% annual interest rate is available, is the service contract a sound economic decision?

47.4) Is storing work-in-process parts a fixed or variable cost?

47.5) Does inspection add value to a product?

REFERENCE

Veilleux, Raymond F. and Louis W. Petro, eds. 1988. *Tool and Manufacturing Engineers Handbook*, Fourth Edition. *Volume 5: Manufacturing Management*. Dearborn, MI: Society of Manufacturing Engineers.

Appendix A

Mathematics

A.1 CIRCLES, ELLIPSES, PARABOLAS, AND HYPERBOLAS

Lines are *first degree* equations because the power of x in the equation is one. Circles, ellipses, parabolas, and hyperbolas are described by *second degree* equations. The general form of a second degree equation is given by:

$$Ax^2 + Bxy + Cy^2 + Dx + Ey + F = 0 \quad (A\text{-}1)$$

This equation describes a set of geometric shapes called *conic sections*. There are various forms of conic sections that can be categorized according to the magnitude of the coefficients $A, B, C, D, E,$ and F (see Table A-1).

A *circle* is the locus or collection of points equidistant from a given point in a plane. The equation for a circle can be expressed in a general form as:

Table A-1. Conic sections

Conic Section	Coefficient
Circle	$B = 0, A = C$ and $B^2 - 4AC < 0$
Ellipse	$B^2 - 4AC < 0$
Parabola	$B^2 - 4AC = 0$
Hyperbola	$B^2 - 4AC > 0$

$$(x - h)^2 + (y - k)^2 = r^2 \quad (A\text{-}2)$$

with center at (h,k) and radius r as shown in Figure A-1(a).

An *ellipse* is the locus of points in a plane, the sum of whose distances from two fixed points (focal points or foci) is constant as shown in Figure A-1(b). The general equation for an ellipse centered at the origin is:

$$\frac{x^2}{a^2} + \frac{y^2}{b^2} = 1 \quad (A\text{-}3)$$

where:

a and b are half the major and minor axis lengths and $a > b$

The foci are located at $(\pm c, 0)$ where:

$$c^2 = a^2 - b^2$$

as shown in Figure A-1(b). The ellipse could also be:

$$\frac{x^2}{b^2} + \frac{y^2}{a^2} = 1, \quad a > b \quad (A\text{-}4)$$

In this case, the foci are located at $(0, \pm c)$, indicating that the y axis is the major axis.

A *parabola* is the locus of points in a plane equidistant from a fixed focal point and a line known as the *directrix* as shown in Figure A-1(c). For a parabola with the vertex at (h,k), the general equation for a parabola in standard position is given by:

$$(x - h)^2 = 4p(y - k) \quad (A\text{-}5)$$

where:

the equation of the directrix line is $y = k - p$ and the focal point location is $(h, k + p)$.

A *hyperbola* is the locus of points in a plane, the difference of whose distances from two fixed points (focal points or foci) is constant as shown in Figure A-1(d).

The general equation describing a hyperbola in standard position centered at the origin opening to the left and right is:

$$\frac{x^2}{a^2} - \frac{y^2}{b^2} = 1 \qquad (A-6)$$

The foci are given by $(\pm c, 0)$ where:

$$c^2 = a^2 + b^2$$

The hyperbola approaches two asymptotes defined by the lines $y = \pm \frac{b}{a} x$.

A.2 TRIGONOMETRIC INDENTITIES

The following is a list of a number of useful trigonometric identities derived from the definitions of the trigonometric functions and the Pythagorean identity. (Note: u and v are any angle.)

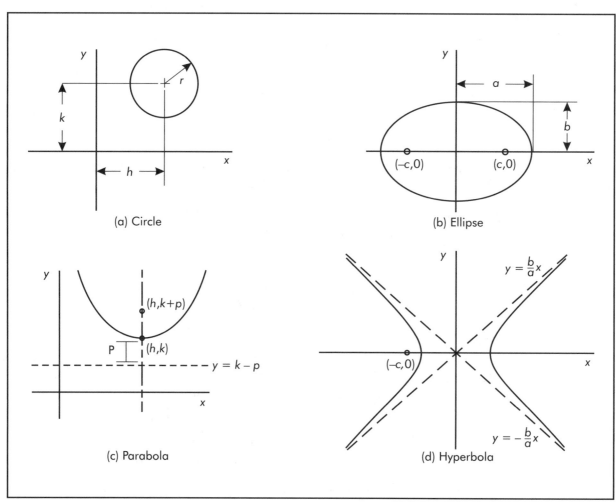

(a) Circle

(b) Ellipse

(c) Parabola

(d) Hyperbola

Figure A-1. Conic sections.

Negative-angle Formulas

$$\sin(-u) = -\sin u;\ \cos(-u) = \cos u;$$
$$\tan(-u) = -\tan u \tag{A-7}$$

$$\csc(-u) = -\csc u;\ \sec(-u) = \sec u;$$
$$\cot(-u) = -\cot u \tag{A-8}$$

Addition Formulas

$$\sin(u \pm v) = \sin u \cos v \pm \cos u \sin v \tag{A-9}$$

$$\cos(u \pm v) = \cos u \cos v \mp \sin u \sin v \tag{A-10}$$

$$\tan(u \pm v) = \frac{\tan u \pm \tan v}{1 \mp \tan u\ \tan v} \tag{A-11}$$

Double-angle Formulas

$$\sin 2u = 2 \sin u \cos u \tag{A-12}$$

$$\cos 2u = \cos^2 u - \sin^2 u$$
$$= 1 - 2 \sin^2 u = 2 \cos^2 u - 1 \tag{A-13}$$

$$\tan 2u = \frac{2 \tan u}{1 - \tan^2 u} \tag{A-14}$$

Half-angle Formulas

$$\sin^2 \frac{u}{2} = \frac{1 - \cos\ u}{2} \tag{A-15}$$

$$\cos^2 \frac{u}{2} = \frac{1 + \cos\ u}{2} \tag{A-16}$$

$$\tan \frac{u}{2} = \frac{1 - \cos\ u}{\sin u} = \frac{\sin\ u}{1 + \cos u} \tag{A-17}$$

A.3 DERIVATIVE AND INTEGRAL FORMULAS

Following are additional derivative and integral formulas to those described in Chapter 1. The notation assumes that f and g are functions of x, and k is a constant.

$$\frac{df^n}{dx} = nf^{n-1}f' \tag{A-18}$$

$$\frac{d}{dx}(\ln x) = \frac{1}{x} \tag{A-19}$$

$$\frac{d}{dx}(e^{kx}) = ke^{kx} \tag{A-20}$$

$$\frac{d}{dx}(\sin x) = \cos x \tag{A-21}$$

$$\frac{d}{dx}(\cos x) = -\sin x \tag{A-22}$$

$$\int x^{-1} dx = \ln x + C \tag{A-23}$$

$$\int e^{ax} dx = \frac{1}{a} e^{ax} + C \tag{A-24}$$

$$\int \sin x\ dx = -\cos x + C \tag{A-25}$$

$$\int \cos x\ dx = \sin\ x + C \tag{A-26}$$

$$\int [f(x) \pm g(x)]\ dx = \int f(x)\ dx \pm \int g(x)\ dx \tag{A-27}$$

A.4 VECTOR OPERATIONS

A.4.1 RECTANGULAR COMPONENTS

The vectors i, j, and k are called *unit vectors* and are defined as vectors of magnitude one directed along the positive x, y, and z axes of a cartesian coordinate system. This is shown in Figure A-2. A vector, A, can be resolved into rectangular components where A_x, A_y, and A_z are the scalar components along each coordinate axis. The components along the x and y coordinate axes are shown in Figure A-3. The vector A can be written as:

$$\boldsymbol{A} = A_x \boldsymbol{i} + A_y \boldsymbol{j} + A_z \boldsymbol{k} \tag{A-28}$$

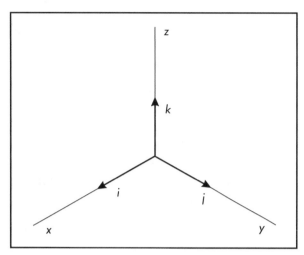

Figure A-2. Unit vectors.

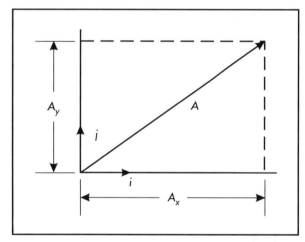

Figure A-3. Resolution of a vector into rectangular components.

A.4.2 VECTOR ADDITION

If the rectangular components are given by:

$$A = A_x i + A_y j \qquad (A\text{-}29)$$

$$B = B_x i + B_y j \qquad (A\text{-}30)$$

then the vector C that is the sum of the two vectors is given by:

$$C = C_x i + C_y j$$
$$= (A_x + B_x)i + (A_y + B_y)j \qquad (A\text{-}31)$$

A.4.3 MAGNITUDE OF A VECTOR

A vector, A, can be defined as a unit vector $\hat{A}$ directed in the same direction as A multiplied by a scalar A that indicates the *magnitude* of the vector. The magnitude of a vector can be found as:

$$|A| = \sqrt{A_x^2 + A_y^2 + A_z^2} \qquad (A\text{-}32)$$

A.4.4 UNIT VECTOR

The unit vector (designated by the caret ^) is oriented in the same direction as A and can be found as:

$$\hat{A} = \frac{A}{|A|} \qquad (A\text{-}33)$$

A.4.5 THE PRODUCT OF A SCALAR AND A VECTOR

The product of a scalar k and a vector P is denoted as kP. It is defined as a vector having the same orientation as P and a magnitude equal to the magnitude of P multiplied by k. Multiplication of a vector and a negative scalar results in a vector having the opposite sense.

A.4.6 SCALAR PRODUCT (DOT PRODUCT)

The scalar product or *dot product* of two vectors, A and B, is defined as the product of the magnitude of the two vectors and the cosine of the angle between the two vectors. The dot product is written as:

$$A \cdot B = |A||B|\cos\theta \qquad (A\text{-}34)$$

$$A \cdot B = B \cdot A \qquad (A\text{-}35)$$

$$A \cdot (B + C) = A \cdot B + A \cdot C \qquad (A\text{-}36)$$

$$A \cdot B = A_x B_x + A_y B_y + A_z B_z \qquad (A\text{-}37)$$

A.4.7 VECTOR PRODUCT (CROSS PRODUCT)

The cross product of two vectors results in a vector that is mutually perpendicular to the two original vectors. The magnitude of the cross product is equal to the product of the magnitude of the two vectors multiplied by the sine of the angle between them:

$$|A \times B| = |A||B|\sin\theta \qquad (A\text{-}38)$$

Cross products are distributive, but they are not commutative. Instead, if the components of the cross product are commuted, the negative of the original result is obtained:

$$A \times B = -(B \times A) \qquad (A\text{-}39)$$

The cross product can be evaluated by resolving A and B into their rectangular components and performing a set of algebraic operations on them. These operations can be summarized by the determinant:

$$C = A \times B = \begin{vmatrix} i & j & k \\ A_x & A_y & A_z \\ B_x & B_y & B_z \end{vmatrix}$$

The components of the cross product C can be evaluated as:

$$C_x = A_y B_z - A_z B_y \qquad (A\text{-}40)$$

$$C_y = A_z B_x - A_x B_z \qquad (A\text{-}41)$$

$$C_y = A_x B_y - A_y B_x \qquad (A\text{-}42)$$

CNC G and M Charts

Computer numerical control (CNC) programming preparatory functions, also called *G-codes*, prepare the control system for implementing the information in the next block of instructions and specify the control mode of the various CNC machining operations. Miscellaneous functions, called *M-functions*, control the auxiliary functions, such as coolant on/off and spindle on/off.

Tables B-1 and B-2 define G-codes for turning and milling respectively. G-codes for turning and milling are generally standardized but can vary from controller to controller.

Table B-3 defines general M-functions for turning and milling. M-functions are also generally standardized but can vary from controller to controller.

Table B-1. G-codes used in turning*

G-code	Function
G00	Positioning (Rapid Traverses)
G01	Linear Interpolation (Feed)
G02	Circular Interpolation Clockwise (CW)
G03	Circular Interpolation Counterclockwise (CCW)
G04	Dwell
G20	Inch Data Input
G21	Metric Data Input
G28	Return to Reference Point
G32	Threading
G36	Automatic Tool Compensation X
G37	Automatic Tool Compensation Z
G40	Tool Nose Radius Compensation Cancel
G41	Tool Nose Radius Compensation Left
G42	Tool Nose Radius Compensation Right
G50	Maximum Speed Setting of Spindle
G70	Finish Cycle
G71	Rough Cutting Cycle of Outer Diameter
G72	Rough Cutting Cycle End Face
G90	Absolute Positioning
G91	Incremental Positioning
G92	Threading Cycle
G94	End Face Cutting Cycle
G90	Absolute Positioning
G96	Constant Surface Speed Control
G98	Feed per Minute
G99	Feed Per Revolution

* G-codes may differ slightly between CNC controllers

Table B-2. G-codes used for milling*

G-code	Function
G00	Position (rapid traverse)
G01	Linear cutting/linear interpolation
G02	Arc interpolation CW
G03	Arc interpolation CCW
G04	Dwell
G10	Program tool compensation input (compensation amount setting)
G11	Program tool compensation input (compensation amount transfer)
G12	Arc cutting CW
G13	Arc cutting CCW
G14	Coordinate reading function
G17	XY plane selection
G18	ZX plane selection
G19	YZ plane selection
G31	Skip function
G40	Tool diameter compensation cancel
G41	Tool diameter compensation (left)
G42	Tool diameter compensation (right)
G43	Tool length compensation
G44	Tool length compensation cancel
G52	Local coordinate system
G53	Work coordinate system offset (selection of the basic machine coordinate system)
G54-59	Work coordinate system offset (selection of the work coordinate system 1-5)
G70	Inch commands
G71	Metric commands
G80	Fixed cycle cancel
G81	Fixed cycle (drilling, spot drilling)
G82	Fixed cycle (drilling, counterboring)
G83	Fixed cycle (deep-hole drilling cycle)
G84	Fixed cycle (tapping cycle)
G85-89	Fixed cycle (boring)
G90	Absolute value command
G91	Incremental value commands
G92	Coordinate system setting
G94	Asynchronous feed command (feed per minute)
G95	Synchronous feed command (feed per revolution)

* G-codes may differ slightly between CNC controllers

Table B-3. General M-functions used in milling and turning

M-function	Function
M00	Program Stop
M01	Optional Stop
M02	End of Program and Tape Rewind
M03	Spindle Start CW
M04	Spindle Start CCW
M05	Spindle Stop
M06	Tool Change
M08	Coolant On
M09	Coolant Off
M30	End of Program and Memory Return
M41	Low Range
M42	High Range
M48	Override Cancel Off
M49	Override Cancel On

* M-functions are standardized but many vary from CNC to CNC machine.

Appendix C

Review Question Answers

PART 1: MATHEMATICAL FUNDAMENTALS

CHAPTER 1: MATHEMATICS

1.1) $x = 4$

1.2) $x = -2$

1.3) $x = 3y/(1-2y)$

1.4) $x = 5$

1.5) $w = 9$

1.6) $x = 82$

1.7) $y_1 = \dfrac{-5 - \sqrt{5}}{2} \approx -3.618$

$y_2 = \dfrac{-5 + \sqrt{5}}{2} \approx -1.382$

1.8) $g_1 = \dfrac{1 - \sqrt{29}}{2} \approx -2.193$

$g_2 = \dfrac{1 + \sqrt{29}}{2} \approx 3.193$

1.9) $r_1 = -\dfrac{7}{2} = -3.5$

$r_2 = \dfrac{1}{3} \approx 0.333$

1.10) $2(30 + 2x)x + 2(40)x = 296$,
$x^2 + 35x - 74 = 0$, $x = 2$
(only one valid solution)

1.11) $2(l - 4)(l - 8) = 256$,
$2l^2 - 24l - 192 = 0$, $l \approx 17.49$, $w \approx 13.49$

1.12) $x = 2.5, y = 0$

1.13) $x = 5, y = 5$

1.14) $x = -\dfrac{3}{4}; \; y = -\dfrac{5}{4}; \; z = \dfrac{13}{4}$

1.15) $x = 1.5$

1.16) $x = 8$

1.17) $x = 258.2$

1.18) $A = \pi(10)(10) + \dfrac{\pi(10)^2}{4} = $ paint
$= 393/5 = 78.5l$

1.19) $y = -2x + 4$

1.20) $y = 1.5x - 6$

1.21) $\cos^{-1} 0.8 \approx 36.87$

1.22) $3^2 + 4^2 = h^2$, $h = 5$

1.23) $\approx 104.5°, 46.6°, 28.9°$

1.24) 7.2

1.25) a. 4/52 = 1/13
b. 2/52 = 1/26
c. 1/4
d. 1/52
e. 12/52 = 3/13

1.26) a. 6/36 = 1/6
b. $P(\text{not } 2) = 1 - P(2) = 35/36$
c. 18/36 = 1/2

1.27) $6! = 720$

1.28) $(30!)/(3! \, 27!) = 4{,}060$

1.29) $P(HH \text{ or } TT) = 1/4 + 1/4 = 1/2$

1.30) a. 75
b. 67.7
c. 14.2

1.31) 55.9%
1.32) $15x^4 + 14x$
1.33) 3
1.34) local maximum at $x = 0$,
       minimum at $x = 8$
1.35) 15

PART 2: PHYSICS AND ENGINEERING SCIENCE

CHAPTER 2: METRICATION/SI SYSTEM

2.1) 5,000 mm
2.2) mm
2.3) 25.4 mm
2.4) 50 Hz
2.5) 3.28 ft
2.6) Pa
2.7) J
2.8) 0.559 mm/rev

CHAPTER 3: LIGHT

3.1) Higher
3.2) 670×10^{-9} m
3.3) No, 3.41×10^{14} Hz
3.4) Green
3.5) 13.5 m
3.6) 1.4 m

CHAPTER 4: SOUND

4.1) 30 dB
4.2) 75 dB, 600 Hz
4.3) 10^{-4} W/m^2
4.4) 66 dB
4.5) 8×10^{-3} W
4.6) 93 Hz

CHAPTER 5: ELECTRICITY AND MAGNETISM

5.1) 24 W
5.2) 0.12 A
5.3) $I = 9.1$ A, $R = 12.1$ Ω
5.4) Electrical energy
5.5) Series

5.6) 7.5 Ω
5.7) $I = 4.5$ A

CHAPTER 6: STATICS

6.1) $R = Pa/(a + b)$
6.2) 100 lb
6.3) T = 1,000 lb
6.4) 141.4 N-m CW
6.5) Slides
6.6) 243 N

CHAPTER 7: DYNAMICS

7.1) 90 m
7.2) 10.2 s
7.3) 47.8 rev
7.4) 6.2 s
7.5) 2.7 ft-lb
7.6) 4.5 in.

CHAPTER 8: STRENGTH OF MATERIALS

8.1) 4,527 psi
8.2) 18,000 psi
8.3) 0.101 in.
8.4) 1.423 in.
8.5) 5.11×10^3 N-m
8.6) 0.0082 rad

CHAPTER 9: THERMAL PROPERTIES OF MATTER

9.1) a. 146° C
       b. 755° R
       c. 419° K
9.2) 178° F
9.3) 70.1° F
9.4) Increases
9.5) Convection

CHAPTER 10: FLUID POWER

10.1) 4.7 psi
10.2) 4.2 ft
10.3) 62.5 lb
10.4) 7.8 m/s
10.5) 981 kPa

PART 3: MATERIALS

CHAPTER 11: MATERIAL PROPERTIES

11.1) Gases, liquids, and solids

11.2) A substance that has no definite shape, but does have a definite volume

11.3) The American Society for Testing and Materials (ASTM) and The International Organization for Standardization (ISO)

11.4) Proportional limit, elastic limit, yield point, yield strength, ultimate strength, breaking (rupture) strength, ductility, and modulus of elasticity

11.5) The elastic limit is the point at which permanent deformation will begin as the stress increases.

11.6) It is the ratio of stress to strain in the elastic region.

11.7) Brinell and Rockwell

11.8) Fatigue properties of a material under test and the number of stress cycles before failure

CHAPTER 12: METALS

12.1) Obstructions in orderly crystal growth

12.2) Lower solidus temperature

12.3) 0.008% – 1.0%

12.4) 1,341° F (727° C)

12.5) Avoid martensite formation

12.6) 275 BHN

12.7) 1,575° F (857° C)

12.8) Lead

12.9) d

12.10) Nodular iron

12.11) 1XXX

12.12) d

CHAPTER 13: PLASTICS

13.1) d

13.2) Addition polymerization and condensation polymerization

13.3) Alternating, block, random, and graft

13.4) High-density polyethylene

13.5) When they contain at least 100 mers

13.6) Semicrystalline

13.7) Polyamide

13.8) Below

CHAPTER 14: COMPOSITES

14.1) resin binder or matrix

14.2) c

14.3) Carbon, aramid, or boron fibers

14.4) It holds the fibers in place and distributes the stress to the fibers.

14.5) When greater strength is required

CHAPTER 15: CERAMICS

15.1) Tungsten carbide

15.2) A material that can withstand extremely high temperatures

15.3) Ionic bonding

15.4) To reduce the melting temperature

15.5) Cubic boron nitride

PART 4: PRODUCT DESIGN

CHAPTER 16: ENGINEERING DRAWING

16.1) Auxiliary view

16.2)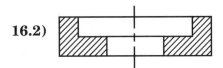

16.3) Baseline

16.4) 0.1 in.

16.5) Hole

16.6) 50-basic size, f-shaft, 6-IT grade

16.7) $.505 \,^{+.004}_{-.000} \, .507 \,^{+.002}_{-.002}$

16.8) Piston $1.000 \,^{+.001}_{-.001}$

Cylinder $1.003 \,^{+.001}_{-.001}$

16.9) 0.0025 in.
16.10) a. average roughness
b. waviness height
c. lay

CHAPTER 17: GEOMETRIC DIMENSIONING AND TOLERANCING

17.1) c
17.2) a
17.3) d
17.4) c
17.5) a
17.6) a
17.7) a
17.8) a
17.9) b
17.10) b

CHAPTER 18: COMPUTER-AIDED DESIGN

18.1) IGES
18.2) Wireframe
18.3) CSG
18.4) Solid modeling
18.5) Stereolithography (SLA)
18.6) No

CHAPTER 19: PRODUCT DESIGN TOOLS

19.1) Organization of process components and standardization
Length of production run
Complexity of scheduling procedures
19.2) a
19.3) Could stand for reliability, quality, testability, etc.
19.4) Decrease
19.5) Severity of the effect
Likelihood of occurrence
Likelihood of detection
19.6) Product planning
19.7) Visual inspection
Production flow analysis
Classification and coding

PART 5: MANUFACTURING PROCESSES

CHAPTER 20: CUTTING TOOL TECHNOLOGY

20.1) Negative rake
20.2) 8.1 minutes
20.3) crater wear
20.4) a
20.5) Emulsified cutting oil

CHAPTER 21: MACHINING

21.1) 382 rpm
21.2) 0.385 in.
21.3) 196 fpm
21.4) 0.70 hp
21.5) 0.0007 in. per tooth
21.6) 0.66 hp

CHAPTER 22: FORMING

22.1) Yes
22.2) Less
22.3) Forward extrusion
22.4) Coining
22.5) 43.8%

CHAPTER 23: SHEET METAL WORKING

23.1) 0.455 in.
23.2) 0.050 in.
23.3) Nibbling
23.4) Flanging
23.5) Stripper

CHAPTER 24: POWDERED METALS

24.1) Yes
24.2) Help the powder fill the die cavity without air pockets
24.3) Green
24.4) Sintering
24.5) Oil impregnation

CHAPTER 25: CASTING

25.1) Shrinkage voids
25.2) Cores

25.3) Investment casting
25.4) No
25.5) Die casting

CHAPTER 26: WELDING/JOINING

26.1) Carburizing
26.2) Gas metal arc welding (also known as MIG or wire welding)
26.3) Stick welding
26.4) Higher
26.5) Ultrasonic welding
26.6) Evaporative adhesives

CHAPTER 27: FINISHING

27.1) External mixing
27.2) Paint
27.3) Cathode

CHAPTER 28: PLASTICS PROCESSES

28.1) Screw diameter and motor horsepower
28.2) Extrusion blow molding and injection blow molding
28.3) Parison
28.4) Polystyrene
28.5) Flash
28.6) To reduce thinning of the sheet

CHAPTER 29: COMPOSITE PROCESSING

29.1) A partially cured composite with fibers aligned parallel to each other
29.2) Resin transfer molding
29.3) Pultrusion
29.4) Roving

CHAPTER 30: CERAMICS PROCESSING

30.1) Rolling and floating
30.2) Tempered
30.3) Water
30.4) Jiggering
30.5) Glazing

CHAPTER 31: PRINTED CIRCUIT BOARD MANUFACTURING AND ASSEMBLY

31.1) Double sided
31.2) Variable center distance (VCD) insertion
31.3) Bridges or icicles
31.4) Reflow soldering
31.5) Stencil printing

PART 6: PRODUCTION SYSTEMS

CHAPTER 32: TRADITIONAL PRODUCTION PLANNING AND CONTROL

32.1) Manufacture-to-stock
32.2) No
32.3) Aggregate
32.4) First-in /first-out
32.5) Time-phased
32.6) Manufacturing resource planning

CHAPTER 33: LEAN PRODUCTION

33.1) Lean
33.2) Kaizen
33.3) One-piece flow
33.4) Takt
33.5) Pull
33.6) Kanban

CHAPTER 34: PROCESS ENGINEERING

34.1) Special
34.2) 6
34.3) Synchronous
34.4) Product-process or cellular
34.5) Preventive
34.6) $P_r = 75\%$
34.7) 11 seconds

CHAPTER 35: INVENTORY MANAGEMENT

35.1) Dependent
35.2) Inventory turns

35.3) 2,236

35.4) Annual usage measured in dollars

35.5) 0

35.6) Left to right

PART 7: AUTOMATED SYSTEMS AND CONTROL

CHAPTER 36: COMPUTER APPLICATIONS/AUTOMATION

36.1) Improve product quality, improve productivity, improve work environment, or improve development time

36.2) Business

36.3) Manufacturing Enterprise Integration

36.4) Level one

CHAPTER 37: MANUFACTURING NETWORKS

37.1) Bandwidth

37.2) Client server

37.3) Fiberoptic

37.4) Bridge

37.5) Star

37.6) Hypertext transfer protocol (HTTP)

CHAPTER 38: CNC MACHINING

38.1) M03

38.2) APT

38.3) Z

38.4) Open-loop

38.5) Resolver

38.6) X

CHAPTER 39: PROGRAMMABLE LOGIC CONTROLLERS

39.1) Relays

39.2) Islands

39.3) Number of I/O

39.4) Relay ladder logic

39.5) Off

CHAPTER 40: ROBOTICS

40.1) Hydraulic

40.2) Degrees

40.3) Adaptive

40.4) Tool coordinate system

40.5) Spherical

CHAPTER 41: AUTOMATED MATERIAL HANDLING AND IDENTIFICATION

41.1) Triangulation

41.2) Smaller

41.3) Width of the narrowest bar

41.4) Radio frequency identification

41.5) Vision system

PART 8: QUALITY

CHAPTER 42: QUALITY ASSURANCE

42.1) QC is reactive in responding to defects and QA is proactive in its approach to defect prevention and reliability.

42.2) Customer

42.3) Appraisal cost

42.4) Facilitate international trade

42.5) No

42.6) U.S. Congress

42.7) Customer focus and satisfaction

CHAPTER 43: STATISTICAL METHODS FOR QUALITY CONTROL

43.1) Assignable variability

43.2) Standard deviation, range

43.3) $158.7 \approx 159$ parts

43.4) 23.05, 19.74, 5.18, 0

43.5) $C_p = 0.61$, process not capable

43.6) 0.48

CHAPTER 44: DIMENSIONAL METROLOGY

44.1) Precision

44.2) Calibration

44.3) Absolute

44.4) 0.081 in.

44.5) Coordinate measuring machine

44.6) Technique error

44.7) Go: $2.1499 \begin{smallmatrix} +.0000 \\ -.0002 \end{smallmatrix}$

No-go: $2.1480 \begin{smallmatrix} +.0002 \\ -.0000 \end{smallmatrix}$

44.8) Go: $3.0000 \begin{smallmatrix} +.0002 \\ -.0000 \end{smallmatrix}$

No-go: $3.0040 \begin{smallmatrix} +.0000 \\ -.0002 \end{smallmatrix}$

PART 9: MANUFACTURING MANAGEMENT

CHAPTER 45: ORGANIZATION AND SUPERVISION

45.1) b

45.2) d

45.3) Gantt chart

45.4) Pareto analysis

45.5) Assets

45.6) Goal setting

CHAPTER 46: LABOR, SAFETY, AND HUMAN FACTORS

46.1) If the strike is unlawful

46.2) c

46.3) 74.4 in. (1,890 mm)

46.4) 90 dBA

46.5) Resonance of internal organs

46.6) Cumulative trauma disorder, for example, carpal tunnel syndrome

CHAPTER 47: ENGINEERING ECONOMICS

47.1) $15,590

47.2) $365

47.3) No, the annualized cost of the service contract option is more expensive

47.4) Variable cost

47.5) No

Physics and Engineering Sciences

D.1 UNITS OF MEASURE

Table D-1. SI derived units*

Quantity	Unit	Symbol	Formula
frequency (of periodic phenomenon)	hertz	Hz	$1/s$
force	newton	N	$kg \cdot m/s^2$
pressure, stress	pascal	Pa	N/m^2
energy, work, quantity of heat	joule	J	$N \cdot m$
power, radiant flux	watt	W	J/s
quantity of electricity, electric charge	coulomb	C	$A \cdot s$
electric potential, potential difference, electromotive force	volt	V	W/A
electric capacitance	farad	F	C/V
electric resistance	ohm	Ω	V/A
electric conductance	siemens	S	A/V
magnetic flux	weber	Wb	$V \cdot s$
magnetic flux density	tesla	T	Wb/m^2
inductance	henry	H	Wb/A
Celsius temperature	degree Celsius[A]	$^\circ C$	$K{-}273$
luminous flux	lumen	lm	$cd \cdot sr$
illuminance	lux	lx	lm/m^2
activity (of a radionuclide)	becquerel	Bq	$1/s$
absorbed dose[B]	gray	Gy	J/kg
dose equivalent	sievert	Sv	J/kg

* Special names, along with their symbols and formulas, adapted from National Bureau of Standards (NBS) Special Publication 330, "The International System of Units (SI)," 1981 edition.

[A] Inclusion in the table of derived SI units with special names approved by the CIPM in 1976.

[B] Related quantities using the same unit are: specific energy imparted, kerma, and absorbed dose index.

Table D-2. Conversion values used to convert from U.S. Customary to SI Metric System.*

To Convert From	To	Multiply By
Acceleration		
ft/s^2	meter per second squared (m/s^2)	3.048 000† E–01
free fall, standard (g)	meter per second squared (m/s^2)	9.806 650† E+00
gal	meter per second squared (m/s^2)	1.000 000† E–02
in./s^2	meter per second squared (m/s^2)	2.540 000† E–02
Angle		
degree	radian (rad)	1.745 329 E–02
minute	radian (rad)	2.908 882 E–04
second	radian (rad)	4.848 137 E–06
grad	degree (angular)	9.000 000† E–01
grad	radian (rad)	1.570 796 E–02
Area		
acre	square meter (m^2)	4.046 873 E+03
are	square meter (m^2)	1.000 000† E+02
barn	square meter (m^2)	1.000 000† E–28
circular mil	square meter (m^2)	5.067 075 E–10
darcy	square meter (m^2)	9.869 233 E–13
ft^2	square meter (m^2)	9.290 304† E–02
hectare	square meter (m^2)	1.000 000† E+04
in.^{2}	square meter (m^2)	6.451 600† E–04
mi^2 (international)	square meter (m^2)	2.589 988 E+06
mi^2 (U.S. statute)	square meter (m^2)	2.589 998 E+06
yd^2	square meter (m^2)	8.361 274 E–01
Bending moment or torque		
dyne $\times$ cm	newton meter (N $\times$ m)	1.000 000† E–07
kgf $\times$ m	newton meter (N $\times$ m)	9.806 650† E+00
ozf $\times$ in.	newton meter (N $\times$ m)	7.061 552 E–03
lbf $\times$ in.	newton meter (N $\times$ m)	1.129 848 E–01
lbf $\times$ ft	newton meter (N $\times$ m)	1.355 818 E+00
Bending moment or torque per unit length		
lbf $\times$ ft/in.	newton meter per meter (N $\times$ m/m)	5.337 866 E+01
lbf $\times$ in./in.	newton meter per meter (N $\times$ m/m)	4.448 222 E+00
Capacity (*see Volume*)		
Density (*see Mass per unit volume*)		

Table D-2. *(continued)*

To Convert From	To	Multiply By
Electricity and magnetism		
abampere	ampere (A)	1.000 000† E+01
abcoulomb	coulomb (C)	1.000 000† E+01
abfarad	farad (F)	1.000 000† E+09
abhenry	henry (H)	1.000 000† E−09
abmho	siemens (S)	1.000 000† E+09
abohm	ohm (Ω)	1.000 000† E−09
abvolt	volt (V)	1.000 000† E−08
ampere hour	coulomb (C)	3.600 000† E+03
EMU of capacitance	farad (F)	1.000 000† E+09
EMU of current	ampere (A)	1.000 000† E+01
EMU of electric potential	volt (V)	1.000 000† E−08
EMU of inductance	henry (H)	1.000 000† E−09
EMU of resistance	ohm (Ω)	1.000 000† E−09
ESU of capacitance	farad (F)	1.112 650 E−12
ESU of current	ampere (A)	3.335 6 E−10
ESU of electric potential	volt (V)	2.997 9 E+02
ESU of inductance	henry (H)	8.987 554 E+11
ESU of resistance	ohm (Ω)	8.987 554 E+11
faraday (based on carbon-12)	coulomb (C)	9.648 70 E+04
faraday (chemical)	coulomb (C)	9.649 57 E+04
faraday (physical)	coulomb (C)	9.652 19 E+04
gamma	tesla (T)	1.000 000† E−09
gauss	tesla (T)	1.000 000† E−04
gilbert	ampere (A)	7.957 747 E−01
maxwell	weber (Wb)	1.000 000† E−08
mho	siemens (S)	1.000 000† E+00
oersted	ampere per meter (A/m)	7.957 747 E+01
ohm centimeter	ohm meter (Ω × m)	1.000 000† E−02
ohm circular-mil per foot	ohm meter (Ω × m)	1.662 426 E−09
statampere	ampere (A)	3.335 640 E−10
statcoulomb	coulomb (C)	3.335 640 E−10
statfarad	farad (F)	1.112 650 E−12
stathenry	henry (H)	8.987 554 E+11
statmho	siemens (S)	1.112 650 E−12
statohm	ohm (Ω)	8.987 554 E+11
statvolt	volt (V)	2.997 925 E+02
unit pole	weber (Wb)	1.256 637 E−07

Table D-2. (*continued*)

To Convert From	To	Multiply By
Energy (includes work)		
British thermal unit (International Table)	joule (J)	1.055 056 E+03
British thermal unit (mean)	joule (J)	1.055 87 E+03
British thermal unit (thermochemical)	joule (J)	1.054 350 E+03
British thermal unit (39° F)	joule (J)	1.059 67 E+03
British thermal unit (59° F)	joule (J)	1.054 80 E+03
British thermal unit (60° F)	joule (J)	1.054 68 E+03
calorie (International Table)	joule (J)	4.186 800† E+00
calorie (mean)	joule (J)	4.190 02 E+00
calorie (thermochemical)	joule (J)	4.184 000† E+00
calorie (15° C)	joule (J)	4.185 80 E+00
calorie (20° C)	joule (J)	4.181 90 E+00
calorie (kilogram, International Table)	joule (J)	4.186 800† E+03
calorie (kilogram, mean)	joule (J)	4.190 02 E+03
calorie (kilogram, thermochemical)	joule (J)	4.184 000† E+03
electronvolt	joule (J)	1.602 19 E–19
erg	joule (J)	1.000 000† E–07
ft × lbf	joule (J)	1.355 818 E+00
ft-poundal	joule (J)	4.214 011 E–02
kilocalorie (International Table)	joule (J)	4.186 800† E+03
kilocalorie (mean)	joule (J)	4.190 02 E+03
kilocalorie (thermochemical)	joule (J)	4.184 000† E+03
kW × h	joule (J)	3.600 000† E+06
therm (European Community)	joule (J)	1.055 06 E+08
therm (U.S.)	joule (J)	1.054 804† E+08
ton (nuclear equivalent of TNT)	joule (J)	4.184 E+09
W × h	joule (J)	3.600 000† E+03
W × s	joule (J)	1.000 000† E+00
Energy per unit area time		
Btu (International Table)/(ft² × s)	watt per square meter (W/m²)	1.135 653 E+04
Btu (International Table)/(ft² × h)	watt per square meter (W/m²)	3.154 591 E+00
Btu (thermochemical)/(ft² × s)	watt per square meter (W/m²)	1.134 893 E+04
Btu (thermochemical)/(ft² × min)	watt per square meter (W/m²)	1.891 489 E+02
Btu (thermochemical)/(ft² × h)	watt per square meter (W/m²)	3.152 481 E+00
Btu (thermochemical)/(in.² × s)	watt per square meter (W/m²)	1.634 246 E+06
cal (thermochemical)/(cm² × min)	watt per square meter (W/m²)	6.973 333 E+02
cal (thermochemical)/(cm² × s)	watt per square meter (W/m²)	4.184 000† E+04
erg/(cm² × s)	watt per square meter (W/m²)	1.000 000† E–03
W/cm²	watt per square meter (W/m²)	1.000 000† E+04
W/in.²	watt per square meter (W/m²)	1.550 003 E+03

Table D-2. (*continued*)

To Convert From	To	Multiply By

Flow (*see Mass per unit time or Volume per unit time*)

Force

To Convert From	To	Multiply By
dyne	newton (N)	1.000 000[†] E–05
kilogram-force	newton (N)	9.806 650[†] E+00
kilopond (kp)	newton (N)	9.806 650[†] E+00
kip (1,000 lbf)	newton (N)	4.448 222 E+03
ounce-force	newton (N)	2.780 139 E–01
pound-force (lbf)	newton (N)	4.448 222 E+00
lbf/lb (thrust/weight [mass] ratio)	newton per kilogram (N/kg)	9.806 650 E+00
poundal	newton (N)	1.382 550 E–01
ton-force (2,000 lbf)	newton (N)	8.896 444 E+03

Force per unit area (*see Pressure*)

Force per unit length

To Convert From	To	Multiply By
lbf/ft	newton per meter (N/m)	1.459 390 E+01
lbf/in.	newton per meter (N/m)	1.751 268 E+02

Heat

To Convert From	To	Multiply By
Btu (International Table) $\times$ ft/(h $\times$ ft^2 $\times$ ° F) (thermal conductivity)	watt per meter kelvin [(W/(m $\times$ K)]	1.730 735 E+00
Btu (thermochemical) $\times$ ft/(h $\times$ ft^2 $\times$ ° F) (thermal conductivity)	watt per meter kelvin [(W/(m $\times$ K)]	1.729 577 E+00
Btu (International Table) $\times$ in./(h $\times$ ft^2 $\times$ ° F) (thermal conductivity)	watt per meter kelvin [(W/(m $\times$ K)]	1.442 279 E–01
Btu (thermochemical) $\times$ in.(h $\times$ ft^2 $\times$ ° F) (thermal conductivity)	watt per meter kelvin [(W/(m $\times$ K)]	1.441 314 E–01
Btu (International Table) $\times$ in./(s $\times$ ft^2 $\times$ ° F) (thermal conductivity)	watt per meter kelvin [(W/(m $\times$ K)]	5.192 204 E+02
Btu (thermochemical) $\times$ in./(s $\times$ ft^2 $\times$ ° F) (thermal conductivity)	watt per meter kelvin [(W/(m $\times$ K)]	5.188 732 E+02
Btu (International Table)/ft^2	joule per square meter (J/m^2)	1.135 653 E+04
Btu (thermochemical)/ft^2	joule per square meter (J/m^2)	1.134 893 E+04
Btu (International Table)/(h $\times$ ft^2 $\times$ ° F) (thermal conductance)	watt per square meter kelvin [(W/(m^2 $\times$ K)]	5.678 263 E+00
Btu (thermochemical)/(h $\times$ ft^2 $\times$ ° F) (thermal conductance)	watt per square meter kelvin [(W/(m^2 $\times$ K)]	5.674 466 E+00
Btu (International Table)/ (s $\times$ ft^2 $\times$ ° F)	watt per square meter kelvin [(W/(m^2 $\times$ K)]	2.044 175 E+04

Table D-2. (*continued*)

To Convert From	To	Multiply By
Heat		
Btu (thermochemical)/ (s × ft^2 × ° F)	watt per square meter kelvin [(W/(m^2 × K)]	2.042 808 E+04
Btu (International Table)/lb	joule per kilogram (J/kg)	2.326 000† E+03
Btu (thermochemical)/lb	joule per kilogram (J/kg)	2.324 444 E+03
Btu (International Table)/ (lb × ° F) (heat capacity)	joule per kilogram kelvin [(J/(kg × K)]	4.186 800† E+03
Btu (thermochemical)/(lb × ° F) (heat capacity)	joule per kilogram kelvin [(J/(kg × K)]	4.184 000† E+03
Btu (International Table)/ft^3	joule per cubic meter (J/m^3)	3.725 895 E+04
Btu (thermochemical)/ft^3	joule per cubic meter (J/m^3)	3.723 402 E+04
cal (thermochemical)/(cm × s × ° C)	watt per meter kelvin [(W/(m × K)]	4.184 000† E+02
cal (thermochemical)/cm^2	joule per square meter (J/m^2)	4.184 000† E+04
cal (thermochemical)/(cm^2 × min)	watt per square meter (W/m^2)	6.973 333 E+02
cal (thermochemical)/(cm^2 × s)	watt per square meter (W/m^2)	4.184 000† E+04
cal (International Table)/g	joule per kilogram (J/kg)	4.186 800† E+03
cal (thermochemical)/g	joule per kilogram (J/kg)	4.184 000† E+03
cal (International Table)/(g × ° C)	joule per kilogram kelvin [(J/(kg × K)]	4.186 800† E+03
cal (thermochemical)/(g × ° C)	joule per kilogram kelvin [(J/(kg × K)]	4.184 000† E+03
cal (thermochemical)/min	watt (W)	6.973 333 E–02
cal (thermochemical)/s	watt (W)	4.184 000† E+00
clo	kelvin square meter per watt (K × m^2/W)	2.003 712 E–01
° F × h × ft^2/Btu (International Table) (thermal resistance)	kelvin square meter per watt (K × m^2/W)	1.761 102 E–01
° F × h × ft^2/Btu (thermochemical) (thermal resistance)	kelvin square meter per watt (K × m^2/W)	1.762 280 E–01
° F × h × ft^2/[Btu (International Table) × in.] (thermal resistivity)	kelvin meter per watt (K × m/W)	6.933 471 E+00
° F × h × ft^2/[Btu (thermochemical) × in.] (thermal resistivity)	kelvin meter per watt (K × m/W)	6.938 113 E+00
ft^2/h (thermal diffusivity)	square meter per second (m^2/s)	2.580 640† E–05
Length		
angstrom	meter (m)	1.000 000† E–10
astronomical unit	meter (m)	1.495 979 E+11
chain	meter (m)	2.011 684 E+01
fathom	meter (m)	1.828 804 E+00
fermi (femtometer)	meter (m)	1.000 000† E–15

Table D-2. (*continued*)

To Convert From	To	Multiply By
Length		
foot	meter (m)	3.048 000[†] E–01
foot (U.S. survey)	meter (m)	3.048 006 E–01
inch	meter (m)	2.540 000[†] E–02
light year	meter (m)	9.460 55 E+15
microinch	meter (m)	2.540 000[†] E–08
micron	meter (m)	1.000 000[†] E–06
mil	meter (m)	2.540 000[†] E–05
mile (international nautical)	meter (m)	1.852 000[†] E+03
mile (U.S. nautical)	meter (m)	1.852 000[†] E+03
mile (international)	meter (m)	1.609 344[†] E+03
mile (U.S. statute)	meter (m)	1.609 347 E+03
parsec	meter (m)	3.085 678 E+16
pica (printer's)	meter (m)	4.217 518 E–03
point (printer's)	meter (m)	3.514 598[†] E–04
rod	meter (m)	5.029 210 E+00
yard	meter (m)	9.144 000[†] E–01
Light		
cd/in.^{2}	candela per square meter (cd/m^2)	1.550 003 E+03
footcandle	lux (lx)	1.076 391 E+01
footlambert	candela per square meter (cd/m^2)	3.426 259 E+00
lambert	candela per square meter (cd/m^2)	3.183 099 E+03
lm/ft^2	lumen per square meter (lm/m^2)	1.076 391 E+01
Mass		
carat (metric)	kilogram (kg)	2.000 000[†] E–04
grain	kilogram (kg)	6.479 891[†] E–05
gram	kilogram (kg)	1.000 000[†] E–03
hundredweight (long)	kilogram (kg)	5.080 235 E+01
hundredweight (short)	kilogram (kg)	4.535 924 E+01
kgf × s^2/m (mass)	kilogram (kg)	9.806 650[†] E+00
ounce (avoirdupois)	kilogram (kg)	2.834 952 E–02
ounce (troy or apothecary)	kilogram (kg)	3.110 348 E–02
pennyweight	kilogram (kg)	1.555 174 E–03
pound (lb avoirdupois)	kilogram (kg)	4.535 924 E–01
pound (troy or apothecary)	kilogram (kg)	3.732 417 E–01
slug	kilogram (kg)	1.459 390 E+01
ton (assay)	kilogram (kg)	2.916 667 E–02
ton (long, 2,240 lb)	kilogram (kg)	1.016 047 E+03
ton (metric)	kilogram (kg)	1.000 000[†] E+03

Table D-2. (*continued*)

To Convert From	To	Multiply By

Mass

To Convert From	To	Multiply By
ton (short, 2,000 lb)	kilogram (kg)	9.071 847 E+02
tonne	kilogram (kg)	1.000 000† E+03

Mass per unit area

To Convert From	To	Multiply By
oz/ft^2	kilogram per square meter (kg/m^2)	3.051 517 E–01
oz/yd^2	kilogram per square meter (kg/m^2)	3.390 575 E–02
lb/ft^2	kilogram per square meter (kg/m^2)	4.882 428 E+00

Mass per unit capacity (*see Mass per unit volume*)

Mass per unit length

To Convert From	To	Multiply By
denier	kilogram per meter (kg/m)	1.111 111 E–07
lb/ft	kilogram per meter (kg/m)	1.488 164 E+00
lb/in.	kilogram per meter (kg/m)	1.785 797 E+01
tex	kilogram per meter (kg/m)	1.000 000† E–06

Mass per unit time (includes flow)

To Convert From	To	Multiply By
perm (0° C)	kilogram per pascal second square meter [kg/(Pa $\times$ s $\times$ m^2)]	5.721 35 E–11
perm (23° C)	kilogram per pascal second square meter [kg/(Pa $\times$ s $\times$ m^2)]	5.745 25 E–11
perm $\times$ in. (0° C)	kilogram per pascal second meter [kg/(Pa $\times$ s $\times$ m)]	1.453 22 E–12
perm $\times$ in. (23° C)	kilogram per pascal second meter [kg/(Pa $\times$ s $\times$ m)]	1.459 29 E–12
lb/h	kilogram per second (kg/s)	1.259 979 E–04
lb/min	kilogram per second (kg/s)	7.559 873 E–03
lb/s	kilogram per second (kg/s)	4.535 924 E–01
lb/(hp $\times$ h) (specific fuel consumption [SFC])	kilogram per joule (kg/J)	1.689 659 E–07
ton (short)/h	kilogram per second (kg/s)	2.519 958 E–01

Mass per unit volume (includes density and mass capacity)

To Convert From	To	Multiply By
grain/gal (U.S. liquid)	kilogram per cubic meter (kg/m^3)	1.711 806 E–02
g/cm^3	kilogram per cubic meter (kg/m^3)	1.000 000† E+03
oz (avoirdupois)/gal (U.K. liquid)	kilogram per cubic meter (kg/m^3)	6.236 021 E+00
oz (avoirdupois)/gal (U.S. liquid)	kilogram per cubic meter (kg/m^3)	7.489 152 E+00
oz (avoirdupois)/in.^{3}	kilogram per cubic meter (kg/m^3)	1.729 994 E+03

Table D-2. (*continued*)

To Convert From	To	Multiply By

Mass per unit volume (includes density and mass capacity)

To Convert From	To	Multiply By
lb/ft^3	kilogram per cubic meter (kg/m^3)	1.601 846 E+01
lb/in.^{3}	kilogram per cubic meter (kg/m^3)	2.767 990 E+04
lb/gal (U.K. liquid)	kilogram per cubic meter (kg/m^3)	9.977 633 E+01
lb/gal (U.S. liquid)	kilogram per cubic meter (kg/m^3)	1.198 264 E+02
lb/yd^3	kilogram per cubic meter (kg/m^3)	5.932 764 E–01
slug/ft^3	kilogram per cubic meter (kg/m^3)	5.153 788 E+02
ton (long)/yd^3	kilogram per cubic meter (kg/m^3)	1.328 939 E+03
ton (short)/yd^3	kilogram per cubic meter (kg/m^3)	1.186 553 E+03

Power

To Convert From	To	Multiply By
Btu (International Table)/h	watt (W)	2.930 711 E–01
Btu (International Table)/s	watt (W)	1.055 056 E+03
Btu (thermochemical)/h	watt (W)	2.928 751 E–01
Btu (thermochemical)/min	watt (W)	1.757 250 E+01
Btu (thermochemical)/s	watt (W)	1.054 350 E+03
cal (thermochemical)/min	watt (W)	6.973 333 E–02
cal (thermochemical)/s	watt (W)	4.184 000† E+00
erg/s	watt (W)	1.000 000† E–07
ft-lbf/h	watt (W)	3.766 161 E–04
ft-lbf/min	watt (W)	2.259 697 E–02
ft-lbf/s	watt (W)	1.355 818 E+00
horsepower (550 ft-lbf/s)	watt (W)	7.456 999 E+02
horsepower (boiler)	watt (W)	9.809 50 E+03
horsepower (electric)	watt (W)	7.460 000† E+02
horsepower (metric)	watt (W)	7.354 99 E+02
horsepower (water)	watt (W)	7.460 43 E+02
horsepower (U.K.)	watt (W)	7.457 0 E+02
kilocalorie (thermochemical)/min	watt (W)	6.973 333 E+01
kilocalorie (thermochemical)/s	watt (W)	4.184 000† E+03
ton of refrigeration (= 12,000 Btu/h)	watt (W)	3.517 E+03

Pressure or stress (force per unit area)

To Convert From	To	Multiply By
atmosphere, standard	pascal (Pa)	1.013 250† E+05
atmosphere, technical (= 1 kgf/cm^2)	pascal (Pa)	9.806 650† E+04
bar	pascal (Pa)	1.000 000† E+05
centimeter of mercury (0° C)	pascal (Pa)	1.333 22 E+03
centimeter of water (4° C)	pascal (Pa)	9.806 38 E+01
dyne/cm^2	pascal (Pa)	1.000 000† E–01
foot of water (39.2° F)	pascal (Pa)	2.988 98 E+03

Table D-2. (continued)

To Convert From	To	Multiply By
Pressure or stress (force per unit area)		
gf/cm^2	pascal (Pa)	9.806 650† E+01
inch of mercury (32° F)	pascal (Pa)	3.386 38 E+03
inch of mercury (60° F)	pascal (Pa)	3.376 85 E+03
inch of water (39.2° F)	pascal (Pa)	2.490 82 E+02
inch of water (60° F)	pascal (Pa)	2.488 4 E+02
kgf/cm^2	pascal (Pa)	9.806 650† E+04
kgf/m^2	pascal (Pa)	9.806 650† E+00
kgf/mm^2	pascal (Pa)	9.806 650† E+06
kip/in.^{2} (ksi)	pascal (Pa)	6.894 757 E+06
millibar	pascal (Pa)	1.000 000† E+02
millimeter of mercury (0° C)	pascal (Pa)	1.333 22 E+02
poundal/ft^2	pascal (Pa)	1.488 164 E+00
lbf/ft^2	pascal (Pa)	4.788 026 E+01
lbf/in.^{2} (psi)	pascal (Pa)	6.894 757 E+03
psi	pascal (Pa)	6.894 757 E+03
torr (mm Hg, 0° C)	pascal (Pa)	1.333 22 E+02
Radiation units		
curie	becquerel (Bq)	3.700 000† E+10
rad	gray (Gy)	1.000 000† E−02
rem	sievert (Sv)	1.000 000† E−02
roentgen	coulomb per kilogram (C/kg)	2.58 E−04
Speed (*see Velocity*)		
Stress (*see Pressure*)		
Temperature		
degree Celsius	kelvin (K)	$T_K = t_{°C} + 273.15$
degree Fahrenheit	degree Celsius (° C)	$t_{°C} = (t_{°F} - 32)/1.8$
degree Fahrenheit	kelvin (K)	$T_K = (t_{°F} + 459.67)/1.8$
degree Rankine	kelvin (K)	$T_K = T_{°R}/1.8$
kelvin	degree Celsius (° C)	$t_{°C} = T_K - 273.15$
Time		
day	second (s)	8.640 000† E+04
day (sidereal)	second (s)	8.616 409 E+04
hour	second (s)	3.600 000† E+03
hour (sidereal)	second (s)	3.590 170 E+03
minute	second (s)	6.000 000† E+01

Table D-2. (*continued*)

To Convert From	To	Multiply By
Time		
minute (sidereal)	second (s)	5.983 617 E+01
second (sidereal)	second (s)	9.972 696 E−01
year (365 days)	second (s)	3.153 600[†] E+07
year (sidereal)	second (s)	3.155 815 E+07
year (tropical)	second (s)	3.155 693 E+07
Torque (*see Bending moment*)		
Velocity (includes speed)**		
ft/h	meter per second (m/s)	8.466 667 E−05
ft/min	meter per second (m/s)	5.080 000[†] E−03
ft/s	meter per second (m/s)	3.048 000[†] E−01
in./s	meter per second (m/s)	2.540 000[†] E−02
km/h	meter per second (m/s)	2.777 778 E−01
knot (international)	meter per second (m/s)	5.144 444 E−01
mi/h (international)	meter per second (m/s)	4.470 400[†] E−01
mi/min (international)	meter per second (m/s)	2.682 240[†] E+01
mi/s (international)	meter per second (m/s)	1.609 344[†] E+03
mi/h (international)	kilometer per hour (km/h)	1.609 344[†] E+00
Viscosity		
centipoise (dynamic viscosity)	pascal second (Pa-s)	1.000 000[†] E−03
centistokes (kinematic viscosity)	square meter per second (m^2/s)	1.000 000[†] E−06
ft^2/s	square meter per second (m^2/s)	9.290 304[†] E−02
poise	pascal second (Pa-s)	1.000 000[†] E−01
poundal-s/ft^2	pascal second (Pa-s)	1.488 164 E+00
lb/(ft-h)	pascal second (Pa-s)	4.133 789 E−04
lb/(ft-s)	pascal second (Pa-s)	1.488 164 E+00
lbf-s/ft^2	pascal second (Pa-s)	4.788 026 E+01
lbf-s/$in.^2$	pascal second (Pa-s)	6.894 757 E+03
rhe	1 per pascal second [1/(Pa-s)]	1.000 000[†] E+01
slug/(ft-s)	pascal second (Pa-s)	4.788 026 E+01
stokes	square meter per second (m^2/s)	1.000 000[†] E−04
Volume (includes capacity)		
acre-foot	cubic meter (m^3)	1.233 489 E+03
barrel (oil, 42 gal)	cubic meter (m^3)	1.589 873 E−01
board foot	cubic meter (m^3)	2.359 737 E−03
bushel (U.S.)	cubic meter (m^3)	3.523 907 E−02
cup	cubic meter (m^3)	2.365 882 E−04

Table D-2. (continued)

To Convert From	To	Multiply By

Volume (includes capacity)

fluid ounce (U.S.)	cubic meter (m^3)	2.957 353 E–05
ft^3	cubic meter (m^3)	2.831 685 E–02
gallon (Canadian liquid)	cubic meter (m^3)	4.546 090 E–03
gallon (U.K. liquid)	cubic meter (m^3)	4.546 092 E–03
gallon (U.S. dry)	cubic meter (m^3)	4.404 884 E–03
gallon (U.S. liquid)	cubic meter (m^3)	3.785 412 E–03
gill (U.K.)	cubic meter (m^3)	1.420 654 E–04
gill (U.S.)	cubic meter (m^3)	1.182 941 E–04
in.^{3}	cubic meter (m^3)	1.638 706 E–05
liter	cubic meter (m^3)	1.000 000† E–03
ounce (U.K. fluid)	cubic meter (m^3)	2.841 307 E–05
ounce (U.S. fluid)	cubic meter (m^3)	2.957 353 E–05
peck (U.S.)	cubic meter (m^3)	8.809 768 E–03
pint (U.S. dry)	cubic meter (m^3)	5.506 105 E–04
pint (U.S. liquid)	cubic meter (m^3)	4.731 765 E–04
quart (U.S. dry)	cubic meter (m^3)	1.101 221 E–03
quart (U.S. liquid)	cubic meter (m^3)	9.463 529 E–04
stere	cubic meter (m^3)	1.000 000† E+00
tablespoon	cubic meter (m^3)	1.478 676 E–05
teaspoon	cubic meter (m^3)	4.928 922 E–06
ton (register)	cubic meter (m^3)	2.831 685 E+00
yd^3	cubic meter (m^3)	7.645 549 E–01

Volume per unit time (includes flow)

ft^3/min	cubic meter per second (m^3/s)	4.719 474 E–04
ft^3/s	cubic meter per second (m^3/s)	2.831 685 E–02
gallon (U.S. liquid)/(hp-h) specific fuel consumption (SFC)	cubic meter per joule (m^3/J)	1.410 089 E–09
in.^{3}/min	cubic meter per second (m^3/s)	2.731 177 E–07
yd^3/min	cubic meter per second (m^3/s)	1.274 258 E–02
gallon (U.S. liquid) per day	cubic meter per second (m^3/s)	4.381 264 E–08
gallon (U.S. liquid) per minute	cubic meter per second (m^3/s)	6.309 020 E–05

Work (see *Energy*)

Note: ESU means electrostatic cgs unit. EMU means electromagnetic cgs unit.

* Courtesy the American Society for Testing and Materials, Standard E380-82.

† Accuracy—this symbol, †, after the sixth decimal place indicates that the conversion factor is exact and that all subsequent digits are zero. All other conversion factors have been rounded.

** Although speedometers may read km/h, the SI unit is m/s.

D.2 CENTROIDS

Center of area (*centroid*) is analagous to center of mass, except it is based on a cross-sectional area rather than mass. Figure D-1 illustrates a center of area or centroid example.

$$\overline{Y} = \frac{\sum\limits_{i=1}^{N} y_i A_i}{\sum\limits_{i=1}^{N} A_i} \qquad (D\text{-}1)$$

$$\overline{X} = \frac{\sum\limits_{i=1}^{N} x_i A_i}{\sum\limits_{i=1}^{N} A_i} \qquad (D\text{-}2)$$

where:

y_i and x_i = location of the center of area of each component with a respect to a datum

$\overline{Y}$ and $\overline{X}$ = location of the center of area for the composite with respect to the datum

A = area of each component

N = number of simple shapes the composite is made of

Figure D-2 shows the location of the centroid on some common two-dimensional objects.

D.3 CURVILINEAR MOTION

Curvilinear motion describes the action of particle travelling in a plane curve. A plane curve may be approximated over a small interval with a circular arc with radius of curvature, r. The motion is characterized by components normal n and tangent t to the curve:

$$a_n = \frac{v^2}{r} \qquad (D\text{-}3)$$

$$a_t = \frac{\Delta v}{\Delta t} \qquad (D\text{-}4)$$

where:

a = acceleration

v = velocity

D.4 MOMENTUM

Linear momentum (p) is given by the product of mass (m) and linear velocity (v):

$$p = mv \qquad (D\text{-}5)$$

Angular momentum (H) is the product of the mass moment of inertia (I) and angular velocity (ω):

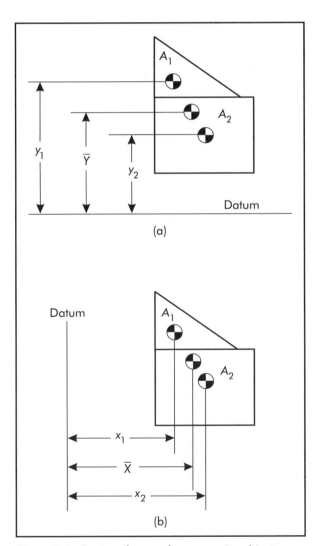

Figure D-1. Center of area of a composite object.

Shape		$\bar{x}$	$\bar{y}$	Area
Triangular area	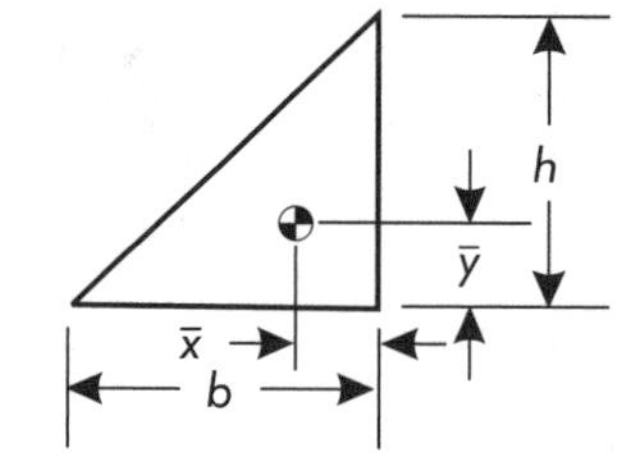	$\dfrac{b}{3}$	$\dfrac{h}{3}$	$\dfrac{bh}{2}$
Quarter-circular area	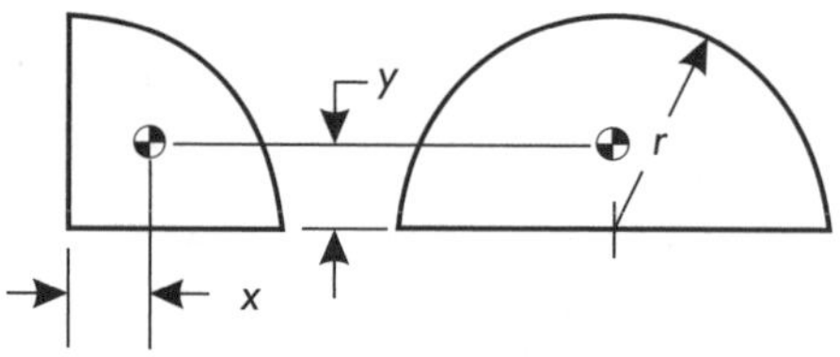	$\dfrac{4r}{3\pi}$	$\dfrac{4r}{3\pi}$	$\dfrac{\pi r^2}{4}$
Semicircular area		0	$\dfrac{4r}{3\pi}$	$\dfrac{\pi r^2}{2}$
Semiparabolic area	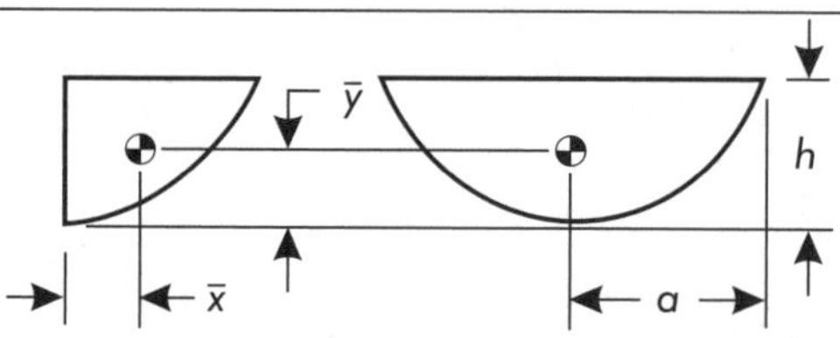	$\dfrac{3a}{8}$	$\dfrac{3h}{5}$	$\dfrac{2ah}{3}$
Parabolic area		0	$\dfrac{3h}{5}$	$\dfrac{4ah}{3}$
Circular sector	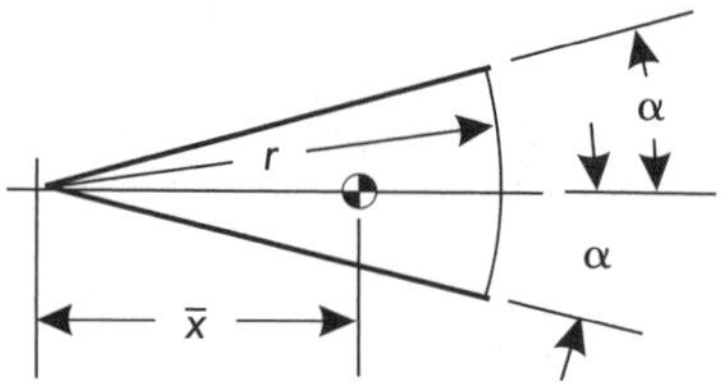	$\dfrac{2r\sin\alpha}{3\alpha}$	0	αr^2

Figure D-2. Centroids.

$$H = I\omega \qquad (D\text{-}6)$$

Relationships between force or moment and changing momentum are:

$$F\Delta t = m\Delta v \qquad (D\text{-}7)$$

$$M\Delta t = I\omega \qquad (D\text{-}8)$$

where:

F = force
M = moment
Δt = time interval the force or moment is applied

$F\Delta t$ is known as an *impulse*. The velocity before force F is applied and after is known as v_1 and v_2 respectively:

$$mv_1 + F\Delta t = mv_2 \qquad (D\text{-}9)$$

$$I\omega_1 + M\Delta t = I\omega_2 \qquad (D\text{-}10)$$

Figure D-3 defines mass moment of inertia (I) for some common shapes.

D.5 POISSON'S RATIO

Poisson's ratio is the ratio of the lateral strain and the axial strain as defined by Eq. D-11 and illustrated in Figure D-4.

Shape		
Slender rod	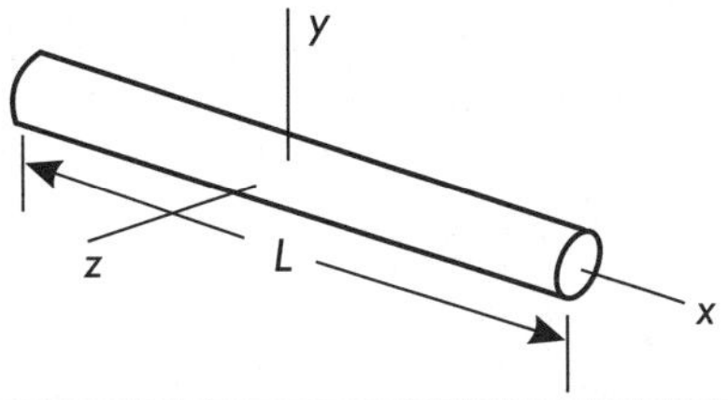	$I_x = I_y = \dfrac{1}{12}\,mL^2$
Thin rectangular plate	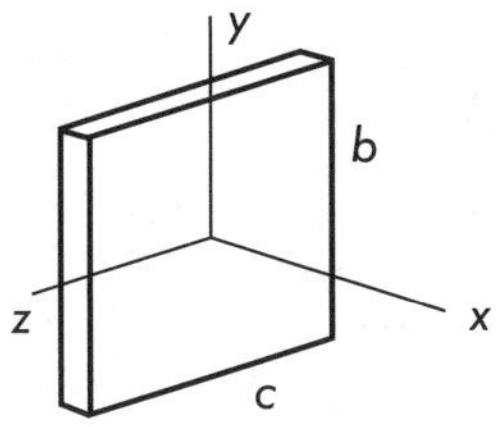	$I_x = \dfrac{1}{12}\,m(b^2 + c^2)$ $I_y = \dfrac{1}{12}\,mc^2$ $I_z = \dfrac{1}{12}\,mb^2$
Rectangular prism	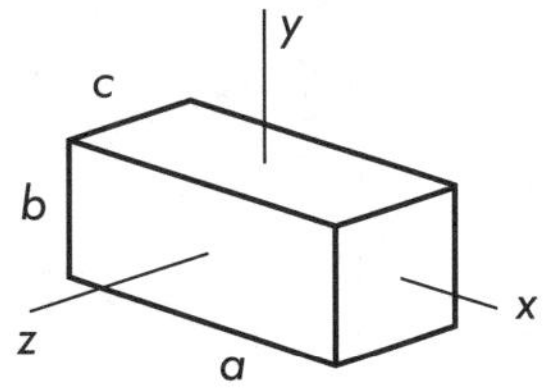	$I_x = \dfrac{1}{12}\,m(b^2 + c^2)$ $I_y = \dfrac{1}{12}\,m(c^2 + a^2)$ $I_z = \dfrac{1}{12}\,m(a^2 + b^2)$
Thin disk	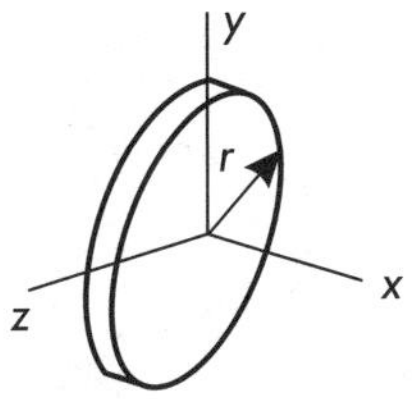	$I_x = \dfrac{1}{2}\,mr^2$ $I_y = I_z = \dfrac{1}{4}\,mr^2$
Circular cylinder	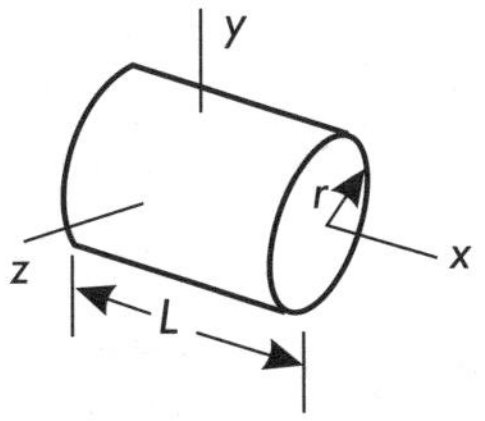	$I_x = \dfrac{1}{2}\,mr^2$ $I_y = I_z = \dfrac{1}{12}\,m(3r^2 + L^2)$

Figure D-3. Mass moment of inertia.

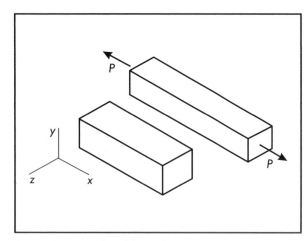

Figure D-4. Axial and lateral strain.

$$v = -\frac{\varepsilon_y}{\varepsilon_x} = -\frac{\varepsilon_z}{\varepsilon_x} \qquad \text{(D-11)}$$

where:

v = Poisson's ratio

ε = strain

x, y, z = direction or axis

D.6 BEAM LOADING

Figure D-5 illustrates common beam loading conditions.

In the cross section of a beam, an internal force referred to as the *shear force* and an internal moment referred to as the *bending moment,* cause the beam to be stressed under loading. Table D-3 defines the maximum shear force (V) and the maximum bending moment (M) for the five loading conditions in Figure D-5.

The maximum bending stress, s, is found by:

$$\sigma = \frac{Mc}{I} \qquad \text{(D-12)}$$

where:

c = distance from the neutral axis to the plane where the bending stress is to be calculated (this is typically the top or bottom surface)

I = area moment of inertia

Table D-3. Important beam formulas

Loading Condition	Maximum Shear Force (V)	Maximum Bending Moment (M)
a	P	PL
b	wL	$\dfrac{wL^2}{2}$
c	$\dfrac{5wL}{8}$	$\dfrac{wL^2}{8}$
d	$\dfrac{P}{2}$	$\dfrac{PL}{4}$
e	$\dfrac{wL}{2}$	$\dfrac{wL^2}{8}$

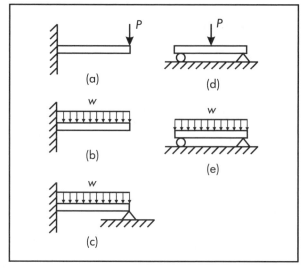

Figure D-5. Typical beam loading conditions.

The area moment of inertia for a rectangular cross section is given by:

$$I = \frac{bh^3}{12} \qquad \text{(D-13)}$$

where:

b = base

h = height

The load is applied in a direction parallel to the height as shown in Figure D-6.

The maximum value of shear stress, τ, for a narrow, rectangular cross-section beam is given by:

$$\tau = \frac{3V_{max}}{2A} \tag{D-14}$$

where:

V_{max} = maximum shear force
A = cross-sectional area of the beam

Table D-4 defines the maximum deflection for the various beam loading conditions illustrated in Figure D-5.

D.7 FLUID CONSERVATION OF MOMENTUM

Conservation of momentum is described by the momentum equation:

$$\Sigma F = \rho Q(v_2 - v_1) \tag{D-15}$$

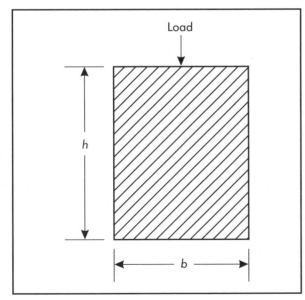

Figure D-6. Rectangular beam cross section.

Table D-4. Important beam deflection formulas

Loading Condition	Maximum Deflection
a	$\dfrac{PL^3}{3EI}$
b	$\dfrac{wL^4}{8EI}$
c	$\dfrac{wL^4}{185EI}$
d	$\dfrac{PL^3}{48EI}$
e	$\dfrac{5wL^4}{384EI}$

where:

ΣF = summation of forces acting on the system
ρ = density of the fluid
Q = volumetric flow rate ($Q = Av$)
A = pipe cross-sectional area
v = fluid velocity

D.8 BUOYANCY

The weight of fluid (W) displaced by an object of volume (V) is given by:

$$W = \gamma V \tag{D-16}$$

where:

γ = specific weight of the fluid

Bibliography

BIBLIOGRAPHY

Amrine, H.T., J.A Ritchey, C.L. Moodie, and J.F. Kmec. 1993. *Manufacturing Organization and Management*, Sixth Edition. Englewood Cliffs, NJ: Prentice-Hall, Inc.

Anton, Howard. 1977. *Elementary Linear Algebra*, Second Edition. New York: John Wiley & Sons.

Atkinson, William. "The Customer-responsive Manufacturing Organization." *Manufacturing Systems*. May 1990: Vol 8.

Bakerjian, Raymond and Philip Mitchell, eds. 1993. *Tool and Manufacturing Engineers Handbook*, Fourth Edition. *Vol. 7: Continuous Improvement*. Dearborn, MI: Society of Manufacturing Engineers.

Besterfield, Dale H. 2000. *Quality Control*, Sixth Edition. Englewood Cliffs, NJ: Prentice-Hall, Inc.

Black Box Catalog. 1998. Lawrence, PA: Black Box Corporation.

Boothroyd, Geoffrey, Peter Dewhurst, and Winston Knight. 1994. *Product Design for Manufacture and Assembly*. New York: Marcel Dekker, Inc.

Bryan, L. A. and E.A. Bryan. 1995. *Programmable Controllers: Theory and Applications*, Second Edition. Atlanta, GA: Industrial Text Company.

Busch, Ted, Roger Harlow, and Richard Thompson. 1998. *Fundamentals of Dimensional Metrology*, Third Edition. Albany, NY: Delmar Publishers, Inc.

Cubberly, William, and Ramon Bakerjian, eds. 1989. *Tool and Manufacturing Engineers Handbook Desk Edition*. Dearborn, MI: Society of Manufacturing Engineers.

DeGarmo, Paul E., J.T. Black, and Ronald A. Kohser. 1996. *Materials and Processes in Manufacturing*. Upper Saddle River, NJ: Prentice-Hall, Inc.

DeGarmo, Paul E., William G. Sullivan, and James A. Bontadelli. 1988. *Engineering Economy*, Eighth Edition. New York: Macmillan Publishing Co.

Dinsdale, Allen. 1986. *Pottery Science: Materials, Process, and Products*. New York: Halsted Press.

Earle, James H. 1990. *Engineering Design Graphics*, Sixth Edition. Reading, MA: Addison-Wesley Publishing Company.

Eary, Donald F. and Gerald E. Johnson. 1962. *Process Engineering for Manufacturing*. Englewood Cliffs, NJ: Prentice-Hall, Inc.

Evans, James R., David R. Anderson, Dennis J. Sweeny, and Thomas A. Williams. 1990. *Applied Production and Operations Managment*, Third Edition. New York: West Publishing Co.

Flinn, Richard A. and Paul K. Trojan. 1990. *Engineering Materials and Their Applications*, Fourth Edition. Boston, MA: Houghton-Mifflin Book Company.

Giesecke, Fredrick E., Alva Mitchell, Henry C. Spencer, Ivan L. Hill, Robert O. Loving, John T. Dygdon, and James E. Novak. 2001. *Engineering Graphics*, Seventh Edition. Upper Saddle River, NJ: Prentice-Hall, Inc.

Goetsch, David L. 1990. *Advanced Manufacturing Technology*. Albany, NY: Delmar Publishers Inc.

Goldman, J. E. 1995. *Applied Data Communications*. New York: John Wiley & Sons, Inc.

Groover, Mikell P. 1996. *Fundamentals of Modern Manufacturing: Materials, Processes, and Systems*. Upper Saddle River, NJ: Prentice-Hall, Inc.

——. 1987. *Automation, Production Systems, and Computer-integrated Manufacturing*. Englewood Cliffs, NJ: Prentice-Hall, Inc.

Halliday, David and Robert Resnick. 1988. *Fundamentals of Physics*, Third Edition. New York: John Wiley & Sons.

Haskins, Robert and Thomas Petit. 1988. "Strategies for Entrepreneurial Manufacturing." *Journal of Business Strategy*, Nov./Dec.

Hayt, William H. and Jack E. Kemmerly. 1987. *Engineering Circuit Analysis*, Third Edition. New York: McGraw-Hill Book Company.

Hibbler, R.C. 1992. *Engineering Mechanics: Dynamics*, Sixth Edition. New York: Macmillan Publishing Co., Inc.

——. 1983. *Engineering Mechanics: Statics*, Third Edition. New York: Macmillan Publishing Co., Inc.

Juran, J.M. and F.M. Gryna. 1988. *Quality Control Handbook*, Fourth Edition. New York: McGraw-Hill Book Company.

Kalpakjian, Serope. 1995. *Manufacturing Engineering and Technology*, Third Edition. New York: Addison-Wesley Publishing Co.

Krulikowski, Alex. 1998. *Fundamentals of Geometric Dimensioning and Tolerancing*, Second Edition. Albany, NY: Delmar Publishers, Inc.

Lin, Jonathan. 1994. *Computer Numerical Control: Essentials in Programming and Networking*. Albany, NY: Delmar Publishers, Inc.

Lokensgard, Erik and Terry Richardson. 1997. *Industrial Plastics*, Third Edition. Albany, NY: Delmar Publishers, Inc.

Luduzinsky, A. 1999. "Open Minded." *Cutting Tool Engineering*, September: 51.

Makris, J. 1998. "DSL, Don't be Duped." *Data Communications*, April.

Margrab, Edward G. 1997. *Integrated Product and Process Design and Development*. New York: CRC Press.

Marks, P. 1994. *Process Reengineering and the New Manufacturing Enterprise Wheel: 15 Processes for Competitive Advantage*. Dearborn, MI: Society of Manufacturing Engineers.

Meredith, Jack R. and Samuel J. Mantel, Jr. 1989. *Project Managment: A Managerial Approach*, Second Edition. New York: John Wiley & Sons.

Mitchell, Philip, ed. 1996. *Tool and Manufacturing Engineers Handbook*, Fourth Edition. *Vol. 8: Plastic Part Manufacturing*. Dearborn, MI: Society of Manufacturing Engineers.

——. 1999. *Tool and Manufacturing Engineers Handbook*, Fourth Edition. *Vol. 9: Material and Part Handling in Manufacturing*. Dearborn, MI: Society of Manufacturing Engineers.

Monden, Yasuhiro. 1998. *Toyota Production System*, Third Edition. Norcross, GA: Engineering and Management Press.

Moran, Michael J. and Howard N. Shapiro. 1995. *Fundamentals of Engineering Thermodynamics,* Third Edition. New York: John Wiley & Sons, Inc.

Nee, John G. 1998. *Fundamentals of Tool Design,* Fourth Edition. Dearborn, MI: Society of Manufacturing Engineers.

Oberg, Erik, Franklin Jones, Holbrook Horton, and Henry Ryffell. 1992. *Machinery's Handbook,* Twenty-fourth Edition. New York: Industrial Press, Inc.

Pfaffenberger, Roger C. and James H. Patterson. 1987. *Statistical Methods for Business and Economics.* Homewood, IL: Richard D. Irwin, Inc.

Pollack, Herman W. 1988. *Materials Science and Metallurgy,* Fourth Edition. Englewood Cliffs, NJ: Prentice-Hall, Inc.

Richardson, Terry. 1987. *Composites: A Design Guide.* New York: Industrial Press, Inc.

Shigley, Joseph E. and Larry D. Mitchell. 1983. *Mechanical Engineering Design,* Fourth Edition. New York: McGraw-Hill Book Company.

Spiegel, Leonard and Goerge Limbrunner. 1999. *Applied Statics and Strength of Materials,* Third Edition. Upper Saddle River, NJ: Prentice-Hall, Inc.

Sullivan, James A. 1989. *Fluid Power: Theory and Applications,* Third Edition. Englewood Cliffs, NJ: Prentice-Hall, Inc.

Waurzyniak, P. 1999. "Robotics Evolution." *Manufacturing Engineering,* February:122.

White, John A. 1987. *Production Handbook,* Fourth Edition. New York: John Wiley & Sons, Inc.

Wick, Charles and Raymond F. Veilleux, eds. 1985. *Tool and Manufacturing Engineers Handbook,* Fourth Edition. *Vol. 3: Materials, Finishing, and Coating.* Dearborn, MI: Society of Manufacturing Engineers.

——. 1987. *Tool and Manufacturing Engineers Handbook,* Fourth Edition. *Vol. 4: Quality Control and Assembly.* Dearborn, MI: Society of Manufacturing Engineers.

Womack, James P., Daniel T. Jones, and Daniel Roos. 1990. *The Machine that Changed the World.* New York: Rawson Associates.

Index